美国大众文化

Critical Readings of American Popular Culture

主　编　金衡山　廖炜春
编　者　孙　超　陆泉枝　周振春
刘　威　张　媛　蒋奇丽

东南大学出版社
·南　京·

图书在版编目(CIP)数据

美国大众文化/金衡山,廖炜春主编.—南京:东南大学出版社,2011.6

ISBN 978-7-5641-2831-9

Ⅰ.①美… Ⅱ.①金… ②廖… Ⅲ.①群众文化-概况-美国-现代 Ⅳ.①G 249.712

中国版本图书馆 CIP 数据核字(2011)第 102607 号

东南大学出版社出版发行

(南京市四牌楼 2 号 邮编 210096)

出版人:江建中

江苏省新华书店经销　　南京新洲印刷有限公司印刷

开本:787mm×1092mm 1/16　印张:16.5　字数:410 千字

2011 年 7 月第 1 版　2011 年 7 月第 1 次印刷

ISBN 978-7-5641-2831-9

印数:1~3000 册　定价:35.00 元

(凡因印装质量问题,可直接向读者服务部调换。电话:025-83792328)

Contents

Chapter 5 Sports: The Cultural Implications in American Sports

Chapter 6 Film: Making Hollywood Dreams

Chapter 7 American Icons: The Worshipped Characters for the Public

导论

大众文化和大众文化批评

大众文化无处不在。或许可以用一个极端比喻说明无处不在的大众文化:就像空气一样,我们时刻呼吸着大众文化。只是这是一个不充分的比喻,因为我们也被大众文化所呼吸。

可以用两个英文词来表明大众文化与我们的紧密关系。一个是 ubiquitous, 意为“无所不在”;另一个是“bombard”, 意为“轰炸”。前一词是形容词,表示状态;后一个是动词,指示程度。大众文化与我们的关系便是一种“无处不在的轰炸”。

当你走进任何一家百货商店,当琳琅满目的商品像潮水一样涌入你的眼帘时;当你在高速公路上行驶,路边的广告牌一个又一个与你“擦肩而过”时;当你打开电视找到你喜欢的节目正看得兴致勃勃,而又因为广告插播不得不暂歇一会时;当你与你的伙伴们进入体育馆改造而成的音乐广场,为你崇拜的歌星不停地挥动手中的荧光棒并高声尖叫时;当你每晚或每个周末一头扎进韩剧、美剧、日剧或不管什么剧而身心皆忘时;当好莱坞或张艺谋、冯小刚、李安、陈可辛们的大片小片遍布全城时;当人们在必胜客前饶有兴趣地排起长队时;当阿迪达斯的“没有不可能”(Impossible is nothing)已经不被看成广告语时;当所有这一切像吃饭睡觉一样被习以为常时,我们的生活也早已经被大众文化包围了。确切地说,应该是被包围得水泄不通。

不过,曾几何时,大众文化这个词并不为我们所熟悉。我们知晓的是另外一个相关词:“文化”。我们进学校,我们读课本,我们听老师讲课,我们受教育;我们所受教育的主要成分是“文化”,我们学文化,成为文化人。这里的“文化”似乎与大众的关系似有似无。这个一直到现在为止依旧存在的“文化”现象实际上是有深厚渊源的。19 世纪英国文化批评大家,马修·阿诺德(Mathew Arnold)在他的名著《文化与无政府状态》(*Culture and Anarchy*)里把文化大致定义为:世界上最优秀的思想和知识/言论(the best that has been thought and known/said in the world)。阿诺德是有感于其时英国社会的道德式微,企图用“文化”来整治各种混杂思想,提供一种高屋建瓴的向心力。文化在他眼中是一种“美好与光明”(sweetness and light)①。这么一种高度浓缩的“文化”一直以来确实成为了我们所受教育的基础,我们可以称之为“高雅文化”,并不一定指“又高又雅”,而是说文化的有限度,即历史上承续和积淀下来的好的、优秀的精神基因,换言之,也就是经典。这种对文化的定义自有其存在的理由,千百年来人类精神生活的延续正是因为有了这种“文化”的支撑的缘故。但是,另一方面,问题也出现了。其一,这种“文化”与当下似有脱节;其二,与日常生活也有隔

---

① 关于阿诺德的论述见《文化与无政府状态:政治与社会批评》,韩敏中译,三联书店,2008。详见正文前“关键词”。

阂(不管是表面的还是深层的)。文化究竟还是与生活息息相关的。阿诺德的同胞,20 世纪的英国文化批评大家,雷蒙德·威廉姆斯(Raymond Williams)在这个方面的论述给了我们诸多启发。在他写于上世纪 50 年代的《文化与社会》(*Culture and Society*)一书中,他指出“文化”一词的定义是在发展中的,其中一个意思是:“文化是一种物质、知识与精神构成的整个生活方式。”“‘文化’原来意指心灵状态或习惯,或者是指知识与道德活动的群体,现在变成也指整个生活方式。”[①]从“心灵状态”和“知识和道德活动”到“生活方式”,文化概念的内涵和外延被大大扩大了。精神的知识活动,也即我们通常在学校里所受的教育,与物质的生活方式构成了“文化”的基础,而后者则应是涵盖日常生活与当下社会的方方面面。于是,大众的内容自然成了“文化”不可或缺的一部分。大众文化自然也是“文化”,而且更是社会,尤其是现当代社会中一个最为活跃的文化领域。

上述从阿诺德到威廉姆斯关于文化的不同定义,其实也粗略勾勒了作为当代人文学科领域一种极具生命力的学术研究趋向的“文化研究”的路径。兴起于威廉姆斯首倡的“文化唯物主义”,兴旺于五六十年代英国伯明翰大学当代文化研究中心[②]的开拓性工作,同时又借助于法国结构主义马克思主义学者阿尔图赛(Louis Althusser)的意识形态国家机器理论以及被西方学者重新发现的上世纪二三十年代意大利共产党领袖葛兰西(Antonio Gramsci)对“市民社会”的分析,“文化研究”在文学、文化、历史、哲学等人文学科领域披荆斩棘,把对广义的文化的研究引向了史无前例的深度。其中,大众文化研究更是被树立为文化研究的风向标,成为了一个新兴的文化研究领域。这当然也与后现代社会氛围在全球的渐趋渐浓不无关联。在后现代主义这个原本属于专门学术语汇而如今早已成为众人口头禅的当下,所谓的高雅的和通俗的、大众的区分越来越失去了原有的分界意义;大众文化或许并不需要与高雅文化一争高下,因为在日常生活越来越与“文化”搭界(或曰“文化化”)的今天,我们的生活方式本身就是一种文化。真所谓文化无处不在。

当然,这种文化首先是大众的。那么,何谓“大众”?同样,我们也可以用两个英文词来表示其含义:第一个是“mass”(常用作复数 masses),即“群体,群众”;第二个是“popular”,意为“通俗的,受欢迎的”。前一个是名词,后一个是形容词,两者的结合便是“受到大众欢迎的”。这可以说是“大众”一词的意义指向。需要注意的是,英文词“mass”可以成为动词“massify”,意为“使……一体化”,也就是说“大众”的一个衍生含义则是“一体化的群体”;“mass”又常常可以和另外一个英文词“production”放在一起使用,即“mass production”,也即“大批量生产”,换言之,大工业生产。也就是说“一体化的群体”成为“大众”的条件应是大工业生产的时代。这绝不仅仅是简单的一两个英文词的意义推演而已。事实如此。文化研究学者斯托里(John Storey)在分析了大众文化的多层含义(比如,通俗的、人民的、非高雅的等等)之后,强调指出不管其有多少层面的含义,有一点是确定的:这是一种唯有在

---

① 雷蒙德·威廉姆斯《文化与社会》,吴松江、张文定译,北京大学出版社,1991,第 19、21 页。

② Center for Contemporary Cultural Studies:1964 年在英国伯明翰大学成立的“当代文化研究中心”,采用马克思主义、后结构主义和女性主义等方法研究文化、媒体等,开创了研究大众文化的新途径。对文化研究作为一门学科的发展有着重要影响。

工业化和城市化兴起后才出现的文化①。通俗文化自古就有,但在此之前不会是"大众的"。打个简单的比方,美国纽约的麦当劳出售的"巨无霸"和中国上海的麦当劳出售的"巨无霸"味道一样之时,正是大众文化流行之日。吃过这两地麦当劳的人都会感到没有什么区别,事实上也不可能有区别存在。工业化的标准生产早已把原本在手工作坊里的经验感觉消弭得无影无踪。

大众文化把大众驱向一体化。这样讲也许有点绝对,或者可以这么说,大众文化"是在特定的时间里一个特定的群体所共有的一种行为和知识"。② 为群体"所共有的"即是指"受欢迎的",而"特定的时间"则是表明大众文化的短暂和变化特征,也就是指大众文化的流行特征。流行通常是说一段时间的流行。尽管如此,大众文化的一体化功能是与生俱来不可改变的,除非产生条件——大工业化生产被改变了。在全球化几近成为现实的今天,这种可能性像是喜马拉雅山顶上的空气,越来越稀薄了。

但是吊诡的是,很多大众文化现象并不是自然而然地随着大工业化的进程而发生并发展的,相反,有不少大众文化往往发端于个体,尤其是个体的反抗行为。比如牛仔裤,特别是被故意磨旧、打洞、截短后的牛仔裤。这些在很多青年中流行的服饰,原本属于青年反文化运动的反抗行为,怪异着装、长发披肩在上世纪60年代中后期的美国是部分青年对社会和政府不满的表示,但是值得注意的是,这种充满个体怨怒情绪的象征很快被转化成了商品。你尽可以通过花钱购得这种象征物以表达你的怨愤,你没有注意到的是,在你穿上了这种现成的象征反抗的服饰时,你已经被商品的制造者们一体化了,或者更确切地说,你,我,还有其他数不胜数的同一服饰的穿戴者们自己把自己一体化了:原本具有的象征意义在商品的流行过程中一点一点被磨蚀掉,取而代之的是一种新的款式的产生。③ 50年代中期"猫王"普莱斯利开创了一代摇滚,他在舞台上摇动双腿这个明显带有性挑逗的标志性动作与50年代美国社会僵化的道德要求形成鲜明的对照,摇滚也因此成为流行乐中的弄潮儿。现在回顾摇滚的历史,其带动社会风尚变化的轨迹依然历历在目;60年代以鲍勃·迪伦(Bob Dylan)为代表的摇滚以及其他各种通俗音乐成为了青年反文化运动和反战运动的急先锋,大众文化与政治运动走到了一起,乃至一时间分不出你我。1969年8月15日—8月18日在纽约附近举行的50万人参加的"伍德斯托克"音乐节既是通俗乐的一次集体嘉年华,也是一次年轻人的政治表白。音乐节的主题"音乐和和平",明显是针对正在不断升级的越战。但是,与此同时摇滚乐也越来越成为唱片公司的挣钱机器,在畅销榜上的名次节节上升的同时,摇滚乐与政治的亲昵关系开始淡化,并最终成为一种个人的偏好。④ 近年来一直热闹非凡的嘻哈音乐的遭遇则是另一个可以说明问题的例子。这种源自牙买加,在纽约布朗克斯区街头黑人青年中发轫,继而在黑人社区风靡一时的融说唱与身体动作于一

---

① John Storey. *Cultural Theory and Popular Culture: An Introduction*, 3rd edition. Peking University Press, 2004, p. 13.

② Michael Petracca and Madeleine Sorapure. *Common Culture: Reading and Writing About American Popular Culture*. New Jersey: Prentice Hall, 2001, p. 4.

③ 关于对牛仔裤的讨论详见约翰·费斯克:《理解大众文化》,王晓玉、宋伟杰译,中央编译出版社,2006,1-13页。

④ 关于60年代通俗乐与政治以及唱片公司的关系可参见约翰·斯托雷:"摇滚霸权:西海岸摇滚乐与美国的越战",载入罗岗、刘象愚主编的《文化研究读本》,中国社会科学出版社,2000。

体的“怪异”音乐，曾经充满了黑人青年的愤懑情绪，在经历了一二十年的“说说唱唱”后最终进入了主流音乐。那嬉笑怒骂的风格还依旧存在，但不过流于形式而已，一个很大的原因是听的人和唱的人都“习以为常”了。

或许可以这样说，流行其实真正发端于“不流行”，也即有着鲜明的个体的、个性的、不趋同的姿态和特征，但是一旦这种“不流行”的姿态被纳入到一体化过程中后，从“不流行”到流行也就开始了。这样一个过程很多时候——套用一句老话——是不以你的意志为转移的。也正是在这个过程的形成中，大众及大众文化呱呱坠地了。

这个过程可以用一个英文词来加以描述：appropriate/appropriation，意为“挪用”，有人翻译为“收编”，这确是可以很好地表达出大众文化的吊诡之处。批评家们则喜欢套用葛兰西的理论来做一番解释。葛兰西在《狱中笔记》中花了相当的精力来讨论“市民社会”（civil society）问题。“市民社会”也即涉及个人生活的社会领域，相对于“市民社会”的则是“政治社会”，也就是常说的“国家”。国家通过政治控制机器如军队、警察、法律等对整个社会发生影响，而相对来说，文化发生影响的一个重要地域则是在“市民社会”，这种影响能够产生效应的一个原因是“市民社会”中的个人对发生影响的文化的认同（consent）。“认同”当然不是随时随地自发地产生的，而是经过了“政治社会”与“市民社会”间的反复“协商”（negotiation），最终才获得了“认同”。促使这种“认同”能够产生的原因是“国家”拥有足够的政治和文化资源，用葛兰西的话说，也就是“霸权”（hegemony），同时“国家”也体认到了个体的需求，于是通过文化和文化人的作用，在个体的认同下，“霸权”得以至少是部分地加以实施。葛兰西本意是要说明资本主义制度中社会控制能够发挥效应的机制是什么①。用这个理论，可以比较清楚地看到大众文化之吊诡或悖论产生的原因。原本来自个体的文化行为经过与“国家”的“协商”，得到了双方的认同，被纳入到“国家”的体系中，并最终得到了流行。在大众文化流行的实际过程中，所谓“国家”则主要体现于工业化大众化的生产体系。

如果说葛兰西揭示了文化之于“市民社会”的重要作用，那么显然受惠于葛兰西理论的阿尔图赛则进一步把这种作用发挥的途径演绎得淋漓尽致。类似于葛兰西的“市民社会”和“政治社会”，阿尔图赛提出了国家机器和国家意识形态机器（Ideological State Apparatuses）的概念。前者指社会的政治控制机器，即军队、法律、警察等，后者则指通过意识形态的途径发挥作用的控制机制。不同于一般见解的是，阿尔图赛把意识形态细分化和扩大化了，意识形态发挥的途径可以见之于学校、家庭、教堂、文化活动、体育活动、出版、工会、党派等等②。换言之，意识形态无处不在，无所不在，意识形态渗透无时无刻不在发生。

---

① Antonio Gramsci. *Selections from the Prison Notebooks*. ed. &tran. Quintin Horae and Geoffrey Nowell Smith. New York: International Publishers, 1999, pp. 4-13. 葛兰西（1891—1937）：哲学家、政治理论家，意大利共产党缔造者和领导者之一，1926 年被意大利法西斯主义者墨索里尼政府投入监狱，判刑 20 年。在狱中写下大量笔记，深入思考资本主义制度下马克思主义的发展情况。1971 年英文版《狱中笔记》出版，对西方左翼思想界产生巨大影响。

② Louis Althusser. “Ideology and Ideology State Apparatuses”, in *Lenin and Philosophy and Other Essays*, tran. Ben Brewster. New York and London: Montly Review Press, 1971, p. 142. 阿尔图赛（1918—1990）：法国马克思主义者，法共党员，其思想对上世纪 60 年代以来的左翼思想界影响深远。

这种理论显然是很有可能背上意识形态绝对化的嫌疑。不过,我们还是可以透过绝对化的阿氏意识形态理论看到一点启示,那就是意识形态与日常生活之间不可分割的关系。如果我们把意识形态换成“文化”(事实上,阿尔图赛的“意识形态”也正是文化研究者眼中的“文化”),那么可以说文化无处不在,无所不在,而能够担当如此重任的“文化”舍去大众文化又能是什么?

上述多少有点玄而又玄的对大众文化的理论言说只是想说明两点:一,大众文化与个体的关系;二,大众文化与社会的关系。从个体到社会,大众文化由此产生,与此同时,需要注意的是,个体并没有在走向社会的过程中(一体化过程)完全丧失个体的自我身份,至少表面上如此(尽管与原来的身份已不相一致)。换言之,大众的另一面是依旧可以沾沾自喜的个体,大众是由这些自我意识颇为强烈的个体组成的,只是处在大众中的个体意识无论如何强烈恐怕也只是大众意识的同谋者而已。于是乎,我们又回到了大众文化的吊诡。

从个体到社会再回到“个体”,这中间经历了大工业生产条件下的一体化过程,期间个体发生了奇妙的改变。这种改变的发生也正是大众文化效应的产生,也就是说,在很大程度上,我们与大众文化互为认同,互相承认,互为一致,大众文化也因此指导我们确定我们是谁,我们要做什么(who we are and what we are going to do),这也就是西方人常说的个人身份问题(self-identity)。同样,我们也可以举个大家熟悉的例子:“没有不可能”在没有成为阿迪达斯的口号之前,也许是一句非常平常的话,也许能从你我他的口中说出;但是一旦这句话与那些闪耀的体育明星们联系在一起,当梅西、贝克汉姆、霍华德们成为了这句话的象征和实践者时,包括你我他在内的大众似乎也在有意无意间发现了这句话的真谛,继而下意识地认同了他们以及他们背后的那句话;更重要的是,与此同时,这种认同似乎还能让我们成为另一个贝克汉姆、梅西、霍华德,或至少是他们的精神(“没有不可能”)的潜在的实践者,正是在这个认同过程发生时,我们变成了一个新的“个体”,一个被赋予了身份的个体。当然,没有我们的认同,“赋予”是不可能发生的。这种互相认同的过程便是大众文化能够产生影响的主要原因。个体—社会—个体,这实在是一个双向的过程。值得注意的是,在大众文化高度发展的今天,社会,也就是产生一体化的工业体系,发挥的作用越来越大。保留个性特征的个体走向社会的大门依旧敞开,大道依然通畅,与此同时,一个又一个人工个体被制造出来,比如好莱坞的明星们,比如被精心包装的歌星们,比如绚烂无比、美轮美奂的商品,比如巧舌如簧但又恰如其分的广告,凡此种种,他们构建了大众文化的主体,也同时构建了我们这个社会的很多价值观念,诸如美丽、勇敢、奋斗、追求、梦想等等。没有了他们,大众们很可能会失去了生活的方向。这便是大众文化的不可或缺的社会影响。

身处这种影响之中的我们是条件反射似地跟着大众文化走,成为一个又一个的粉丝成员之一,还是在迷恋、享受、欣赏或者拥戴的同时也能时不时地抽身出来,冷眼旁观一下,问问自己那玩意到底为何物。这种态度或者是姿态即使不是有意为之,也应是有了些许批评的味道了。大众文化不是洪水猛兽,用不着、也不可能拒之门外,但是研究一下大众文化的缘起,了解一点其各种表现渠道,如广告、体育、电影、媒体等中的大众文化因子,以及发生的作用,这多少会有助于我们了解所处这个社会的文化运作机制,而这实际上也就是在做着批评的工作了。

在当今社会,美国是大众文化的大本营。尽管新近遭遇了百年未遇的金融危机,尽管自上世纪70年代以来美国衰退论不绝于耳,尽管面临为媒体所津津乐道的“金砖四国”(中国，俄罗斯，印度，巴西）等新兴国家的全面挑战，美国至少在当下仍然是世界头号强国。很多人反对全球化的一个理由便是在他们眼中全球化实际上就是美国化，而美国化的一个重要内容则是美国的大众文化在全世界的广为传播。君不见好莱坞电影大片在我们这里大有占据半壁江山之势，美国的快餐店在很多人的心目中几近成为西餐的代名词，NBA 的球星们也早已把北京、上海等地当成了另一个主赛场——至少是娱乐的主场，从“猫王”到杰克逊再到麦当娜，美国的歌星们也俨然成为我们的通俗乐中的经典。随之而来的则是美国的价值观，如个体主义、美国梦、平等、自由、民主等等。要了解美国和美国社会，美国大众文化无疑是一个很好的渠道。

本书是一部有关美国大众文化的阅读文选，收集了与大众文化相关的消费文化、广告、电视、体育、音乐、电影、大众偶像等方面的各类文章。一方面，读者可以从这些文章中了解近几十年来美国大众文化的方方面面；另一方面，这些文章不只是单单介绍大众文化，更主要的是，文章的作者都是用一种批评的眼光来看待大众文化，所以你读到的除了相关知识之外，更多的是精湛的评论，犀利的批判，深邃的思想，生动的文笔。此外，文章作者切入论题的方法则可以大大拓宽我们的视野，提升我们看问题的水平。在这些文章里，大众文化被置于美国社会的各个层面和价值体系中加以讨论。比如，美国梦在广告中的巧妙体现，棒球、美式橄榄球和高尔夫球与美国梦的关系，体育与政治、性别等的微妙联系，NBA 中黑人球员与白人球员的风格区别以及背后的原因，美国文化的标志之一——牛仔裤与美国价值的凸现，百货公司与超级市场的区别以及与消费者的关联，商品包装的学问和意义，美国电视中超级脱口秀的渊源与社会问题的关系，看电视对个体行为的影响，电视内容与实际生活的区别，好莱坞电影中的美国价值观，电影中的“神话”构架，西部片的道德诉诸，芭比娃娃、飞人乔丹、超人等这些美国偶像的社会成因，对摇滚乐、“猫王”等的争议性讨论，嘻哈音乐的起源和发展以及影响等等。所有这些都给我们提供了深入了解美国大众文化的途径，同时也让我们深刻体味到了大众文化批评和批判的意义所在。了解大众文化，评述大众文化，实际上也是审视我们自己，因为我们都是文化大众中的一员。我们呼吸大众文化，因为我们的呼吸，大众文化也培育了我们。

书中所有文章都不是学究性的理论篇章，尽管理论的影子随处可见。围绕具体例子，深入探析，同时上升到一定的理论高度，这些是很多文章的特征。为阅读方便，我们对文章中的很多内容，特别是涉及美国大众文化的专有名词都加了注释，这些注释可以给读者提供诸多相关方面的知识。

每个专题包括 3 ~ 6 篇文章，前面有一个总论，引介此专题以及各篇文章的大致内容，每篇文章前也有一个简短介绍，文后有一些问题供读者参考。大多数专题还附有一篇（有的多于一篇）关于此专题的历史介绍，从中可以知道该专题的历史沿革和发展，非常有助于对该专题的全面了解。每篇文章都附有一些图片，可资对文章的形象化解读。大众文化本身就是活的文化物件，无论是音乐、广告或者体育，没有亲临实际的参与，无论如何也谈不上会有亲密的接触，更遑论评述了。建议本书的读者在阅读文章的同时，还可以做一些专门的研究，比如在网上搜查相关内容，再结合文章观点，做出自己的评价，这样肯定会有丰厚的收益。

本书大部分文章选自美国的大学教材。如：Sonia Maasik and Jack Solomon. *Signs of Life in the USA: Readings on Popular Culture for Writers*, 4th edition. Boston/New York: Bedfords/

St. Martin's, 2003. Michael Petracca and Madeleine Sorapure. *Common Culture: Reading and Writing About American Popular Culture*, *3rd edition*. New Jersey: Upper Saddle River, 2001. Katherine Anne Ackley. *Perspectives on Contemporary Issues: Readings Across the Disciplines*, 3rd edition. Heine: Thomson, 2003. M. Thomas Inge, ed.. *Concise Histories of American Popular Culture*. Westport, Connecticut: Greenwood Press, 1982. 有些文章选自网上材料。

本书是集体劳动的成果，每个专题由一个人负责注释、编辑。具体分工如下：消费文化（蒋奇丽），广告（张媛），通俗音乐（刘威），电视（周振春），体育（陆泉枝），电影（廖炜春），偶像（孙超）。他们中有些是华东师范大学美国研究中心在读研究生，怀着对大众文化的热爱和关心，全身心投入工作，尽管初涉学术，但已显示出很强的发展潜力。作为主编，我们要向他们及所有参加本书编辑的其他人员表示衷心感谢。

本书可以作为大学英语专业高年级拓展课教材，或非英语专业选修课教材，也可以用作美国研究专业研究生教材。对大众文化和美国社会感兴趣的读者，本书也是很好的阅读对象。

苏格拉底说过，未经审视的生活是没有价值的。大众文化无处不在，对大众文化的审视和批评也应时时跟上。由此，我们更能清楚我们是谁。

金衡山　廖炜春

华东师范大学美国研究中心

2011-3

Chapter 1 Consumer Culture

The Passion of Consumption and the Consumer Society

消费热情与消费社会

If you were given a blank check to purchase anything—and everything—you wanted, what would you buy? Make a list and then annotate that list with brief explanations for why you want each item. Do your choices say something about yourself that you want others to know? Do they send an image?

Now consider the things you do own. Make another list and annotate it too. Why did you buy this item or that? Which were presents that reflect someone else's tastes and desires? What compromises did you have to make in choosing one item over another? How often did price or quality affect your decisions? How often did style or image? Are the images sent by your actual possessions any different from the ones sent by your ideal ones? Why? Or why not?

Such questions are a good place to begin a semiotic analysis of American consumer culture, for every choice you make in the products you consume, from clothing to furniture to cars to electronics and beyond, is a sign, a signal you are sending to the world about yourself. Those aren't just a pair of shoes you're wearing: They're a statement about your identity. That's not just a collection of CDs. It's a message about your worldview. Indeed, your music collection may say more about you than anything else you own.

To read the signs of American consumption, it is best to start with yourself, because you've already got an angle on the answers. But be careful and be honest. Remember, a cultural sign gets its meaning from the system, or code, in which it appears. Its significance does not lie in its usefulness but rather in its symbolism, in the image it projects, and that image is *socially constructed.* You didn't make it by yourself. To decode your own possessions, you've got to ask yourself what you are trying to say with them and what you want other people to think about you. And you've got to remember the difference between fashion and function.

The point is that when you interpret a cultural sign, the actual object is not what is meaningful in a simply semiotic analysis. What matters is the overall cultural system, the social context, in which that object appears. A highly portable, wireless communication box is not a sign in itself. It becomes a sign only when seen in relation to other objects and other signs.

When analyzing a consumer sign, you will often find yourself referring to particular decades in which certain popular fads and trends were prominent, for the decade in which a given style appears may be an essential key to the system that explains it. Have you ever wondered why American cultural trends seem to change with every decade, why it is so easy to speak of the sixties or the seventies or the eighties and immediately recognize the popular styles that dominated each decade? Have you ever looked at the style of a friend and thought, "Oh, she's so seventies"? Can you place an Earth Shoe① at the drop of a hat, or a Nehru jacket②? A change in the calendar always seems to herald a change in style in a consuming culture. But why?

The decade-to-decade shift in America's pop cultural identity goes back a good number of years. It is still easy, for example, to distinguish Fitzgerald's Jazz Age③ twenties from John Steinbeck's wrathful thirties④. The fifties, an especially connotative decade, raise images of ducktail haircuts and poodle skirts, drive-in culture and Elvis⑤, family sitcoms and white-bread innocence, while the sixties are remembered for acid rock, hippies, the student revolution, and back-to-the-land communes. We remember the seventies as a pop cultural era divided between disco, Nashville⑥, and John Travolta⑦ as dominant pop icons. The boom-boom eighties gave us Wall Street glitz and the yuppie invasion. Indeed, each decade since the first World War—which, not accidentally happens to coincide roughly with the rise of modern advertising and mass production—seems to carry its own consumerist style.

It's no accident that the decade-to-decade shift in consumer styles coincides with the advent of modern advertising and mass production because it was mass production that created a need for constant consumer turnover in the first place. Mass production, that is, promotes stylistic change because with so many products being produced, a market must be created to consume all of them, and this means constantly consuming more. To get consumers to keep buying all the new stuff, you have to convince them that the stuff they already have has gone out of style. Why else, do you think, do fashion designers completely redesign their lines each year? Why else do car manufacturers annually change their color schemes and body shapes when the old model year seemed good enough? The new designs aren't simply functional improvements (though they are

---

① 1970年代发明于斯堪的纳维亚的一种反传统的鞋子。该鞋鞋底较厚,鞋跟较细。穿上它,如同走在沙滩上。

② 尼赫鲁式上衣,源于印度。

③ 菲茨杰拉德,美国著名作家,著作有《了不起的盖茨比》、《夜色温柔》等。作品中反映了20世纪20年代美国社会的享乐主义等社会风气,该时期也被称为美国的爵士时代。

④ 约翰·斯坦贝克,美国著名作家,1939年出版小说《愤怒的葡萄》,反映上世纪30年代大萧条时期的社会。

⑤ 艾尔维斯·普莱斯利,"猫王",20世纪世界流行音乐重要人物,50年代摇滚乐的奠基者。

⑥ 纳什维尔,20世纪50年代逐渐开始成为美国乡村音乐大本营,许多音乐追随者来到这里。Nashville sound 成为乡村音乐的代名词。

⑦ 约翰·特拉沃尔塔,美国演员,1975年出演电视系列剧《欢迎回来,科特》,一炮而红;1977年和1978年又因主演《周末狂热》和《油脂》达到事业高峰。

marketed as such), they are inducements to go out and replace what you already have to avoid appearing out of fashion. Just think: If you could afford to buy any car that you want, what would it be? Would your choice a few years ago have been the same?

Mass production, then, creates consumer societies based on the constant production of new products that are intended to be disposed of with the next product year. But something happened along the way to the establishment of our consumer culture: **We began to value consumption more than production.** Listen to the economic news: consumption, not production, is relied upon to carry America out of its economic downturns. When Americans stop buying, our economy grinds to a halt. Consumption lies at the center of our economic system now and the result has been a transformation in the very way we view ourselves.

It has not always been thus in America, however. Once, Americans prided themselves on their productivity. In 1914, for example, the poet Carl Sandburg① boasted of a Chicago that was "Hog butcher for the world, Tool maker, Stacker of Wheat, Player with Railroads and the Nation's Freight Handler." One wonders what Sandburg would think of the place today. From the south shore east to the industrial suburb of Gary Indiana②, Chicago's once-proud mills and factories rust in the winter wind. The broken windows of countless tenements stare blindly at the Amtrak③ commuter lines that transport the white-collared brokers of the Chicago Mercantile Exchange to the city center, where trade today is in commodity futures, not commodities. Even Michael Jackson, Gary's most famous export, rarely goes home.

Meanwhile, a few hundred miles to the northwest, Bloomington④, Minnesota, buzzes with excitement. For there stands the Mall of America⑤, a colossus of consumption so large that it contains within its walls a seven-acre Knott's Berry Farm⑥ theme park, with lots of room to spare. You can find almost anything you want in the Mall of America, but most of what you will find won't have been manufactured in America. The proud tag "Made in the USA" is an increasingly rare item.

It's a long way from Sandburg's Chicago to the Mall of America, a trip that traverses America's shift from a producer to a consumer economy. This shift is not simply economic; it is behind a cultural transformation that is shaping a new mythology within which we define ourselves, our hopes, and our desires.

---

① 卡尔·桑德堡,美国"城市诗人",后半生在芝加哥度过,芝加哥被美国人视为"大肩膀城市"(City of the big Shoulder),即出自他的一首诗《芝加哥》。

② 该城市以炼钢厂著称。

③ 美国铁路客运公司。

④ 美国明尼苏达州第五大城市。

⑤ 全美最大的购物娱乐中心。其中一个特点是娱乐及休闲设施比例高,内有主题公园、水族馆、高尔夫球场、电影院及其他传统娱乐设施。另外还有520间零售专卖店,80多家餐饮店。该商场总建筑面积达420万平方尺。

⑥ 诺氏果园,美国主题游乐公园。1940年首个诺氏果园对外开放。每年万圣节前后都会举办诺氏恐怖园活动。

To live in a consumer culture is not simply a matter of shopping, however; it is also a matter of being. For in a consumer society you are what you consume, and the entire social and economic order is maintained by the constant encouragement to buy. The ubiquity of television and advertising in America is a direct reflection of this system, for these media deliver the constant stimulus to buy through avalanches of consuming images. Consider how difficult it is to escape the arm of the advertiser. You may turn off your TV set, but a screen awaits you at the checkout counter of your supermarket, displaying incentives to spend your money. If you rush to the rest room to hide, you may find advertisements tacked to the stalls. If you log onto the Internet, advertisements flash on the screen. Resistance is useless. Weren't you planning to do some shopping this weekend anyway?

In a cultural system where our identities are displayed in the products we buy, it accordingly behooves us to pay close attention to what we consume and why. From the cars we drive to the clothes we wear, we are enmeshed in a web of consuming images. …

In this chapter, Anne Norton gives us a semiotic analysis of shopping malls, mail-order catalogues, and the Home Shopping Network, focusing on the ways in which they construct a language of consumption tailored to specific consumer groups. Rachel Bowlby provides an analysis of the experience of shopping itself, at the same time, giving a critical account of the meaning of consumption for different people. Fred Davis surveys the history of blue jeans and how they have been transformed from an emblem of labor to one of leisure. Loretta Carrillo shows us a detailed picture of the development of American fashion since the early seventeenth century. With these readings done, you will come to know much about the passion of consumption in America and its various cultural implications.

Lesson 1 The Signs of Shopping

解读购物

ANNE NORTON

Introduction

Shopping malls are more than places to shop, just as mail-order catalogues are more than simple lists of goods. Both malls and catalogues are coded systems that not only encourage us to buy but, more profoundly help us to construct our very sense of identity, as stated in the J. Peterman catalogue that "constructs the reader as a man of rugged outdoor interests, taste and money". Thus, shopping is not merely aimed at meeting your material needs but also cultural and even political pursuits. In this selection from *Republic of Signs* (1993), Anne Norton (b. 1954), a professor of political science at the University of Pennsylvania, analyzes the many ways in which malls, catalogues and home shopping networks sell you what they want by telling you who you are.

Text

Shopping at the Mall

The mall has been the subject of innumerable debates. Created out of the modernist impulse for planning and the centralization of public activity, the mall has become the distinguishing sign of suburban decentralization, springing up in unplanned profusion. Intended to restore something of the lost unity of city life to the suburbs, the mall has come to export styles and strategies to stores at the urban center. Deplored by modernists, it is regarded with affection only by their postmodern foes. Ruled more by their content than by their creators' avowed intent, the once sleek futurist shells have taken on a certain aura of postmodern playfulness and popular glitz.

The mall is a favorite subject for the laments of cultural conservatives and others critical of the culture of consumption. It is indisputably the cultural locus of commodity fetishism. It has been noticed, however, by others of a less condemnatory disposition that the mall has something of the mercado, or the agora, about it. It is both a place of meeting for the young and one of the rare places where young and old go together. People of different races and classes, different occupations, different levels of education meet there. As M. Pressdee[①] and John Fiske[②] note,

---

① M. Pressdee (1944—2009),以犯罪文化学研究著称,作品关注青年社会及其犯罪文化,著有 *Agony or Ecstasy*: *Broken Transitions and the New Social State of Working-class Youth in Australia* 等。

② John Fiske, 1939 年生于英国,著名传播学学者,著有 *Understanding Popular Culture* (1989), *Television Culture* (1987)等。

however, though the mall appears to be a public place, it is not. Neither freedom of speech nor freedom of assembly is permitted there. Those who own and manage malls restrict what comes within their confines. Controversial displays, by stores or customers or the plethora of organizations and agencies that present themselves in the open spaces of the mall, are not permitted. These seemingly public spaces conceal a pervasive private authority.

The mall exercises its thorough and discreet authority not only in the regulation of behavior but in the constitution of our visible, inaudible, public discourse. It is the source of those commodities through which we speak of our identities, our opinions, our desires. It is a focus for the discussion of style among peripheral consumers. Adolescents, particularly female adolescents, are inclined to spend a good deal of time at the mall. They spend, indeed, more time than money. They acquire not simple commodities (they may come home with many, few, or none) but a well-developed sense of the significance of those commodities. In prowling the mall they embed themselves in a lexicon of American culture. They find themselves walking through a dictionary. Stores hang a variety of identities on their racks and mannequins. Their window displays provide elaborate scenarios conveying not only what the garment is but what the garment means.

A display in the window of Polo provides an embarrassment of semiotic riches. Everyone, from the architecture critic at the *New York Times* to kids in the hall of a Montana high school, knows what Ralph Lauren① means. The polo mallet and the saddle, horses and dogs, the broad lawns of Newport②, Kennebunkport③, old photographs in silver frames, the evocation of age, of ancestry and Anglophilia④, of indolence and the Ivy League⑤, evoke the upper class. Indian blankets and buffalo plaids, cowboy hats and Western saddles, evoke a past distinct from England but nevertheless determinedly Anglo.

Polo Brand Logo　Polo 商标

Walking from one window to another, observing one another, shoppers, especially the astute and observant adolescents, acquire a facility with the language of commodities. They learn not only words but a grammar. Shop windows employ elements of sarcasm and irony strategies of

① Polo：由美国设计师 Ralph Lauren 于 1967 年创立的高端休闲时装品牌。

② New Port：纽波特，位于美国罗德岛州。

③ Kennebunkport：位于缅因州。

④ Anglophilia：对英国人民、文化及习俗的极度崇尚。

⑤ Ivy League：常青藤联合会，指美国东部一些名牌大学（包括哈佛、耶鲁、哥伦比亚、普林斯顿、康奈尔、布朗、达特茅斯和宾夕法尼亚大学）。

inversion and allusion. They provide models of elegant, economical, florid, and prosaic expression. They teach composition.

The practice of shopping is, however, more than instructive. It has long been the occasion for women to escape the confines of their homes and enjoy the companionship of other women. The construction of woman's role as one of provision for the needs of the family legitimated her exit. It provided an occasion for women to spend long stretches of time in the company of their friends, without the presence of their husbands. They could exchange information and reflections, ask advice, and receive support. As their daughters grew, they would be brought increasingly within this circle, included in shopping trips and lunches with their mothers. These would form, reproduce, and restructure communities of taste.

The construction of identity and the enjoyment of friendship outside the presence of men was thus effected through a practice that constructed women as consumers and subjected them to the conventions of the market-place. Insofar as they were dependent on their husbands for money, they were dependent on their husbands for the means to the construction of their identities. They could not represent themselves through commodities without the funds men provided, nor could they, without money, participate in the community of women that was realized in "going shopping." Their identities were made contingent not only on the possession of property but on the recognition of dependence.

Insofar as shopping obliges dependent women to recognize their dependence, it also opens up the possibility of subversion (Fiske 13-42). The housewife who shops for pleasure takes time away from her husband, her family and her house and claims it for herself. Constantly taught that social order and her private happiness depend on intercourse between men and women, she chooses the company of women instead. She engages with women in an activity marked as feminine, and she enjoys it. When she spends money, she exercises an authority over property that law and custom may deny her. If she has no resources independent of her husband, this may be the only authority over property she is able to exercise. When she buys things her husband does not approve—or does not know of—she further subverts an order that leaves control over property in her husband's hands (Bowlby 22).

Her choice of feminine company and a feminine pursuit may involve additional subversions. As Fiske and Pressdee recognize, shopping without buying and shopping for bargains have a subversive quality. This is revealed, in a form that gives it additional significance, when a saleswoman leans forward and tells a shopper, "Don't buy that today it will be on sale on Thursday." Here solidarity of gender (and often of class) overcome, however partially and briefly the imperatives of the economic order.

Shoppers who look, as most shoppers do, for bargains, and salespeople who warn shoppers of impending sales, see choices between commodities as something other than the evidence and the exercise of freedom. They see convert direction and exploitation; they see the withholding of information and the manipulation of knowledge. They recognize that they are on enemy terrain and that their shopping can be, in *Michel de Certeau's*① term, a "guerrilla raid". This recognition in practice of the presence of coercion in choice challenges the liberal conflation of choice and consent.

Shopping at Home

Shopping is an activity that has overcome its geographic limits. One need no longer go to the store to shop. Direct mail catalogues, with their twenty-four-hour phone numbers for ordering, permit people to shop where and when they please. An activity that once obliged one to go out into the public sphere, with its diverse array of semiotic messages, can now be done at home. An activity that once obliged one to be in company if not in conversation, with one's compatriots can now be conducted in solitude.

The activity of catalogue shopping, and the pursuit of individuality are not, however, wholly solitary. The catalogues invest their commodities with vivid historical and social references. The J. Peterman② catalogue, for example, constructs the reader as a man of rugged outdoor interests, taste, and money. He wears "The Owner's Hat" or "Hemingway's Cap," a leather flight jacket or the classic "Horseman's Duster," and various other garments identified with the military athletes, and European imperialism. The copy for "The Owner's Hat" naturalizes class distinctions and, covertly racism:

> Some of us work on the plantation.
> Some of us own the plantation.
> Facts are facts.
> This hat is for those who own the plantation. (The J. Peterman)

Gender roles are strictly delineated. The copy for a skirt captioned "Women's Legs" provides a striking instance of the construction of the gaze as male, of women as the object of the gaze:

> just when you think you see something, a shape you think you recognize, it's gone and then it begins to return and then it's gone and of course you can't take your eyes off it.
>
> Yes, the long slow motion of women's legs. Whatever happened to those things at carnivals that blew air up into girls'

The J. Peterman catalogue
色彩丰富的邮寄广告

① Michel de Certeau(1925—1986),法国社会科学家、文化理论家,著有 *Culture in the Plural*, *The Practice of Everyday Life* 等。

② 由 J. Peterman 于 1987 年创办的邮寄商品零售公司。通过一些极具炫耀的文字宣传商品的特征,描述异域故事,以获得购买者的青睐。

skirts and you could spend hours watching. (ibid 5)

"You," of course, are male. There is also the lace blouse captioned Mystery: "lace says yes at the same time it says no." (ibid 3) Finally there are notes of imperialist nostalgia: the Sheapherd's Hotel (Cairo) ① bathrobe and white pants for "the bush" and "the humid hell-holes of Bombay and Calcutta②." (ibid 17)

> It may no longer be unforgivable to say that the British left a few good things behind in India and in Kenya, Singapore, Borneo③, etc., not the least of which was their Englishness. (ibid 20)

As Paul Smith observes, in his reading of their catalogues, the Banana Republic④ has also made capital out of imperial nostalgia (Smith 128-148).

The communities catalogues create are reinforced by shared mailing lists. The constructed identities are reified and elaborated in an array of semiotically related catalogues, one who orders a spade or a packet of seeds will be constructed as a gardener and receive a deluge of catalogues from plant and garden companies. The companies themselves may expand their commodities to appeal to different manifestations of the identities they respond to and construct. Smith and Hawken, a company that sells gardening supplies with an emphasis on aesthetics and environmental concern, puts out a catalogue in which a group of people diverse in age and in their ethnicity wear the marketed clothes while gardening, painting, or throwing pots. Williams-Sonoma⑤ presents its catalogue not as a catalogue of things for cooking but as "A Catalog for Cooks." The catalogue speaks not to need but to the construction of identity.

The Nature Company⑥ dedicates its spring 1990 catalogue "to trees," endorses Earth Day, and continues to link itself to the Nature Conservancy through posters and a program in which you buy a tree for a forest restoration project. Here, a not-for-profit agency is itself commodified, adding to the value of the commodities offered in the catalogue. In this catalogue, consumption is not merely a means for the construction and representation of the self, it is also a means for political action. Several commodities are offered as "A Few Things You Can Do" to save the earth: a string shopping bag, a solar battery recharger, a home newspaper recycler. Socially conscious, shopping is a liberal practice in every sense. It construes shopping as a form of election, in which one votes for good commodities or refuses one's vote to candidates whose practices are ethically suspect. In this respect, it reveals its adherence to the same ideological presuppositions that

---

① 位于埃及开罗的一家著名酒店,从19世纪后期到20世纪50年代曾声名远扬。
② 印度西部港口城市孟买,东北部港口城市加尔各答。
③ 婆罗洲(东南亚加里曼丹岛的旧称)。
④ 起源于1978年的美国时尚品牌公司,现属于盖普(GAP)时尚品牌公司。
⑤ 家具装饰公司,于1956年开设第一家店面,销售厨房用具及家居用品。
⑥ 成立于1972年,总部位于加州伯克利的连锁零售店,销售科普玩具、望远镜、艺术品、CD等。

structure television's Home Shopping Network① and other cable television sales shows.

…

The semiotic identification of consumption as an American activity indeed, a patriotic one, is made with crude enthusiasm on the Home Shopping Network and other video sales shows. Red, white, and blue figure prominently in set designs and borders framing the television screen. The Home Shopping Network presents its authorities in an office conspicuously adorned with a picture of the Statue of Liberty. Yet the messages that the Home Shopping Network sends its customers—that you can buy as much speech as you can afford, that you are recognized by others in accordance with your capacity to consume—do much to subvert the connection between capitalism and democracy on which this semiotic identification depends②.

Works Cited

Bowlby, R. *Just Looking: Consumer Culture in Dreiser, Gissing, and Zola.* London: Methuen, 1985.

Fiske, John. *Reading the Popular*. Boston: Unwin Hyman [now Routledge], 1989.

Smith, Paul. "Visiting the Banana Republic." *Universal Abandon*? ed. Andrew Ross for *Social Text.* Minneapolis: University of Minnesota Press, 1988.

The J. Peterman Company Owner's Manual No. 5. The J. Peterman Company. 2444 Palumbo Drive, Lexington, Ky 40509.

Questions to Consider

1. What does Norton mean when she claims that the suburban shopping mall appears to be a public place but in fact is not?
2. What is Norton's interpretation of Ralph Lauren's Polo line?
3. How is shopping a subversive activity for women, according to Norton?
4. How do mail-order catalogues create communities of shoppers, in Norton's view?
5. Behind the detailed and even vivid depiction of different shopping processes lies Norton's sharp criticism of shopping as a way of distorting a person's behavior, and to a large degree, democratic system in the society. How do you understand it?

---

① HSN，24 小时电视购物频道。

② 购买力与民主似乎成正比，但这恰恰是对民主的讽刺。

Lesson 2 The Haunted Superstore

徘徊于商场

RACHEL BOWLBY

Introduction

The experience of modern shopping is as complex as the corridors of an IKEA① furniture warehouse, at once magical and as Rachel Bowlby, the author of this essay, suggests in this analysis of department stores and supermarkets, insidious. Dazzled by goods, you may feel trapped in an environment for which there is no way out—especially if the computerized cash registers are down. And what is more, it produces a feeling of confinement deep in your mind at the time when you are possessed with ecstasy in what has been shopped. Mixing psychology and history, Bowlby meditates upon the complex, and often contradictory nature of shopping, exploring its gender implications and its diferences when viewed from a European and an American perspective. The author of *Just Looking*: *Consumer Culture in Dreiser*, *Gissing and Zola* (1985), *Shopping with Freud* (1992) and *Carried Away*: *The Invention of Modern Shopping* (2001), from which this selection is taken, Bowlby teaches English, French, and American Studies at the University of York.

Text

Saturday, 21 **September** 1996;
IKEA, **Purley Way**, **South London**

It is late in the afternoon and the lines of wide carts loaded up with flatpacks of future furniture stretch back from the row of checkouts. Back and back, right into the warehouse section, they bump up against the people still trying to pick out their own cardboard packages and happily oblivious, as yet, to the fate in store for them.

The IKEA Building, in blue and yellow, the color of the national flag of Sweden

宜家家居，外墙为经典的蓝色与黄色，即瑞典国旗的颜色

But gradually the news is getting through. The computers are down; all the purchase transactions are having to be done manually. The prospect of a

① 宜家家居于1943年创建于瑞典，截至2008年12月为止宜家在全世界的36个国家和地区中拥有292家大型门市，是全球最大的家具家居用品商家。

handwritten receipt from IKEA seems quaintly unreal. Nobody, nothing moves, forward or backwards. Nobody protests. Nobody seems to be talking to anyone else, passing the time in complaint or chat. We all stand sullenly by our carts, keeping our places, half heartedly trying to decode the announcements. And nobody walks out, back through the store or out past the checkouts, leaving their cart behind.

We just can't leave now. These carts bear the tangible results of an afternoon's hard work. It may have been fun at the time, but now the prospect of going home empty-booted obliterates that from view. If we let go of the goods, we would have nothing to show for all this time and effort. And we are attached to these things already. This big brown box contains what a joyous, newly verbal two-year-old, still trailing clouds of consumerly innocence, is already proudly calling "my IKEA bed." Here we are, voluntarily trapped inside a store that we are unable to leave. Why did we come here in the first place? What is keeping us here? Is our behavior perverse, a stubborn refusal to give up? Or is it calmly rational, suffering the short-term frustrations and making the best of a bad situation? In this IKEA world there isn't much to choose between the two, or much to choose at all.

The checkout come to a dead halt is a long-standing nightmare for retailers. For decades, self-service stores of all kinds have sought to ease what they recognize as that difficult moment when customers finally emerge from the dreamier delights of trolley-filling to reach the point of purchase. There, reality intrudes in the form of the monetary transaction, and the trance of the aisles is broken by a slow line at the checkout. For supermarkets, barcode technology was the godsend of the 1980s; but shut down the computers, and chaos—slow despondency—is come again.

IKEA with the computers down might be a comic vision of a late twentieth-century nightmare. We are familiar with tales of shopping as exploitation, addiction, false allure. As we wait, the frame for pondering the experience is already there for us: the store that you can't get out of as a microcosm of this consumer world, where shopping is endless and always, everywhere the same. One IKEA is much like another, each as reproducibly "Swedish" as the next, from Leeds to Groningen① and from Paris to New Jersey. For critics of over-consumption, the over-stark contrast between movement and stoppage, dream and reality that the stores seek to parry is ever present—not the avoidable contingency or the dreaded emergency but the staple metaphor of shopping as hellish confinement.

Consumer culture lends itself to images of unconscious imprisonment. The deluded are unaware that their desires are for worthless or superfluous things, or that they are shaped—if not entirely created—by the skills and tricks of advertising and other forms of presentation. They do not know that there is a better and freer world than the shopping world in which they find themselves; for them it has no exit, nor do they seek one.

① Leeds：英国北部城市利兹。Groningen：荷兰东北部城市格罗宁根。

Opposite dark pictures like these stand their mirror images: shopping as freedom of choice, pleasure, material progress. Instead of confinement, darkness, hidden controls, shopping in its positive guise appears as sheer heaven of more prosaically as the proud symbol of modern mobility. People are no longer restricted to their traditional horizons, whether geographical, social, or psychological; consumer choice epitomizes their liberty to move away from old constrictions, to indulge the freedom of new desires and demands, and to take on different identities as they wish. This is also the dream world of shopping's own self images, its beautiful stores and its glossy advertisements, where people's desires are treated as forever open to change and fulfilment. ...

Supermarket①, Anywhere, Around 1999

Here you are in the middle of the things. You are halfway through your list. You steer your way smoothly up and down, putting out your hand to take something at intervals, and placing it in your trolley. You know what you want, what it looks like, whereabouts it will be. You see different categories of product, differences between labels and brands and sizes that enable you to home in quickly on what you are seeking. This, not that. When you have finished, the seventeen items you have expertly selected from among the twenty thousand or so different possibilities are checked through: one by one. A job has been efficiently done.

King Kullen of New York, the first supermarket in the world.

金库伦联合商店,世界上最早的超级市场,1930 年建于纽约。

Here you are in the middle of the things. You have been here for quite a while. Twenty minutes, maybe half an hour. You came in to get something for tonight and thought you might as well stock up a bit while you were here. Everywhere around you are colors, letters, figures, pictures, all made to attract you. This and that. There is always something new or something on offer. If something appeals, you'll pick it up, perhaps put it back. But your mind is not really on what you're buying or looking at; you're thinking of other things. You will be here for some time, and eventually you will depart, with the same seventeen things.

What is the difference between the two? None, from the point of view of the receipt, which lists everything both shoppers buy in all-informing detail. To all supermarket intents and purposes, they are one and the same person; and maybe they are. In another life, on another day, the first shopper might easily slip into becoming the second, and the second, when pressed, might find herself or himself acting like the first.

---

① 超级市场最早产生于 1930 年的美国纽约。1930 年 8 月,美国人迈克尔·库仑(Michael Cullen)在美国纽约州开设了第一家超级市场——金库仑联合商店。

The first shopper thinks of herself as in control, taking what she wants and only what she wants. The second shopper sees herself as comfortably susceptible to all the attractions of the place. The first shopper knows about the second and regards her with a certain affectionate scorn. The second shopper knows about the first and thinks she is missing out on the pleasure of shopping. Both, as well, partly share the other's opinion of them. And the first would also confess that she gets a certain pleasure out of her efficiency, while the second would declare that she also uses the time in the supermarket productively, unwinding the rest of her day as she drifts. Both, at times, when in a particular frame of mind, become the other one. The first is sometimes waylaid by a striking new product, while the second rushes urgently past, blind to everything but the two or three things she came in for.

Both, in one way are figments or manufactures of the marketing imagination. Once upon a time, in the 1960s, it was principally the second shopper who featured, and she was dim and dazed, a childlike housewife passively picking up brightly colored things she had no thought to resist. Nowadays the shopper is viewed positively as the rational planner who knows what she wants and competently makes her selection. The upgraded version of the second shopper, meanwhile, is no longer seen as necessarily stupid, but as someone who simply enjoys what others regard as a chore. These characters, and others too, and mixes of all of them, have filtered into shopping consciousness, to become the cartoon versions or templates of how we regard our own behavior. Like the products surrounding us, images of shoppers supply the background to the way that we experience and talk about whatever it might be that we are doing when we shop.

Some may see themselves as more involved or more detached than others, and certainly there is every possible gradation of difference between people's individual consumerly practices and ways of thinking. For what it's worth, shopping seems to be a part of everyday life in which people positively enjoy discussing their own peculiarities, as well as other people's, and often with much more subtlety than is shown by official psychologists of consumer behavior seeking to make predictable sense of shopping. But even when people identify themselves as non-shoppers, or anti-consumers, there is no getting away from the surrounding wash of consumerly ways of representing human choices and feelings, in which we are all immersed.

On the one hand, there is a semi-technical language, derived from the big academic business of consumer psychology that has entered everyone's vocabulary for describing or experiencing their own behavior. Solemnly or ironically or both, with a knowing mixture of mastery and susceptibility we refer to "loss-leaders①" and describe our "impulse purchases②" or avoidance of them. Marketing language may also be applied more widely. The "sell-by-date③", heralded as an important breakthrough for food retailing in the early 1970s, moved out of the store in the 1990s to

① 低价促销,通过价格战略吸引顾客,争取市场份额。
② 未经计划的、不由自主的购物行为。
③ 保质期,最迟销售期。

be used in relation to anything passé①; now the expression has probably passed its own. We can speak the marketing language, we know what is being done to us; but this same language also shapes our understanding.

On the other hand, arguments about shopping and consumption involve much more than the situations in which actual buying takes place. Thirty or forty years ago, the phrase "consumer society" usually suggested a deluded, essentially female population of the unresisting victims of manipulative advertising and vulgar, alluring displays. The implication might have been that too much of their life was shopping; but the consumers of "consumer society" were not represented as being anything other than shoppers. Now in a remarkable rhetorical turnabout, the consumer has been elevated to a status of exemplary good sense in areas extending far beyond shopping itself, with the name implying not a situation of vulnerability or delusion but quite the contrary. The consumer has ceased to be seen as part of a jellishly susceptible mass, having become instead an individual endowed with rights of which, by implication, his or her previous incarnations had been deprived. She (or he) is no longer a fool, but the model of modern individuality the one who, as patient or passenger or parent, demands and gets the deal to which, implicitly, she was always entitled but that she was never granted before.

In the course of this process, the consumer has lost her sex. "He or she" is rhetorically removed from the picture of real shopping, where men and women remain readily distinguishable. In terms of perceptions of shopping (and women), the shift is crucial. Ceasing to be seen as passive, exploited, and dim, the consumer has ceased to be seen as female.

The Department Store and the Supermarket

Though it wouldn't be obvious from a glance at the customers in IKEA today, the history of shopping is largely a history of women, who have overwhelmingly been the principal shoppers both in reality and in the multifarious representations of shopping. This history began to gather momentum in the middle of the nineteenth century when department stores entered the world. Their splendid new buildings and permanent exhibitions of lovely new things brought middle-class women into town to engage in what was historically a new activity: a day's shopping. They were places of leisure and luxury offering women the image of a life that they could then, in fantasy if not in substance, take home with them. So after the frustrations of IKEA, and before we embark upon the intricacies of the supermarket's many small histories, let us dwell for a

Macy's : A department store in New York.
梅西百货,纽约曼哈顿市中心的标志之一。

① 过期,过时。

moment in the more leisurely spaces of its principal predecessor as a revolutionary new idea in shopping.

The department store offered an experience of aristocratic grandeur to every woman customer. There, she could act the queen and be treated like royalty. Department stores flattered women into seeing themselves as part of a beautiful environment; they fostered a sense of perpetual and limitless desire for things, in a kind of socialized abandonment. Loosened longings blended and unfixed existing social differences: New shopping instincts made no distinction of class, just as anyone might look like a lady.

In the nineteenth century was the department store; in the twentieth century was the supermarket. Department-store shopping was leisured, middle-class, metropolitan. Supermarkets and self-service, the great retailing innovations of the twentieth century, came from the opposite directions. Instead of luxury, they offered functionality and standard products; instead of the pleasures of being served, consumers could congratulate themselves on saving money by doing the work themselves. Food shopping was associated with necessity and routine, whereas department stores had promoted a sense of goods that engendered new desires and possibilities, out of the ordinary. It was the difference between going shopping—an open-ended, pleasurable, perhaps transgressive experience—and doing the shopping, a regular task to be done with the minimum expenditure of time, labor, and money.

But in many ways, department stores and supermarkets belong together. Both are large-scale institutions, selling a vast range of goods under one roof and making use of modern marketing principles of rapid turnover and low profit margins①. Both rely on economies of scale through their large selling areas, and through direct buying in bulk from producers or manufacturers. Both were taken, when they first appeared on the scene, as emblematic of contemporary developments not only in marketing, but in social life more generally: cities and leisure in one case, suburbs and cars in the other.

Both came to be represented in terms of magic and enchantment, seen as either pleasurable or insidious. Department stores, and supermarkets in their later developments, dazzled with their lighting and displays of goods so beautiful, or so much. Like the supermarket, the department store presented a new kind of indoor retailing space, which was open, with goods on display for looking at, and with no sense that customers had to come in with a definite intention to buy. Both were thought to produce in their female customers states of mind removed from the normal: the collective ecstasy of the nineteenth-century crowd of women in front of an array of heavenly new fabrics, or the hypnotic trance of the 1950s housewife numbed by the Muzak② as she glides along the aisles.

Yet the differences between the two kinds of store count far more than the similarities in their

① rapid turnover and low profit margin: 快速资金周转,薄利多销。

② 一种背景音乐。

respective mythologies. First, in what they sell. The department store offered everything and anything, though with a concentration on clothes and furnishings. The supermarket is associated with something the department store did not always sell: food. Whereas the department stores were represented as bringing the glamour of fashion to the middle classes, supermarkets brought cheap food to "the masses." In one case, luxury items are offered to a class aspiring to an image of affluence and a sex aspiring to an image of beauty; in the other, necessities are made available to all.

The department store is European; the supermarket is American. The association in the first case is false, in the sense that department stores appeared in the United States at more or less the same time as in Paris or London or Berlin. In the second case, it's right, but the contrast functions to reinforce other distinctions. The department store is considered to be feminine, frivolous, French, and fashionable; in its Parisian form, it is one of the emblems of nineteenth-century modernity for Walter Benjamin's① retrospect in the first part of the twentieth. The supermarket, massive and materialistic, figures as an American invention subsequently exported to Europe; and it was.

The department store was called (by Emile Zola②) "the cathedral of modern commerce," (Zola 258) it was also a "palace" for the middle classes. As a cathedral, it took over from religion; it had its consecrated building, and its own rituals and festive seasons in the form of designated times for sales and events in relation to particular themes and product groups: linens, toys, oriental rugs, autumn and spring fashions; winter and summer sales. The plain checkout visible at the end of each supermarket aisle hardly offers itself as an altar, though the uproar in the early 1990s in England about Sunday opening may suggest that the weekly shopping trip is indeed in some sense a symbolic replacement for the traditional family ritual.

As a palace, the department store offered a spectacle of opulence accessible to anyone who cared to enter and participate in an image of the aristocratic life. In the first American supermarkets, the show was less a planned or beautiful display than a performance or stunt. This was later to appear as a markedly dirty trick. In the 1960s, at the height of consumerist protests against exploitation by the big food corporations, the supermarket took on dramatically negative appearances, as a "jungle" (Giordan) or "trap" (Cross), both giving titles to influential books of the period. The images imply primitive aggression but also a space of confusion or imprisonment from which you cannot escape. Where the department store invites you in, the supermarket grabs you and won't let you out.

The differences between the images of the two kinds of store are today much less clear than they were. Supermarkets sell many kinds of product apart from food. Like department stores in

① 瓦尔特·本雅明(1892—1940),德国现代卓有影响的思想家、哲学家和马克思主义文学批评家,其重要作品包括《发达资本主义时代的抒情诗人》、《单向街》、《机械复制时代的艺术作品》和《巴黎拱廊街》等。

② 埃米尔·左拉(1840—1902),法国作家。代表作:《萌芽》、《娜娜》、《卢贡-马卡尔家族》等。

their heyday, they try to present themselves as places for comfortably spending some time, with refreshments and rest rooms provided. Not the least remarkable feature of IKEA is that it seems to combine, in almost parodically differentiated sequence, the two forms of shopping, in history and experience. It is both department store and supermarket, both leisure and work, the one and then the other as though in artificial textbook separation.

…

These two versions of modern shopping, as labor or leisure, the pleasurable or the functional, are installed as co-present orientations in the minds of shoppers, as much as in the layout and self presentation of shops themselves. At IKEA on that unusual afternoon, it was easy enough for one to pinpoint a moment when shopping shifted its meaning decisively from enjoyment to imposition. But much of the strangeness of shopping and consuming can come from the difficulty of knowing, experientially or otherwise, the difference between shopping's delights and its demands.

Works Cited

Cross, Jennifer. *The Supermarket Trap: The Consumer and the Food Industry.* Bloomington: Indiana UP, 1970.

Giordan, Marion. *The Consumer Jungle*. London: Fontana, 1974.

Zola, Emile. *Au Bonheur des Dames*. Paris Garnier Fiammarion, 1971.

Questions to Consider

1. What are the two kinds of shoppers whom Bowlby describes and marketers imagine?
2. Describe in your own words Bowlby's analytic opposition between the image of the department store and the image of the supermarket. What evidence does she advance to illustrate these images? How adequate do you find that evidence?
3. How has the image of the consumer changed in recent years, according to Bowlby?
4. What support does Bowlby offer to demonstrate her contention that the consumer has ceased to "be seen as female"? Do you find that support to be adequate?
5. There are two kinds of critical judgments referred by the author to the consumers in the modern society. What are they? And do you agree with them?

Lesson 3 Blue Jeans

牛仔裤

FRED DAVIS

Introduction

Blue jeans are almost certainly America's greatest contribution to fashion history and in this analysis, which originally appeared in his book *Fashion Culture and Identity* (1992), the author, Fred Davis(1925—1992), a former professor of sociology at the University of California at San Diego, shows how this staple of the American wardrobe has become a symbol of many of our most enduring, and contradictory cultural values through a historical demonstration of the shifting implied meaning of blue jeans. At once an emblem of democratic populism and elite status symbol, blue jeans are part of an American dialectic, Davis argues, in which "status and antistatus, democracy and distinction," are in a constant flux, moving with the tides of history itself. What is worth particular attention is how the fashion industry has incorpated the social meanings into the product for its promotion, through which process it has gained a right to formulate some of the key concepts in the social and cultural system.

How blue jeans survived redefinitions.
千变万化,还是牛仔裤(酷)。

Text

The new clothes [jeans] express profoundly democratic values. There are no distinctions of wealth or status, no elitism; people confront one another shorn of these distinctions.

——CHARLES A. REICH①
The Greening of America

Throughout the world, the young and their allies are drawn hypnotically to denim's code of hope and solidarity—to an undefined vision of the energetic and fraternal Americanness inherent in them all.

——KENNEDY FRASER②
"That Missing Button"

---

① Charles A. Reich (1928—):美国学者,耶鲁大学教授。*The Greening of America* (1970)是他写的关于赞颂 1960 年代反文化运动的一部著作。

② Kennedy Fraser (1948—):出生于英国的美国时尚评论家,著有 *Fashionable Mind——Reflections on Fashion 1970-1981*(1981)。

Since the dawn of fashion in the West some seven hundred years ago, probably no other article of clothing has in the course of its evolution more fully served as a vehicle for the expression of status ambivalences and ambiguities than blue jeans. Some of the social history supporting this statement is by now generally well known. First fashioned in the mid-nineteenth-century American West by Morris Levi Strauss①, a Bavarian Jewish peddler newly arrived in San Francisco, the trousers then as now were made from a sturdy, indigo-dyed cotton cloth said to have originated in Nimes, France. (Hence the anglicized contraction to denim from the French de Nimes.) A garment similar to that manufactured by Levi Strauss for goldminers and outdoor laborers is said to have been worn earlier in France by sailors and dockworkers from Genoa, Italy, who were referred to as "genes"; hence the term jeans. The distinctive copper riveting at the pants pockets and other stress points were the invention of Jacob Davis, a tailor from Carson City, Nevada, who joined the Levi Strauss firm in 1873, some twenty years after the garment's introduction.

More than a century went by, however, before this workingman's garment attained the prominence and near-universal recognition it possesses today. For it was not until the late 1960s that blue jeans, after several failed moves in previous decades into a broader mass market, strikingly crossed over nearly all class, gender, age, regional, national, and ideological lines to become the universally worn and widely accepted item of apparel they are today. And since the crossover, enthusiasm for them has by no means been confined to North America and Western Europe. In former Soviet bloc countries and much of the Third World, too, where they have generally been in short supply, they remain highly sought after and hotly bargained over.

A critical feature of this cultural breakthrough is, of course, blue jeans' identity change from a garment associated exclusively with work (and hard work, at that) to one invested with many of the symbolic attributes of leisure: ease, comfort, casualness, sociability and the outdoors. Or, as the costume historians Jasper and Roach-Higgins (1987) might put it, the garment underwent a process of cultural authentication that led to its acquiring meanings quite different from that with which it began. In bridging the work/leisure divide when it did, it tapped into the new consumer-goods-oriented, postindustrial affluence of the West on a massive scale. Soon thereafter it penetrated those many other parts of the world that emulate the West.

But this still fails to answer the questions of why so rough-hewn, durably hued, and crudely tailored a piece of clothing should come to exercise the fascination it has for so many diverse societies and peoples, or why within a relatively short time of breaking out of its narrow occupational locus it spread so quickly throughout the world. Even if wholly satisfactory answers elude us, these questions touch intimately on the twists and turns of status symbolism②. ...

To begin with, considering its origins and longtime association with workingmen, hard

---

① Morris Levi Strauss：李维斯牛仔裤品牌创始人。李维·施特劳斯 1853 年从德国巴伐利亚来到美国旧金山，1873 年开始创立李维斯品牌，1920 年开始生产现代牛仔裤。

② twists and turns of status symbolism：（社会）地位象征的曲折变化。

physical labor, the outdoors, and the American West, much of the blue jeans' fundamental mystique seems to emanate from populist sentiments① of democracy, independence, equality, freedom, and fraternity. This makes for a sartorial symbolic complex② at war, even if rather indifferently for nearly a century following its introduction, with class distinctions, elitism, and snobbism, dispositions extant nearly as much in jeans-originating America as in the Old World. It is not surprising, therefore, that the first non-"working stiffs" to become attached to blue jeans and associated denim wear were painters and other artists, mainly in the southwest United States, in the late 1950s and 1940s (Friedmann 1987). These were soon followed by "hoodlum" motorcycle gangs ("bikers") in the 1950s and by New Left③ activists and hippies in the 1960s (Belasco n. d.). All these groups (each in its own way of course) stood strongly in opposition to the dominant conservative, middle-class, consumer-oriented culture of American society. Blue jeans, given their origins and historic associations, offered a visible means for announcing such antiestablishment sentiments. Besides, jeans were cheap, and, at least at first, good fit hardly mattered.

Whereas by the late 1950s one could in some places see jeans worn in outdoor play by middle-class boys, until well into the 1960s a truly ecumenical acceptance of them was inhibited precisely because of their association with (more, perhaps, through media attention than from firsthand experience) such disreputable and deviant groups as bikers and hippies. Major sales and public relations campaigns would be undertaken by jeans manufacturers to break the symbolic linkage with disreputability and to convince consumers that jeans and denim were suitable for one and all and for a wide range of occasions (Belasco n. d.). Apparently such efforts helped; by the late 1960s blue jeans had achieved worldwide popularity and, of greater relevance here, had fully crossed over the occupation, class, gender, and age boundaries that had circumscribed them for over a century.

What was it—and, perhaps, what is it still—about blue jeans? Notwithstanding the symbolic elaborations and revisions (some would say perversions) to which fashion and the mass market have in the intervening years subjected the garment, there can be little doubt that at its crossover phase its underlying symbolic appeal derived from its antifashion significations: its visually persuasive historic allusions to rural democracy, the common man, simplicity, unpretentiousness, and, for many, especially Europeans long captivated by it, the romance of the American West with its figure of the freespirited, self-reliant cowboy.

But as the history of fashion has demonstrated time and again, no vestmental symbol is inviolable. All can, and usually will be, subjected to the whims of those who wish to convey more or different things about their person than the "pure" symbol in its initial state of signification communicates. Democratic, egalitarian sentiments notwithstanding, social status still counts for

① populist sentiments：平民主义的、民粹主义的思想，指倾向于社会平等的思想和情绪。
② a sartorial symbolic complex：男式服饰系列。
③ New Left：指 1960 年代以大学生反抗运动为主的新左派，强调建立有更多人参与的民主社会。

too much in western society to permanently suffer the proletarianization that an unmodified blue-jean declaration of equality and fraternity projected①. No sooner, then, had jeans made their way into the mass marketplace than myriad devices were employed for muting and mixing messages, readmitting evicted symbolic allusions, and, in general, promoting invidious distinctions among classes and coteries of jean wearers. Indeed, to the extent that their very acceptance was propelled by fashion as such, it can be said an element of invidiousness was already at play. For, other things being equal and regardless of the "message" a new fashion sends, merely to be "in fashion" is to be one up on those who are not as yet.

Elite vs. Populist Status Markers

Beyond this metacommunicative function, however, the twists, inversions, contradictions, and paradoxes of status symbolism to which blue jeans subsequently lent themselves underscore the subtle identity ambivalences plaguing many of their wearers. In a 1973 piece titled "Denim and the New Conservatives," Kennedy Fraser (1981, 92) noted several such, perhaps the most ironic being this:

> Some of the most expensive versions of the All-American denim theme have come bouncing into our stores from European manufacturers. The irresistible pull of both European fashion and denim means that American customers will pay large sums for, say, French blue jeans despite the galling knowledge that fashionable young people in Saint-Tropez② are only imitating young people in America, a country that can and does produce better and cheaper blue jeans than France.

By 1990 a nearly parallel inversion seemed about to occur in regard to the garment's Post-1950s image as leisure wear, although for destination other than fields and factories. With the introduction of Men's fall fashions for the year featuring "urban denim," a spokesman for the Men's Fashion Association said (Hofmann 1990): "It's not just about cowboys and country and western any more. It used to be that denim meant play clothes; now men want to wear it to the office the next day."

worn out short blue jeans.
酷裤喜欢否?

Framing the garment's status dialectic was the contest of polarities, one pole continuing to emphasize and extend blue jeans' "base-line" symbolism of democracy, utility, and

---

① 此句的大意为:尽管美国流行民主和平等观念,但对于社会地位的重视使得牛仔裤所指向的"无产化"意向(平等,博爱)不可能被完全接受。

② Saint-Tropez: 圣特罗佩,法国南部城市。

classlessness, the other seeking to reintroduce traditional claims to taste, distinction, and hierarchical division. (Any individual wearer, and often the garment itself, might try to meld motifs from both sides in the hope of registering a balanced, yet appropriately ambivalent, statement.)

Conspicuous Poverty: Fading and Fringing

From the"left" symbolic (and not altogether apolitical) pole came the practice of jean fading and fringing. Evocative of a kind of conspicuous poverty, faded blue jeans and those worn to the point of exposing some of the garment's warp and woof① were soon more highly prized, particularly by the young, than new, well-blued jeans. Indeed, In some circles worn jeans commanded a higher price than new ones. As with Chanel's little black dress, it cost more to look "truly poor" than just ordinarily so, which new jeans by themselves could easily accomplish. But given the vogue that fading and fringing attained, what ensued in the marketplace was predictable: Jeans manufacturers started producing prefaded, worn-looking, stone-or acid-washed jeans. These obviated, for the average consumer if not for the jeans connoisseur disdainful of such subterfuge, the need for a long break-in period.

Labeling, Ornamentation, and Eroticization

From the"right" symbolic pole② emerged a host of stratagems and devices, all of which sought in effect to de-democratize jeans while capitalizing on the ecumenical appeal they had attained: designer jeans, which prominently displayed the label of the designer; jeans bearing factory sewn-in embroidering, nailheads, rhinestones, and other decorative additions, specially cut and sized jeans for women, children, and older persons; in general, jeans combined (with fashion's sanction) with items of clothing standing in sharp symbolic contradiction of them, e. g. sports jackets, furs, dress shoes, spiked heels, ruffled shirts, or silk blouses.

Jeans for gals,牛仔女裤,突出性感。

Paralleling the de-democratization of the jean, by the 1970s strong currents toward its eroticization were also evident. These, of course, contravened the unisex, de-gendered associations the garment initially held for many: the relative unconcern for fit and emphasis on comfort; the fly front for both male and female; the coarse denim material, which, though it chafed some, particularly women, was still suffered willingly. Numerous means were found to invest the jean and its associated wear with gender-specific, eroticized meaning. In the instance of women—and this is more salient sociologically since it was they who had been de-feminized by donning the blatantly masculine blue jeans in the first place—these included the

① warp and woof: 基础,基本东西。

② "right":"右翼"的,指改变牛仔裤原有的平民化意蕴,即所谓的"去民主化"。与此词相对的则是"left","左翼"的,指突出牛仔裤的平民风格,如故意弄旧、弄破等(见文中前一段)。

fashioning of denim material into skirts, the "jeans for gals" sales pitches of manufacturers, the use of softer materials, cutting jeans so short as to expose the buttocks, and, in general, the transmogrification of jeans from loose-fitting, baggy trousers into pants so snugly pulled over the posterior as to require some women to lie down to get into them. So much for comfort, so much for unisexuality! Interestingly in the never-ending vestmental dialectic on these matters baggy jeans for women again became fashionable in the mid-1980s.

Designer Jeans

Of all of the modifications wrought upon it, the phenomenon of designer 15 jeans speaks most directly to the garment's encoding of status ambivalences. The very act of affixing a well-known designer's label—and some of the world's leading hautes couturiers in time did so—to the back side of a pair of jeans has to be interpreted, however else it may be seen, along Veblenian① lines, as an instance of conspicuous consumption, in effect, a muting of the underlying rough-hewn proletarian connotation of the garment through the introduction of a prominent status market. True, sewing an exterior designer label onto jeans—a practice designers never resort to with other garments—was facilitated psychologically by the prominent Levi Strauss & Co. label, which had from the beginning been sewn above the right hip pocket of that firm's denim jeans and had over the years become an inseparable part of the garment's image. It could then be argued, as it sometimes was, that the outside sewing of a designer label was consistent with the traditional image of blue jeans. Still, Yves Saint Laurent, Oscar de la Renta, or Gloria Vanderbilt②, for that matter, are not names to assimilate easily with Levi Strauss, Lee, or Wrangler③, a distinction hardly lost on most consumers.

But as is so characteristic of fashion, every action elicits its reaction. No sooner had the snoblike, status-conscious symbolism of designer jeans made its impact on the market than dress coteries emerged whose sartorial stock-in-trade was a display of disdain for the invidious distinctions registered by so obvious a status ploy. This was accomplished mainly through a demonstration of hyperloyalty to the original, underlying egalitarian message of denim blue jeans. As Kennedy Fraser (1981, 93) was to observe of these countercyclicists in 1973:

> The denim style of the more sensitive enclaves of the Village, the West Side, and SoHo is the style of the purist and neo-ascetic. Unlike the "chic" devotee of blue jeans, this loyalist often wears positively baggy denims, and scorns such travesties as embroideries and

---

① Veblenian: Thorstein Veblen (1857—1929)，美国经济学家，在 1899 年出版的《有闲阶级的理论》(*Theory of Leisure Class*)一书中提出夸耀性消费(conspicuous consumption)思想，即有闲阶级的一部分通过消费表明自己的社会地位。

② Yves Saint Laurent, Oscar de la Renta, or Gloria Vanderbilt: 伊夫·圣罗兰，奥斯卡·德拉伦塔，格萝拉·范德比，都是高级时装品牌。

③ Lee, or Wrangler: 牛仔裤品牌。

nailheads. To underline their association with honesty and toil, the denims of choice are often overalls.

Not long after, the"positively baggy denims" of which Fraser speaks—this antifashion riposte to fashion's prior corruption of denim's 1960s-inspired rejection of status distinctions—were themselves, with that double reflexive irony at which fashion is so adept, assimilated into the fashion cycle. Then those "into" denim styles could by "dressing down" stay ahead of—as had their older, first-time-around denim-clad siblings of the sixties—their more conformist, "properly dressed" alters.

Conclusion

And so… do the dialectics of status and antistatus, democracy and distinction, inclusiveness and exclusiveness pervade fashion's twists and turns; as much, or even more, with the workingman's humble blue jeans as with formal dinner wear and the evening gown.

But such is fashion's way. If it is to thrive it can only feedoff the ambiguities and ambivalences we endure in our daily lives and concourse, not only over those marks of social status considered here but equally over such other key identity pegs as age, gender, and sexuality, to mention but the most obvious. Were it the case, as some scholars have maintained, that fashion's sole symbolic end was registering and re-registering invidious distinctions of higher and lower, or better and lesser—that is, distinctions of class and social status—it would hardly have enough "to talk about", certainly not enough to account for its having thrived in Western society for as long as it has. But, as we have already seen…, it does have more to say: about our masculinity and feminity, our youth and age, our sexual scruples or lack thereof, our work and play, our politics, national identity, and religion. This said, one need not take leave of what has engaged us here, that rich symbolic domain that treats of the deference and respect we accord and receive from others (what Max Weber① meant by status), in order to appreciate that fashion is capable of much greater subtlety, more surprises, more anxious backward glances and searching forward gazes than we credit it with.

Works Cited

Belasco, Warren A. n. d. "Mainstreaming Blue Jeans: The Ideological Process, 1945—1980." Unpublished.

Fraser, Kennedy. *The Fashionable Mind*. New York: Knopf, 1981.

Friedmann, Daniel. *Une Histoire du blue jean*. Paris: Ramsay, 1987.

Hoffmann, Deborah. "New Urbanity for Denim and Chambray." *New York Times,* Sept. 24, 1990.

① Max Weber (1864—1920):德国社会学家,对现代社会学理论做出重要贡献。

Jasper, Cynthia R., and Mary Ellen Roach-Higgins. "History of Costume: Theory and Instruction." *Clothing and Textile Research Journal* 5, no. 4 (Summer): 1-6, 1987.

Reich, Charles A. *The Greening of America*. New York: Crown, 1970.

Questions to Consider

1. Why, according to Davis, were jeans linked with "disreputability" (para. 6) until the mid-1960s?
2. In Davis's view what enabled jeans to "crossover" (para. 2) from being disreputable to fashionable?
3. Summarize in your own words the ambivalence between "democracy and distinction" (para. 17) or "left" (para. 12) and "right" (para. 15) that Davis ascribes to jeans since the 1960s.
4. How does Davis interpret the advent of designer jeans?
5. How does the fashion industry make use of the shifting and ambivalent meanings of jeans for the promotion of their products, and at same time, how are the social meanings of jeans are created around this product?

Historical Perspective **历史视角**

Fashion

时尚

LORETTA CARRILLO

One of the many ways in which the Jamestown① Settlers of 1607 reflected their status as English colonists was in their style of clothing. Men dressed in standard doublet, trunk hose and boots while women wore wide, cut-away farthingales and stiff, straight bodices. Half a century later in the 1650s the Virginia Cavaliers② were still following the London dress fashions. Men wore knickerbockers gathered with ribbons at the knees and women wore the latest fashions of billowing sleeves and gummed, black silk patches of stars or crescent moons on the face. The southern Virginia wilderness settlers, on the other hand, were much less fashionably dressed. Their clothing was in the popular mode, but was of a more simple cut and made of leather and homespun fabrics. North and South Carolina frontier dress followed similar fashions as the rest of the region with the exception of Charleston③ where fashionable dress was featured when the city became a fashionable cultural center in the late eighteenth century.

The fashions of the New England Pilgrim settlers at Plymouth conformed generally to the current English dress mode but were stripped of ornamentation. The Pilgrim men wore the traditional doublet and hose and the women simple farthingales. Their dress, however, had been influenced to a degree by Dutch fashion, since the Pilgrims had spent many years in exile in the Low Countries④. The Puritans of Massachusetts Bay—who came later to the New World, having departed directly from the mother country, dressed in the current English mode more faithfully than their Pilgrim counterparts. In time, New England society developed a heterogeneous population consisting of Puritan ecclesiastics⑤, merchants and merchant adventurers, yeomen and tenant farmers, and African slaves, all of whose rank in society was reflected in their dress. The Puritan fathers dressed in the severe Puritan garb of broad-brimmed hat, black doublet, coarse stockings and heavy, square-toed shoes. They attempted to lay down dress codes by sermonizing

---

① 位于弗吉尼亚州,依詹姆士河,建于 1607 年。常被认为是英国在美国的第一个殖民地所在,其名字来自英皇詹姆士一世。

② 弗吉尼亚州支持英国查理一世统治的保王党员。

③ 位于南卡罗纳州,18 世纪中叶成为南部殖民地区的贸易重心。

④ 包括荷兰、比利时、卢森堡。

⑤ 清教传教士。

against extravagance in dress, but had little success in doing so. The merchant class dressed much as did the Virginia colonists while the wealthy classes in both colonies followed London high fashions. The tenant farmer class dressed as simply as did their counterparts in England while the slaves were relegated to hand-me-downs and crudely constructed clothing of coarse fibers.

During this period and continuing for the better part of America's fashion history, wearing fashionable clothing was directly related to a person's social standing in the community, since only wealthy persons could afford imported clothing and fine silks and satins. Upper-class women in the seventeenth century Virginia and New England colonies were dressed in silks, fur-lined hoods, lace, and ribbons. Less wealthy persons relied on coarse fibers and crude construction which attempted, more often unsuccessfully, to follow fashionable styles.

In other developing regions, the same class distinctions could be seen in fashions. The Quaker① settlers of Pennsylvania were of the peasant class and wore sober, plain dress in the style of the period. Philadelphia, on the other hand, grew into a bustling trade center by the late eighteenth century where imported dresses and fabrics made the wealthy class as well attired as their counterparts in New England and Virginia.

Later, the American Revolution and the resulting stress on equalitarianism popularized more simple, less ornamented dress. In more practical terms, the growing emphasis on simplicity was a result of the cut-off of commerce between the colonies and Europe, due to the British blockade. Hatred of the British allowed a greater French influence on American fashions after the 1783 peace treaty; nevertheless, the mother country's dress continued to predominate over American fashion styles.

By the late 1700s, powdered wigs and frilled shirts were no longer fashionable for men, and male dress settled into a variation of the recognizable form known today as jacket and trousers. Influenced by post-revolutionary French fashions, women's dress in America underwent a "Classical Revival" that featured short-bodiced gowns, high waistlines and low necklines. During this time period, but on another front, Westward expansion② in America gave rise to a more rugged lifestyle reflected in the functional, simple clothing of the frontier settlers. From Canada to Spanish Florida, Texas, and the Southwest, the hunting smock, loose tunic, moccasins, and leggings were standard men's dress. Much use was made of animal hides③ and furs for jackets and caps. Women's dress was hardly fashionable but was sturdy, useful, and made of crude homespuns. Unlike the leisured classes of the colonies and their descendants, the frontier families had greater use for functional as opposed to purely fashionable, ornamented dress. Spanish colonization of the United States Southwest introduced the prevailing Spanish and Mexican mode of dress to the region. In addition, the functional *vaquero* or Mexican cowboy attire greatly

① 贵格会教徒,教友派信徒。可追溯至17世纪中叶英格兰和威尔士的基督教运动。他们相信普通人可以和上帝直接交流。

② 开始于1776年美国独立后,是美国扩大领土版图及开发西部的过程。

③ 兽皮。

influenced the dress of the American cowboy and frontiersman.

The increasing industrialization of America in the early 1800s created a thriving American textile industry which accounted for enormous increases in cotton production over the period 1815-1830. The single invention that democratized fashion in America as well as in England was the sewing machine, invented in 1830 by the French tailor Barthelemy Thimmonier but patented in the United States in 1851 by Issac Singer as a more elaborate instrument with eye-point needle and under-thread shuttle. The sewing machine allowed fashion as an industry to form quickly, and exporters, importers, wholesalers, and department and retail stores quickly developed to participate in the burgeoning trade. As the American clothing industry continued to grow, the large labor force required to run the industry inevitably exerted an important influence from 1900 onward when the International Ladies Garment Workers Union① organized to demand reform of appalling working conditions in the factories.

Further allowing the middle-class women in America access to stylish clothing was the development of the paper pattern industry. In the 1850s, women could obtain basic paper dress patterns in women's magazines, either diagrammed or printed as tissue supplements. Enterprising women and men such as Madame Ellen Louise Demorest and William Jennings Demorest along with Ebenezer Butterick and James McCall recognized the current and potential market for patterns and developed the industry so that by the 1860s a thriving market for patterns copied from English and Parisian designers in several sizes with explicit sewing instructions were available in department stores, retail outlets and mail order houses to middle and lower class women.

The American paper pattern industry not only brought fashionable dress to the average woman, but it also created a fashion press. In 1860, the Demorests introduced *Madame Demorest's Quarterly Mirror of Fashions* devoted exclusively to fashion news, and they later inserted a fashion section in the weekly *New York Illustrated News*. Butterick's dress pattern business was so successful that by 1867 he issued the *Ladies Report of New York Fashions*, and in the 1870s he had established wholesale depots in Chicago and Montreal for Butterick patterns.

Other more established women's periodicals such as *Godey's Ladies Book, Peterson's Magzine, Leslie's,* and *Harper's Bazaar* which carried diagrams and tissue supplements found competition in the newer fashion journals. So established was the paper pattern industry by the late 1800s that the 1876 Centennial Exhibition② at Philadelphia displayed two pavilions of women's paper dress patterns, one by the Demorests and the other by Ebenezer Butterick.

An important feature of women's fashions during the mid-nineteenth century which focused attention on women's health rather than on the aesthetics of fashion was the Dress Reform Movement of the 1850s. This small but vocal group in America protested against the dangerous,

---

① 1900年成立于纽约,是最早吸纳女性会员的工会之一,在1920和1930年代的美国劳工社会起过重要作用。

② 庆祝《独立宣言》签署一百周年纪念。是美国首次世界博览会,吸引了大约一千万游客,美国五分之一的人口来此参观。

constricting features of tight bodices that threatened women's health and anatomical development. The cumbersome bustles and dragging trains that collected street filth were also presented as dangerous features of popular women's fashions of the period. In protest, Amelia Bloomer[1] introduced the knee-length skirt worn over baggy trousers known as "Bloomers," but the outfit was never generally accepted. Only at the century's end was it used and then simply as a cycling outfit. Similar dress reform groups in England and Germany also did not fare well with either popular or mass fashions.

Amelia Bloomer in her "Bloomer suit"
穿着女士长裤的 Amelia Bloomer

Haute couture[2] had formally emerged in Paris and London when in the late 1850s "couturiers" such as Charles Frederick Worth[3] designed garments for European nobility and the upper classes and displayed and sold specially designed and manufactured garments in elite salons. During the early twentieth century in America, New York City, Boston, and Chicago emerged as the country's fashion capitals, all of which took their cues from Paris. The heart of the clothing industry in America, however, was the mass production of clothes, including copies of designers' styles which provided the average woman her level of haute couture.

Gloria Swanson in 1921
1921 年衣着艳丽的葛罗莉亚·史旺逊

By 1914, World War I brought the fashion business to a halt in Europe, and America was subsequently cut off from European designers. Edna Woofman Chase, editor of *Vogue*, responded by putting on a fashion show with live models to show original American designs. After the war, Hollywood and its stars and American culture itself began to have a greater share of influence upon American fashion. The Jazz Age[4] produced Hollywood stars such as Pola Negri[5],

① Amelia Bloomer(1818—1894),美国早期女权运动倡导者,经她提倡女士长裤(bloomer)风行一时。

② 高级女子时装制作。

③ Charles Frederick Worth(1825—1895),高级女子时装之父,生于英国,其作品在法国生产制作。

④ 爵士时代:一战后至大萧条前,传统的清教道德土崩瓦解,享乐主义开始大行其道。

⑤ Pola Negri(1894—1987),生于波兰,1917 年到柏林拍片,获得成功后进入美国影坛。曾主演《包法利夫人》、《帝国饭店》等多部影片。

Gloria Swanson[①], and Greta Garbo[②] all of whom popularized bobbed hair, cloche hats[③], heavy eye-makeup and the "vamp" look. Also originating during this decade was the cocktail dress, shortened calf-length dresses, lowered waistlines and strap shoes for women while for men the grey-flannel trousers or "Oxford Bags[④]" became popular. The high fashion designer, Coco Chanel, greatly influenced the fashions of the decade when she introduced a simple, natural look in the boxy suit which resembled the convent uniform she had worn as a girl. The Chanel look made women appear young and boyish in contrast to the popular Oriental designs of one of Chanel's counterparts in Paris, Paul Poiret. Chanel also facilitated mass manufacture of couture designs by using simple fabrics such as jersey and cotton which made copying easier. Lastly, the period was known for such fashion items as the "Eton Crop" hairdo[⑤], long strings of pearls and "slave" bracelets.

In reaction against the boyish look generated by the Chanel suit and hip-length waist dresses of the 1920s, the fashions of the early 1930s were influenced by Italian-born designer Schiaparelli[⑥] and stressed normal waistlines, rounded bust, longer hair and lowered, mid-calf dress and skirt lengths. The Depression and its hardships inevitably influenced fashions of the latter part of the decade. A more masculine trend appeared in ladies suits which emphasized wider shoulders and shoulder pads; however, the short, full-skirted, ballet-length, dinner dress became very popular in America during the period and contrasted sharply with the severe day suit. Despite catastrophic financial setbacks of the decade, the 1930s was also the period when designers and manufacturers stressed the importance of accessories and presented coordinated collections of handbags, shoes, and gloves.

Inevitably, World War II influenced fashions of the 1940s, for the better part of the decade featured the "Austerity Look." Fashion historians point out that this decade marks the first time fashion was dictated by the masses and not by elite designers. Skirt lengths were short, jackets were long and square-shouldered, and hair was set in rolls at the nape of the neck and tied with scarves knotted at the top of the head. This "no-frills" look appeared to suit the world's anxious, wartime mood. Claire McCardell[⑦] further pioneered an "American Look[⑧]" that was essentially casual when she revealed a taste for simple fabrics such as seersucker, cotton, and voile. In many

---

① 葛罗莉亚·史旺逊(1899—1983),美国演员。默片时期最为著名的女演员及时尚偶像。最著名的作品是1950年的《日落大道》(*Sunset Boulevard*)。

② 嘉宝(1905—1990),生于瑞士,好莱坞电影史上最著名女星之一,曾获奥斯卡终身成就奖。1920年进入演艺圈,1941年息影。曾主演《安娜·卡列尼娜》等作品。

③ 钟形女帽。

④ 受剑桥学生青睐的一种宽松下垂的裤子。

⑤ 一种女士短发,流行于1920年代,妇女往往配以钟形女帽。

⑥ Schiaparelli(1890—1973),生于罗马贵族家庭,设计的服装色彩和想像力丰富,具有超现实主义特点,并大胆地将艺术与服装相结合,气势直逼20年代由Chanel创造的黑裙天下。

⑦ Claire McCardell(1905—1958),成衣设计师。

⑧ 一种认为服装应该是"大众的,休闲的"的理念,反对当时法国式正装。

ways, McCardell may have set the precedent for the casual look Americans have since preferred in their clothing, epitomized in the American love for denim which blossomed in the 1960s.

On the high fashion scene, Christian Dior soon tired of the austerity look and introduced "The New Look" in 1947 which reigned for the entire decade of the 1950s. Round shoulders, corseted waists, long, billowing skirts, dinner gloves and stiletto high-heeled shoes signaled a return to femininity and prosperity. An interesting and important feature of wartime austerity which Dior incorporated into high fashion and popularized was the use of synthetic fibers such as Rayon and Lurex. Though previously despised, the artificial fibers which later included Banlon and Orlon proved durable, easy to care for and an attractive alternative to natural fibers.

The decade of the 1950s is critical to American fashion history because it marks America's complete dominance in the ready-to-wear trade. Ready-to-wear clothing had been an infant industry in the post Civil War period and had blossomed in the last decade of the century. By the decade of the 1950s, the American ready-to-wear production and merchandizing experts had so perfected their trade that millions of profit dollars were being made on copies of European haute couture designer clothing. In time, European designer houses as a group saw the light and eventually set up boutiques in America to sell their own copies. But by the early 1960s, they had rivals in American designers such as Bill Blass①, Geoffrey Beene and Calvin Klein who were all making huge profits from off-the-rack copies of clothing designed specifically for the ready-to-wear market. These fashions stressed the casual, suburban lifestyle that came to dominate the American scene. By 1966, individual American ready-to-wear designer houses could boast of profits in the $200 million range.

The 1960s was indisputably the decade of ready-to-wear, denim and blue jeans, pop fashions, including mini skirts, vinyl dresses, unisex clothing and the breakdown of all classic fashion rules in America and in Europe as well. Fashion was now ruled over by the middle and working classes, by youth and, to a great extent, not by dictates at all but by personal taste. British ready-to-wear designer Mary Quant popularized denim and above-the-knee hemlines and model Twiggy, with her long, lean, boyish figure, popularized the mini skirt. The Hippie culture in the late 1960s influenced mass fashion by popularizing peasant garments and miring clashing patterns and textures of clothing. Fashion personalities such as Jacqueline Kennedy were created by the now neatly organized New York fashion press. As an avid consumer of fashion, Jackie Kennedy exerted enormous influence over popular fashion trends for the entire decade, making everything from low-heeled buckle shoes to Spanish mantillas popular. The 1960s were important, too, because the decade marked the period when men's fashions were given more attention by high-fashion designers Pierre Cardin and John Weitz.

The Hippie craze for ethnic and peasant dress was carried over into the early 1970s and

---

① 1922年生于美国印第安纳州，17岁到纽约，在纽约帕森设计学院学习时装设计。1970年收购Maurice Rentner公司并改名为Bill Blass。其服装设计极富想像力，华丽雍容却不入俗套。

assimilated by high fashion. The mood in dress, however, was still anti-haute couture, with jeans, work clothes, and casual sports-wear predominating. The pantsuit for both casual and evening wear was most popular with women in the early 1970s while hemlines came to below-the-knee in mid-decade, several years after the public completely rejected the mini-length hemline. In the late 1970s, London's punk rock look, complete with leather jackets, dyed purple and pink hair and safety pin earrings, influenced American fashion, particularly the youth in urban centers.

A sizable reaction against the tough, punk look in the early 1980s, however, has been the "classic" look which stresses a simple, neat and tailored appearance. The fashion extravagances of the 1960s have given way in the 1980s to a casual though refined appearance that is essentially conservative and traditional. This trend has influenced women's fashions, particularly the way in which women dress in the business world. The recent flurry of "Dressing for Success" books and manuals attempt to show women executives, administrators, office managers and other businesswomen how to dress in order to be accepted into management and business circles. The stress is usually on conservative, tailored fashions that purportedly show women appropriately dressed for the serious, no-frills world of work.

On the more popular level, contemporary popular fashion, interestingly, again puts emphasis upon the couture designers who had been told in the 1960s to take their cues from popular fashion. The craze now appears to be for the designer label—Bill Blass, Dior, Givenchy, Calvin Klein—on everything from jeans to scarves, perfume, and luggage. After two decades of stress upon individuality and personal taste in fashion, the American public of the early 1980s now values the designer label, apparently for its declaration of status and wealth. More importantly, perhaps, the American fashion consumer craves designer labels on everything from sunglasses to brassieres in order to affirm its own ability to buy items that previously were reserved only for the wealthy, elite class.

Chapter 2 Advertising

The Signs of Advertising in America
解读广告

Let's start with an example. Here is a very simple advertisement for a Timex watch. A picture of the watch, a short statement, a tag with information about the watch and the familiar Timex slogan, some small print at the bottom: there doesn't seem to be much more to it than that. But appearances can be deceiving—and indeed, they often are in advertisements.

The ad is centered on a simple statement: "If you think it's cool, it is." The longest word in the sentence is only five letters, reminding us of other familiar advertising slogans such as "Just do it," "Coke is it," and "I love what you do for me." In addition to their quite basic vocabulary, these slogans share a certain quality of vagueness: the "it" in "Just do it," like the "it" in "Coke is it" and the "what" in the Toyota slogan, are what semioticians might call "floating signifiers": their meaning is open and flexible, determined substantially by the reader of the ad. The same can be said for the "it" in this Timex ad: does "it" refer only to the watch? If so, why doesn't the statement say, "If you think *this watch* is cool, it is"? Clearly, an all-encompassing word like "it" allows the statement to be about more than just the watch.

Even more interesting in this ad is the word "cool": what exactly is "cool"? It's a word that we all define differently, and Timex invites us here to take our own definition of "cool" and associate it with the watch. Whatever each of us thinks of as "cool," that's what this watch is. While vagueness usually leads to poor communication, you can see how it's used effectively here by the advertiser: "cool" tells us virtually nothing about the watch, but makes us feel good about it nonetheless. And of course, "cool" appeals to a certain audience: precisely the young, upscale, Generation X types who might be reading *Icon*, the glossy and expensive new "thoughtstyle" magazine in which we found the ad. So, targeting a smaller audience, Timex can afford to be more specific than Coke can be when it claims to be "it". Still, the watch is "cool" rather than "groovy" (too old) or "the bomb" (too new). In that one word alone and in the way it's used, we can see the ad hard at work trying to make its product appealing to potential customers.

When we look at the slogan in the Timex ad, we can also see a degree of complexity behind its seeming simplicity. Even if we accept that the word "it" refers only to the watch, the sentence invites two different interpretations:

1. "If you think this watch is cool, well, you're right, because it is."
2. "If you think this watch is cool, then it is (because you say it is)."

This is a fine difference, but an important one. The first way of reading the sentence suggests that the watch is naturally, essentially cool, and so the reader is to be congratulated on being perceptive enough to see coolness when he or she comes across it. In the second reading, the watch isn't naturally cool at all; it's the reader who decides that the watch is cool. Either way, the reader of the ad gets a compliment and perhaps an ego-boost: either he or she is cool enough to recognize a cool watch, or he or she has the power to determine coolness. The first option might appeal to a more insecure sort of reader, someone who fears that he or she can't distinguish cool from uncool. The second reading confirms the confidence of a more secure reader, someone who knows perfectly well what's cool and what isn't. In other words, the statement appeals simultaneously to both the "wanna-be cools" and the "already cools" who might be reading *Icon*.

The appeal of the advertisement, however, goes beyond this. It is not just to show and tell. In effect, it's a form of behavior modification, a psychological strategy designed not only to inform you about products but to persuade you to buy them by making associations between the products and certain pleasurable experiences that may have nothing to do with the product at all, like sex or a promise of social superiority, or simply by making you laugh.

Usually an effective piece of advertisement follows three stages in the making process:

—**substituting images of desire for the actual products**—Coca Cola ads, for example, don't really sell soda: they sell images of fun, or popularity, or of sheer celebrity, promising a gratifying association with the likes of celebrities like Whitney Houston, the "real thing①".

—**transforming desire into necessity**—again, take Coca Cola for an example, it promises the real pleasure for you, the "real thing" is something you can not do without.

—**the commodification of desire**—this is the last but more important stage in the ad making process; by associating logically unrelated desire with an actual product and by making it become a necessary product in your life, it reflects the process of a shift from a producing economy to a consuming economy, the key point of which is the process of commodification. A commodity is the link between the visible product and invisible desire. The latter is embodied in the commodification of the former; meanwhile, the cultural values are added to the products to speed up the commodification of desire with the help of ads. **"Desire is what loosens the pocketbook strings."** And what makes this happen, largely, is due to the appeal of not merely the product itself but its

① 可口可乐公司广告用语:It's the real thing (1969)。其他不同年代的用语还有:Coke is it! (1982), Make it Real (2005)等。1986 年著名黑人女歌手惠特尼·休斯顿为可口可乐公司演唱低糖可乐(diet coke)产品主打歌曲"Just for the Taste of it."

cultural images through the transformation of advertisements. Accordingly, advertisements also carry much of political, religious, ethical, historical and economical messages. It, thus, becomes a social institution that shapes our life in various ways.

Several readings in this chapter explain in further detail the ways in which we can be influenced if not really manipulated by advertising. In *Master of Desire: The Culture of American Advertising* Jack Solomon probes into the structure of advertising from the perspective of American culture, the American dream in particular. Focuing on the paradoxical elements in the American dream, Solomon finds admen make full use of this cultural pattern and their products appeal to the psychological impulse of desire deeply rooted in the minds of the ordinary American people. This psychological exploration is further pushed forward by Jib Fowles in the essay *Advertising's Fifteen Basic Appeals*. He points out a variety of strategies advertisements use to appeal to our emotions even though we may think we are making product choices using our intellect. In different people's eyes, advertisements may mean different things. William Lutz seems to hold a critical attitude toward those admen who always use those "weasel words" in their advertising language. As a result, misleading can be a real possiblity for many ads.

In any way, whatever your view of advertising, keep in mind as you read the following articles that everything in advertisements—from sexy models to simple black and white pictures of watches—exist solely for three well-calculated reasons: to sell, sell and sell.

Lesson 4 Masters of Desire: The Culture of American Adertising

欲望大师:美国的广告文化

JACK SOLOMON

Introduction

Advertising campaigns come and go, as do the products they promote, but what does not change so quickly are the cultural patterns that advertisers rely on to work their magic. For as Jack Solomon(b. 1954) argues in this excerpt from *The Signs of Our Time* (1988), advertising does not work in a vacuum: it plays on deeply held cultural values and desires to stimulate consumption. To analyze an ad, then, is to analyze the culture in which it appears. As far as this excerpt is concerned, the relation between American Dream and various kinds of ads turn out to be the main point of attention. A professor of English at California State University, Northridge, Solomon is also the author of *Discourse and Reference in the Nuclear Age*(1988) and the coeditor (with Sonia Maasik) of *California Dreams and Realities* (1999).

Text

> Amongst democratic nations, men easily attain a certain equality of condition; but they can never attain as much as they desire.
>
> ——ALEXIS DE TOCQUEVILLE①

On May 10, 1831, a young French aristocrat named Alexis de Tocqueville arrived in New York City at the start of what would become one of the most famous visits to America in our history. He had come to observe firsthand the institutions of the freest, most egalitarian society of the age, but what he found was a paradox. For behind America's mythic promise of equal opportunity, Tocqueville discovered a desire for *unequal* social rewards, a ferocious competition for privilege and distinction. As he wrote in his monumental study, *Democracy in America:*

> When all privileges of birth and fortune are abolished, when all professions are

---

① Alexis-Charles-Henri Clérel de Tocqueville (1805—1859):法国著名政治思想家和历史学家托克维尔,著有 *Democracy in America*(1835)和 *Regime and the Revolution*(1856)。在这两部著作中,他探寻了西方社会中不断增强的平等性对个人和国家的影响。游访美国后,他写下 *Democracy in America*(1835),如今被视为是社会学和政治科学的早期经典作品。

accessible to all, and a man's own energies may place him at the top of any one of them, an easy and unbounded career seems open to his ambition. ...But this is an erroneous notion, which is corrected by daily experience. [For when] men are nearly alike, and all follow the same track, it is very difficult for any one individual to walk quick and cleave a way through the same throng which surrounds and presses him.

Yet walking quick and cleaving a way is precisely what Americans dream of. We Americans dream of rising above the crowd, of attaining a social summit beyond the reach of ordinary citizens. And therein lies the paradox.

The American dream, in other words, has two faces: the one communally egalitarian and the other competitively elitist. This contradiction is no accident; it is fundamental to the structure of American society. Even as America's great myth of equality celebrates the virtues of mom, apple pie, and the girl or boy next door, it also lures us to achieve social distinction, to rise above the crowd and bask alone in the glory. This land is your land and this land is my land, Woody Guthrie's① populist anthem tells us, but we keep trying to increase the "my" at the expense of the "your". Rather than fostering contentment, the American dream breeds desire, a longing for a greater share of the pie. It is as if our society were a vast high-school football game, with the bulk of the participants nosily rooting in the stands while, deep down, each of them is wishing he or she could be the star quarterback or head cheerleader.

For the semiotician, the contradictory nature of the American myth of equality is nowhere written so clearly as in the signs that American advertisers use to manipulate us into buying their wares. "Manipulate" is the word here, not "persuade"; for advertising campaigns are not sources of product information, they are exercises in behavior modification. Appealing to our subconscious emotions rather than to our conscious intellects, advertisements are designed to exploit the discontentments fostered by the American dream, the constant desire for social success and the material rewards that accompany it. America's consumer economy runs on desire, and advertising stokes the engines by transforming common objects—from peanut butter to political candidates—into signs of all the things that Americans covet most.

But by semiotically reading the signs that advertising agencies manufacture to stimulate consumption, we can plot the precise state of desire in the audiences to which they are addressed. Let's look at a representative sample of ads and what they say about the emotional climate of the country and the fast-changing trends of American life. Because ours is a highly diverse, pluralistic society, various advertisements may say different things depending on their intended audiences, but in every case they say something about America, about the status of our hopes, fears, desires, and beliefs.

---

① 又作 Woodrow Wilson(1912—1967),美国著名的创作型歌手兼民乐音乐人,他的作品题材广泛,涉及政治、民俗、童谣和即兴创作等。他最有名的歌曲是 This Land Is Your Land (1940),流行于美国校园。

We'll begin with two ad campaigns conducted by the same company that bear our Alexis de Tocqueville's observations about the contradictory nature of American society: General Motors' campaigns for its Cadillac and Chevrolet lines. First, consider an early magazine ad for the Cadillac Allanté①. Appearing as a full-color, four-page insert in *Time*, the ad seems to say "I'm special—and so is this car" even before we've begun to read it. Rather than being printed on the ordinary, flimsy pages of the magazine, the Allanté spread appears on glossy coated stock. The unwritten message here is that an extraordinary car deserves an extraordinary advertisement, and that both car and ad are aimed at an extraordinary consumer, or at least one who wishes to appear extraordinary compared to his more ordinary fellow citizens.

An advertisement for Cadillac Allanté (1987) with the following words: "Allanté merges European road manners with Cadillac comfort and convenience. Cadillac specified that allanté coachwork be designed and handcrafted by Pininfarina of Italy—designer of Ferrari Testarossa and Rolls-Royce Camargue."

Allanté 融汇欧洲车型的风尚和卡迪拉克(Cadillac)的舒适与便捷。卡迪拉克之 Allanté 特别由意大利 Pininfarina 设计公司亲自设计,该公司曾设计了 Ferrari Testarossa 和 Rolls-Royce Camargue。

(具有欧洲顶级设计水准的 Cadillac Allanté,带给美国人别样的身份自豪感。)

Ads of this kind work by creating symbolic associations between their product and what is most coveted by the consumers to whom they are addressed. It is significant, then, that this ad insists that the Allanté is virtually an Italian rather than an American car, an automobile, as its copy runs, "Conceived and Commissioned by America's Luxury Car Leader—Cadillac" but "Designed and Handcrafted by Europe's Renowned Design Leader—Pininfarina②, SpA, of Turin, Italy." This is not simply a piece of product information, it's a sign of the prestige that European luxury cars enjoy in today's automotive marketplace. Once the luxury car of choice for America's status drivers, Cadillac has fallen far behind its European competitors in the race for the prestige market. So the Allanté essentially represents Cadillac's decision, after years of resisting the trend toward European cars, to introduce its own European import—whose high cost is clearly printed on the last page of the ad. ...

American companies manufacture status symbols because American consumers want them. As Alexis de Tocqueville recognized a century and a half ago, the competitive nature of democratic

① Allanté 是 Cadillac(凯迪拉克系列)推出的第一款超奢华敞篷车,1987 年出品,1993 年停产。

② Pininfarina S. p. A. 是一个意大利的汽车设计公司,在意大利 Turin 省的 Cambiano 从事汽车车身的设计和制造。很多高端的汽车制造商都雇佣 Pininfarina 进行汽车设计。

societies breeds a desire for social distinction, a yearning to rise above the crowd. But given the fact that those who do make it to the top in socially mobile societies have often risen from the lower ranks, they still look like everyone else. In the socially immobile societies of aristocratic Europe, generations of fixed social conditions produced subtle class signals. The accent of one's voice, the shape of one's nose, or even the set of one's chin immediately communicated social status. Aside from the nasal bray and uptilted head of the Boston Brahmin①, Americans do not have any native sets of personal status signals. If it weren't for his Mercedes-Benz and Manhattan townhouse, the parvenu Wall Street millionaire often couldn't be distinguished from the man who tailors his suits. Hence, the demand for status symbols, for the objects that mark one off as a social success, is particularly strong in democratic nations—stronger even than in aristocratic societies, where the aristocrat so often looks and sounds different from everyone else.

Status symbols, then, are signs that identify their possessors' place in a social hierarchy, markers of rank and prestige. We can all think of any number of status symbols—Rolls-Royces, Beverly Hills② mansions, even Shar Pei puppies③ (whose rareness and expense has rocketed them beyond Russian wolfhounds as status pets and has even inspired whole lines of wrinkle-faced stuffed toys)—but how do we know that something *is* a status symbol? The explanation is quite simple: when an object (or puppy!) either costs a lot of money or requires influential connections to possess, anyone who possesses it must also possess the necessary means and influence to acquire it. The object itself really doesn't matter, since it ultimately disappears behind the presumed social potency of its owner. Semiotically, what matters is the signal it sends, its value as a sign of power. One traditional sign of social distinction is owning a country estate and enjoying the peace and privacy that attend it. Advertisements for Mercedes-Benz, Jaguar, and Audi automobiles thus frequently feature drivers motoring quietly along a country road, presumably on their way to or from their country houses. …

Ads that are aimed at a broader market take the opposite approach. If the American dream encourages the desire to "arrive," to vault above the mass, it also fosters a desire to be popular, to "belong." Populist④ commercials accordingly transform products into signs of belonging, utilizing such common icons as country music, small-town life, family picnics, and farmyards. All of these icons are incorporated in GM's "Heartbeat of America" campaign for its Chevrolet line. Unlike the Seville commercial, the faces in the Chevy ads look straight at us and smile. Dress is casual; the mood upbeat. Quick camera cuts take us from rustic to suburban to urban scenes, creating an American montage filmed from sea to shining sea. We all "belong" in a Chevy.

Where price alone doesn't determine the market for a product, advertisers can go either way.

---

① Boston Brahmins 也被称作波士顿第一家庭(First Families of Boston),自称是建立波士顿城的英国新教徒的后代,被视为是构成东海岸历史核心的要素之一。他们常常与 Boston Brahmin 口音联系在一起。

② Beverly Hills 是位于加州洛杉矶西部的一个城市,在 2007 年的时候被列为全美最贵的房价市场,一个中等房屋要价 2200 万美元。

③ 沙皮狗,原产自中国,身上皱纹很深,舌头呈蓝黑色,曾经被 *Time* 杂志列为世界珍奇狗种之一。

④ 平民主义者。

Both Johnnie Walker and Jack Daniel's are better-grade whiskies, but where a Johnnie Walker ad appeals to the buyer who wants a mark of aristocratic distinction in his liquor, a Jack Daniel's ad emphasizes the down-home, egalitarian folksiness of its product. Johnnie Walker associates itself with such conventional status symbols as sable coats, Rolls-Royces, and black gold; Jack Daniel's gives us a Good Ol' Boy① in overalls. In fact, Jack Daniel's Good Ol' Boy is an icon of backwoods independence, recalling the days of the moonshiner and the Whisky Rebellion of 1794②. Evoking emotions quite at odds with those stimulated in Johnnie Walker ads, the advertisers of Jack Daniel's have chosen to transform their product into a sign of America's populist tradition. The fact that both ads successfully sell whisky is itself a sign of the dual nature of the American dream. …

Johnnie Walker (1988)

Jack Daniel's (1986)

同是 80 年代的广告,Johnnie Walker 将自己与建国之父联系在一起,传播高雅的贵族气息;而 Jack Daniel's 则平易近人,突显普通人的友情,散发浓郁的亲切感。

Populist advertising is particularly effective in the face of foreign competition. When Americans feel threatened from the outside, they tend to circle the wagons and temporarily forget their class differences. In the face of the Japanese automotive "invasion," Chrysler runs populist commercials in which Lee Iacocca③ joins the simple folk who buy his cars as the jingle "Born in America④" blares in the background. Seeking to capitalize on the popularity of Bruce

---

① Good Ol' Boy 是一个美国俚语,可用来描述一个人为人谦和、社会名声好。

② The Whiskey Rebellion 是 18 世纪 90 年代发生在美国西部的一场抵制政府运动,运动产生的根源在于美国西部对以东部为基础的政府表示不满。这场运动得名于西部人民反对政府在 1791 年对威士忌征收消费税,运动在 1794 年达到高潮。

③ 美国著名商界人士,1978 年任 Chrysler 集团总裁兼首席执行官,在 1980 年代重振了 Chrysler 集团。

④ Bruce Springsteen 在 1984 年创作并演唱的一首歌。歌词涉及越战对美国的影响,被广泛地认为是一首爱国主义的圣歌。

Springsteen's *Born in the USA* album, these ads gloss over Springsteen's ironic lyrics in a vast display of flag-waving. Chevrolet's "Heartbeat of America" campaign attempts to woo American motorists away form Japanese automobiles by appealing to their patriotic sentiments.

The patriotic iconography of these campaigns also reflects the general cultural mood of the early to mid-1980s. After a period of national anguish in the wake of the Vietnam War and the Iran hostage crisis①, America went on a patriotic binge. American athletic triumphs in the Lake Placid and Los Angeles Olympics introduced a sporting tone into the national celebration, often making international affairs appear like one great Olympiad in which America was always going for the gold. In response, advertisers began to do their own flag-waving.

The mood of advertising during this period was definitely upbeat. Even deodorant commercials, which traditionally work on our self-doubts and fears of social rejection, jumped on the bandwagon. In the guilty sixties②, we had ads like the "Ice Blue Secret" campaign③ with its connotations of guilt and shame. In the feel-good Reagan④ eighties, "Sure" deodorant commercials featured images of triumphant Americans throwing up their arms in victory to reveal—no wet marks! Deodorant commercials once had the moral echo of Nathaniel Hawthorne's guilt-ridden *The Scarlet Letter*⑤; in the early eighties they had all the moral subtlety of *Rocky Ⅳ*⑥, reflecting the emotions of a Vietnam-weary nation eager to embrace the imagery of America Triumphant. …

Live the Fantasy

By reading the signs of American advertising, we can conclude that America is a nation of fantasizers, often preferring the sign to the substance and easily enthralled by a veritable Fantasy Island of commercial illusions. Critics of Madison Avenue⑦ often complain that advertisers create consumer desire, but semioticians don't think the situation is that simple. Advertisers may give shape to consumer fantasies, but they need raw material to work with, the subconscious dreams and desires of the marketplace. As long as these desires remain unconscious, advertisers will be able to exploit them. But by bringing the fantasies to the surface, you can free yourself from advertising's often hypnotic grasp.

---

① 伊朗人质危机。伊朗伊斯兰革命后,美国大使馆被占领,66 名美国外交官和平民被扣留为人质。这场人质危机开始于 1979 年 11 月 4 日,一直持续到 1981 年 1 月 20 日才结束,长达444 天。

② 美国的 60 年代充满着反文化思潮和社会改革,与反性别歧视和种族歧视紧密相联。

③ 一场猜测一种名叫 Blue Moon 的冰激凌的成分的广告活动。Blue Moon 是一种炫蓝色冰激凌,只在美国中西部有卖。

④ 罗纳德·威尔逊·里根(Ronald Wilson Reagan, 1911—2004),1981 年至 1989 年间任美国第 40 届总统。

⑤ 《红字》(1850),美国小说家 Nathaniel Hawthorne 的经典名著。

⑥ *Rocky Ⅳ*(1985)是史泰隆 Rocky 系列电影的第四部。

⑦ 位于纽约曼哈顿的一条南北走向的大道。在上世纪 20 年代,这个地区的广告业迅速发展,"Madison Avenue"从此成为广告业的代名词。

I can think of no company that has more successfully seized upon the subconscious fantasies of the American marketplace—indeed the world marketplace—than McDonald's. By no means the first nor the only hamburger chain in the United States, McDonald's emerged victorious in the "burger wars" by transforming hamburgers into signs of all that was desirable in American life. Other chains like Wendy's①, Burger King, and Jack-In-The-Box② continue to advertise and sell widely, but no company approaches McDonald's transformation of itself into a symbol of American culture.

McDonald's success can be traced to the precision of its advertising. Instead of broadcasting a single "one-size-fits-all" campaign at a time, McDonald's pitches its burgers simultaneously at different age groups, different classes, even different races (Budweiser beer, incidentally, has succeeded in the same way). For children, there is the Ronald McDonald③ campaign, which presents a fantasy world that has little to do with hamburgers in any rational sense but a great deal to do with the emotional desires of kids. Ronald McDonald and his friends are signs that recall the Muppets, *Sesame Street*④, the circus, toys, storybook illustrations, even *Alice in Wonderland*. Such signs do not signify hamburgers. Rather, they are displayed in order to prompt in the child's mind an automatic association of fantasy, fun and McDonald's.

Mac Tonight of McDonald's
麦当劳创造出独特的"Mac Tonight"文化,将麦当劳供应早、中饭快餐的形象,提升至提供晚餐并晚间娱乐场所的高度。

The same approach is taken in ads aimed at older audiences—teens, adults, and senior citizens. In the teen-oriented ads we may catch a fleeting glimpse of a hamburger or two, but what we are really shown is a teenage fantasy: groups of hip and happy adolescents singing, dancing, and cavorting together. Fearing loneliness more than anything else, adolescents quickly respond to the group appeal of such commercials. "Eat a Big Mac," these ads say, "and you won't be stuck home alone on Saturday night."

To appeal to an older and more sophisticated audience no longer so afraid of not belonging and more concerned with finding a place to go out to at night, McDonald's has designed the elaborate "Mac Tonight" commercials, which have for their backdrop a nightlit urban skyline and at their center a cabaret pianist with a moon-shaped head, a glad manner, and Blues Brothers⑤ shades. Such signs prompt an association of McDonald's with

① 一家全球连锁的快餐店,全称 Wendy's Old Fashioned Hamburgers。据 2010 年 3 月数据显示,Wendy's 是世界第三大汉堡快餐店。

② Robert O. Peterson 在 1951 年创建的快餐店,总部在加利福利亚州。

③ 麦当劳叔叔,麦当劳快餐店的一个小丑吉祥物。

④ 芝麻街,美国一套著名的儿童教育电视节目,使用大量的布偶(Muppet)作主角。

⑤ 美国的一支布鲁斯和灵歌复兴乐队,由 Dan Aykroyd 和 John Belushi 在 1978 年组建成立。

nightclubs and urban sophistication, persuading us that McDonald's is a place not only for breakfast or lunch but for dinner too, as if it were a popular off-Broadway nightspot, a place to see and be seen. Even the parody of Kurt Weill's "Mack the Knife" theme song that Mac the Pianist performs is a sign, a subtle signal to the sophisticated hamburger eater able to recognize the origin of the tune in Bertolt Brecht's *Threepenny Opera*①.

For yet older customers, McDonald's has designed a commercial around the fact that it employs a large number of retirees and seniors. In one such ad, we see an elderly man leaving his pretty little cottage early in the morning to start work as "the new kid" at McDonald's, and then we watch him during his first day on the job. Of course he is a great success, outdoing everyone else with his energy and efficiency, and he returns home in the evening to a loving wife and a happy home. One would almost think that the ad was a kind of moving "help wanted" sign (indeed, McDonald's *was* hiring elderly employees at the time), but it's really just directed at consumers. Older viewers can see themselves wanted and appreciated in the ad—and perhaps be distracted from the rationally uncomfortable fact that many senior citizens take such jobs because of financial need and thus may be unlikely to own the sort of home that one sees in the commercial. But realism isn't the point here. This is fantasyland, a dream world promising instant gratification no matter what the facts of the matter may be.

Practically the only fantasy that McDonald's doesn't exploit is the fantasy of sex. This is understandable, given McDonald's desire to present itself as a family restaurant. But everywhere else, sexual fantasies, which have always had an important place in American advertising, are beginning to dominate the advertising scene. You expect sexual come-ons in ads for perfume or cosmetics or jewelry—after all, that's what they're selling—but for room deodorizers? In a magazine ad for Claire Burke② home fragrances, for example, we see a well-dressed couple cavorting about their bedroom in what looks like a cheery preparation for sadomasochistic exercises. Jordache③ and Calvin Klein pitch blue jeans as props for teenage sexuality. The phallic appeal of automobiles,

An ad for Listerine mouthwash: "How is your breath today? If it's bad, you won't be welcome ... Play safe ... use Listerine."

"您的口气今天好吗？如果不好，您将不受欢迎。保险起见，请用Listerine。"

（谁也不想成为一个不受欢迎的人吧？Listerine基于人们害怕被孤立、遭排斥的心理，打出这幅广告。）

---

① "Mack the Knife"是由 Kurt Weill 谱曲，德国戏剧家 Bertolt Brecht 填词，为歌剧 *The Threepenny Opera* 所作的一首歌曲。该歌剧 1928 年在柏林首演，这首歌成为衡量流行歌曲好坏的标尺。

② 家庭芳香用品的一个品牌，产品有如香薰烛台等。

③ 服装公司，出品衬衫、牛仔裤、外套等。

traditionally an implicit feature in automotive advertising, becomes quite explicit in a Dodge commercial that shifts back and forth from shots of a young man in an automobile to teasing glimpses of a woman—his date—as she dresses in her apartment.

The very language of today's advertisements is charged with sexuality. Products in the more innocent fifties were "new and improved," but everything in the eighties is "hot!"—as in "hot woman," or sexual heat. Cars are "hot." Movies are "hot." An ad for Valvoline① pulses to the rhythm of a "heat wave, burning in my car." Sneakers get red hot in a magazine ad for Travel Fox② athletic shoes in which we see male and female figures, clad only in Travel Fox shoes, apparently in the act of copulation—an ad that earned one of *Adweek*'s③ annual "badvertising" awards for shoddy advertising.

The sexual explicitness of contemporary advertising is a sign not so much of American sexual fantasies as of the lengths to which advertisers will go to get attention. Sex never fails as an attention-getter, and in a particularly competitive, and expensive, era for American marketing, advertisers like to bet on a sure thing. Ad people refer to the proliferation of TV, radio, newspaper, magazine, and billboard ads as "clutter," and nothing cuts through the clutter like sex. …

Madison Avenue has also framed ad campaigns around the cultural prestige of high-tech machinery. This is especially the case with sports cars, whose high-tech appeal is so powerful that some people apparently fantasize about *being* sports cars. At least, this is the conclusion one might draw form a Porsche commercial that asked its audience, "If you were a car, what kind of car would you be?" As a candy-red Porsche speeds along a rain-slick forest road, the ad's voice-over describes all the specifications you'd want to have if you *were* a sports car. "If you were a car," the commercial concludes, "you'd be a Porsche."

In his essay "Car Commericals and *Miami Vice*④," Todd Gitlin⑤ explains the semiotic appeal of such ads as those in the Porsche campaign. Aired at the height of what may be called America's "myth of the entrepreneur," these commercials were aimed at young corporate managers who imaginatively identified with the "lone wolf" image of a Porsche speeding through the woods. Gitlin points out that such images cater to the fantasies of faceless corporate men who dream of entrepreneurial glory, of striking out on their own like John DeLorean⑥ and telling the

① 美国最大的汽油生产商之一。

② 休闲鞋、运动鞋的一个品牌。

③ 美国广告业的一本周刊,1978 年首次出版。

④ *Miami Vice* 是 Michael Mann 为美国 NBC 电视台编写的电视剧,其特点是运用大量的音乐和视觉效果来讲述故事。

⑤ Todd Gitlin,美国社会学家、政论家、小说家、文化评论人。

⑥ John Zachary DeLorean (1925—2005),美国工程师和汽车工业的执行官,创建了 DeLorean Motor Company,并发了著名的 Pontiac GTO 高性能豪华跑车。1982 年被指控贩卖毒品而被捕,贩毒的行为是为了给在挣扎中的公司筹款,公司同年宣布破产。John 最后成功洗脱罪名。

boss to take his job and shove it. But as DeLorean's spectacular failure demonstrates, the life of the entrepreneur can be extremely risky. So rather than having to go it alone and take the risks that accompany entrepreneurial independence, the young executive can substitute fantasy for reality by climbing into his Porsche—or at least that's what Porsche's advertisers wanted him to believe. ...

In short, the Porsche campaign is a sign of a new mythology that is emerging before our eyes, a myth of the machine, which is replacing the myth of the human. The iconic figure of the little tramp caught up in the cogs of industrial production in Charlie Chaplin's *Modern Times* signified a humanistic revulsion to the age of the machine. Human beings, such icons said, were superior to machines. Human values should come first in the moral order of things. But as Edith Milton suggests in her essay "The Track of the Mutant," we are now coming to believe that machines are superior to human beings, that mechanical nature is superior to human nature. Rather than being threatened by machines, we long to merge with them. ... In such an age it should come as little wonder that computer-synthesized Max Headroom① should be a commercial spokesman for Coca-Cola, or that Federal Express should design a series of TV ads featuring mechanical-looking human beings revolving around strange and powerful machines.

Fear and Trembling in the Marketplace

While advertisers play on and reflect back at us our fantasies about everything from fighter pilots to robots, they also play on darker imaginings. If dream and desire can be exploited in the quest for sales, so can nightmare and fear.

The nightmare equivalent of America's populist desire to "belong," for example, is the fear of not belonging, of social rejection, of being different. Advertisements for dandruff shampoos, mouthwashes, deodorants, and laundry detergents ("Ring Around the Collar②!") accordingly exploit such fears, bullying us into consumption. Although ads of this type are still around in the 1980s, they were particularly common in the fifties and early sixties, reflecting a society still reeling from the witch-hunts of the McCarthy years③. When any sort of social eccentricity or difference could result in a public denunciation and the loss of one's job or even liberty, Americans were keen to conform and be like everyone else. No one wanted to be "guilty" of smelling bad or of having a dirty collar.

"Guilt" ads characteristically work by creating narrative situations in which someone is "accused" of some social "transgression," pronounced guilty, and then offered the sponsor's

① 英国的一部科幻电视剧，可口可乐公司在进行"新可乐(New Coke)"运动的时候，以该片的主角 Max Headroom 为产品代言人。

② Wisk 清洁剂在 1968 年的广告词。

③ 上世纪 50 年代的美国笼罩在"麦卡锡主义(McCarthyism)"的阴影下，参议员约瑟夫·麦卡锡(Joseph Raymond McCarthy)煽起全国性的反共运动，大肆渲染共产党侵入政府和舆论界，煽动人们互相揭发，迫使许多著名人士遭受证据不充分的怀疑、控告和迫害。

product as a means of returning to "innocence." Such ads, in essence, are parodies of ancient religious rituals of guilt and atonement, whereby sinning humanity is offered salvation through the agency of priest and church. In the world of advertising, a product takes the place of the priest, but the logic of the situation is quite similar.

In commercials for Wisk detergent, for example, we witness the drama of a hapless housewife and her husband as they are mocked by the jeering voices of children shouting "Ring Around the Collar!" "Oh, those dirty rings!" the housewife groans in despair. It's as if she and her husband were being stoned by an angry crowd. But there's hope, there's help, there's Wisk. Cleansing her soul of sin as well as her husband's, the housewife launders his shirts with Wisk, and behold, his collars are clean. Product salvation is only as far as the supermarket. ...

If guilt looks backward in time to past transgressions, fear, like desire, faces forward, trembling before the future. In the late 1980s, a new kind of fear commercial appeared, one whose narrative played on the worries of young corporate managers struggling up the ladder of success. Representing the nightmare equivalent of the elitist desire to "arrive," ads of this sort created images of failure, storylines of corporate defeat. In one ad for Apple computers, for example, a group of junior executives sits around a table with the boss as he asks each executive how long it will take his or her department to complete some publishing jobs. "Two or three days," answers one nervous executive. "A week, on overtime," a tight-lipped woman responds. But one young up-and-comer can have everything ready tomorrow, today, or yesterday, because his department uses a Macintosh desktop publishing system. Guess who'll get the next promotion?

...

The Future of an Illusion

There are some signs in the advertising world that Americans are getting fed up with fantasy advertisements and want to hear some straight talk. Weary of extravagant product claims and irrelevant associations, consumers trained by years of advertising to distrust what they hear seem to be developing an immunity to commercials. At least, this is the semiotic message I read in the "new realism" advertisements of the eighties, ads that attempt to convince you that what you're seeing is the real thing, that the ad is giving you the straight dope, not advertising hype.

You can recognize the "new realism" by its camera techniques. The lighting is usually subdued to give the ad the effect of being filmed without studio lighting or special filters. The scene looks gray, as if the blinds were drawn. The camera shots are jerky and off-angle, often zooming in for sudden and unflattering close-ups, as if the cameraman was an amateur with a home video recorder. In a "realistic" ad for AT&T, for example, we are treated to a monologue by a plump stockbroker—his plumpness intended as a sign that he's for real and not just another actor—who tells us about the problems he's had with his phone system (not AT&T's) as the camera jerks around, generally filming him from below as if the cameraman couldn't quite fit his equipment into the crammed office and had to film the scene on his knees. "This is no fancy advertisement," the ad tries to convince us, "this is sincere."

An ad for Miller draft beer tries the same approach, recreating the effect of an amateur videotape of a wedding celebration. Camera shots shift suddenly from group to group. The picture jumps. Bodies are poorly framed. The color is washed out. Like the beer it is pushing, the ad is supposed to strike us as being "as real as it gets."

Such ads reflect a desire for reality in the marketplace, a weariness with Madison Avenue illusions. But there's no illusion like the illusion of reality. Every special technique that advertisers use to create their "reality effects" is, in fact, more unrealistic than the techniques of "illusory" ads. The world, in reality, doesn't jump around when you look at it. It doesn't appear in subdued gray tones. Our eyes don't have zoom lenses, and we don't look at things, with our heads cocked to one side. The irony of the "new realism" is that it is more unrealistic, more artificial, than the ordinary run of television advertising.

But don't expect any truly realistic ads in the future, because a realistic advertisement is a contradiction in terms. The logic of advertising is entirely semiotic: It substitutes signs for things, framed visions of consumer desire for the thing itself. The success of modern advertising, its penetration into every corner of American life, reflects a culture that has itself chosen illusion over reality. At a time when political candidates all have professional image-makers attached to their staffs, and the President of the United States can be an actor who once sold shirt collars, all the cultural signs are pointing to more illusions in our lives rather than fewer—a fecund breeding ground for the world of the advertiser.

Questions to Consider

1. Describe in your own words the paradox of the American dream, as Solomon sees it.
2. In Solomon's view, why do status symbols work particularly well in manipulating American consumers?
3. What is a "guilt" ad, according to Solomon, and how does it affect consumers?
4. Why, according to Solomon, has McDonald's been so successful in its ad campaigns?
5. What relationship does Solomon see between the "new realism" of some ads and the paradoxes of the American dream?

Lesson 5 Advertising's Fifteen Basic Appeals

广告的巨大诱惑

JIB FOWLES

Introduction

We are confronted daily by hundreds of ads, only a few of which actually attract our attention. These few do so, according to Fowles, through"something primary and primitive, an emotional appeal, that in effect is the thin edge of the wedge, trying to find its way into a mind." In the following essay, Jib Fowles looks at how advertisements work by examining the emotional, subrational appeals that they employ.

Underlying Fowles's psychological analysis of advertising is the assumption that advertisers try to circumvent the logical, cautious, skeptical powers we develop as consumers, to reach, instead, the "unfulfilled urges and motives swirling in the bottom half of our minds." In Fowles's view, consumers are well advised to pay attention to these underlying appeals in order to avoid responding unthinkingly. A professor of communication at the University of Houston-Clear Lake, Jib Fowles has written extensively on advertisments and popular culture. His book *The Case for Television Violence and Advertising and Popular Culture* (1996) has caught much attention in the academic world.

Text

EMOTIONAL APPEALS

The nature of effective advertisements was recognized full well by the late media philosopher Marshall McLuhan①. In his *Understanding Media*, the first sentence of the section on advertising reads, "The continuous pressure is to create ads more and more in the image of audience motives and desires."

By giving form to people's deep-lying desires, and picturing states of being that individuals privately yearn for, advertisers have the best chance of arresting attention and affecting communication. And that is the immediate goal of advertising: to tug at our psychological shirt sleeves and slow us down long enough for a word or two about whatever is being sold. We glance

① Herbert Marshall McLuhan (1911—1980),加拿大著名教育家、哲学家和学者。他的学说被认为是媒体理论的奠基石。他提出著名的"媒介就是信息"(The medium is the message.)和"地球村"(global village)的概念。

at a picture of a solitary rancher at work, and "Marlboro" slips into our minds.

…

An advertisement communicates by making use of a specially selected image (of a supine female, say, or a curly-haired child, or a celebrity) which is designed to stimulate "subrational impulses and desires" even when they are at ebb, even if they are unacknowledged by their possessor. Some few ads have their emotional appeal in the text, but for the greater number by far the appeal is contained in the artwork. This makes sense, since visual communication better suits more primal levels of the brain. … Many ads seem to be saying, "If you have this need, then this product will help satisfy it." It is a primitive equation, but not an ineffective one for selling.

Thus, most advertisements appearing in national media can be understood as having two orders of content. The first is the appeal to deep-running drives in the minds of consumers. The second is information regarding the good[s] or service being sold: its name, its manufacturer, its picture, its packaging, its objective attributes, its functions. …

Sometimes there is an apparently logical link between an ad's emotional appeal and its product information. It does not violate common sense that Cadillac automobiles be photographed at country clubs, or that Japan Air Lines be associated with Orientalia①. But there is no real need for the linkage to have a bit of reason behind it. Is there anything inherent to be the connection between Salem cigarettes and mountains, Coke and a smile, Miller Beer and comradeship? The link being forged in minds between product and appeal is a pre-logic one.

A Coke and a smile
可乐与微笑,让人倍感亲切与友谊。

…

When enough advertisements are examined in this light, it becomes clear that the emotional appeals fall into several distinguishable categories, and that every ad is a variation on one of a limited number of basic appeals. …

Advertisements can appeal to:

1. The need for sex
2. The need for affiliation
3. The need to nurture
4. The need for guidance
5. The need to aggress
6. The need to achieve
7. The need to dominate

---

① 东方学,东方史料或东方文物。

8. The need for prominence
9. The need for attention
10. The need for autonomy
11. The need to escape
12. The need to feel safe
13. The need for aesthetic sensations
14. The need to satisfy curiosity
15. Physiological needs: food, drink, sleep, etc…

FIFTEEN APPEALS

1. *Need for sex.*

…

Brooke Shields in the Calvin Klein (1980).

作者认为这个广告旨在激起人们获得关注的渴望,而不是对性的关注。

The fascinating thing is not how much sex there is in advertising, but how little. Contrary to impressions, unambiguous sex is rare in these messages. Some of this surprising observation may be a matter of definition: the Jordache ads with the lithe, blouse-less female astride a similarly clad male is clearly an appeal to the audience's sexual drives, but the same cannot be said about Brooke Shields① in the Calvin Klein commercials. Directed at young women and their credit-card carrying mothers, the image of Miss Shields instead invokes the need to be looked at. Buy Calvins and you'll be the center of much attention, just as Brooke is, the ads imply; they do not primarily inveigle their target audience's need for sexual intercourse.

…

2. *The need for affiliation*

…

In any case, the need to associate with others is widely invoked in advertising and is probably the most prevalent appeal.

…

According to Henry Murray②, the need for affiliation consists of 24 desires "to draw near and enjoyably cooperate or reciprocate with another; to please and win affection of another; to adhere

---

① Brooke Christa Shields (生于 1965 年),美国演员,1980 年出演 Calvin Klein 的广告。

② Henry Alexander Murray (1893—1988),美国著名心理学家,著有 *Explorations in Personality*(1938)等书。本文也借鉴了他的有关人的性格构成的 20 种动机的观点。

and remain loyal to a friend." The manifestations of this motive can be segmented into several different types of affiliation, beginning with romance.

Courtship may be swifter nowadays, but the desire for pair-bonding is far from satiated. Ads reaching for this need commonly depict a youngish male and female engrossed in each other. The head of the male is usually higher than the female's, even at this late date; she may be sitting or leaning while he is standing. They are not touching in the Smirnoff vodka ads, but obviously there is an intimacy, sometimes frolicsome, between them.

Warm family feelings are fanned in ads when another generation is added to the pair. Hallmark Cards brings grandparents into the picture, and Johnson and Johnson Baby Powder has Dad, Mom, and baby, all fresh from the bath, encircled in arms and emblazoned with "Share the Feeling." A talc has been fused to familial love.

Friendship is yet another form of affiliation pursued by advertisers. Two women confide and drink Maxwell House coffee together; two men walk through the woods smoking Salem cigarettes. …

As well as presenting positive images, advertisers can play to the need for affiliation in negative ways, by invoking the fear of rejection. If we don't use Scope①, we'll have the "Ugh! Morning Breath" that causes the male and female models to avert their faces. Unless we apply Ultra Brite② or Close-Up③ to our teeth, it's good-bye romance. Our family will be cursed with "House-a-tosis④" if we don't take care. …

3. *Need to nurture.* Akin to affiliative needs is the need to take care of small, defenseless creatures—children and pets, largely. … Murray uses synonyms like "to feed, help, support, console, protect, comfort, nurse, heal." A strong need it is, woven deep into our genetic fabric, for if it did not exist we could not successfully raise up our replacements. When advertisers put forth the image of something diminutive and furry, something that elicits the word "cute" or "precious," then they are trying to trigger this motive. We listen to the childish voice singing the Oscar Mayer wiener song⑤, and our next hotdog purchase is prescribed. Aren't those darling kittens something, and how did this Meow Mix⑥ get into our shopping cart?

This pitch is often directed at women, as Mother Nature's chief nurturers. …But it is not

---

① 一种漱口水品牌。

② 美国牙膏品牌,在 1970 年代名声鹊起。其广告语:"Ultrabrite gives your mouth …[bling]…sex appeal!(Ultrabrite,性感你的牙齿!)"功劳显赫。

③ 另一种漱口水,原产印度。

④ 指房间里挥之不去的难闻的气味。

⑤ Oscar Mayer 是美国著名的肉制品和冷冻食品公司,隶属美国最大的食品公司——卡夫食品有限公司(Kraft Foods)。这里提到的 Oscar Mayer 广告歌词如下:"Oh I wish I were an Oscar Mayer Wiener. That is what I'd truly like to be. Cause if I were an Oscar Mayer Wiener, every one would be in love with me."(哦,我真希望自己就是奥斯卡美雅肉肠,那是我心所想。因为如果我是一只奥斯卡美雅肉肠,人人都会跟我坠入情网。)

⑥ 一种猫食品牌,由 Meow Mix Company 出品。

women alone who can be touched by this appeal. The father nurses his son Eddie through adolescence while the John Deere① lawn tractor survives the years. Another father counts pennies with his young son as the subject of New York Life Insurance comes up.

…

4. *Need for guidance.* The opposite of the need to nurture is the need to be nurtured: to be protected, shielded, guided. …

Robert Young recommends Sanka Coffee. (1970s)
Robert Young"爸爸"级别的形象,给人厚实的信任感。

Parent-like figures can successfully call up this need. Robert Young recommends Sanka coffee, and since we have experienced him for twenty-five years as television father and doctor, we take his word for it. …

Often it is tradition or custom that advertisers point to and consumers take guidance from. … We conform to traditional male/female roles and age-old social norms when we purchase Barclay② cigarettes, which informs us "The pleasure is back."

The product itself, if it has been around for a long time, can constitute a tradition. …Kool-Aid③ says "You loved it as a kid. You trust it as a mother," hoping to get yet more consumers to go along.

5. *Need to aggress.* The pressures of the real world create strong retaliatory feelings in every functioning human being. Since these impulses can come forth as bursts of anger and violence, their display is normally tabooed. Existing as harbored energy, aggressive drives present a large, tempting target for advertisers. It is not a target to be aimed at thoughtlessly, though, for few manufacturers want their products associated with destructive motives. There is always the danger that, as in the case of sex, if the appeal is too blatant, public opinion will turn against what is being sold. …

Better disguised aggressive appeals are less likely to backfire: Triumph cigarettes has models making a lewd gesture with their uplifted cigarettes, but the individuals are often laughing and usually in close company of others. When Exxon said, "There's a Tiger in your tank," the implausibility of it concealed the invocation of aggressive feelings. …

6. *Need to achieve.* This is the drive that energizes people, causing them to strive in their lives and careers. According to Murray, the need for achievement is signaled by the desires "to accomplish something difficult. To overcome obstacles and attain a high standard. To excel one's

---

① 即 Deere & Company,由 John Deere(1804—1886)在 1837 年创立,系著名农业机械生产商。

② 巴克利香烟,由布朗·威廉姆森烟草公司(Brown & Williamson Tobacco Corp.)于上世纪 80 年代推出。其颇受争议的地方是,它的广告宣称其 99% 无焦油。

③ 美国卡夫食品(Kraft Foods)出品的一种混合风味饮料。

self. To rival and surpass others." A prominent American trait, it is one that advertisers like to hook on to because it identifies their product with winning and success.

The Cutty Sark① ad does not disclose that Ted Turner② failed at his latest attempt at yachting's America Cup; here he is represented as a champion on the water as well as off in his television enterprises. If we drink this whiskey, we will be victorious alongside Turner. …

Sports heroes are the most convenient means to snare consumers' need to achieve, but they are not the only one. Role models can be established, or the advertiser can establish a prize: two neighbors play one-on-one basketball for a Michelob beer in a television commercial, while in a print ad a bottle of Johnnie Walker Black Label has been gilded like a trophy.

Any product that advertises itself in superlatives—the best, the first, the finest—is trying to make contact with our needs to succeed. …

7. *Need to dominate.* This fundamental need is the craving to be powerful—perhaps omnipotent, as in the Xerox ad where Brother Dominic③ exhibits heavenly powers and creates miraculous copies. Most of us will settle for being just a regular potentate, though. We drink Budweiser because it is the King of Beers, and here comes the powerful Clydesdales④ to prove it. A taste of Wolfschmidt vodka and "The spirit of the Czar lives on."

The need to dominate and control one's environment is often thought of as being masculine, but as close students of human nature advertisers know, it is not so circumscribed. Women's aspirations for control are suggested in the campaign theme, "I like my men in English Leather⑤, or nothing at all." The females in the Chanel No. 19 ads are "outspoken" and wrestle their men around. …

8. *Need for prominence.* Here comes the need to be admired and respected, to enjoy prestige and high social status. …

Beefeater gin⑥ represents itself as "The Crown Jewel of England" and uses no illustrations of jewels or things British, for the words are sufficient indicators of distinction. Buy that gin and you will rise up the prestige hierarchy, or achieve the same effect on yourself with Seagram's 7 Crown⑦, which ambiguously describes itself as "classy."

Being respected does not have to entail the usual accoutrements of wealth: "Do you know who I am?" the commercials ask, and we learn that the prominent person is not so prominent without

---

① 一个调和型苏格兰威士忌的系列品牌。

② Robert Edward ("Ted" Turner III),出生于1938年,美国媒体界巨头和慈善家,1980年创建美国CNN有线电视;1998年向联合国捐献10亿美元,建立了联合国基金会(United Nations Foundation)。Turner 11岁时首次参加帆船比赛,并在1964年参加奥运会选拔赛,在1993年入选美洲杯名人堂。

③ 施乐打印机系列广告"施乐僧"中的主角。

④ 百威啤酒旗下的一个啤酒品牌。

⑤ 一款男士香水,由Dana设计公司于1949年推出。

⑥ 英国James Burrough公司生产的一种杜松子酒。

⑦ 又名Seagram's Seven,是由Diageo公司生产的一种美国威士忌。

his American Express[①] card.

9. *Need for attention.* The previous need involved being *looked up to*, while this is the need to be *looked at*. The desire to exhibit ourselves in such a way as to make others look at us is a primitive, insuppressible instinct. The clothing and cosmetic industries exist just to serve this need, and this is the way they pitch their wares. Some of this effort is aimed at males, as the ads for Hathaway[②] shirts and Jockey underclothes. But the greater bulk of such appeals is targeted singlemindedly at women. …

If I buy Calvin Klein jeans, consumers infer, I'll be the object of fascination. The desire for exhibition has been most strikingly played to in a print campaign of many years' duration, that of Maiden-form lingerie. The woman exposes herself, and sales surge. … The same appeal works for cosmetics and lotions. …

10. *Need for autonomy* . … The focus here is upon the independence and integrity of the individual; this need is the antithesis of the need for guidance and is unlike any of the social needs. "If running with the herd isn't your style, try ours," says Rotan-Mosle[③], and many Americans feel they have finally found the right brokerage firm.

The photo is of a red-coated Mountie[④] on his horse, posed on a snow-covered ledge; the copy reads, "Windsor—One Canadian stands alone." This epitome of the solitary and proud individual may work best with male customers, as may Winston's[⑤] man in the red cap. But one-figure advertisements also strike the strong need for autonomy among American women. As Shelly Hack[⑥] strides for Charlie perfume, females respond to her obvious pride and flair; she is her own person. …

Like many psychological needs, this one can also be appealed to in a negative fashion, by invoking the loss of independence or self-regard. Guilt and regrets can be stimulated: "Gee, I could have had a V-8[⑦]." Next time, get one and be good to yourself.

11. *Need to escape.* An appeal to the need for autonomy often co-occurs with one for the need to escape, since the desire to duck out of our social obligations, to seek rest or adventure, frequently takes the form of one-person flight. The dashing image of a pilot, in fact, is a standard way of quickening this need to get away from it all.

---

① 又作"AmEx"或"Amex",是一个全球性的财务服务公司,成立于1850年。该公司最有名的产品是信用卡、收费卡和旅行支票。

② 全称 C. F. Hathaway Company,美国一家生产男士衬衫的公司。

③ 提供银行投资和证券经纪服务的公司。

④ 加拿大皇家警察,全称 The Royal Canadian Mounted Police (RCMP),成立于1920年。

⑤ 温斯顿香烟,雷诺烟草公司(RJ Reynolds Tobacco Company)出品,1954年进入美国,1966—1972年间全美香烟销量冠军,其广告词功不可没:"Winston tastes good like a cigarette should."(Winston,品出烟本味)。

⑥ 美国演员和模特,出生于1947年,曾出演电影 *Charlie's Angles*(1979—1980)。

⑦ 内燃机的汽缸排列型式之一。一般使用在中高端车辆上。8个汽缸分成两组,每组4个,成V型排列。

Freedom is the pitch here, the freedom that every individual yearns for whenever life becomes too oppressive. Many advertisers like appealing to the need for escape because the sensation of pleasure often accompanies escape, and what nicer emotional nimbus could there be for a product? "You deserve a break today," says McDonald's, and Stouffer's frozen foods chime in, "Set yourself free." …

There are varieties of escape, some wistful like the Boeing "Someday" campaign of dream vacations, some kinetic like the play and parties in soft drink ads. But in every instance, the consumer exposed to the advertisement is invited to momentarily depart his everyday life for a more carefree experience, preferably with the product in hand.

12. *Need to feel safe.* Nobody in their right mind wants to be intimidated, menaced, battered, poisoned. We naturally want to do whatever it takes to stave off threats to our well-being, and to our families. It is the instinct of self-preservation that makes us responsive to the ad of the St. Bernard① with the Keg of Chivas Regal. …

In the interest of keeping failure and calamity from our lives, we like to see the durability of products demonstrated. Can we ever forget that Timex takes a licking and keeps on ticking? …We want to be safe and secure; buy these products, advertisers are saying, and you'll be safer than you are without them.

13. *Need for aesthetic sensations.* There is an undeniable aesthetic component to virtually every ad run in the national media: the photography or filming or drawing is near-perfect, the type style is well chosen, the layout could scarcely be improved upon. Advertisers know there is little chance of good communication occurring if an ad is not visually pleasing. Consumers may not be aware of the extent of their own sensitivity to artwork, but it is undeniably large. …

J & B scotch② says "It whispers" and shows a bucolic scene of lake and castle.

14. *Need to satisfy curiosity.* …Human beings are curious by nature, interested in the world around them, and intrigued by tidbits of knowledge and new developments. Trivia, percentages, observations counter to conventional wisdom—these items all help sell products. Any advertisement in a question-and-answer format is strumming this need. A dog groomer has a question about long distance rates, and Bell Telephone has a chart with all the figures. …

15. *Physiological needs.* …In this final category are clustered appeals to sleeping, eating, drinking. The art of

An ad for the Red Lobster restaurant

美食似乎触手可及，让人垂涎欲滴。

① 瑞士阿尔卑斯山的一种大型犬，因其在阿尔卑斯山的救援故事而出名。

② Justerini & Brooks (J & B)，一种苏格兰调和威士忌。

photographing food and drink is so advanced, sometimes these temptations are wondrously caught in the camera's lens: the crab meat in the Red Lobster restaurant ads can start us salivating, the Quarterpounder① can almost be smelled, the liquor in the glass glows invitingly. Imbibe, these ads scream.

STYLES

Some common ingredients of advertisements were not singled out for separate mention in the list of fifteen because they are not appeals in and of themselves. They are stylistic features, influencing the way a basic appeal is presented. The use of humor is one, and the use of celebrities is another. A third is time imagery, past and future, which goes to several purposes.

…

Roughly fifteen percent of all advertisements incorporate a celebrity, almost always from the fields of entertainment or sports. The approach can also prove troublesome for advertisers, for celebrities are human beings too, and fully capable of the most remarkable behavior. If anything distasteful about them emerges, it is likely to reflect on the product. …An untimely death can also react poorly on a product. But advertisers are willing to take risks because celebrities can be such a good link between producers and consumers, performing the social role of introducer. …

The past and future, being outside our grasp, are exploited by advertisers as locales for the projection of needs. History can offer up heroes (and call up the need to achieve) or traditions (need for guidance) as well as art objects (need for aesthetic sensations). Nostalgia is a kindly version of personal history and is deployed by advertisers to rouse needs for affiliation and for guidance; the need to escape can come in here, too. The same need to escape is sometimes the point of futuristic② appeals but picturing the avant-garde can also be a way to get at the need to achieve.

ANALYZING ADVERTISEMENTS

When analyzing ads yourself for their emotional appeals, it takes a bit of practice to learn to ignore the product information (as well as one's own experience and feelings about the product). But that skill comes soon enough, as does the ability to quickly sort out from all the non-product aspects of an ad the chief element which is the most striking, the most likely to snag attention first and penetrate brains farthest. …

Another clue: the viewing angle which the audience has on the ad's subjects is informative. If the subjects are photographed or filmed from below and thus are looking down at you, then the need to be guided is a good candidate for the ad's emotional appeal. If, on the other hand, the

① 一种中间夹肉饼的汉堡,其得名于因它做熟前重约1/4磅,在麦当劳等快餐店出售。

② Futurism,未来主义,发端于20世纪的一种艺术思潮,最早出现在意大利,认为近代的科学技术和工业交通改变了人类的物质生活方式,因而人类的精神生活也必须随之改变。

subjects are shot from above and appear deferential, then other needs are being appealed to.

To figure out an ad's emotional appeal, it is wise to know (or have a good hunch about) who the targeted consumers are; this can often be inferred from the magazine or television show it appears in. ...

It would be convenient if every ad made just one appeal, were aimed at just one need. Unfortunately, things are often not that simple. A cigarette ad with a couple at the edge of a polo field is trying to hit both the need for affiliation and the need for prominence; depending on the attitude of the male, dominance could also be an ingredient in this. ... Better ads, however, seem to avoid being too diffused; in the study of post-World War II advertising described earlier, appeals grew more focused as the decades passed. As a rule of thumb, about sixty percent have two conspicuous appeals; the last twenty percent have three or more. Rather than looking for the greatest number of appeals, decoding ads is most productive when the loudest one or two appeals are discerned, since those are the appeals with the best chance of grabbing people's attention.

Finally, analyzing ads does not have to be a solo activity and probably should not be. The greater number of people there are involved, the better chance there is of transcending individual biases and discerning the essential emotional lure built into an advertisement.

...

A productive understanding is that advertising messages involve costs and benefits at both ends of the communications channel. For those few ads which do make contact, the consumer surrenders a moment of time, has the lower brain curried, and receives notice of a product; the advertiser has given up money and has increased the chance of sales. In this sort of communications activity, neither party can be said to be the loser.

Questions to Consider

1. Fowles's basic claim in this essay is that advertisers try to tap into basic human needs and emotions, rather than consumers' intellect. How does he go about proving this claim? What examples or other proof strike you as particularly persuasive? Where do you see weaknesses in Fowles' argument?
2. What do advertisers assume about the personality of the consumer, according to Fowles? How do these assumptions contribute to the way they sell products? Do you think that these assumptions about personality are correct? Why or why not?
3. Working with Fowles's list of the fifteen appeals of advertising, survey a recent magazine, looking at all the ads and categorizing them based on their predominant appeal. In an essay, describe what your results tell you about the magazine and its readership. Based on your survey, would you amend Fowles's list? What additions or deletions would you make?

Lesson 6 With These Words I Can Sell You Anything

只要有这些字眼儿，什么都能卖出去

WILLIAM LUTZ

Introduction

William Lutz has become a nationally known figure for his analyses of language in advertisements and other public statements. A professor of English at Rutgers University, Lutz is former chair of the Committee on Public Doublespeak of the National Council of Teachers of English and former editor of the *Quarterly Review of Doublespeak*. He has written many books including *Beyond Nineteen Eighty-Four* (1984), *Doublespeak: From "Revenue Enhancement" to "Terminal Living": How Government, Business, Advertisers, and Others Use Language to Deceive* (1990), *The New Doublespeak: Why No One Knows What Anyone's Saying Anymore* (1997), etc. The following passage is from *Doublespeak* in which Lutz decodes most of the "weasel words"—fancy empty words—advertisers employ in their advertisements and warns consumers to be critical-minded and read advertisers literally.

Text

One problem advertisers have when they try to convince you that the product they are pushing is really different from other, similar products is that their claims are subject to some laws. Not a lot of laws, but there are some designed to prevent fraudulent or untruthful claims in advertising. Even during the happy years of nonregulation under President Ronald Reagan, the FTC① did crack down on the more blatant abuses in advertising claims. Generally speaking, advertisers have to be careful in what they say in their ads, in the claims they make for the products they advertise. Parity claims are safe because they are legal and supported by a number of court decisions. But beyond parity claims there are weasel words.

Advertisers use weasel words to appear to be making a claim for a product when in fact they are making no claim at all. Weasel words get their name from the way weasels eat the eggs they find in the nests of other animals. A weasel will make a small hole in the egg, suck out the insides, then place the egg back in the nest. Only when the egg is examined closely is it found to be hollow. That's the way it is with weasel words in advertising: Examine weasel words closely and you'll find that they're as hollow as any egg sucked by a weasel. Weasel words appear to say one

① Federal Trade Commission，是独立于美国政府的机构，它的主要任务是保护消费者，消除并防止反竞争的商业行为，例如垄断。

thing when in fact they say the opposite, or nothing at all.

Help—The Number One Weasel Word

The biggest weasel word used in advertising doublespeak is *help*. Now *help* only means to aid or assist, nothing more. It does not mean to conquer, stop, eliminate, end, solve, heal, cure, or anything else. But once the ad says *help*, it can say just about anything after that because *help* qualifies everything coming after it. The trick is that the claim that comes after the weasel word is usually so strong and so dramatic that you forget the word *help* and concentrate only on the dramatic claim. You read into the ad a message that the ad does not contain. More importantly, the advertiser is not responsible for the claim that you read into the ad, even though the advertiser wrote the ad so you would read that claim into it.

The next time you see an ad for a cold medicine that promises that it "helps relieve cold symptoms fast," don't rush out to buy it. Ask yourself what this claim is really saying. Remember, *helps* means only that the medicine will aid or assist. What will it aid or assist in doing? Why, "relieve" your cold "symptoms." *Relieve* only means to ease, alleviate, or mitigate, not to stop, end, or cure. Nor does the claim say how much relieving this medicine will do. Nowhere does this ad claim it will cure anything. In fact, the ad doesn't even claim it will *do* anything at all. The ad only claims that it will aid in relieving (not curing) your cold symptoms, which are probably a runny nose, watery eyes, and a headache. In other words, this medicine probably contains a standard decongestant and some aspirin. By the way, what does *fast* mean? Ten minutes, 1 hour, 1 day? What is fast to one person can be very slow to another. *Fast* is another weasel word. …

An ad for Rice Krispies with the words "Now helps support your child's immunity".

Rice Krispies:"现在帮助您的孩子增强免疫力。"

注意广告里出现的"黄鼠狼词汇"(weasel words)—"helps"。

Help is such a useful weasel word that it is often combined with other action-verb weasel words such as *fight* and *control*. Consider the claim, "Helps control dandruff symptoms with regular use." What does it really say? It will assist in controlling (not eliminating, stopping, ending, or curing) the *symptoms* of dandruff, not the cause of dandruff nor the dandruff itself. What are the symptoms of dandruff? The ad deliberately leaves that undefined, but assume that the symptoms referred to in the ad are the flaking and itching commonly associated with dandruff. But just shampooing with *any* shampoo will temporarily eliminate these symptoms, so this shampoo isn't any different from any other. Finally, in order to benefit from this product, you must use it regularly. What is "regular use"—daily, weekly, hourly? Using another shampoo "regularly" will have the same effect. Nowhere does this advertising claim say this particular shampoo stops, eliminates, or cures dandruff. In fact, this claim says nothing at all, thanks to all the weasel words.

…

Virtually Spotless

One of the most powerful weasel words is *virtually*, a word so innocent that most people don't pay any attention to it when it is used in an advertising claim. … What does *virtually* mean? It means "in essence or effect, although not in fact." Look at that definition again. *Virtually* means *not in fact*. It does *not* mean "almost" or "just about the same as," or anything else. … The next time you see the ad that says that this dishwasher detergent "leaves dishes virtually spotless," just remember how advertisers twist the meaning of the weasel word *virtually*. You can have lots of spots on your dishes after using this detergent and the ad claim will still be true, because what this claim really means is that this detergent does not *in fact* leave your dishes spotless. Whenever you see or hear an ad claim that uses the word *virtually*, just translate that claim into its real meaning. So the television set that is "virtually trouble free" becomes the television set that is not in fact trouble free, the *virtually foolproof operation* of any appliance becomes an operation that is in fact not foolproof, and the product that "virtually never needs service" becomes the product that is not in fact service free.

New and Improved

If *new* is the most frequently used word on a product package, *improved* is the second most frequent. In fact, the two words are almost always used together. It seems just about everything sold these days is "new and improved." …

What makes a product "new"? Some products have been around for a long time, yet every once in a while you discover that they are being advertised as "new." Well, an advertiser can call a product new if there has been "a material functional change" in the product. What is "a material functional change"? you ask. Good question. In fact it's such a good question it's being asked all the time. It's up to the manufacturer to prove that the product has undergone such a change. And if the manufacturer isn't challenged on the claim, then there's no one to stop it. Moreover, the change does not have to be an improvement in the product. One manufacturer added an artificial lemon scent to a cleaning product and called it "new and improved," even though the product did not clean any better than without the lemon scent. The manufacturer defended the use of the word *new* on the grounds that the artificial scent changed the chemical formula of the product and therefore constituted "a material functional change."

Which brings up the word *improved*. When used in advertising, *improved* does not mean "made better." It only means "changed" or "different from before." So, if the detergent maker puts a plastic pour spout on the box of detergent, the product has been "improved," and away we go with a whole new advertising campaign. Or, if the cereal maker adds more fruit or a different kind of fruit to the cereal, there's an improved product. …

New is just too useful and powerful a word in advertising for advertisers to pass it up easily. So they use weasel words that say "new" without really saying it. One of their favorites is *introducing*, as in, "Introducing improved Tide," or "Introducing the stain remover." The first is simply saying, here's our improved soap; the second, here's our new advertising campaign for our detergent. Another favorite is *now*, as in, "Now there's Sinex①," which simply means that Sinex is available. Then there are phrases like "Today's Chevrolet," "Presenting Dristan②," and "A fresh way to start the day." The list is really endless because advertisers are always finding new ways to say *new* without really saying it. …

Acts Fast

Acts and *works* are two popular weasel words in advertising because they bring action to the product and to the advertising claim. When you see the ad for the cough syrup that "Acts on the cough control center," ask yourself what this cough syrup is claiming to do. Well, it's just claiming to "act," to do something, to perform an action. What is it that the cough syrup does? The ad doesn't say. It only claims to perform an action or do something on your "cough control center." By the way, what and where is your "cough control center"? I don't remember learning about that part of the body in human biology class.

Ads that use such phrases as "acts fast," "acts against," "acts to prevent," and the like are saying essentially nothing, because *act* is a word empty of any specific meaning. The ads are always careful not to specify exactly what "act" the product performs. Just because a brand of aspirin claims to "act fast" for headache relief doesn't mean this aspirin is any better than any other aspirin. What is the "act" that this aspirin performs? You're never told. Maybe it just dissolves quickly. Since aspirin is a parity product③, all aspirin is the same and therefore functions the same.

Works Like Anything Else

If you don't find the word *acts* in an ad, you will probably find the weasel word *works*. In fact, the two words are almost interchangeable in advertising. Watch out for ads that say a product "works against," "works like," "works for," or "works longer." … *Works*, like *acts*, is basically a word empty of any specific meaning.

Like Magic

Whenever advertisers want you to stop thinking about the product and start thinking about

---

① 一种缓解鼻充血的喷雾剂，由宝洁公司(Procter & Gamble)的分公司 Vicks 出品。

② 一种缓解鼻充血的喷雾剂。

③ 指一个商品类别或商品系列，在这个类别或系列中，不同品牌的商品拥有同样的功效，使得不同品牌的商品完全可以互相替代。

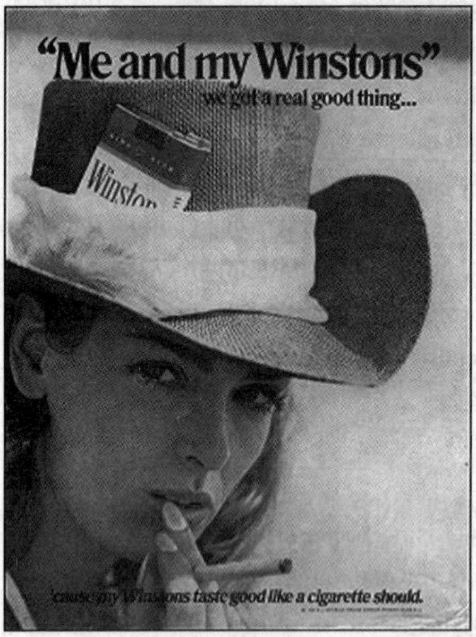

An ad for Winston cigarette with the sentence: "cause my Winstons taste good like a cigarette should."

Winston 牌香烟:"因为我的 Winston 味道之美正如烟该有的味道。"

（烟究竟应该是什么味道呢？这完全取决于个人定义。但 Winston 的广告却企图告诉你答案。这里用"like"这个"黄鼠狼字词"，让消费者自己去补充并想像广告里没有说出的内容。）

something bigger, better, or more attractive than the product, they use that very popular weasel word, *like*. The word *like* is the advertiser's equivalent of a magician's use of misdirection. *Like* gets you to ignore the product and concentrate on the claim the advertiser is making about it. "For skin like peaches and cream" claims the ad for a skin cream. What is this ad really claiming? It doesn't say this cream will give you peaches-and-cream skin. There is no verb in this claim, so it doesn't even mention using the product. How is skin ever like "peaches and cream"? Remember, ads must be read literally and exactly, according to the dictionary definition of words. The ad is making absolutely no promise or claim whatsoever for this skin cream. If you think this cream will give you soft, smooth, youthful-looking skin, you are the one who has read that meaning into the ad.

The wine that claims "It's like taking a trip to France" wants you to think about a romantic evening in Paris as you walk along the boulevard after a wonderful meal in an intimate little bistro. Of course, you don't really believe that a wine can take you to France, but the goal of the ad is to get you to think pleasant, romantic thoughts about France and not about how the wine tastes or how expensive it may be. That little word *like* has taken you away from crushed grapes into a world of your own imaginative making. Who knows, maybe next time you buy wine, you'll think those pleasant thoughts when you see this brand of wine, and you'll buy it. Or, maybe you weren't even thinking about buying wine at all, but now you just might pick up a bottle the next time you're shopping. Ah, the power of *like* in advertising. …

Can It Be Up to the Claim?

Analyzing ads for doublespeak requires that you pay attention to every word in the ad and determine what each word really means. Advertisers try to wrap their claims in language that sounds concrete, specific, and objective, when in fact the language of advertising is anything but. Your job is to read carefully and listen critically so that when the announcer says that "Crest can be of significant value …" you know immediately that this claim says absolutely nothing. … The ad for Crest only says that using Crest "can be" of "significant value." What really throws you off in this ad is the brilliant use of *significant*. It draws your attention to the word *value* and makes you forget that the ad only claims that Crest "can be." The ad doesn't say that Crest *is* of value, only that it is "able" or "possible" to be of value, because that's all that *can* means. …

Unfinished Words

Unfinished words are a kind of "up to" claim in advertising. The claim that a battery lasts "up to twice as long" usually doesn't finish the comparison—twice as long as what? A birthday candle? A tank of gas? A cheap battery made in a country not noted for its technological achievements? The implication is that the battery lasts twice as long as batteries made by other battery makers, or twice as long as earlier model batteries made by the advertiser, but the ad doesn't really make these claims. You read these claims into the ad, aided by the visual images the advertiser so carefully provides.

Unfinished words depend on you to finish them, to provide the words the advertisers so thoughtfully left out of the ad. Pall Mall cigarettes were once advertised as "A longer finer and milder smoke." The question is, longer, finer, and milder than what? … "Magnavox[①] gives you more" doesn't tell you what you get more of. More value? More television? More than they gave you before? It sounds nice, but it means nothing, until you fill in the claim with your own words, the words the advertiser didn't use. Since each of us fills in the claim differently, the ad and the product can become all things to all people, and not promise a single thing.

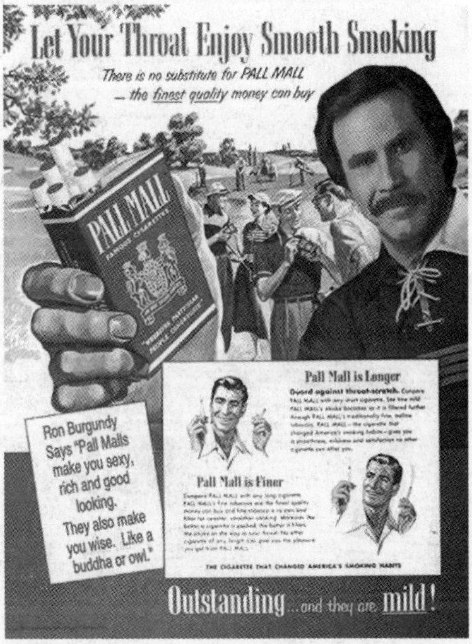

There is no substitute for PALL MALL—the finest quality money can by.

Pall Mall cigarette is Longer and Finer! Pall Malls make you sexy, rich and good looking. They also make you wise. Like a Buddha or owl.

PALL MALL 无可取代——你所能买到的最好的香烟。

Pall Mall 牌香烟更长、更雅致！Pall Malls 让你性感、富贵、好看。还让你智如菩萨，明如猫头鹰。

Unfinished words abound in advertising because they appear to promise so much. More importantly, they can be joined with powerful visual images on television to appear to be making significant promises about a product's effectiveness without really making any promises. In a television ad, the aspirin product that claims fast relief can show a person with a headache taking the product and then, in what appears to be a matter of minutes, claiming complete relief. This visual image is far more powerful than any claim made in unfinished words. Indeed, the visual image completes the unfinished words for you, filling in with pictures what the words leave out. …

---

① 美国一家电子公司，成立于 1917 年。

Combining Weasel Words

A lot of ads don't fall neatly into one category or another because they use a variety of different devices and words. Different weasel words are often combined to make an ad claim. The claim, "Coffee-Mate gives coffee more body, more flavor," uses unfinished words (*more* than what?) and also uses words that have no specific meaning (*body* and *flavor*). Along with *taste, body* and *flavor* mean nothing because their meaning is entirely subjective. In you, *body* in coffee might mean thick, black, almost bitter coffee, while I might take it to mean a light brown, delicate coffee. Now, if you think you understood that last sentence, read it again, because it said nothing of objective value; it was filled with weasel words of no specific meaning: *thick, black, bitter, light brown*, and *delicate*. Each of those words has no specific, objective meaning, because each of us can interpret them differently.

Tide gets clothes cleaner than any soap! Yes, Tide washes cleaner.

汰渍洁衣,所向无敌。是的,汰渍洗得更干净。

Try this slogan: "Looks, smells, tastes like ground-roast coffee." So, are you now going to buy Taster's Choice[①] instant coffee because of this ad? *Looks, smells,* and *tastes* are all words with no specific meaning and depend on your interpretation of them for any meaning. Then there's that great weasel word *like*, which simply suggests a comparison but does not make the actual connection between the product and the quality. Besides, do you know what "ground-roast" coffee is? I don't, but it sure sounds good. So, out of seven words in this ad, four are definite weasel words, two are quite meaningless, and only one has any clear meaning. ...

Other Tricks of the Trade

Advertisers' use of doublespeak is endless. Rosser Reeves[②] has explained advertising's function this way: to make something out of nothing. The best way advertisers can make something out of nothing is through words. Although there are a lot of visual images used on television and in magazines and newspapers, every advertiser wants to create that memorable line that will stick in the public consciousness. I am sure pure joy reigned in one advertising agency when a study found that children who were asked to spell the word *relief*

---

① 又作 Nescafé Taster's Choice, Nestlé 旗下一个咖啡品牌,其历史可追溯到 1930 年代。在美国, Nescafé 的品牌名字一直沿用到 1960 年代,随后 Nestlé 公司用"Taster's Choice"取代了以前的 Nescafé。2003 年,公司又重回到 Nescafé,所以现在常作 Nescafé Taster's Choice。

② Rosser Reeves (1910—1984),美国广告人和电视广告先锋。

promptly and proudly respond **r-o-l-a-i-d-s**①.

The variations, combinations, and permutations of doublespeak used in advertising go on and on, running from the use of rhetorical questions ("Wouldn't you really rather have a Buick?" "If you can't trust Prestone②, who can you trust?") to flattering you with compliments ("The lady has taste." "We think a cigar smoker is someone special." "You've come a long way, baby."). …

A more subtle approach is the ad that proclaims a supposedly unique quality for a product, a quality that really isn't unique. "If it doesn't say Goodyear③, it can't be polyglas." Sounds good, doesn't it? Polyglas is available only from Goodyear because Goodyear copyrighted that trade name. …

Since we like to think of ourselves as living in a technologically advanced country, science and technology have a great appeal in selling products. Advertisers are quick to use scientific doublespeak to push their products. There are all kinds of elixirs, additives, scientific potions, and mysterious mixtures added to all kinds of products. Gasoline contains "HAT," "F-310," "Platformate," and other chemical-sounding additives, but nowhere does an advertisement give any real information about the additive.

Shampoo, deodorant, mouthwash, cold medicine, sleeping pills, and any number of other products all seem to contain some special chemical ingredient that allows them to work wonders. "Certs contains a sparkling drop of Retsyn④." So what? What's "Retsyn"? What's it do? What's so special about it? When they don't have a secret ingredient in their product, advertisers still find a way to claim scientific validity. …

Advertising Doublespeak Quick Quiz

Now it's time to test your awareness of advertising doublespeak. The following is a list of statements from some recent ads. Your job is to figure out what each of these ads really says.

Domino's pizza:	"Because nobody delivers better."
Sinutab:	"It can stop the pain."
Tums:	"The stronger acid neutralizer."
Maximum Strength Dristan:	"Strong medicine for tough sinus colds."
Listermint:	"Making your mouth a cleaner place."
Cascade:	"For virtually spotless dishes nothing beats Cascade."

① 强生公司旗下的一个解酸药的品牌,最著名的是它70年代的广告,其广告词深入人心:"How do you spell relief?" "R-O-L-A-I-D-S."

② Honeywell推出的一款防冻剂。

③ 美国一款轮胎品牌。Goodyear早在1925年就使用软式小飞船(blimp)做广告。

④ Certs:1956年进入美国市场的一个薄荷糖品牌;Retsyn是一种氢化棉籽油、葡萄糖酸铜和调味品的混合物,Certs的成分之一。

Nuprin:	"Little. Yellow. Different. Better."
Anacin:	"Better relief."
Sudafed:	"Fast sinus relief that won't put you fast asleep."
Advil:	"Advanced medicine for pain."
Ponds Cold Cream:	"Ponds cleans like no soap can."
Miller Lite Beer:	"Tastes great. Less filling."
Philips Milk of Magnesia:	"Nobody treats you better than MOM (Philips Milk of Magnesia)."
Bayer:	"The wonder drug that works wonders."
Cracker Barrel:	"Judged to be the best."
Knorr:	"Where taste is everything."
Anusol:	"Anusol is the word to remember for relief."
Dimetapp:	"It relieves kids as well as colds."
Liquid Drāno:	"The liquid strong enough to be called Drāno."
Johnson & Johnson Baby Powder:	"Like magic for your skin."
Puritan:	"Make it your oil for life."
Pam:	"Pam, because how you cook is as important as what you cook."
Ivory Shampoo and Conditioner:	"Leave your hair feeling Ivory clean."
Tylenol Gel-Caps:	"It's not a capsule. It's better."
Alka-Seltzer Plus①:	"Fast, effective relief for winter colds."

The World of Advertising

... Every word in an ad is there for a reason; no word is wasted. Your job is to figure out exactly what each word is doing in an ad—what each word really means, not what the advertiser wants you to think it means. Remember, the ad is trying to get you to buy a product, so it will put the product in the best possible light, using any device, trick, or means legally allowed. Your only defense against advertising (besides taking up permanent residence on the moon) is to develop and use a strong critical reading, listening, and looking ability. Always ask yourself what the ad is *really* saying. When you see ads on television, don't be misled by the pictures, the visual images. What does the ad *say* about the product? What does the ad *not* say? What information is missing

① Sinutab:一种止疼片。Tums:一种抗酸剂。Listermint:一种漱口水。Cascade:一种洗碗剂。Nuprin:一种消炎止痛药。Anacin:一种止痛药。Sudafed:一种鼻炎药。Advil:一种止痛药。Ponds Cold Cream:旁氏冷霜卸妆膏。Philips Milk of Magnesia:一种通便剂。Cracker Barrel:美国一家连锁餐馆和商店。Knorr:一种配料汤粉。Anusol:一种痔疮药。Dimetapp:一种感冒药。Liquid Drāno:一种静脉注射剂。Puritan:一种食用油。Pam:一种用来防止食物粘锅的烹饪喷雾。Tylenol Gel-Caps:一种止痛胶囊。Alka-Seltzer Plus:一种感冒药。

from the ad? Only by becoming an active, critical consumer of the doublespeak of advertising will you ever be able to cut through the doublespeak and discover what the ad is *really* saying.

Questions to Consider

1. Make a list of the brand name products you have used today. Which, if any, did you buy because of claims made in their advertisements?
2. Bring copies of magazine or newspaper advertisements to class and do a careful analysis of their language and the way in which they manipulate consumers. What "weasel" words do you find in the ads? What unfinished words or words with no special meaning do you find?
3. Discuss the extent to which you think it matters that advertisements use meaningless, empty words. That is, do you think the use of "weasel" words in advertisements is a fair practice? Is anyone harmed by such words? Why should consumers care "what the ad is *really* saying"?

***Historical Perspective* 历史视角**

Advertising

广告

ELIZABETH WILLIAMSON

Advertising has been described as an institution, a business, and industry, a discipline, a profession, a science, an art, and a talent. It has been defined as news, salesmanship in print, and mass communication. Some of the best minds in the business, outside the business, and on the fringes of the business have attempted to define and deal with this elusive subject. Scholars and advertising men themselves have examined the political, economic, social, ethical, historical, and religious aspects of advertising. Each of them has told us what advertising is, how it works, how it should work, and why it does not work; each has told us that advertising either deceives, informs, pleases, or frightens us.

Advertising has been attacked and defended by almost every segment of society. When it is advantageous, someone will admit to having used or even liked advertising. When it is not, the vindictiveness against advertising flies, even from public relations, marketing, and retailing specialists. Some popular culture books deal with advertising, but generally by including disparaging remarks. Examine a typical American history book and you will probably find little or no mention of advertising. Yet, to look at the advertisements of a nation is essentially to view most aspects of its existence. Advertising is the story of a nation's people. And, although advertising certainly did not originate in America, this country has probably done more than any other nation to use and foster advertising. It has been said that some foreign politicians have observed American advertisements as a gauge for measuring and understanding America's tastes and values. Advertising is probably the most pervasive form of popular culture and, surprisingly, has rarely been examined from this perspective.

Although the origins of advertising have been traced back to several very early sources, no one is exactly sure when the trade began. However, several evidences of written advertisements have been discovered and offered as the first recorded efforts in selling. The ones most often suggested are a Babylonian clay tablet announcing the services of an ointment dealer, scribe, and shoemaker, and a piece of papyrus from the ruins of Thebes offering a reward for the return of runaway slaves. The early history of advertising, replete with its accounts of Grecian town criers and Roman shop signs, is a fascinating one, and the reader is advised to consult the definitive histories listed elsewhere in this essay for a more thorough survey of early advertising history. Because of space limitations, we must necessarily begin with colonial America, which was beginning to implement already existing advertising methods, especially the shop sign and posted notices.

Advertising in America, which grew in conjunction with the expanding colonial economy, found its greatest impetus in newspapers, once the press had won its right to exist. As early as 1704 *The Boston Newsletter* carried advertisements for the return of some men's clothing and for the reward and capture of a thief. By the time of the Revolution, there were some thirty newspapers in America, each carrying substantial amounts of advertisements, mostly classified and local.

Although American advertising had reached a considerable sophistication and circulation, it was Benjamin Franklin who has earned—along with his many other credits—the title of father of American advertising, because he made important improvements in advertising methods. As a printer and a newspaperman, Franklin made major changes in the style and format of American advertisements. Most newspaper advertisements, which consisted of three-and four-line notices, were printed in various and uneven typefaces and were difficult to read. Franklin cleaned up the ads by separating individual notices with white spaces and then by adding bolder headings, thus making each ad distinctive from the rest. To make the advertisements even more distinctive, Franklin began using illustrations representative of the individual advertiser. He experimented with different symbols, such as ships, tools, horses, and books, which indicated the general contents of the advertisements. These symbols ranged in size from one and one-quarter inches to half columns and full columns and served as either borders or major graphics for the advertisements. …

Although some men like Franklin led the way in improving advertising, the general state of advertising was a poor one. Most ads were simply notices for goods, services, land out west, slaves, or lost items. Advertisements were also used to attack competition and to announce the newest wonder drugs. Fraudulent medicine men and patent medicines, most often cited for giving advertising a disreputable image, would remain problems for advertisers for a long time.

Most of the advertisements of the shopkeepers of the late eighteenth century were directed toward the upper classes. Long notices informed the wealthy readers of the latest imported goods from England, Holland, and the Far East. Quality fabrics like chintzes and taffetas, and fragrant balms, spices, and perfumes were signs of wealth and prestige in the New World. The words "imported" and "just arrived" in an advertisement spoke of America's taste and the advertiser's audience, both of which changed after the revolutionary war. After the long struggle with England for independence, America felt drastic changes both socially and economically, and advertisements of that period reflected those changes. Once fashionable to own goods "just imported," it was now fashionable and more feasible to purchase "American-made" products, a tag that began to appear regularly in advertisements.

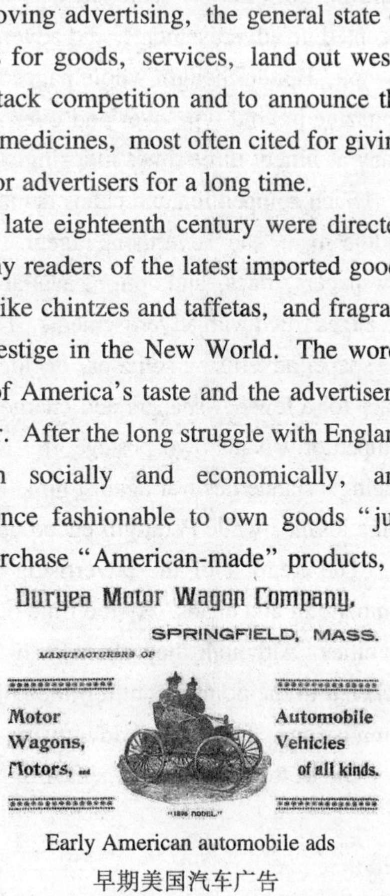

Early American automobile ads
早期美国汽车广告

Newspaper growth matched the increasing American population and income, and, by 1820, some five hundred newspapers were serving more than nine million Americans. Although advertisements were still of uneven quality, they were almost certain to be read since advertisements, a little more than legal notices, flooded the newspapers. Newspapers prided themselves on the number, not the quality, of the ads that appeared in their pages. And the American reading public accepted the inundation of advertisements, along with the editorial policies of American newspapers, which remained highly partisan.

Technological advances in the early 1800s created many kinds of changes in the format and production of newspapers, especially in price reduction. The first penny newspaper, *The New York Sun*, was a 9 ×12 tabloid that rapidly reached a circulation of twenty thousand. Benjamin Day, its founder, soon met competition from a very shrewd editor, reporter, and founder of *The New York Herald* —James Gordon Bennett. Bennett charged two pennies for his paper and soon its circulation doubled that of the *Sun*. Both men experimented with advertisements. Day created a section called "Wants" and charged advertisers fifty cents per ad per day. Bennett immediately created the "Personals" column whose contents read much like those of today.

Bennett saw the power and profit in advertising and soon added restrictions to advertisers in his newspaper. At first he limited the time that a single advertisement could run to two weeks, but he later changed the limitation to one day. He also banned the use of illustrations. His idea was to give all advertisements equal importance and impact. Advertisers protested, but the *Herald's* circulation and the need for and effectiveness of advertising forced the advertisers to submit to Bennett's rules.

Bennett was successful in implementing his restrictions for a brief time until Robert Bonner of *The New York Ledger* matched wits with Bennett and won. Bonner, whose pulp magazine itself accepted no advertisements, did advertise for his magazine elsewhere. Deciding to break Bennett's boycott, Bonner bought whole pages in the *Herald* and simply repeated the announcement for his magazine in bold type over and over again. Sometimes he repeated a complete advertisement as many as ninety-three times in a single issue of the *Herald*.

Such competition and chaos demanded some sort of order, which soon arose in the form of a middle man, the advertising agent. Someone had to inform the advertiser about the various newspapers, rates, and options available to him, and someone had to help the newspaperman keep his pages filled with advertisements. The first advertising agent, Volney B. Palmer, who began as a newspaper advertising solicitor, decided to go "independent" and established several offices selling space for a few newspapers and charged a 25 percent commission for each advertisement. His first competitor was his own protégé, S. M. Pettingill, whom Palmer tried to run out of business by waging a slanderous war against him. Palmer was unsuccessful, however. In fact, Palmer ended up going insane, while Pettingill ended up as a very successful advertising agent and copywriter.

The creation of the advertising agent, which worked for a while, soon created its own competition and chaos. By the time of the Civil War, there were some twenty agents operating in ten cities. Although they claimed to follow the rates established by the newspapers, they often dickered to the point of cutting the editors' rates a healthy percentage, thus increasing their own commissions. The shrewd advertising agent became a wealthy man easily enough.

Out of the advertising agent struggle emerged a man who added stability and respectability to a floundering, but possibly good, system. George P. Rowell① bought mass space in one hundred papers across the country and contracted to advertisers. Rowell also guaranteed payment to the newspapers for any ads for which he received a commission. He believed in truth in advertising and even wrote in an essay, "Honesty is by all odds the very strongest point which can be crowded in an ad." Rowell, in addition to his devotion to honesty, is known as the founder of *Printer's Ink* and as the publisher of the first American newspaper directory that gave estimates of the nation's newspaper rates and circulation.

Although Rowell stressed the need for honesty in advertising, he and many other agents made a great deal of money during the Civil War by advertising patent medicines. While it is easy for us today to point a finger at such men and such practices, it would be wise for us to reconsider the times. Even religious publications—the predecessors of magazines and the most influential medium in post-Civil War America—contained inordinate amounts of patent medicine② advertisements. In fact, patent medicine advertising comprised 75 percent of all advertising in religious publications. Many temperance papers carried advertisements for medicines that were eighty-proof alcohol.

However, once the secret formulas of patent medicine began to be exposed, the public responded by showing disapproval of both the promoters of the products and of the advertising men. One result of the consumers' behavior was that certain advertising men again tried to clean up their unsavory reputation. F. Wayland Ayer, founder of N. W. Ayer and Son, became personally interested in the reputation of advertising after an associate made disparaging remarks about the nature of Ayer's business. Ayer responded by trying further to stabilize Rowell's efforts to establish rates between advertiser, publisher, and agent. Ayer initiated the open contract, which stipulated the amount of money that would be spent on advertising costs plus the agent's commission. The greatest impact of Ayer's system was that it became clear that the agent represented the advertiser. Ayer is also credited with being the man who first studied the market and produced the first marketing survey.

Most efforts to establish a greater rapport between agents and clients focused on newspaper activity since the few magazines that were successful in the mid-century refused to carry advertisements. J. Walter Thompson③ was the first advertising man to convince magazine publishers to accept advertisements. His success plus several events in the last three decades of the nineteenth century made magazines and magazine advertising the new American craze. Technological advances such as the Hoe④ high-speed rotary press and the halftone method of reproducing photographs, in addition to a reduction in second-class postal rates, and a 50 percent increase in the literacy rate, all contributed to the mass circulation of magazines. Mass magazines introduced Americans to the

---

① George P. Rowell (1839—1908),美国广告界的重要人物。

② patent medicine:一种合成药,其药效颇受怀疑。制药商在推广这种合成药的过程中,运用了很多当时领先的广告和营销技巧,因此它的兴起是广告业发展的一个重要标志。

③ James Walter Thompson (1847—1928):广告技术先锋,JWT 广告公司以他名字命名。

④ Richard Hoe (1812—1886):美国发明家,发明转轮式印刷机。

nationwide sale of products and to national advertising. ...

The twentieth century heralded in the age of American advertising. Outdoor advertising, the oldest form of the profession, received a new face when the first electric sign was erected in New York in 1891. Retailers actively engaged in advertising. Copywriter Claude Hopkins① gave Americans a breakfast product "shot from guns," in addition to giving copy a new status in the advertising campaign. Americans were bombarded with advertising. Newspapers, magazines, transit ads, billboards, posters, and window displays echoed America's progress. The age of mass production, mass selling, and mass advertising had arrived. And Americans appeared to love it. Broadway, "The Great White Way②," attracted thousands of tourists, as did the Hudson River steamboat excursions to Albany, during which passengers gazed at the lighted billboards that lined the riverbanks.

But many people began to worry about the moral, psychological, and physical effects that such mass production and mass selling would have on the American public. Outsiders (and insiders, too) wrote exposés attacking the new American way and fraudulent advertising; while on the other side, advertisers themselves grouped together to create organizations and clubs to regulate their own profession. Vigilance committees and campaigns to promote truth in advertising sprang up overnight. Agencies such as the Better Business Bureau, the Association of National Advertising Managers, and the American Association of Advertising Agencies developed policies to improve the effectiveness of advertising and to protect the consumer from fraudulent claims. *Printer's Ink,* the leading advertising trade paper, created a model statute for the regulation of advertising; it vowed to "punish untrue, deceptive, or misleading advertising." In 1916 advertising gained some crucial respectability when President Woodrow Wilson addressed the Associated Advertising Clubs of the World in Philadelphia.

The struggle between advertising groups and consumer groups continued, as did American prosperity, through the 1920s. Advertising benefited greatly from the prosperity and, at the same time, congratulated itself for its contributions to America's growth. The December 7, 1929 issue of *The Saturday Evening Post* carried 154 pages of advertising in a 268-page publication that sold for five cents. Another new medium of the 1920s—the radio—brought advertising billings to three and one-half billion dollars by the end of the decade.

In addition to the stockmarket crash of 1929 and the ensuing economic upheavals, advertisers had to struggle against other factors throughout the 1930s. Muckrakers launched new attacks; the Robinson-Patman Act of 1936③ protected the little merchant from unfair competition by the big

---

① Claude C. Hopkins (1866—1932):最伟大的广告先锋之一。他认为广告就是为了销售,广告的成败也应该由它所带来的销售结果来进行评价和判断。

② "The Great White Way"指的是 Broadway 大街上的灯,它们照亮了 Broadway,使黑夜变"白",所以称为"The Great White Way"。

③ 又作 Anti-Price Discrimination Act,美国一部联邦法,禁止生产商的反竞争行为,尤其是价格歧视。

businessman; the Wheeler-Lea Act of 1938① gave the Federal Trade Commission② more power over advertising; and the Federal Food, Drug, and Cosmetic Act of 1938③ gave the administration authority over packaging and labeling.

But in spite of controls and criticism, advertising continued to survive and prosper. Radio remained the major advertising medium until the emergence of television, which quickly gave advertising a new source of expression, new challenges, and new problems. How successfully advertising will survive the electronic age, the problems of shortages, and an uncertain American economic future cannot be accurately predicted. But one thing is certain: advertising will face the new challenges just as it faced the ones presented to it throughout its early history in America.

---

① 美国一部联邦法,禁止商业中的不公平、欺骗行为,以保护消费者权益和商业竞争。

② Federal Trade Commission(FTC):(美国)联邦贸易委员会,成立于1914年,它的主旨是保护消费者,防止反竞争的商业行为。

③ 美国国会1938年通过的一套法案,授权美国食品与药物管理局(U. S. Food and Drug Administration)对食品、药物和化妆品进行安全检查。

Chapter 3 Pop Music

Excitements, Emotions and Controversies

流行音乐:躁动、情感和争议

A naked man, arms outstretched suggestive of Christ on the cross or an Olympian swimmer about to take the plunge, stands atop a cassette deck. Electric pulses from the tape player reach his brain through headphones as he gazes heavenward as if in a trance. The phrase "Be the music" scrolls about his midsection, concealing—perhaps replacing—his maleness, as the music fills his every cell. Such is the power music has over us, it suggests that it can take us over completely—mentally, physically, emotionally.

By virtue of its sheer volume, rhythm, and encompassing presentation, music has the capacity to take us to "completely different" psychic spaces. It can lift us from our ordinary sense of reality and profoundly affect our moods, emotions, energy level, and even our level of sexual arousal. Furthermore, the lyrics, when combined with these powerful aural appeals, become all the more potent and suggestive, influencing our feelings of isolation or belonging, our relation to parents and friends, our attitudes toward authority figures, our notions about romance, and our views about gender and race.

The articles in this chapter discuss the pervasive power of pop music in modern society and the ways in which people are "constructed" by what they hear—that is, how their beliefs, values, attitudes, and morals are shaped by the music they listen to. In "Hip-Hop Nation: There's More to Rap Than Just Rhythms and Rhymes", the authors explore rap as a predominant music form in contemporary America and discuss hip-hop's social and historical roots, tracing its origin back to Bronx, New York. Special attention is paid to the relationship between rap and African-American culture, the responses of the black community towards hip-hop's move to the white mainstream, and their way of maintaining their own culture. A timeline "20 years of hip-hop" is also provided in the end of the article to help the readers have a historical overview of rap's development.

There is no doubt that music can affect people's mood, thought and emotion. Over the past years, rock music has been criticized variously as wicked, immoral, and depraved for its relationship with violence and the possibility of encouraging young people to transgress the boundaries imposed by civilized society. Leonard Pitts launches a sort of attack against some pop music which "fell into the toilet". And he attributes it to the lack of honest criticism on pop culture typified in people's attitude toward Presley's hips. Isabelle Leymarie, in "Rock 'N' Revolt", also concentrates on rock as a powerful art form, but does not consider rock music as completely negative. By examining different cultures, societies, music forms and the way music is being used in different countries, the author tries to answer the question that whether music incites certain behavior or it is simply a reflection of the culture that produces it. Her article offers a general view of the importance of music in different cultures and its impact on our lives.

As you read these essays, perhaps hooked up to your Walkman and blasting the latest Christina Aguilera, Beyonce Knowles, Linkin Park, Justin Timberlake or Tupac posthumous release, or you can switch to the music video channel to take a glance of Elvis Presley or Michael Jackson's dance, you might consider the implications of music, the messages embodied in their lyrics and rhythm, and the pleasure and possible dangers inherent in letting popular music move you to a "completely different" frame of mind.

Lesson 7 Hip-Hop Nation: There's More To Rap Than Just Rhythms and Rhymes

嘻哈国度:说唱乐,不只是节奏和旋律

MELISSA AUGUST, LESLIE EVERTON BRICE LAIRD HARRISON, TODD MMURPHY, AND DAVID E. THIGPEN

Introduction

In this article, co-written by a group of young experts in rap and hip-hop music, the authors argue that rap has become a predominant force in American popular culture and has found its way into a wide variety of other artistic forms, such as literature and film. The authors provide an encapsulated view of hip-hop's social and historical roots, noting that this pop-music force derived originally from Bronx, New York, with inspiration from some role-related musical activities in Kingston, Jamaica. They supplement that historical overview with a timeline at the end of the article, chronicling notable points in rap's development. Finally, the authors explore the popularity of this musical form with white audience and discuss the responses of the African-American community to this mainstream "appropriation" of an originally black art form, namely the danger of being deprived of the politically critical edge and used merely as profit-making machinery.

Text

... Rap music was once called a fad, but it's now celebrating a 20th anniversary of sorts. The first hip-hop hit, "Rapper's Delight" by the Sugar Hill Gang①, came out in 1979. Hip-hop got its start in black America, but now more than 70% of hip-hop albums are purchased by whites. In fact, a whole generation of kids—black, white, Latino, Asian—has grown up immersed in hip-hop. "I'm hip-hop every day," declares 28-year old Marlon Irving, a black record-store employee in Portland, Ore. "I don't put on my hip-hop." Says Sean Fleming, a white 15-year-old from Canton, Ga.: "It's a totally different perspective and I like that about it." Adds Katie Szopa, 22, a white page at NBC in New York City: "You do develop a sense of self through it. You listen and you say, 'Yeah, that's right.'"

Hip-hop represents a realignment of America's cultural aesthetics. Rap songs deliver the message,

---

① Sugar Hill Gang: 糖山帮,来自布朗克斯区的说唱乐队,以其韵文般的歌曲引起听众的共鸣,代表作有"Rapper's Delight"。

again and again, to keep it real. The poet Rainer Maria Rilke① wrote that "a work of art is good if it has sprung from necessity." Rap is the music of necessity, of finding poetry in the colloquial, beauty in anger, and lyricism even in violence. Hip-hop, much as the blues and jazz did in past eras, has compelled young people of all races to search for excitement, artistic fulfillment and even a sense of identity by exploring the black underclass. "And I know because of [rapper] KRS-1②," the white ska-rap singer Bradley Nowell③ of Sublime once sang in tribute to rap. Hip-hop has forced advertisers, filmmakers and writers to adopt "street" signifiers like cornrows and terms like player hater. Invisibility has been a long-standing metaphor for the status of blacks in America. "Don't see us / but we see you," hip-hop band the Roots raps on a new song. Hip-hop has given invisibility a voice.

But what does that voice have to say?

…

Hip-hop is perhaps the only art form that celebrates capitalism openly. To be sure, filmmakers pore over weekend grosses, but it would be surprising for a character in a Spielberg film to suddenly turn toward the camera and shout, "This picture's grossed $100 million, y'all! Shout out to DreamWorks④!" Raps' unabashed materialism distinguishes it sharply from some of the dominant musical genres of the past century. For example, nobody expects bluesmen to be money-makers—that's why they're singing the blues. It's not called the greens⑤, after all. As for alternative rockers, they have the same relationship toward success that one imagines Ally McBeal⑥ has toward food: even a small slice of pie leaves waves of guilt. Rappers make money without remorse. "These guys are so real, they brag about money," says Def Jam's Simmons⑦. "They don't regret getting a Coca-Cola deal. They brag about a Coca-Cola deal."

…

Madison Avenue⑧ has taken notice of rap's entrepreneurial spirit. Tommy Hilfiger⑨ has positioned his apparel company as the clothier of the hip-hop set, and he now does a billion dollars a year in oversize shirts, loose jeans and so on. "There are no boundaries," says Hilfiger. "Hip-hop has created a style that is embraced by an array of people from all backgrounds and races." However, fans

---

① Rainer Maria Rilke (1875—1926)：奥地利诗人里尔克，其作品充满了颓废情调和神秘色彩，追求诗歌的形式美和音乐性。

② KRS-1 (1965—)：原名 Laurence Krisna Parker，他和 DJ Scott La Rock 两人组成的 Boogie Down Productions(BDP)是上世纪 80 年代众多具有影响力的嘻哈团体之一。

③ Bradley Nowell (1968—1996)：来自加州的乐队 Sublime 的主唱兼吉它手。

④ DreamWorks：梦工厂是美国排名前十位的一家电影洗印、制作和发行公司，同时也是一家电视游戏、电视节目制作公司。

⑤ 布鲁斯源自黑人音乐，音调多为悲伤、忧郁，布鲁斯唱者不是为挣钱而做，他们不是那种挣钱的人(greens)。

⑥ Ally McBeal：美剧《甜心俏佳人》的女主角。

⑦ Def Jam's Simmons: Russell Simmons(1957—)，美国企业家，著名嘻哈音乐品牌 Def Jam 的创办人之一。

⑧ Madison Avenue：纽约曼哈顿区的一条著名大街；美国许多广告公司的总部都集中在这条街上。

⑨ Tommy Hilfiger (1951—)：唐美 · 希绯格，美国知名服装设计师，创建了同名服装品牌。

are wary of profiteers looking to sell them back their own culture. Says Michael Sewell, 23, a white congressional staff member and rap fan: "I've heard rap used in advertising, and I think it's kind of hokey—kind of a goofy version of the way old white men perceive rap."

But the ads are becoming stealthier and streetier. Five years ago, Sprite① recast its ads to rely heavily on hip-hop themes. Its newest series features several up-and-coming rap stars (Common, Fat Joe, Goodie Mob②) in fast-moving animated clips that are intelligible only to viewers raised on Bone-Thugs-N-Harmony③ and Playstation④. According to Sprite brand manager Pina Sciarra, the rap campaign has quadrupled the number of people who say that Sprite is their favorite soda.

Hollywood too is feeling the rap beat. After Lauryn Hill⑤ passed on a role in *The Cider-House Rules*(an adaptation of the John Irving⑥ book), filmmakers cast hip-hop soul singer Erykah Badu⑦. Ice Cube⑧, who has appeared in such movies as *Boyz N the Hood and Fridays*, will soon star with George Clooney⑨ in the Gulf War thriller *Three Kings*. Queen Latifah⑩, featured in the recent film *Living Out Loud*, is now set to be the host of a TV talk show. …

Poetic language emerges out of the ruins of prose.

—Jean-Paul Sartre⑪, *Art and Action*

The hip-hop world began in the Bronx in 1971. Cindy Campbell needed a little back-to-school money, so she asked her brother Clive to throw a party. Back in Kingston, Jamaica, his hometown, Clive used to watch dancehall revelers. He loved reggae, Bob Marley and Don Drummond and the Skatalites⑫. He loved the big sound systems the deejays had, the way they'd "toast" in a singsong voice before each song. When he moved to the U. S. at age 13, he used to tear the speakers out of abandoned cars and hook them onto a stereo in his room.

The after-school party, held in a rec room of a Bronx high-rise, was a success: Clive and Cindy

---

① Sprite:雪碧,可口可乐公司旗下的一个著名商标。

② Fat Joe, Goodie Mob:肥仔乔,纽约说唱巨头之一; 正义暴民,美国的一支南部嘻哈说唱团体。

③ Bone-Thugs-N-Harmony:一支来自俄亥俄州克里夫兰市格兰维尔地区的说唱乐团,以其快速的说唱风格和和声而著名。

④ Playstation:日本索尼旗下的新力电脑娱乐 SCEI 家用电视游戏机。

⑤ Lauryn Hill (1975—):劳伦·希尔,美国著名说唱歌手、演员和制作人。

⑥ John Irving (1942—):约翰·欧文,美国当代作家,他的作品呈现出高超的叙述技巧、独特的原创性和优美的文学性,代表作有《盖普眼中的世界》等。

⑦ Erykah Badu (1971—):埃里卡·巴杜,美国说唱歌手、演员。

⑧ Ice Cube (1969—):艾斯·库伯,美国说唱歌手、演员、编剧、导演和制作人,曾是美国洛杉矶著名说唱组合 N. W. A 的核心成员之一。

⑨ George Clooney (1961—):乔治·克鲁尼,好莱坞著名男星。

⑩ Queen Latifah (1970—):奎因·拉蒂法,美国知名嘻哈女歌手、演员、主持人。

⑪ Jean-Paul Sartre (1905—1980):让-保罗·萨特,法国哲学家、戏剧家,存在主义的代表人物之一。

⑫ Bob Marley, Don Drummond, the Skatalites: 都是当时雷鬼音乐的代表人物。

charged 25 [cents] for girls and 50 [cents] for boys, and it went till 4 A. M. Pretty soon Clive was getting requests to do more parties, and in 1973 he gave his first block party. He was Kool Herc① now—that was the graffito tag he used to write on subway cars—and he got respect ... Joseph Saddler loved music too. He thought Kool Herc was a god—but he thought he could do better. Saddler figured most songs had only about 10 seconds that were good, that really got the party going, so he wanted to stretch those 10 seconds out, create long nights of mixing and dancing. Holed up in his Bronx bedroom, he figured out a way to listen to one turntable on headphones while the other turntable was revving up the crowd. That way a deejay could keep two records spinning seamlessly, over and over again. Herc was doing it by feel. Saddler wanted the show to be perfect.

Grandmaster Flash 和他的 the Furious Five 是嘻哈史上最伟大的革新者,他们将原本只是派对背景音乐的嘻乐带到了新的高度。

So he became Grandmaster Flash②. He played his turntables as if he were Jimi Hendrix③, cuing records with his elbow, his feet, behind his back. He invented "scratching"—spinning a record back and forth to create a scratchy sound. He tried rapping, but he couldn't do it, so he gathered a crew around him—the Furious Five, rap's first supergroup. ...

We in the '90s And finally it's looking good / Hip-hop took it to billions I knew we would.

——Nas④, We Will Survive

All major modern musical forms with roots in the black community—jazz, rock, even gospel—faced criticism early on. Langston Hughes⑤, in 1926, defended the blues and jazz from cultural critics. Hard-core rap⑥ has triumphed commercially, in part, because rap's aesthetic of sampling connects it closely to what is musically palatable. Some of the songs hard-core rappers sample are surprisingly mainstream. DMX⑦ raps about such subjects as having sex with bloody corpses. But one of his songs,

---

① Kool Herc (1955—): 本名 Clive Campbell, 美国著名 DJ, 他改良了音响的声音系统, 使得它可发出更大更有爆发力的声响.

② Grandmaster Flash (1958—): 原名 Joseph Saddler, 美国著名 DJ, 是史上第一人借由多张黑胶, 用手搓动唱片改变歌曲的安排、段落和重复(称为"Break"), 现在我们称之为 Scratching(刮碟)。他和他的团体 Furious Five(愤怒五人组)为 hip-hop 音乐带来巨大的派对功能和娱乐性。

③ Jimi Hendrix(1942—1970): 摇滚历史上最伟大的电吉他天才, 他在电吉他演奏技巧方面的贡献是革命性的, 并间接促使了重金属音乐的诞生。1970 年因过量服用安眠药剧烈呕吐窒息而死。

④ Nas (1973—): 美国说唱歌手 NAS(纳斯), 被称为纽约的说唱皇帝, 东岸的领军人物。也被誉为街头诗人, 其作品"It was written"和"I can"被认为是 rap 界的经典。

⑤ Langston Hughes (1902—1967): 兰斯顿·休斯, 美国黑人诗人, 被誉为"黑人民族的桂冠诗人"。

⑥ Hard-core: 硬核说唱, 嘻哈说唱形式的一种, 是一种极具力量感的音乐形式。

⑦ DMX (1970—): Dark Man X 的缩写, 原名 Earl Simmons, 美国说唱歌手。

"I Can Feel It," is based on Phil Collins'[①] easy-listening staple "In the Air Tonight." Jay-Z's[②] hit song "Hard-Knock Life" draws from the musical *Annie*. Tupac's[③] Changes uses Bruce Hornsby[④]. Silkk the Shocker[⑤] samples the not-so-shocking Lionel Richie[⑥].

The underlying message is this: the violence and misogyny and lustful materialism that characterizes some rap songs are as deeply American as the hokey music that rappers appropriate[⑦]. The fact is, this country was in love with outlaws and crime and violence long before hip-hop—think of Jesse James[⑧], and Bonnie and Clyde[⑨]—and then think of the movie *Bonnie and Clyde*, as well as *Scarface* and the *Godfather* saga[⑩]. In the movie *You've Got Mail*[⑪], Tom Hanks even refers to the Godfather trilogy as the perfect guide to life, the I-Ching[⑫] for guys.

…

Corporate America's infatuation with rap has increased as the genre's political content has withered. Ice Cube's early songs attacked white racism; Ice-T[⑬] sang about a Cop Killer; Public Enemy[⑭] challenged listeners to "fight the power." But many newer acts such as DMX and Master P[⑮] are focused almost entirely on pathologies within the black community. They rap about shooting other blacks but almost never about challenging governmental authority or encouraging social activism. "The stuff today is not revolutionary," says Bob Law, vice president of programming at WWRL, a black talk-radio station in New York City. "It's just, 'Give me a piece of the action.'"…

---

① Phil Collins (1951—)：菲尔·柯林斯，美国著名摇滚歌手，八座格莱美奖得主、美国音乐奖最佳摇滚艺术家。

② Jay-Z (1969—)：美国嘻哈音乐艺术家、企业家，于2008年4月4日与著名歌手碧昂丝结婚。

③ Tupac (1971—1996)：全名 Tupac Shakur，美国说唱巨星、演员和诗人。

④ Bruce Hornsby (1954—)：美国歌手和钢琴家。

⑤ Silkk the Shocker (1975—)：原名 Vyshonn King Miller，美国说唱歌手、演员和企业家。

⑥ Lionel Richie (1949—)：莱昂纳尔·里奇，上世纪80年代美国摇滚乐坛最耀眼的歌星之一，是两次奥斯卡电影歌曲奖得主及誉满全球的歌曲"We Are The World"、"Say You Say Me"的共同作曲者。

⑦ 一方面说唱中的暴力、厌女症、物欲、贪婪本身反映了社会的问题，另一方面这些内容也吸引了很多眼球，唱片公司牢牢抓住了这种链接，把音乐的揭露和反抗特征转化成了挣钱的润滑剂，而这正是美国社会的特征。

⑧ Jesse James (1847—1882)：杰西·詹姆斯，美国强盗，也是詹氏-杨格强盗团伙最有名的成员。

⑨ Bonnie and Clyde：美国经济大萧条时期出名的雌雄大盗，他们的故事后被改编成同名电影。

⑩ *Scarface*, *Godfather*：电影《疤面煞星》、《教父》，都是美国著名的黑帮片。

⑪ *You've Got Mail*：电影《电子情书》，汤姆·汉克斯和梅格·瑞恩共同主演的一部爱情喜剧。

⑫ I-Ching：《易经》，这里指《教父》系列给男人提供指导。

⑬ Ice-T (1958—)：嘻哈历史上最重要的歌手与创作人之一，匪帮说唱(Gangsta Rap)的真正创始人和实践者。

⑭ Public Enemy：美国著名的嘻哈组合，其歌词关注黑人社会和困扰黑人的各种问题。

⑮ Master P (1970—)：原名 Percy Miller，美国说唱巨星，企业家。

At first I did not know what I wanted. But in the end I understood the language. I understood it, I understood it, I understood it all wrong perhaps. That is not what matters ... Does this mean that I am freer than I was?

——Samuel Beckett[①], *Malloy*

In Mill Valley, Calif., in a one-bedroom apartment above a coin-operated laundry, Andre Mehr, a white 17-year-old with a crew cut, and Emiliano Obiedo, a ponytailed 16-year-old who is half white and half Hispanic, are huddled over a PC. A beat spirals up. Obiedo offers some advice, and Mehr clatters away at the keyboard. They are making music. Once they settle on a beat. Obiedo will take a diskette bearing a rhythm track home and lay down some rhymes. Soon they hope to have enough for a CD. Boasts Obiedo: "I'm going to change rap."

Across the country, similar scenes are playing out as kids outside the black community make their own hip-hop or just listen in. Some say they don't pay much attention to the lyrics, they just like the beat. "I can't relate to the guns and killings," says Mehr. Others are touched more deeply. Says 15-year-old Sean Fleming: "I can relate more and get a better understanding of what urban blacks have to go through."

Todd Boyd, a professor of critical studies at the University of Southern California, says rap can bring races together: "It's a little more difficult to go out and talk about hate when your music collection is full of black artists. That is not to say that buying an OutKast[②] record is the same as dealing with real people, but it is reason to hope." Ice Cube is a bit more cynical: "It's kinda like being at the zoo. You can look into that world, but you don't have to touch it. It's safe."

Nonblack performers are increasingly drawing from rap. Beck[③] expertly combined folk and hip-hop. Hanson[④]'s hit "MMMBop" included deejay scratching. Portishead[⑤] refashioned hip-hop into ethereal trip-hop. Singer Beth Orton[⑥], whose enchantingly moody album *Central Reservation* is due out in March, blends folksy guitars with samples and beats. Doug Century, author of *Street Kingdom: Five Years inside the Franklin Avenue Posse*, studied hip-hop culture as he documented the lives of gang members; he predicts white acts will eventually dominate rap, just as white rockers pushed out rock's black forerunners. "It's possible that in 15 years all hip-hop will be white." Century says. "[Then] black youth culture will transform itself again."

---

① Samuel Beckett (1906—1989):20 世纪爱尔兰、法国作家,荒诞派戏剧的重要代表人物,代表作《等待戈多》。

② OutKast:美国南方脏口说唱乐园,是极少的既获得商业成功又赢得评论界称赞的说唱乐团之一。

③ Beck (1944—):全名 Jeff Beck,美国著名摇滚吉他手。

④ Hanson:美国一支创作型乐队,由三个亲兄弟组成,音乐类型介于摇滚和流行之间,代表作有"MMMBop"等。

⑤ Portishead:来自英国南部港口布里斯托尔的一支乐队,神游舞曲(trip-hop)的代表乐队。

⑥ Beth Orton (1970—):贝斯 · 奥顿,英国歌手,她将传统民谣与神游舞曲结合起来,开创出自己独特的音乐风格。

Already the white b-boy has become an iconic figure—ridiculed in movies like *Can't Hardly Wait* and the forthcoming *Go*, and in songs like Offspring's[1]"Pretty Fly (for a White Guy)." In "Pretty Fly" the punk band Offspring mocks whites who adopt hip-hop styles, singing, "He may not have a clue / And he may not have style / But every-thing he lacks / Well he makes up in denial." Irish-American rap-rocker Everlast, whose new CD, *Whitey Ford Sings the Blues*, has proved to be a commercial hit, says the song makes him laugh: "They ain't talking about me, 'cause I'll beat the s— out of every one of those guys." In fact, Everlast feels confident enough about his standing in the rap world to take a verbal swipe at Puffy Combs[2]: "I don't think Puffy really cares about what he's doing. He's a brilliant businessman, but he's no different from the Backstreet Boys or the Spice Girls because he's just creating a product."

曾经的嘻哈偶像、说唱音乐教父Puffy Combs,同时也是最具商业头脑的艺人之一,成功从明星身份转变为商业巨亨。

Wu-Tang Clan producer-rapper RZA[3] is also concerned about maintaining standards. He believes many performers are embracing the genre's style—rapping—but missing its essence, the culture of hip-hop. "I don't think the creativity has been big. I think the sales have been big, and the exposure has been big," says RZA. "Will Smith is rap. That's not hip-hop. It's been a big year for rap. It's been a poor year for hip-hop."

…

Other groups, signed to major labels, are trying to perpetuate rap's original spirit of creativity. The rapper Nas' forthcoming album *I Am…the Autobiography* promises to be tough, smart and personal. And the Atlanta-based duo OutKast's current album, *Aquemini*, weaves chants, neo-soul and hip-hop into an enthralling mix. Says OutKast's Big Boi: "We're not scared to experiment."

One of the most ambitious new CDs is the Roots[4]' *Things Fall Apart* (named after the book by the Nigerian Nobel laureate Chinua Achebe[5]). The CD features live instrumentation, lyrics suitable for a poetry slam and a cameo from Erykah Badu. Roots drummer Ahmir hopes, in the future, the more creative wing of performers in hip-hop will form a support network. "There are

---

① Offspring:来自加州的朋克摇滚乐队,创作了半说唱的形式的热门歌曲"Pretty Fly (For a White Guy)"。

② Puffy Combs (1969—):美国说唱歌手、服装设计师、唱片制作人和企业家。创建了著名的坏小子唱片公司(Bad Boy Records)和嘻哈服装品牌 Sean John。

③ RZA (1969—): Robert Fitzgerald Diggs, 美国说唱歌手、演员和制作人,是嘻哈乐队 Wu-tang Clan(武当派)的成员之一。

④ Roots:美国爵士嘻哈乐团,融合爵士疯克等音乐风格,代表专辑"The Tipping Point"。

⑤ Chinua Achebe (1930—):钦努阿·阿契贝,尼日利亚小说家、诗人,曾获诺贝尔文学奖。

some people in hip-hop that care about leaving a mark," he says. There are some of us that look at *Innervisions*① as a benchmark, or *Blood on the Tracks* or *Blue* or *Purple Rain*②. Leaving a mark is more important than getting a dollar. I think Lauryn's album is one of the first gunshots of hip-hop art the world is going to get.

You could get the money / You could get the power But keep your eyes on the final hour.

——Lauryn Hill, Final Hour③

It's Puffy's 29th birthday party, and the celebration is being held on Wall Street. Inside the party, women in thongs dance in glass cages. Above the door a huge purple spotlight projects some of Puffy's corporate logos: Bad Boy (his record company) and Sean John (his new clothing label). But where's Puffy?

The music stops. The crowd parts. Muhammad Ali④ arrives. He's only the appetizer. The score to Rocky booms over the speakers. Only then does Puffy enter, in a light-colored three-piece suit. Forget being street. He's Wall Street, he's Madison Avenue, he's le Champs Elysees⑤. Donald Trump⑥ is at his side. It's Puffy's moment. His album *No Way Out* played on some familiar gangsta themes, but it's a smash hit. Puffy is a household name, a brand name. In fact his name comes up again and again, in gossip columns and other people's rap songs. He has transformed himself into a human sample. He is swallowed by the crowd.

You are at the Emporio Armani store on Fifth Avenue in down-town Manhattan. There's a benefit here tonight for the Refugee Project, a nonprofit organization Lauryn Hill founded to encourage social activism among urban youth. Hill is here, and the cameras are flashing. Her musical performance on *Saturday Night Live*⑦ has boosted her album back to the upper reaches of the charts. In a few days she will receive 10 Grammy nominations, the most ever by a female artist.

She never did do that *SNL* skit about the hooker. She says she feels too connected to hip-hop to do a movie or TV role that might compromise the message in her music. She addresses the crowd. "I'm just a vehicle through which this thing moves." she says. "It's not about me at all."

---

① *Innervisions*:《内在视觉》,美国传奇黑人音乐家、24 座格莱美奖杯获得者史蒂夫·汪德(Stevie Wonder)的专辑。

② 都是一些非常有名的摇滚唱片,像 *Blood on the Tracks* 是美国摇滚男歌手 Bob Dylan 的著名黑胶唱片。

③ 美国著名蓝调歌手劳伦·希尔(Lauryn Hill)的唱片"The Miseducation of Lauryn Hill"中的一首歌曲。

④ Muhammad Ali (1942—):穆罕默德·阿里,拳王阿里,美国历史上第一位三次夺得重量级拳王称号的运动员。

⑤ le Champs Elysees:香榭丽舍大街,巴黎城一条著名的大街,国际知名品牌的汇集之地。

⑥ Donald Trump (1946—):唐纳德·特朗普,美国知名亿万富翁,曾是美国最知名的房地产商之一,后投资创办热门真人秀节目《飞黄腾达》。

⑦ *Saturday Night Live*:《周六夜现场》是一个每周六深夜播出、90 多分钟的美国综艺节目,每期都有不同的客座主持人与音乐人加入。

You think back to some of the rappers you've talked to—Jay-Z, Nas, the Roots, Grandmaster Flash. A record cues up in your mind: "Ain't no stopping us now. …"

20 YEARS OF HIP-HOP

1979 THE SUGAR HILL GANG. Six years after Kool Herc introduced rap to partyers in the Bronx, the Sugar Hill Gang serves it up to a national audience in the form of the classic catchy song Rapper's Delight.

1984 RUSSELL SIMMONS. He co-founds Def Jam Recordings and goes on to become one of the richest, most influential forces in pop music.

1984 RUN-D. M. C. Hailing from Hollis, Queens, the supergroup rocks the house and introduces some rap signifiers—gold chains and untied sneakers.

1986 BEASTIE BOYS. The white rap trio's mix of hard rock and hip-hop make License to III a favorite at frat parties everywhere and the first rap album to hit the top of the charts.

1988 THE SOURCE. Harvard undergrads Jon Shecter and David Mays publish the first issue of their hip-hop mag out of their dorm room. Although it no longer has the field to itself and isn't even the largest publication covering the rap scene today, the Source remains a widely read source on hip-hop.

1989 N. W. A. The California act's Straight Outta Compton sparks gangsta rap and foreshadows the Los Angeles uprising of '92.

1989 2 LIVE CREW. (Remember "Me so horny?") This proudly foulmouthed group is pushed into the national spotlight in a-Florida battle over freedom of speech.

1990 VANILLA ICE. Admit it. You like Ice, Ice Baby. And so do the 7 million others who buy this one-hit wonder's To the Extreme.

1990 WILL SMITH. The sitcom The Fresh Prince of Bel-Air debuts on NBC, bringing suburban-flavored rap to the small screen. A new acting star is born.

1991 NEW JACK CITY. The crime thriller co-starring Ice-T is a surprise box-office hit and helps usher in a new genre of urban films, such as Boyz N the Hood and Menace II Society.

1992 SISTER SOULJAH. Her music and its message become a campaign issue when presidential candidate Bill Clinton attacks her militant views on race.

1993 SNOOP DOGGY DOGG. The pop-gangsta rapper releases Doggystyle, and it immediately rockets to the No. 1 spot on the charts.

1996 THE FUGEES. The trio's album The Score features head-bobbing beats, reggae and smart lyrics. It becomes a world-Wide smash.

1996 TUPAC SHAKUR. The year after he releases his best album, Me Against the World, the rapper dies in a drive by killing.

1997 BIGGIE SMALLS. The Notorious B. I. G. is shot. His album Life After Death is a hit.

1997 PUFF DADDY. His galvanizing rendition of I'll Be Missing you at the MTV Music Awards awakens millions of pop fans and ushers in a new era of positivism in hip-hop.

1998 BULWORTH. Warren Beatty's comedy uses the language of rap to critique politics.

1999 LAURYN HILL. She grabs 10 Grammy nods, begins first solo tour and eyes a film career.

Questions to Consider

1. What concrete examples do the authors of this article cite to support their article's thesis: that hip-hop is today's pervasive pop-music form? Based on your own experience, what additional examples can you cite? Are there any other pop-music forms that have similar influence, in your experience?
2. In what ways, according to this article, has hip-hop music and culture infiltrated and dramatically changed institutions of the American financial mainstream, such as advertising, fashion, literary publishing, and the Hollywood film industry?
3. Outline the historical roots of hip-hop, as laid out in this article. What social and/or personal concerns does this music reflect? What, according to this article, is the thematic function of "the violence and misogyny and lustful materialism that characterize some rap songs"?
4. What is the influence of hip-hop on the "nonblack" American youth culture, according to this article? How do some African-American critics feel about hip-hop's move into the white mainstream and provide easy ways for the industry to make profit?

Lesson 8 Rock 'N' Revolt
摇滚和反叛

ISABELLE LEYMARIE

Introduction

Isabelle Leymarie is a Franco-American jazz pianist, dancer and musicologist. She holds a Ph. D from Columbia University in ethnomusicology. Her study, "Salsa and Migration," appeared in an anthology of writing on Puerto Rico entitled *The Commuter Nation* (1992). In this article, the author discussed the relationship between music and violence—whether music induces violent behavior or is simply a reflection of the culture that produces it. The impact of music on human physiology and psychology was also discussed. It is believed that music can affect a person's mood, emotion and thought. Several studies were conducted to find out the impact of music on different cultures. The article goes beyond the relationship between music and violence by asking musicians to develop an ethic position in their art. It analyzes different cultures, different societies, different music forms and the way music is being used around the world, and gives a deep understanding about the importance of music and its impact on our lives.

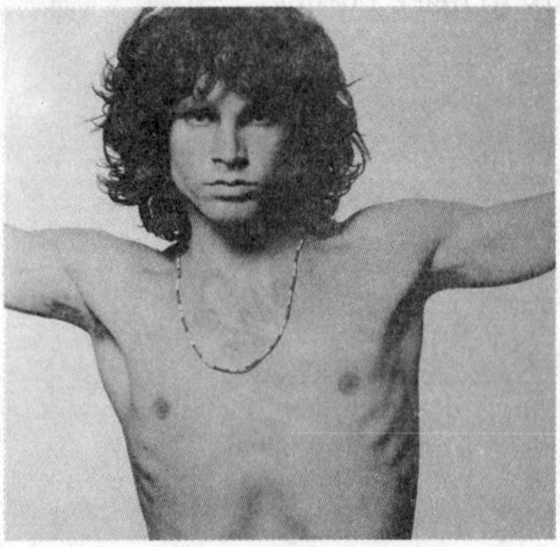

吉姆·莫里森(Jim Morrison)无疑是西方流行音乐史上一颗不可磨灭的明星,在成为历史后,"大门"的音乐和莫里森的传奇仍然令一代又一代的摇滚乐爱好者为之迷狂。1993 年,吉姆·莫里森和"大门"的名字被收入"摇滚名人堂"(the Rock and Roll Hall of Fame)。

Text

Rock, a musical and social phenomenon of unprecedented scope and intensity raises in acute form the question of the relationship between music and violence. Its history has been fraught with violence. Jim Morrison①, leader of The Doors, apostle of sex, alcohol, and LSD②, died young, of a heart attack in his bathtub in Paris. Stars Jimi Hendrix and Janis Joplin③ both died of drug overdoses. Acid rock has become synonymous with punks and English

---

① Jim Morrison (1943—1971):吉姆·莫里森,著名摇滚歌星。他的乐队"大门"(The Doors)是 20 世纪 60 年代最重要的乐队之一,它的名称来自威廉·布莱克的一句诗:"感知的大门敞开了"。

② LSD:学名"麦角酸二乙酰胺",一种致幻剂,滥用后可造成精神和行为的改变。

③ Janis Joplin (1943—1970):著名的白人摇滚女歌手,以其自信、性感、直率、嘶哑甚至邋遢肮脏的方式以及触电般的舞台表演,征服了亿万观众。1970 年因吸食过量海洛因突然死亡。

football riots. The fans of Metallica and Guns n' Roses have burned cars, and during a recent concert in Montreal they wrecked a stadium and injured twelve people. The Sex Pistols① proclaimed in their song "Anarchy in the UK": "I wanna destroy passers-by, for I wanna be anarchy." John Phillips, a member of The Mamas and The Papas②, was reported by musicologist David Tame as claiming that any rock group can whip a crowd into a hysterical frenzy by carefully controlling a sequence of rhythms. In 1967 he went ahead and did just that in Phoenix. When Bell's Angels roughed up spectators during a Rolling Stones concert in California, rocker Mick Jagger③ remarked that "Something like this happens every time I play that song."

米克·贾格尔(Mick Jagger),滚石乐队主唱。

Although physically less conspicuous, violence is also expressed in the lyrics of urban music such as rap (a recent hit by star rapper Ice-T④ is entitled "Cop Killer") and free jazz⑤("We are not angry young men, we are enraged!" proclaimed saxophonist Archie Shepp in the late 1960s). Here, violence is palpable in lyrics, song titles, public statements by musicians, and in the music itself: the mega-volumes, "fuzz" effects, and distortions of rock, the hammer beats of rap, the shrieking saxophones and cascading notes of jazz, and the amplified bass of reggae⑥. Violence is also associated with other types of music. In Stanley Kubrick's film *A Clockwork Orange*⑦, the hero, Alex, driven crazy by the sounds of Beethoven, jumps out of a window. In Cuba during the 1920s and 1930s, concerts by rival band playing the popular music known as *son* degenerated into brawls which had to be broken up by the police.

虽然性手枪乐队(Sex Pistols)只存在了短短2年,但其朋克革命精神——与世界彻底的决裂和完全的自我毁灭,创造了摇滚乐最危险的历史。

① Sex Pistols:朋克音乐的先驱级乐队之一,以各种尖锐、猥亵的方式抨击当时的社会制度。"性手枪"用让人崩溃的音乐和噪音,反映出当时英国年青一代绝望、醒悟的情感。

② The Mamas and the Papas:美国民谣摇滚乐队,主唱为John Phillips,其代表作有"California Dreaming",是电影《阿甘正传》的一首插曲。

③ Mick Jagger(1943—):滚石乐队(the Rolling Stones)的主唱,摇滚乐有史以来最有影响力的主唱之一。

④ Ice-T (1959—):Hip-Hop历史上最重要的歌手与创作人之一,西海岸(加州)一切辉煌的起源,Gangsta Rap的真正创始人和实践者。

⑤ Free jazz:自由爵士出现于上世纪60年代,一批先锋派乐手使爵士乐达到了一种"无法之法乃为至法"的境界。他们反对以往爵士乐的一切传统,采用惊人的自由调性,极力地破坏音乐的结构和调性。

⑥ Reggae:雷鬼音乐;教父Bob Marley由斯卡(Ska)和洛克·斯代迪(Rock Steady)音乐演变而来的一种牙买加流行音乐。

⑦ *A Clockwork Orange*:电影《发条橙》,由美国著名导演斯坦利·库布里克执导,影片以第一人称的形式讲述了一个名叫阿历克斯的少年犯的故事。

贾尼斯·乔普林(Janis Joplin)去世时才27岁,正式的唱歌生涯也只有几年,却给人留下了难以磨灭的印象。她是白人,但她的歌唱风格体现了黑人才具备的Soul的精神和特征。在“模仿”盛行的流行音乐界,很难有人能模仿出另一个Joplin来。

Violence, in more controlled forms, is present in many musical traditions, old and new: in the wailing of women in the funeral lamentations of Macedonia; in certain Senegalese songs whose lyrics pour out a stream of bitter invective against new wives brought into a household; in the drumbeats of African *griot*① storytellers which once stimulated the ardor of warriors and today perform a similar role for the participants in traditional wrestling matches. It is found in martial music, in hunting calls, and in filmed thrillers where it plays a crucial role in setting the mood.

Violence is also present in classical music such as Handel's "Saul"②, Beethoven's *Eroica Symphony* ③, in operas generally such as those of Verdi④, who once said that he sought to express "passions above all else" and almost all of whose heroines die tragic deaths, in Mahler's *Fourth Symphony*⑤, in Berlioz's *Symphonie Fantastique*⑥, with its dramatic *Dies irae*, and in Stravinsky's *The Rite of Spring*⑦, in which a virgin, sacrificed to the gods, dances herself to death (a riot broke out during the first performance). One could continue the list indefinitely.

An Extraordinary Power

Is it possible, asks musicologist Gilbert Rouget in his book on music and trance, that music may be endowed with a magical power capable of whipping people into the state of madness which

---

① Griot:格里奥,是一种职业,是民间的诗人和乐师,神话传说和历史故事的记诵者,宗教和民俗仪式上的巫师和歌者。

② George Frideric Handel (1685—1759):乔治·弗里德里希·亨德尔,著名的英籍德国作曲家。代表作有《阿尔米拉》、《尼罗》、《哈利路亚》等。《扫罗》(*Saul*)是其创作的清唱剧。

③ *Eroica Symphony*:德国作曲家贝多芬的降E大调第三交响曲,被称为《英雄交响曲》。

④ Giuseppe Verdi(1813—1901):威尔第,意大利伟大的歌剧作曲家,是19世纪意大利歌剧复兴时期最具代表性的歌剧作曲家。

⑤ Gustav Mahler (1860—1911):古斯塔夫·马勒,杰出的奥地利作曲家及指挥家,代表作有交响乐《巨人》、《复活》和《大地之歌》等。

⑥ Berlioz (1863—1869):柏辽兹,法国作曲家,法国浪漫乐派的主要代表人物,著有《幻想交响曲》(*Symphonie Fantastique*)。

⑦ Stravinsky (1882—1971):美籍俄罗斯作曲家,西方现代音乐的主要代表人物之一,《春之祭》(*The Rite of Spring*)是其经典作品之一。

the ancient Greeks called *mania*? Or does it have no objective reality? Rouget cites Timotheus of Miletus[①], who lived in the fourth century B. C. and once said that music was capable of tempting Alexander away from a banquet to take up arms, and then of luring him back again to his guests with a lilting harmony. Rouget also quotes Boethius, who claimed that the Dorian mode[②] inspired virtue, whereas the Phrygian mode[③] aroused passion and violence, and refers to Aristotle's theory of the ethos of modes, which was similar to that of Boethius. He concludes that music can induce a trance in some cases and calm in others, and that it "derives its power from its integration into a given set of representations."

It is true that in order to grasp the symbolism in a particular type of music it is essential to be familiar with the set of representations into which it is integrated and the context in which it is performed. In the West, for example, the major modes evoke elation and rejoicing and the minor modes inspire melancholy, while in the East other modes such as Arab *maqam*[④] and Indian *ragas*[⑤] evoke totally different emotional moods. Similarly, drums and trumpets are regarded as martial instruments and flutes are associated with pastoral. All this is bound up with mental associations that are to a large extent culturally determined.

Leibniz[⑥] spoke of the "anxiety-causing effect" of dissonance, and yet today dissonances, which have become commonplace in contemporary music, have lost much of their disquieting character (even Chopin's mazurkas, when first performed, were criticized for their "dissonance"). Verdi's use of double basses to introduce the final scene of *Othello,* Berlioz's use of percussion instruments in the *Symphonie Fantastique* and Alfred Hitchcock's use of violins to heighten dramatic tension, are all illustrations of the way in which musical choices are both personal and culturally determined.

And yet music, when considered as a group of organized sounds and hence as a purely acoustic phenomenon, is also known to produce certain physiological and psychological effects which have been scientifically documented. Certain rhythms and sound frequencies, for example, can accelerate or slow down the human metabolic rate and even induce hypnosis. John Diamond, a specialist in behavioral physiology, has shown the relative strength of certain muscles, a function which is easily measurable, varies according to the type of music to which people are listening. Animals and plants are also known to react physically to music. According to studies carried out in India, Russia, and the United States, plants seem to hate "heavy metal" rock music and twist

---

① Timotheus of Milētus (c. 446—357 B. C)：古希腊音乐家米利都人提摩太，传说他为西特拉琴加了一根弦，从而使音乐变得更为复杂。

② Dorian Mode：多里安调式，中古调式的一种，即大调 2 级音阶。

③ Phrygian Mode：弗利几亚调式，中古调式的一种，即大调 3 级音阶。

④ Maqam：玛卡姆，阿拉伯音乐的曲调以四音列为基础，各种不等的音程构成了多种类型的四音列，两个以上的四音列可以组合成一种调式。在阿拉伯音乐中有 100 多种这样的调式，它们被称之为玛卡姆。

⑤ Ragas：拉迦，印度古典音乐的一种调式，以其如怨如诉、绵延不断的旋律著称。

⑥ Leibniz (1646—1716)：全名 Gottfried Wilhelm von Leibniz，德国伟大的科学家、哲学家。"世界上没有两片完全相同的树叶"就是出自他之口。

themselves as far away as possible from the offending loud-speaker while they adore classical violin and will grow even more lushly to the sounds of disco.

Noise engenders violence; it can even drive people to suicide. Some artificial noises, especially those which emanate from continuous-frequency engines, have been found to have a pathological effect on the body's cellular structure, and can sometimes cause cancer, while natural sounds, like those of waves, the warbling of birds, and certain types of classical or African music, can create a sense of well-being and even a healing effect by harmonizing with our biorhythms.

In recent years, the practice of music therapy has enjoyed considerable popularity. Members of the Research Group in Pediatric Anaesthesiology at the Hospital for Sick Children in Paris and doctors in many American hospitals have used carefully selected types of music to reduce their patients' dependency on tranquillizers. In *The Burmese Harp* (1956), a fine film by the Japanese director Kon Ichkawa, a soldier-musician saps his comrades' will to fight whenever he plays and sings.

Study of the relationship between music and violence also raises the question of the political aspect of music. In many parts of the world, musicians such as the bards of Nepal, the *griots* or the musicians of Ethiopia are perceived as pariahs or as socially inferior and are believed to lead dissolute lives and be addicted to drugs and alcohol. Music has often been used as an instrument of domination. In some African societies, *mirliton* reed pipes and other instruments provide a musical accompaniment during the ritual parading of masks, which women and children must not see and which perpetuate male dominance.

The French writer Jacques Attali① has observed that in Western societies the upper classes have always encouraged artistic creation, but only in order to maintain the established order and legitimize their own authority. In the 1950s, the Dominican dictator Rafael Trujilloy Molina encouraged the practice of the *merengue*, a dance closely related to the samba, but gave orders that the musicians should sing his praises and exiled those who opposed him. In many countries, music has become a form of propaganda or been appropriated by the Church, and judgments about music have been an endorsement of manipulation and intolerance.

Authoritarian colonial regimes arbitrarily associated drums with violence and debauchery and long banned black music. The "New Age" writer Corinne Hélène② claims that jazz and juvenile delinquency go hand in hand. But this baseless claim is fraught with prejudice, for how can the

① Jacques Attali (1943—):法国政治和经济学学者,长期担任密特朗总统的特别顾问,著有《大爆炸》、《危机之后》等作品。

② Corinne Hélène (1882—1975):美国作家,致力于探求古代的智慧,代表作 *The New Age Bible Interpretation*。

beautiful and expressive phrasing of a Sarah Vaughan[①] or an Ella Fitzgerald[②] be associated with juvenile delinquency? Why should jazz as a whole be connected with this social problem when most young jazz musicians are now graduates of music conservatories and universities and the overwhelming majority of jazz fans are intellectuals? How indeed, when music, for many deprived black and Hispanic adolescents of America's urban ghettos, far from leading to delinquency, is often a lifeline?

In the United States, moral-majority pressure groups have stigmatized some rock records as "obscene", in the hope of getting them withdrawn from the market, but they also tried to ban the Robert Mapplethorpe photo[③] exhibition and other artistic events which did not correspond with their ideals. On the other hand, some kinds of music such as "Muzak[④]", which supposedly increase consumer sales and induce people in restaurants to eat more but are actually a form of audio-brainwashing and noise pollution, are broadcast all day long in shopping centers and other public areas.

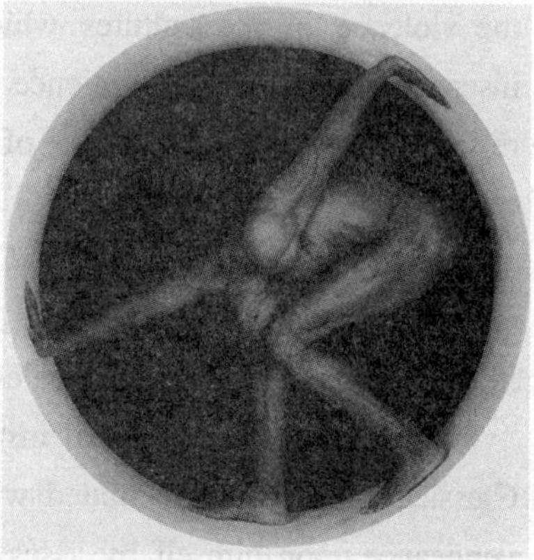

罗伯特·梅普勒索普(Robert Mapplethorpe)的人体摄影作品最后出来的效果虽然非常具有震撼力,但是可以看出他在拍摄这些照片时候所具有的刻意。他对画面构成比例、人体姿势安排、造型、用光等方面均有严密的考虑,因而在形式表现上总是以无以复加的完美先声夺人。

Jacques Attali has also remarked that "show business, the star system, and the hit parade are signs of deep-rooted institutional and cultural colonization." In this context music, through a sometimes violent protest against official art and the mechanization of society becomes a means of fighting authority. "Music exists," adds Jacques Attali, "to help us hear the sound of change. It forces us to invent new categories, to come up with a new momentum capable of rejuvenating a view of society that has become ossified, trapped, moribund." This is partly true of rock and its rebellious anti-establishment stance, and of jazz, rap and reggae—all musical forms which proclaim their black identity and have rejected old models along with the hypocrisy and inhumanity of materialism. In certain ritualized settings, notably during festivals, subversive songs are often used to express grievances against the establishment.

---

① Sarah Vaughan (1924—1990):美国著名爵士女歌手,她天生有很好的嗓音和宽广的音域,可以唱出四个八度的音域。她注重爵士乐的即兴演唱,进入一种自发性的独唱领域。

② Ella Fitzgerald (1917—1996):爵士三女伶之一的急智歌后,被誉为"爵士第一夫人"(First Lady of Song),以其纯洁的音色、近乎完美无缺的分节和音准著称。

③ Robert Mapplethorpe (1946—1989):美国摄影家罗伯特·梅普勒索普,其作品通过独特手法表现男性人体美,并以其表现内容惊世骇俗的摄影作品一跃成为西方现代艺术史与现代摄影史上引人注目的"异端"。

④ Muzak:缪扎克音乐,一种通过线路向机场、商场、餐馆等播放的背景录音音乐。

A Yearning for Harmony

Does music engender violence or does it express violence? And if it does express violence, does it, by sublimating violent impulses and dissipating tensions, play a cathartic role and "soothe the savage breast"? Music, for Attali, is the "audible tape of society's vibrations and signs." It is undeniably deeply rooted in the collective psychology: rock, rap, free jazz, and reggae all express the violence of the cultures which have bred them. But people and their environment are inseparable: the pent-up violence in the individual affects society and vice versa. While music reflects the collective *gestalt*① of a society, its particular form of expression also reflects the emotions of the musician.

In China, Egypt, India, and ancient Greece, music was believed to possess a certain ethical value and the power to uplift or debase the soul. In ancient China, the imperial government existed in harmony with the twelve celestial tones, and during the Confucian Chin dynasty, certain "virtuous" songs and musical instruments were reputed to temper the harshness of the regime. Classical music is also imbued with spirituality: Mozart's Don Giovanni② brings down divine vengeance upon himself by assassinating a nobleman and burns in hell for it. Liszt aspired to compose inspirational works, and although Wagner's *Tetralogy*③ (the four opera *Ring* cycle) expresses both the fall of humanity cut adrift from the gods and the distress of the artist faced with the world's misfortunes, Wagner had a deeply moral view of art.

The French sociologist Jean Duvignaud④ has written that art expresses "nostalgia for a lost form of communication in the shape of a forbidden dream that is continually revived by the irrepressible desire of the human emotional impulse." He goes on to say that a successful work of art "rebuilds behind the self a unity which pieces together the shards of a divided humanity". Now that idealism has been demolished and the philosophy of music has become a thing of the past, while the media (which tend to put the visual image before the musical message) bombard us with vulgar and iconoclastic music, it is more than ever incumbent on musicians and artists in general to adopt an ethical position. The most influential creators of the twentieth century, notably the film-makers whose art is one of our era's most powerful forms of expression—artists such as Kurosawa, Ozu, and Satyajit Ray⑤ —have been passionate humanists.

Musical eurhythmics presupposes both inner and outer harmony peace with oneself and with

---

① Gestalt：格式塔，主要指完形，即具有不同部分分离特性的有机整体。格式塔心理学创始人主张格式塔效应的普遍有效性，强调经验和行为的整体性。

② Don Giovanni：莫扎特的两幕歌剧《唐璜》。剧中的主人公唐璜是中世纪西班牙的一个专爱寻花问柳的胆大妄为的典型人物。他本质上是反面人物，但又具有一些正面的特点。

③ 德国音乐家瓦格纳作曲及编剧的一部大型音乐剧，于1848年开始创作，至1874年完成，历时共26年。创作灵感来自北欧神话的故事及人物，特别是冰岛家族传说。

④ Jean Duvignaud (1921—2007)：法国小说家和社会学家让·杜维纳，著有《戏剧社会学》等书。

⑤ 黑泽明，小津安二郎，萨耶吉特·雷伊，都是当代的著名电影导演。

the universe. Violence, in its latent form, is an intrinsic part of human nature and of the universe generally. But when violence is unleashed and expressed, often in a paroxysm, in music or other art forms, it is a paroxysm either of social unrest or of inner imbalance or torment, emotional deprivation, and arrested development.

And just as the wind can rise from a gentle breeze to a raging hurricane, so music can enchant or destroy us. It is for musicians to create works which enrich life, which contribute to the harmony of humanity, without compromising the quality of their art (some forms of therapeutic music, such as "New Age①" music, do not really have any aesthetic value).

However, when music achieves perfection, it allows us to catch a glimpse of the divine; it becomes, according to a Buddhist belief, the most refined art, the path to enlightenment. According to the Taoist sage, Zhuangzi, "Music allows man to remain pure, simple, sincere, and in this way to rediscover his primitive emotions." (A few centuries later, Wagner would also use music to explore primitive forms of expression.) The great violinist Yehudi Menuhin② once observed that "music creates order out of chaos." Nietzsche's humorous conclusion was that "Without music, life would be a mistake."

Questions to Consider

1. How would you answer Leymarie's question, "Does music engender violence or does it express violence"? Discuss whether you think music creates violent behavior or simply reflects the culture that produces it.
2. Leymarie gives examples of the way in which certain mental associations with music "are to a large extent culturally determined" (paragraph 6 and 7). Can you give other examples of the point she makes in this section of her essay?
3. Give examples of musicians or musical groups who have made political statements through their music, especially those who use music as "a means of fighting authority". Discuss the effect you see from their political statements.
4. Leymarie discusses her subject objectively for the most part, but she offers her own opinions from time to time, as for instance, when she says that "New Age" music does "not really have any aesthetic value." Find passages in which she makes her own subjective comments, and discuss whether you agree with her opinions or not.

---

① New Age：新世纪音乐，也被翻译成新纪元音乐，是种宁静、安逸、闲息的音乐，纯音乐作品占的比重较多。其重点是营造出大自然平静的气氛或宇宙浩瀚的感觉，洗涤听者的心灵，令人心平气和。

② Yehudi Menuhin (1916—1999)：耶胡迪·梅纽因，美国著名的小提琴家，他的演奏具有高超的技巧、独特的气质和动人的魅力。

Lesson 9 The Lessons of Presley's Hips

猫王舞步的启示

LEONARD PITTS JR.

Introduction

Leonard Pitts Jr. has written a twice-weekly column on pop culture, social issues, and family life for the *Miami Herald* since 1994 and KRT News Service since 1995 and is now syndicated by Tribune Media Services. He has also freelanced for national magazines and written and produced numerous radio programs. A 1992 Pulitzer Prize finalist, he has won a number of awards, including the 2001 American Society of Newspaper Editors Awards for distinguished writing. He is author of the book *Becoming Dad: Black Men and the Journey to Fatherhood* (1990). This article appeared in syndication in August 2000. In this article, the author started from the 15-year-old son's question to talk about modern society's loss of capacity to properly judge over popular culture. He argues that our culture has already become "too cool to take offense, too jaded for questions of decency and so filled with attitude that we disconnect from our own feelings, our own barometers of right and wrong."

20世纪世界流行音乐发展历史中最重要的人物是谁？答案毋庸置疑，那就是"猫王"埃尔维斯·普雷斯利。The Hillbilly Cat，这个绰号是狂热的美国南方歌迷为他取的昵称。

Text

Last week, my 15-year-old son asked me to explain Elvis Presley①'s hips.

What was the big deal, he asked. Why was there such an outcry, such public anger, over this guy's gyrating pelvis?

I didn't have to reach too far for an answer. I explained how each rhythmic thrust of this white country boy's hips came like a dagger to the heart of American hypocrisy on the dangerous subjects of sex and race. Told how he liberated a nation in spite of itself, got it all shook up so that nearly half a

---

① Elvis Presley (1935—1977)：艾尔维斯·普莱斯利，又称"猫王"(The Hillbilly Cat)。20世纪50年代，猫王的音乐开始风靡世界。他的音乐超越了种族以及文化的疆界，将乡村音乐、布鲁斯音乐以及山地摇滚乐融会贯通，形成了具有鲜明个性的独特曲风，强烈地震撼了当时的流行乐坛，并让摇滚乐如同旋风一般横扫了世界乐坛。

century later, he's a pop culture demigod while the people who decried his music seem short-sighted, censorious—quaint.

不羁天性而富有感召力的舞台表现力成为了猫王的标签,也使他成为世人狂热崇拜的明星。

Easy question. Except, as I thought about it later, it occurred to me that while the answer I'd given was correct, it was also incomplete. Because if it's true that Elvis' hips represent a victory by the forces of progress, amity and good rockin' tonight, it's also perversely true that we've been hobbled by that victory ever since.

More to the point, that victory is part of the reason pop culture fell into the toilet sometime in the last generation. And that instead of climbing out, it's doing the backstroke. Indeed, that it swims proudly in matters excretory, masturbatory, penile, puerile, bigoted and foul. From the potty-mouthed tykes of "South Park①" to the hateful gay-bashing of rapper Eminem② to the lewd butt-worshipping of the music video channel, it's become nearly impossible to absorb popular culture without also absorbing slop that would embarrass a reasonably respectable pig③.

Eminem是嘻哈界极少数成功的白人歌手之一,他也因为歌词的内容渗透着"反同性恋"、"厌恶女性"的情绪,也因过分描绘"暴力"而倍受争议。

Worse, you can't even complain about it without worrying that people will think you some priggish, humorless prude. Which is why, over the years, the complaining has nearly stopped. Granted, when a given piece of work offends a particular constituency—if an Eminem insults gays, let's say—you can expect representatives of that group to register a complaint. But a general sense of outrage? No. That's a capacity we seem to have lost.

It's a loss that traces directly to the fight over the hips of Elvis. Not that they were the only battleground. The same war was waged, after all, over Little Richard's mascara, the Beatles' hair, Lenny Bruce's language, the

---

① South Park:美国喜剧中心(Comedy Central)制作的一部剪纸百拍动画剧集,经常通过歪曲式的摹仿来讽刺和嘲弄美国文化和社会时事的方方面面,挑战了许多根深蒂固的观念和禁忌。

② Eminem:埃米纳姆,美国歌手。其风格类型为硬核说唱(Hardcore Rap)。他最大的突破就是证明白人也能介入到黑人一统天下的说唱界中,而且获得巨大的成功。

③ 流行文化在一些人眼里是那么邋遢、肮脏、怪异,要想拥抱流行文化而不接受让那些很是体面的人大皱眉头的东西,这近乎是不可能的事。但是,另一方面,因为害怕被指责为正人君子而放弃提出正当的批评则让社会丧失了判断的标准。这是此文的要旨所在。

每当猫王演唱到激越之处时，那独特的标志性的扭胯摇摆，立刻引起歌迷们声嘶力竭的狂叫。

Smothers Brothers' politics①. Now like Elvis, all those people stand vindicated, acclaimed as performers who changed the architecture of art and hurried the Zeitgeist② along. And history's judgment of the people who fought them has been harsh. They seem, in hindsight, stuffy, silly, self-righteous and out of touch.

It's a verdict that unavoidably colors any attempt to offer honest criticism of the state of pop culture today. We've learned to fear history's hindsight—this present raunch, might one day be judged genius—so instead of complaining, we nod and smile at stuff we hate③. Like Bill Clinton, we obsess over legacy.

Take, for example, the recent Entertainment Weekly④ cover story about the sewer pop culture has become. Writer Lisa Schwarzbaum⑤ seemed ill at ease with her own premise, worried that, in pronouncing certain aspects of the culture offensive, she might damage her reputation as an arbiter of edgy entertainment. Writing the piece "makes me sound like Bill Bennett⑥ with a wedgie," she fretted.

猫王将黑人和白人音乐十分自然地融为一体，并以其独特的夸张、刺激的动作和热情奔放的舞蹈相结合，使摇滚乐成为平民大众喜闻乐见的艺术形式。

As a former full-time critic of pop music, I understand the apprehension. I also understand that something's wrong when people are too fearful of history's judgment to voice honest misgivings.

Understand: the issue is not freedom of speech. Pop culture has an absolute constitutional right to swim in the toilet and I'm opposed to ham-handed government attempts to take that right away. We ought to understand by now that taste is, by definition, subjective; I may draw the line in a different place than you.

But here's the question: What happens when no one has the guts to draw the line anywhere?

---

① 这里的例子皆指一些反文化运动代表人物的颠覆性行为，比如摇滚歌手小理查德（Little Richard）的烟熏妆，披头士乐队（The Beatles）成员离经叛道的发型，喜剧演员莱尼布鲁斯（Lenny Bruce）大胆的台词，以及乡村合唱团斯莫瑟兄弟（Smothers Brothers）在自己的电视节目专栏中对政治调侃的态度。

② Zeitgeist：时代精神。

③ 昔日的混混成为了今天的天才，历史的"后视"让我们闭嘴，即使有不满也不敢说出。由此，大众文化缺少了批评的氛围。

④ Entertainment Weekly：美国的著名杂志《娱乐周刊》，1990 年创刊，侧重于影视娱乐领域的新闻。

⑤ Lisa Schwarzbaum：利萨·施瓦兹鲍姆，美国作家，1991 年加入《娱乐周刊》，成为该杂志的两位重要影评家之一。

⑥ William (Bill) Bennett（1943—）：美国保守派著名人物，学者，曾在 1985—1988 任里根政府教育部长，反对设立多元文化课程，极力捍卫美国传统价值，成为卫道派代表。

We're finding the answer now and it's not pretty. We've become a people too cool to take offense, too jaded for questions of decency and so filled with attitude that we disconnect from our own feelings, our own barometers of right and wrong. We took the wrong lessons from Elvis' hips.

And we're getting the pop culture we deserve.

Questions to Consider

1. In what way did "Elvis's hips represent a victory," according to Pitts? What does Pitts mean when he says, "[T] hat victory is part of the reason pop culture fell into the toilet some time in the last generation"? Discuss your response to that remark. Can you think of other examples that would illustrate his point?
2. To what extent do you agree with Pitts's opinion that "we seem to have lost" the capacity to be outraged by anything in popular music today (paragraph 4)? Do you agree that we as a culture are "too cool to take offense, too jaded for questions of decency, ... [too] disconnect[ed] from our own feelings...of right and wrong"?
3. Pitts says in paragraph 8 and 9: "Understand: The issue is not freedom of speech.... But here's the question: What happens when no one has the guts to draw the line anywhere?" Discuss your understanding of his point here and the extent to which you agree with him.

Historical Perspective **历史视角**

Music

音乐

MARK W. BOOTH

While thoughtful attention to popular music is relatively new, the music itself has been vigorously alive in this country for a long time. Some of the music brought to the New World by the colonists was serious academic music; some was what we now call *folk music*, belonging to the community by tradition and freely. Some, however, was popular music, printed and sold in broadsides and song books or performed by professional entertainers to paying audiences. The source of this popular music was the mother countries of the new Americans, chiefly England. The same ballads sold in the streets of London were sold in the colonial American cities and towns; the same ballad operas and other musical entertainments were heard in English and American theaters.

During the eighteenth century an increasing amount of this popular music was written in the colonies for colonists. During the years of the Revolution, the sentiments of Americans were expressed in anti-British broadsides that could hardly have been imported, but a significant number of these broadsides were specific parodies of British songs. They set anti-British words to British music. As such they remained, however rebellious, colonial popular music. The forms of the lyrics as well as of the music were indebted to the model brought over from England.

To decide, then, where we can mark the beginning of American popular music, it is necessary to find the stage in the developing history of music that has been enjoyed by Americans where not only the actual writing, printing, and selling of the music take place on American ground, but where the product itself has an American quality—some flavor that is not borrowed or inherited.

English music remained in the American marketplace throughout the nineteenth century, but it gradually became mixed with, then edged by, popular music that is distinctly native. Where this genuine American popular music really began cannot be said for certain. A sign of the beginning can be located in 1827. Among the few scattered relics of the music sold or professionally performed a century and a half ago that we know were hits of the day, two songs suggest in retrospect that that year marks a turning point. In *Variety Music Cavalcade 1620—1969*, Julius Mattfeld①, the editor, lists four prominent songs for 1827 and of the four, two, "My Long-Tail

① Julius Mattfeld (1893—1968)：曾担任国家广播馆(National Broadcasting Library)管理员。本文所指的著作 *Variety Music Cavalcade 1620—1969* 按照时间顺序介绍了美国流行音乐的发展,此书于1971年出版。

Blue" and "The Coal-Black Rose," were popularized by the minstrel singer George Washington Dixon①. Dixon, whom Mattfeld calls "a Negro minstrel②," was a white man performing in blackface. He was neither the first nor the most successful performer in that masquerade tradition, which was still alive more than a century later, but he can be taken to represent with these two hits an emblem, or a portent, of the course of American popular music. The native American note we are looking for was struck in the meeting of Afro-American and Euro-American styles.

Most popular songs in the years after 1827 continued to be the work of English writers or indistinguishable from English work; tunes continued to be borrowed, as the tunes of "Yankee Doodle" and "The Star-Spangled Banner③" had been borrowed, from English songs, but a new way had been opened. The music that slaves brought with them from west Africa evolved into an Afro-American folk music and then evolved into a variety of styles of professional performance for black audiences. In themselves these styles are an American popular music. Throughout their history, in all their forms, they have also exerted an influence on the shaping of the rest of American popular music.

扬基曲(Yankee Doodle)是美国的爱国歌曲,多年来一直被当作美国非正式的第二国歌。

Alec Wilder④ argues that the first truly native American popular songs are those a generation after George Washington Dixon, at the next stage of interaction between black and white music, the songs of Stephen Foster⑤. Foster was influenced not only by the minstrel mimicry of slave music but also by Negro church music. After Foster's death in 1864, Wilder contends, the disruption of the Civil War and Reconstruction in the lives and culture of black men and women kept black music away from the ears of white Americans, and popular music entered a recession that ended in the 1890s when the sounds of ragtime⑥ played by young black pianists began to be heard by a white public. The distinctively American feeling that derived from ragtime rhythm enters the mainstream of those

① George Washington Dixon (1801—1861):美国歌手、演员和报刊编辑。因扮演黑人而成名,有人认为他可能是美国历史上第一个尝试白人扮演黑人的演员。前文所提到的"My Long-Tail Blue"和"The Coal-Black Rose"皆为其代表歌曲。

② Minstrel:19世纪起源于美国的黑人剧团的演出,常由白人扮演黑人演唱黑人歌曲。

③ "Yankee Doodle"又叫扬基曲,早在北美独立战争以前这首歌就在英国殖民地非常流行;在独立战争期间,北美大陆军采用扬基曲作为他们自己的歌。"The Star-Spangled Banner"是美国国歌。这两首歌皆借用了英国歌曲的曲调。

④ Alec Wilder(1907—1980):美国作曲家,他的作品很好地结合了爵士、流行和经典音乐的元素。

⑤ Stephen Foster(1826—1864):美国作曲家,作有《故乡的亲人》、《我的肯塔基故乡》等200首歌曲,其中很多都是广为流传的著名歌曲。

⑥ Ragtime:一种采用黑人旋律,依切分音法(Syncopation)循环主题与变形乐句等法则结合而成的早期爵士乐,盛行于第一次世界大战前美国经济十分繁荣的时期。

斯蒂芬·福斯特(Stephen Foster),被誉为第一位伟大的美国音乐家,他的音乐作品很好地融合了黑人民歌的特点。

major songwriters of the twentieth century whose work Wilder traces. Often very remote from ragtime—or from the successors of ragtime, blues and jazz—American music continued to show the rhythmic and harmonic signs of inspiration from the black tradition, from Tin Pan Alley①to swing bands② to rock, with a contribution by the way to country and western.

Popular music is a marketplace art. American popular music was the commercial extension of the eighteenth-century publishing and theater business as it had evolved in London and been imitated in New York. This publishing and theater system, in nineteenth-century American cities and towns, met with an American buying public and gradually learned to offer that public music flavored by American folk music styles, most distinctively black music. The evolution came slowly, and when something clearly American predominated at the end of the nineteenth century, it was the product both of American musicians and of the American genius for commercial promotion. A massive market was sought out, or built, by promoters and salesmen for shows, for sheet music, and for pianos to play the music. Some of the sold entertainment still had, at the turn of the century, the prestige of being European, but the booming American music business drew on a growing body of native writers and performers and sold to a public gaining in cultural self-confidence in spite of itself.

Thomas Edison③ built the first phonograph in 1877, but for half a century phonograph records would be only a smaller or larger minority of popular music sales. Joseph Murrells④, in his *Book of Golden Discs*, supplies the lore of successful recordings: the first to sell a million in 1902 and a couple of dozen of them by the 1920s for home phonographs and juke boxes⑤.

At the opening of the twentieth century the decisive influence of the ragtime pianists fell on white audiences tiring of the minstrel show and willing to pay to hear black performers. At the

---

① Tin Pan Alley:叮砰巷,是个地名,位于纽约第28街(第五大道与百老汇街之间),19世纪末20世纪初这里是流行音乐发行人和作曲家的集中区。叮砰巷音乐指美国传统的流行音乐,50年代摇滚乐的出现使传统的叮砰巷歌曲在整个流行音乐中的地位受到了挑战。

② Swing Bands:摇摆乐队。摇摆乐起源于1930年前后,是爵士乐的重要流派之一,最明显的特征是其让人一听便想随之舞动的摇摆节奏。

③ Thomas Edison(1847—1931):爱迪生,美国电学家和发明家,他发明了留声机、电灯、电话、电报、电影等,为人类的文明和进步作出了巨大的贡献。

④ Joseph Murrells(1890—1952): *Book of Golden Discs* 的编纂者,书中记录了一些销售过百万的唱片,该书于1974年出版。

⑤ Juke boxes:点唱机。

same time the American band was being heard everywhere, promoted by John Philip Sousa①, the most successful musician of his time, and testifying among other things to pugnacious nationalism. Both phenomena would modulate into dance bands playing vigorous dance music. Burgeoning displays of sheet music in neighborhood stores, often music calling itself *rag*, attracted a diverse public, much of which never heard the concerts of the creators of ragtime. Modest as well as prosperous homes had a keyboard, either a piano or the less expensive reed organ: the industry built 107,000 harmoniums a year in 1900, and 177,000 pianos. By 1909, the figure was 364,000 pianos. Piano music was available beyond the proportion of the population that could play: by 1925, more than half the pianos produced were automatics, using player rolls for current hits (see Cyril Ehrlich②, *The Piano: a History*). Such instruments, giving out more and better sound than the evolving phonograph had yet mastered, tuned the audience more closely than ever before to the latest fad in music.

A boom in social dancing began during the second decade of the twentieth century, along with the first recognition of music called *jazz*. Nat Shapiro③ quotes *Variety* as estimating that in the mid-1920s there were 60,000 dance bands playing on the dance floors of jazz age America. Beginning in 1920, radio broadcasting brought recorded and live music into homes, posing an economic challenge to pianos and combining with the Depression in 1929 to decimate record and phonograph sales. The music that America absorbed through these media came mostly from New York, from Tin Pan Alley publishing houses and from the flourishing Broadway stage, reproduced also in vaudeville houses across the country. When in the middle of the 1920s recording engineers developed microphones to replace recording horns, a new softer "crooning" performance became possible and stylish on records and over the radio.

Al Jolson④'s songs on screen in 1927 opened another medium. When the Depression crippled the New York musical theater, Hollywood studios became the patrons of much of professional songwriting, for the movies that were the country's largest entertainment indulgence during the 1930s. The record industry struggled back late in the decade, dominated by the big swing bands and their vocalists. As the war overtook the United States, a significant economic struggle surfaced in musical entertainment. The American Society of Composers, Authors, and Publishers (ASCAP)⑤ had been formed in 1914 to collect performance royalties⑥ for the owners of song copyrights. By 1939 it held monopoly power over popular music performance, and a contract

---

① John Philip Sousa (1854—1932):美国作曲家、军乐指挥家,一生作有大量军乐曲和轻歌剧、歌曲等,被誉为"进行曲之王"。

② Cyril Ehrlich (1925—2004):美国社会和经济历史学家,有多本有关音乐方面的著作。文中提到的 *The Piano: a History* 于 1990 年出版。

③ Nat Shapiro (1922—1983):美国爵士作曲家和唱片制作人。

④ Al Jolson (1886—1950):美国演员和歌手,为立陶宛籍犹太人,1893 年随父母来到美国。他演唱过的知名歌曲有《我的妈咪》和《四月的阵雨》。

⑤ ASCAP:美国作曲家、作家与出版商协会,成立于 1914 年的非盈利性组织,旨在保护音乐版权。

⑥ royalties:版税。

dispute with radio broadcasters led to the formation of Broadcast Music Incorporated (BMI)① as a rival guild. Following a ten-month interval in 1941 during which no ASCAP music could be played on the radio, causing a boom in classical, folk, and public domain music generally, ASCAP entered into a new broadcast contract, but BMI continued and grew. BMI, growing out of the dispute where its rival stood for established interests, came to represent popular music from outside the New York-Hollywood establishment, and local markets compared with the network emphasis of ASCAP. An institution had appeared to reflect the regional, rural, and minority interests in the music world that would gain great audience support after the war.

When the war ended, the entertainment industry responded to the ready money of a new public, more urbanized, but less in touch with Broadway sophistication, and with expanding young families preparing to be the next generation of popular music consumers——raised with unprecedented pocket money and leisure time and with an unsuspected susceptibility to the energies of rock and roll they would first hear in 1954. Carl Betz② describes the recording industry in the years after the war as dividing its market in the interest of stability and consequently producing for the general market dull, or at least highly controlled and predictable, music. Small independent record companies sold to the country and Western and rhythm and blues markets, while the major companies guided the music of the largest pop market down a narrow channel, with a slow succession of new songs and much repetitive recording by competing stars.

Rock and roll, which the industry learned to ride to a staggering new sales volume, also jarred that industry into new patterns: new companies, new small-group recording economics, new audience definitions, and new relationships to radio broadcasting. Some of the story can be told in terms of technical innovations. Television as the surging home entertainment medium turned radio stations toward the disc jockey format of record programming. New sizes, speeds, and materials for the records themselves may have had wide implications. Belz makes an interesting analysis of the cultural meaning of the shift from 78 to 45 rpm③ records, as stream-lining the experience of recorded music toward casualness, especially for young audiences, while their parents bought the more substantial 33 long-playing records that emerged at the same time in the early 1950s. The later movement of rock and its audience into long-playing records reflects the triumphing cultural and economic power of the same young generation, along with a growing seriousness and self confidence of the makers of rock music.

The relationship of popular culture to ideology in the 1960s and into the 1970s has become of interest to academic sociology, although the alarmed interest of politicians has given way to accommodation. The relationship of the entertainment favored by highly visible classes of teen-

---

① BMI：美国广播音乐公司，成立于 1939 年，和 ASCAP 一样是美国三大版权组织之一，BMI 代表作曲家、音乐出版人等收取版税。

② Carl Betz (1921—1978)：美国知名演员，曾主演 ABC 电视剧集《唐娜 · 里德秀》(*Donna Reed Show*)。

③ rpm: revolution per minute, 指播放唱片的每分钟转速。

agers and young adults to the behavior of that audience, and especially its use of drugs, is probably now still too current an issue for full perspective and confident judgment. The history of popular music suggests that it is very unlikely that musical entertainment can induce new behavior, or even introduce new ideas to the audience it must court in order to sell itself. Though popular music has been blamed in the past for undermining community standards or otherwise damaging society, it is a new phenomenon for popular music to have the pervasive presence that prosperity and the portable radio and tape deck have given it lately, and for such conspicuous economic power to be vested in a youth audience. The history of popular music that is now happening cannot be fully schematized and managed by the patterns of earlier popular music. Its development has always been contingent, surprising, and even discontinuous except when we rationalize it with hindsight, and it is continuing that unpredictable development now.

As rock has evolved in the last quarter of a century and brought, among other things, self conscious seriousness to popular music, it has prompted an immense volume of reportage and analysis, much of it empty but some perceptive and judicious. The attention that rock has demanded has occasioned the first widespread, serious critical attention to the popular arts in general. Nostalgia, publicity promotion, and the university environment of a part of the proprietary audience of rock have contributed to the growing critical and scholarly interest in popular music of the past as well as the present. We are in the process of discovering a heritage; it is certain to contribute to the understanding of our own culture.

Chapter 4 Television

The Cultural Impacts of Television
电视及其文化影响力

We might often find ourselves more engaged, more entertained, and even more emotionally touched by what we watch on television than by our own experiences in real life.

Some critics even suggest that people regard what they see on television as more real than what goes on around them and thus virtually narrow their world to what comes to them on "the tube." Paradoxically, television's greatest benefit is its potential to broaden our experience, to bring us to places we could never visit, to people we could never meet, and to a range of ideas otherwise unavailable to many people.

This complex relationship between television and people as individuals and as a society leads thoughtful people to examine closely the way television diverts our attention from what could be our own rich, nonmediated experiences; the way it entertains and informs us through otherwise inaccessible experiences; the way it shapes our perceptions of the world around us.

Some important questions are raised in regard to this ubiquitous medium. Why do Americans spend so much time watching television? What essential needs and desires does television satisfy? How accurately does television represent reality? How strongly do its distortions of reality affect our ideas and behavior? To what extent does television intervene in our everyday lives, influencing families and communities, domestic space, and leisure time?

There is some expansion on these questions and focus on two popular television genres—talk shows and soap operas. In this chapter, the writers use a variety of critical methods to uncover meanings beneath the surface that passive observers (as most of us often are) internalize with little awareness.

This chapter consists of four articles, each of which reflects one particular aspect of the television culture to provide readers with a brief understanding of it.

In *The Oprah Winfrey Show and The Talk-Show Furor*, the author Steven D. Stark made a point that talk shows are pushing the boundaries of what the American culture says is acceptable through examining how Oprah Winfrey always got her way and analyzing the social forces behind the reality. By looking at the way the talk-show genre operates in the case of the Oprah Winfrey show as well as others, Stark offers a clue to its cultural significance.

In *Life According to TV*, Harry Waters summarized the research by George Gerbner, a noted cultural critic and communications scholar, who, through breaking TV viewers into different categories, identifies the way television influences people's perception towards the surrounding world to the extent it even creates a distorted reality. Ended with comments from network officials, Waters offers readers a much balanced conclusion.

《疯狂的主妇》第五季
(2008—2009)

In *Soaps Day and Night*, Ronald Berman contends that soap operas, much like to serial fiction, contain similar social values that mirror different socioeconomic stratum. By contrasting nighttime and daytime soap operas, Berman identifies the marked class difference between them in view of its portrayal of the role of wealth and states of mind.

In *Television and Cultural Behavior*, Conrad P. Kottak attributes students' classroom behavior patterns to their television watching—the process that he terms "teleconditioning." In Kottak's view, television, the same as other cultural and societal institutions, reflects certain knowledge, beliefs and expectations, which has a significant influence on viewers' collective behaviors.

1939 GE HM171
美国通用电气公司 1939 年生产的电视机

As you hone your own critical abilities you will go beyond being a passive observer to become an active, critically engaged viewer.

Lesson 10 Televison and Cultural Behavior

电视与文化行为

CONRAD P. KOTTAK

Introduction

Implicitly arguing with other scholars who might see television as trivial—and against distinctions between 'high' and 'light' forms of culture—Kottak takes television as his cultural artifact and object of study. The crux of his argument is that years of television watching have fundamentally conditioned the behavior of post-1955 generations of Americans, and that this "teleconditioning" has caused them to adopt behavior styles learned while watching TV. To develop his somewhat unorthodox thesis, Kottak connects his role as a teacher to the role of the television set in modern life. According to Kottak, these behavior patterns manifest themselves in his classroom, where his students react to the "live" instructor—namely, himself—as they would to a TV screen.

For Kottak, television is as powerful as our other societal and cultural institutions—such as family, church, and state—and his attempt to subject it to traditional anthropological study includes the use of academic language and the creation of new terminology such as "teleconditioning." The essay, meanwhile, also provides us with much information about some of the important TV serials over the past decades, which is quite helpful in understanding the American society during the same period of time.

A well known scholar of anthropology at the University of Michigan, Kottak is the author of *Prime-Time Society: An Anthropological Analysis of Television and Culture* (1990).

Text

Why should a cultural anthropologist, trained to study primitive societies, be interested in television, which is the creation of a complex, industrial society? My interest in television's impact on human social behavior arose mainly through contacts with young Americans. These include my children, their friends, and particularly the college students at the University of Michigan to whom I have been teaching introductory anthropology since 1968.

Most of the freshmen I have taught during the past decade were born after 1955. They belong to the first generation raised after the almost total diffusion of television into the American home. Most of these young Americans have never known a world without TV. The tube has been as much a fixture in their homes as mom or dad. Considering how common divorce has become, the TV set even outlasts the father in many homes. American kids now devote 22-30 hours to television each week. By the end of high school, they will have spent 22,000 hours in front of the set, versus only

11,000 in the classroom (*Ann Arbor News* 1985b). Such prolonged exposure must modify Americans' behavior in several ways.

I have discussed the behavior modification I see in my classroom with university colleagues, and many say they have observed similar changes in students' conduct. The thesis to be defended in this essay is somewhat different from those of other studies about television's effects on behavior. Previous researchers have found links between exposure to media content (for example, violence) and individual behavior (hyperactivity, aggression, "acting out"). I also believe that content affects behavior. However, I make a more basic claim: The very habit of watching television has modified the behavior of Americans who have grown up with the tube.

Anyone who has been to a movie house recently has seen examples of TV conditioned behavior—teleconditioning. People talk, babies cry, members of the audience file in and out getting snacks and going to the bathroom. Students act similarly in college courses. A decade ago, there was always an isolated student who did these kinds of things. What is new is a behavior pattern, characteristic of a group rather than an individual. This cultural pattern is becoming more and more pronounced, and I link it directly to televiewing. Stated simply, the pattern is this: Televiewing causes people to duplicate inappropriately, in other areas of their lives, behavior styles developed while watching television.

Some examples are in order. Almost nothing bothers professors more than having someone read a newspaper in class. If lecturers take their message and teaching responsibilities seriously, they are understandably perturbed when a student shows more interest in a sports column or "Doonesbury[①]." I don't often get newspapers in class, but one day I noticed a student sitting in the front row reading a paperback novel. Irritated by her audacity, I stopped lecturing and asked "Why are you reading a book in my class?" Her answer: "Oh, I'm not in your class. I just came in here to read my book."

How is this improbable response explained? Why would someone take the trouble to come into a classroom in order to read? The answer, I think is this: Because of televiewing, many young Americans have trouble reading unless they have background noise. Research confirms that most Americans do something e1se while watching television. Often they read. Even I do it. When I get home from work I often turn on the television set, sit down in a comfortable chair, and go through the mail or read the newspaper.

Research on television's impact in other countries confirms that televiewing evolves through certain stages. The first stage when sets are introduced is rapt attention, gazes glued to the screen. Some of us can remember from the late 1940s and 1950s sitting in front of our first TV, dumbly watching even test patterns. Later, as the novelty diminishes, viewers become progressively less attentive. Televiewers in Brazil, whom I began studying systematically in 1983, had already

① Doonesbury：由 Garry Trudeau 创作的连载连环画，内容以各种各样的人物的生活或是冒险经历为主，包括美国总统和该连环画的主人公，一个中年再婚的父亲 Michael Doonesbury。

moved past the first stage, but they were still much more attentive than Americans.

…

The student who came to my class to read her novel was simply an extreme example of a culture pattern derived from television. Because of her lifelong TV dependency, she had trouble reading without background noise. It didn't matter to her whether the background hum came from a stereo, a TV set, or a live professor. Accustomed to machines that don't talk back, she probably was amazed that I noticed her at all. Perhaps my questioning even prompted her to check her set that night to see if someone real was lurking inside.

Another example of a televiewing effect is students' increasing tendency to enter and leave classrooms at will. Of course, individual students do occasionally get sick or have a dentist's appointment. But here again I'm describing a group pattern rather than individual idiosyncrasies①. Only during the past few years have I regularly observed students getting up in mid-lecture, leaving the room for a few minutes, then returning. Sometimes they bring back a canned soft drink.

These students intend no disrespect. They are simply transferring a home-grown pattern of snack-and-bathroom break from family room to classroom. They perceive nothing unusual in acting the same way in front of a live speaker and fellow students as they do when they watch television. (A few students manage to remain seated for only 10-15 minutes. Then they get up and leave the classroom. They are exhibiting a less flattering pattern. Either they have diarrhea, as one student told me he did, or they have decided to shut off the "set" or "change channels.")

Today, almost all Americans talk while watching television. Talking is becoming more common in the classroom, as in the movie house, and this also illustrates television's effects on our collective behavior. Not only do my students bring food and drink to class, some lie down on the floor if they arrive too late to get a seat. I have even seen couples kissing and caressing just a few rows away.

New examples of teleconditioning pop up all the time. In each of the past two semesters that I've taught introductory anthropology, at least one student has requested that I say publicly "Happy Birthday" to a friend in the class. These students seem to perceive me as a professorial analog of Willard Scott, NBC's Today show weatherman, who offers birthday greetings (to people 100 and over). Long ago I put into my syllabus injunctions against reading newspapers and eating crunchy foods in class. Last semester I felt compelled to announce that I "don't do birthdays."

All these are examples of effects of televiewing on social behavior of young Americans. They are not individual idiosyncrasies (the subject matter of psychology) but new culture patterns that have emerged since the 1950s. As such they are appropriate objects for anthropological analysis. Culture, as defined by anthropologists, consists of knowledge, beliefs, perceptions, attitudes, expectations, values, and patterns of behavior that people learn by growing up in a given society. Above all else, culture consists of shared learning. In contrast to education, it extends well beyond

---

① idiosyncrasies：特质，奇怪的或不同寻常的习惯或行为模式。

what we learn in school, to encompass everything we learn in life. Much of the information that contemporary Americans share comes from their common exposure to the mass media, particularly television.

TV CONTENT'S CULTURAL IMPACT

TV content's impact on American culture enters the story when we consider that contemporary Americans share common information and experiences because of the programs they have seen. Again, I learn from my students. The subject matter of introductory anthropology includes the kinship systems of the United States and other societies. One habit I acquired about five years ago takes advantage of my students' familiarity with television. My practice is to illustrate changes in American family structure and household organization by contrasting television programs of the 1950s with more recent examples.

Three decades ago, the usual TV family was a nuclear family consisting of employed father (who often knew best), homemaker mother, and children. Examples include *Father Knows Best, Ozzie and Harriet* and *Leave It to Beaver*①. These programs, which were appropriate for the 1950s, are out of sync with the social and economic realities of the late 1980s. Only 16 million American women worked outside the home in 1950, compared with three times that number today. By the mid-1980s, fewer than 10 percent of American households had the composition that was once considered normal: breadwinner father, homemaker mother, and two children. Still, today's college students remain knowledgeable about these 1950s shows through syndicated reruns. Afternoon television is a pop culture museum that familiarizes kids with many of the same images, characters, and tales that their parents saw in recent days of yore.

Despite *The Brady Buch*'s less-than-stellar primetime ratings and having won no awards, the show would become a true cultural phenomenon, enduring in the minds of Americans for decades.

尽管 *The Brady Bunch* 在黄金时段播出之后的收视率不够理想，也没有赢得任何奖项，但是该剧仍然成为了一个真正的文化现象，在美国人的记忆中留存了数十年之久。

Virtually all my students have seen reruns of the series *The Brady Bunch*②. Its family

---

① *Father Knows Best*：全称为 *Hogan Knows Best*，美国电视剧，剧情主要围绕着职业摔跤手 Hulk Hogan 的家庭生活而展开；*Ozzie and Harriet*：全称为 *The Adventures of Ozzie and Harriet*，美国广播公司于 1952 年至 1966 年间推出的情景喜剧，由现实生活中的 Nelson 家族真人出演；*Leave It to Beaver*，上世纪 50 年代至 60 年代间上映的家庭情景喜剧，其剧情主要围绕着一个好奇而又天真的小男孩 Theodore "Beaver" Cleaver 在家里、学校以及近郊的冒险经历而展开。

② *The Brady Bunch*：由美国广播公司于 1969 年至 1974 年间播出的电视情景喜剧。其剧情围绕着一个混合家庭 the Bradys 而展开。

In the *New York Herald Tribune*, John Crosby stated *Leave It to Beaver* was "charming and sincere" and featured "the wonderful candor and directness with which children disconcert and enchant you."

John Crosby,公认的知名电视评论员,在《纽约先驱论坛报》上刊文,评价 *Leave It to Beaver* 这部情景喜剧"真诚而又充满魅力",特别是该剧凸显了"孩子们在惊慌失措时表现出来的坦诚与率真,因而令人为之着迷"。

organization provides an interesting contrast with earlier programs. It illustrates what anthropologists call "blended family organization." A new (blended) family forms when a widow with three daughters marries a widower with three sons. Blended families have been increasing in American society because of more frequent divorce and remarriage. However, a first spouse's death may also lead to a blended family, as in *The Brady Bunch*. During *The Brady Bunch*'s first run, divorce remained controversial and thus could not give rise to the Brady household.

The occupation of Mike, the Brady husband-father, a successful architect, illustrates a trend toward upper-middle-class jobs and lifestyles that continues on American television today. TV families tend to be more professional, more successful, and richer than the average real-life family. More recent examples include the Huxtables (*The Cosby Show*)① and the Keatons (*Family Ties*)②. There are also ultra-rich night-time soap families such as the Carringtons③ of *Dynasty* and the Ewings of *Dallas*. Mike and Carol Brady were wealthy enough to employ a housekeeper, Alice. Mirroring American culture when the program was made, the career of the wife-mother was part time and subsidiary, if it existed at all. Back then, women like Carol Brady who had been lucky enough to find a wealthy husband didn't compete with other women—even professional housekeepers—in the work force.

I use familiar examples like *The Brady Bunch* to teach students how to draw the genealogies and kinship diagrams that anthropologists use routinely in fieldwork and in making cross-cultural comparisons. TV family relationships may be represented with the same symbols and genealogical charts used for the Bushmen of the Kalahari Desert④ of southern Africa, or any other society. In particular, I chart changes in American family organization, showing how real-life changes have been reflected in television content, with which students tend to be familiar. *The Brady Bunch*, for

① the Huxtables:美国国家广播公司于 1984 年至 1992 年间推出的电视情景喜剧 *The Cosby Show* 中,居住在纽约市布鲁克林区的富有的非裔美国家庭。该剧故事情节即是围绕着 Huxtable 家族而展开。

② the Keatons:美国国家广播公司于 1982 年至 1989 年间推出的电视情景喜剧 *Family Ties* 中的主要家庭。该剧故事情节围绕着年轻的共和党人 Alex P. Keaton 与其父母之间的关系而展开。

③ the Carringtons:美国广播公司于 1981 年至 1989 年间推出的肥皂剧 *Dynasty* 中的美国样板核心家庭。

④ Bushmen of the Kalahari Desert:the Kalahari Desert 指的是位于非洲南部的面积达九十万平方公里的沙质土壤区域;The Bushmen 指的是两万年以来一直居住在这一地区,从事狩猎与采集活动的部落。

example, illustrates a trend toward showing nontraditional families and households. We also see this trend in day-time soaps and in prime time, with the marital breakups, reconciliations, and extended family relationships of *Dallas, Dynasty, Falcon Crest*①, and *Knot's Landing*②. The trend toward newer household types is also obvious in *Kate &Allie* and *The Golden Girls*.

Students enjoy learning about anthropological techniques with culturally familiar examples. Each time I begin my kinship lecture, a few people in the class immediately recognize (from reruns) the nuclear families of the 1950s. They know the names of all the Cleavers—Ward, June, Wally, and Beaver③. However, when I begin diagramming the Bradys, my students can't contain themselves. They start shouting out "Jan," "Bobby," "Greg," "Cindy," "Marsha," "Peter," "Mike," "Carol," "Alice④." The response mounts. By the time we get to Carol and Alice, almost everyone is taking part in my blackboard kinship chart. Whenever I give my Brady Bunch lecture, Anthropology 101 resembles a revival meeting. Hundreds of young natives shout out in unison names made almost as familiar as their parents' through television reruns.

As the natives take up this chant—learned by growing up in post-1950s America—there is an enthusiasm, a warm glow, that my course will not recapture until next semester's rerun of my Brady Bunch lecture. It is as though my students find nirvana, religious ecstasy, through their collective remembrance of the Bradys, in the ritual-like incantation of their names.

Given my own classroom experiences, I was hardly surprised to read that in a 1986 survey of 1,550 American adults, more people said they got pleasure from TV than from sex, food, liquor, money, or religion. In that survey, people indicated which of the following "give a great deal of pleasure and satisfaction." The percentages were as follows:

watching TV	68
friends	61
helping others	59
vacations	58
hobbies	56
reading	55
marriage	45
sexual relationships	42

---

① *Falcon Crest*:1981 年至 1990 年间哥伦比亚广播公司推出的黄金时间档肥皂剧。该剧情节围绕着加利福尼亚州从事葡萄酒业的两大富有家族 Gioberti 和 Channing 家族之间的世仇而展开。

② *Knot's Landing*:1979 年至 1993 年间,哥伦比亚广播公司推出的黄金时间档肥皂剧。剧情背景设置在加利福尼亚州洛杉矶的一个虚构濒海郊区,故事情节围绕着四对夫妇的生活而展开。

③ the Cleavers:指的是美国广播公司于 1969 年至 1974 年间播出的电视情景喜剧 *Leave It to Beaver* 中的主要家庭,其中 Ward 与 June 分别是父亲和母亲,Wally 是 Beaver 的兄弟。而 Beaver 则是该剧的主人公 Theodore "Beaver" Cleaver。

④ 美国广播公司于 1969 年至 1974 年间播出的电视情景喜剧 *The Brady Bunch* 中的人物名字。

food	41
money	40
sports	32
religion	32

Furthermore, when people were asked what they liked to do for relaxation, watching TV again topped the list, followed by just relaxing and doing nothing, vacationing, music, reading and going out to eat. Sex and religion were each chosen by a mere one percent.

THE CULTURAL DIMENSION

I often wonder how my more traditional colleagues in anthropology have managed to avoid becoming interested in television—so striking are the behavioral modifications it has wrought in the natives we see and talk to most frequently: our fellow citizens in modern society. Nationwide and ubiquitous, television cuts across demographic boundaries. It presents to diverse groups a set of common symbols, vocabularies, information, and shared experiences. Televiewing encompasses men and women of different ages, colors, classes, ethnic groups, and levels of educational achievement. Television is seen in cities, suburbs, towns, and country—by farmers, factory workers, and philosophers (although the last may be loath to admit it).

Television is stigmatized as trivial by many people (particularly orthodox intellectuals). However, it is hardly trivial that the average American household has more television sets (2.2 per home) than bathrooms. Given the level of television's penetration of the modern home, we should hardly ignore its effects on socialization and enculturation. The common information that members of a mass society come to share as a result of watching the same thing is indisputably *culture* as anthropologists use the term. This anthropological definition of culture encompasses a much broader spectrum of human life than the definition that focuses on "high culture"—refinement, cultivation, taste, sophistication, education, and appreciation of the fine arts. From the anthropological perspective, not just university graduates, but all people are cultured.

Anthropology's subject matter must include features of modern culture that some regard as too trivial to be worthy of serious study, such as commercial television. As a cultural product and manifestation, a rock star may be as interesting as a symphony conductor, a comic book as significant as a book-award winner. It is axiomatic in anthropology that the most significant cultural forces are those that affect us every day of our lives. Particularly important are those features influencing children during **enculturation** —the process whereby one grows up in a particular society and absorbs its culture.

Culture is collective, shared, meaningful. It is transmitted by conscious and unconscious learning experiences. People acquire it not through their genes, but as a result of growing up in a particular society. Hundreds of culture-bearers have passed through the Anthropology 101 classroom over the past decade. Many have been unable to recall the full names of their parents' first cousins. Some have forgotten a grandmother's maiden name, and few contemporary students know many Biblical or Shakespearean characters. Most, however, have no trouble identifying names and relationships in mythical families that exist only in televisionland.

As the Bible, Shakespeare, and classical mythology did in the past, television influences the names we bestow on our children and answer to all our lives. For example, "Jaime" rose from 70th to 10th most popular girl's name within two years of the debut of *The Bionic Woman*①, whose title character was Jaime Sommers. The first name of the program's star, Lindsay Wagner, also became popular. *Charlie's Angels* boosted "Tiffany" and "Sabrina." Younger kids are named "Blake," "Alexis," "Fallon," and "Krystle" (spellings vary) after *Dynasty's* Carringtons. In other cultures children still receive names of gods (Jesus, Mohammed) and heroes (Ulysses). The comparably honored Olympians② of contemporary America lead their glamorous, superhuman lives not on a mountaintop, but in a small square box. We don't even have to go to church to worship them, because we can count on them to come to us in weekly visitations.

Psychologists are still debating the precise effects of television on *individual* behavior and psychopathology; TV murders and car chases may indeed influence kids toward aggressive or destructive behavior. However, television's *cultural* effects are indubitable. Examples of the medium's impact on U. S. culture—on the collective behavior and knowledge of contemporary Americans—are everywhere.

My conclusions about television can be summarized as follows: New culture patterns related to television's penetration of the American home have emerged since the 1950s. As technology, television affects collective behavior, as people duplicate, in many areas of their lives, habits developed while watching TV. Television content also influences mass culture because it provides widely shared common knowledge, beliefs, and expectations.

I became interested in television because I saw that its effects are comparable to those of humanity's most powerful traditional institutions—family, church, state, and education. Television is creating new cultural experiences and meanings. It is capable of producing intense, often irrationally based, feelings of solidarity and *communitas* ("community feeling") shared widely by people who have grown up within the same cultural tradition. Nothing so important to natives could long escape the eye of the anthropologist.

Questions to Consider

1. Kottak coins the term "teleconditioning" to refer to certain television-induced patterns of behavior and provides several examples drawn from movie audiences and students in his classes. What other sorts of behavior have you observed recently that might be the result of teleconditioning?

---

① *The Bionic Woman*:美国广播公司与国家广播公司于 1976 年至 1978 年间播出的电视剧,剧情围绕着 Jaime Sommers,一个意外受伤而致残的职业网球选手,在接受了仿生学改造获得了超乎常人的能力之后的故事而展开。

② Olympians:古希腊神话中中居住在奥林帕斯山上的诸神。此处意指影视剧中公众熟知的人物。

2. Does Kottak's assertion that behaviors like reading newspapers and drifting in and out of class have increased since the 1960s? Support his analysis or are there other conditions that could have contributed to this change?
3. Kottak suggests that television is as powerful an institution in influencing cultures as "family, church, state, and education". Do you think Kottak's assessment is accurate or does he exaggerate his case?
4. Have you been"teleconditioned" the same way Kottak's students behave?

Lesson 11 Life According to TV ①

活在电视中

HARRY WATERS

Introduction

The world of television directly influences how people see the "real" world around them. So says George Gerbner, a noted cultural critic and communications scholar. Gerbner and his staff spent over fifteen years studying the televised programs America matches. Their results paint a damning picture of the TV industry. In the following essay, Harry Waters summarizes Gerbner's research about how the televised world matches up to "reality" and to people's perception of reality. To that end, Gerbner breaks the television—viewing audience into a number of different representative categories—gender, age, race, and lifestyle, just to name a few—and he observes how people in each category are portrayed in different television shows. Frequently, Gerbner's results, as detailed by Waters, are surprising.

Text

The late Paddy Chayefsky②, who created Howard Beale③, would have loved George Gerbner④. In "Network," Chayefsky marshaled a scathing, fictional assault on the values and methods of the people who control the world's most potent communications instrument. In real life, Gerbner, perhaps the nation's foremost authority on the social impact of television, is quietly using the disciplines of behavioral research to construct an equally devastating indictment of the medium's images and messages. More than any spokesman for a pressure group, Gerbner has become the man that television watches. From his cramped, book-lined office at the University of Pennsylvania springs a steady flow of studies that are raising executive blood pressures at the networks' sleek Manhattan command posts.

George Gerbner's work is uniquely important because it transports the scientific examination of television far beyond familiar children-and-violence arguments. Rather than simply studying the

---

① 该文刊登于1982年12月6日出版的《新闻周刊》(*Newsweek*)上。虽然距现在时间相隔近三十年,但是所言及内容今天很多依然如此。

② Paddy Chayefsky: Sidney Aaron "Paddy" Chayefsky(1923—1981),美国戏剧作家、电影剧本作家和小说家,唯一一位三次荣获奥斯卡最佳剧本奖的电影剧本作家,被认为是"电视黄金时代"最知名的剧作家。

③ Howard Beale: 1976年电影 *Network* 中的主人公。

④ George Gerbner(1919—2005): 传播学教授,涵化理论(cultivation theory)的创始人。

link between violence on the tube and crime in the streets, Gerbner is exploring wider and deeper terrain. He has turned his lens on TV's hidden victims—women, the elderly, blacks, blue-collar workers and other groups—to document the ways in which video-entertainment portrayals subliminally condition how we perceive ourselves and how we view those around us. Gerbner's subjects are not merely the impressionable young; they include all the rest of us. And it is his ominous conclusion that heavy watchers of the prime-time mirror are receiving a grossly distorted picture of the real world that they tend to accept more readily than reality itself.

The 63-year-old Gerbner, who is dean of Penn's Annenberg School of Communications①, employs a methodology that meshes scholarly observation with mundane legwork. Over the past 15 years, he and a tireless trio of assistants (Larry Gross, Nancy Signorielli and Michael Morgan) videotaped and exhaustively analyzed 1, 600 prime-time programs involving more than 15, 000 characters. They then drew up multiple-choice questionnaires that offered correct answers about the world at large along with answers that reflected what Gerbner perceived to be the misrepresentations and biases of the world according to TV. Finally, these questions were posed to large samples of citizens from all socioeconomic strata. In every survey, the Annenberg team discovered that heavy viewers of television (those watching more than four hours a day), who account for more than 30 percent of the population, almost invariably chose the TV-influenced answers, while light viewers (less than two hours a day), selected the answers corresponding more closely to actual life. Some of the dimensions of television's reality warp②:

SEX

Male prime-time characters outnumber females by 3 to 1 and, with a few star-turn exceptions③, women are portrayed as weak, passive satellites to powerful, effective men. TV's male population also plays a vast variety of roles, while females generally get typecast as either lovers or mothers. Less than 20 percent of TV's married women with children work outside the home—as compared with more than 50 percent in real life. The tube's distorted depictions of women, concludes Gerbner, reinforce stereotypical attitudes and increase sexism. In one Annenberg survey, heavy viewers were far more likely than light ones to agree with the proposition: "Women should take care of running their homes and leave running the country to men."

AGE

People over 65, too, are grossly underrepresented on television. Correspondingly, heavy-

---

① Penn's Annenberg School of Communications：宾夕法尼亚州立大学下属传播学院，该学院于1958年创立。George Gerbner 曾于1964年至1989年间担任该学院的系主任。

② Some of the dimensions of television's reality warp：电视中所呈现出的现实在以下层面上往往是扭曲的。

③ star-turn exceptions：指的是与前文相对，由于明星加入而带来的例外情况。

viewing Annenberg respondents believe that the elderly are a vanishing breed, that they make up a smaller proportion of the population today than they did 20 years ago. In fact, they form the nation's most rapidly expanding age group. Heavy viewers also believe that old people are less healthy today than they were two decades ago, when quite the opposite is true. As with women, the portrayals of old people transmit negative impressions. In general, they are cast as silly, stubborn, sexually inactive and eccentric. "They're often shown as feeble grandparents bearing cookies," says Gerbner. "You never see the power that real old people often have. The best and possibly only time to learn about growing old with decency and grace is in youth. And young people are the most susceptible to TV's messages."

RACE

The problem with the medium's treatment of blacks is more one of image than of visibility. Though a tiny percentage of black characters come across as "unrealistically romanticized," reports Gerbner, the overwhelming majority of them are employed in subservient, supporting roles—such as the white hero's comic sidekick①. "When a black child looks at prime time," he says, "most of the people he sees doing interesting and important things are white." That imbalance, he goes on, tends to teach young blacks to accept minority status as naturally inevitable and even deserved. To access the impact of such portrayals on the general audience, the Annenberg survey forms included questions like "Should white people have the right to keep blacks out of their neighborhoods?" and "Should there be laws against marriages between blacks and whites?" The more that viewers watched, the more they answered "yes" to each question.

WORK

Heavy viewers greatly overestimated the proportion of Americans employed as physicians, lawyers, athletes and entertainers, all of whom inhabit prime-time in hordes. A mere 6 to 10 percent of television characters hold blue-collar or service jobs vs. about 60 percent in the real work force. Gerbner sees two dangers in TV's skewed division of labor. On the one hand, the tube so overrepresents and glamorizes the elite occupations that it sets unrealistic expectations among those who must deal with them in actuality. At the same time, TV largely neglects portraying the occupations that most youngsters will have to enter. "You almost never see the farmer, the factory worker or the small businessman." he notes. "Thus not only do lawyers and other professionals find they cannot measure up to the image TV projects of them, but children's occupational aspirations are channeled in unrealistic directions." The Gerbner team feels this emphasis on high-powered jobs poses problems for adolescent girls, who are also presented with views of women as homebodies. The two conflicting views, Gerbner says, add to the frustration over choices they have to make as adults.

---

① sidekick:指电影或电视主角身边的配角,通常是出于调节气氛的目的而设置。

HEALTH

Although video characters exist almost entirely on junk food and quaff alcohol 15 times more often than water, they manage to remain slim, healthy and beautiful. Frequent TV watchers, the Annenberg investigators found, eat more, drink more, exercise less and possess an almost mystical faith in the curative powers of medical science. Concludes Gerbner: "Television may well be the single most pervasive source of health information. And its over-idealized images of medical people, coupled with its complacency about unhealthy life-styles, leaves both patients and doctors vulnerable to disappointment, frustration and even litigation."

CRIME

On the smallscreen, crime rages about 10 times more often than in real life. But while other researchers concentrate on the propensity of TV mayhem to incite aggression, the Annenberg team has studied the hidden side of its imprint: fear of victimization. On television, 55 percent of prime-time characters are involved in violent confrontations once a week; in reality, the figure is less than 1 percent. In all demographic groups in every class of neighborhood, heavy viewers overestimated the statistical chance of violence in their own lives and harbored an exaggerated mistrust of strangers—creating what Gerbner calls "mean-world syndrome." Forty-six percent of heavy viewers who live in cities rated their fear of crime "very serious" as opposed to 26 percent for light viewers. Such paranoia is especially acute among TV entertainment's most common victims: women, the elderly, non-whites, foreigners and lower-class citizens.

Video violence, proposes Gerbner is primarily responsible for imparting lessons in social power: it demonstrates who can do what to whom and get away with it. "Television is saying that those at the bottom of the power scale cannot get away with the same things that a white, middle-class American male can," he says. "It potentially conditions people to think of themselves as victims."

The Washington Post criticized Prison Break for its "somber pretentiousness" and "uniformly overwrought" performances.

《华盛顿时报》批评《越狱》，认为该剧充斥着"阴郁做作"和"千篇一律，花里胡哨"的表演。

At a quick glance, Gerbner's findings seem to contain a cause-and-effect, chicken-or-the-egg question. Does television make heavy viewers view the world the way they do or do heavy viewers come from the poorer, less experienced segment of the populace that regards the world that way to begin with? In other words, does the tube create or simply confirm the unenlightened attitudes of its most loyal audiences? Gerbner, however, was savvy enough to construct a methodology largely immune to such criticism. His samples of heavy viewers cut across all ages, incomes, education levels and ethnic backgrounds—and every category displayed the same tube-induced misconceptions of the world outside.

Needless to say, the networks…, their responses tend

to be tinged with a singular respect for Gerbner's personal and professional credentials. The man is no ivory-tower recluse. During World War II, the Budapest-born Gerbner parachuted into the mountains of Yugoslavia to join the partisans fighting the Germans. After the war, he hunted down and personally arrested scores of high Nazi officials. Nor is Gerbner some videophobic vigilante. A Ph. D. in communications, he readily acknowledges TV's beneficial effects, noting that it has abolished parochialism reduced isolation and loneliness and provided the poorest members of society with cheap, plug-in exposure to experiences they otherwise would not have. Funding for his research is supported by such prestigious bodies as the National Institute of Mental Health, the Surgeon General's office, and the American Medical Association, and he is called to testify before congressional committees nearly as often as David Stockman①.

MASS ENTERTAINMENT

When challenging Gerbner, network officials focus less on his findings and methods than on what they regard as his own misconceptions of their industry's function. "He's looking at television from the perspective of a social scientist rather than considering what is mass entertainment," says Alfred Schneider, vice president of standards and practices at ABC. "We strive to balance TV's social effects with what will capture an audience's interests. If you showed strong men being victimized as much as women or the elderly, what would comprise the dramatic conflict? If you did a show truly representative of society's total reality, and nobody watched because it wasn't interesting, what have you achieved?"

CBS senior vice president Gene Mater also believes that Gerbner is implicitly asking for the theoretically impossible. "TV is unique in its problems," says Mater. "Everyone wants a piece of the action. Everyone feels that their racial or ethnic group is underrepresented or should be portrayed as they would like the world to perceive them. No popular entertainment form, including this one, can or should be an accurate reflection of society."

On that point, at least, Gerbner is first to agree; he hardly expects television entertainment to serve as a mirror image of absolute truth. But what fascinates him about this communications medium is its marked difference from all others. In other media, customers carefully choose what they want to hear or read: a movie, a magazine, a bestseller. In television, notes Gerbner, viewers rarely tune in for a particular program. Instead, most just habitually turn on the set—and watch by the clock rather than for a specific show. "Television viewing fulfills the criteria of a ritual." he says. "It is the only medium that can bring to people things they otherwise would not select." With such unique power, believes Gerbner, comes unique responsibility: "No other

① David Stockman:美国政客和商人,1977—1981 年间任密歇根州共和党国会议员,并于 1981—1985 年间担任政府管理和预算办公室主任。

medium reaches into every home or has a comparable, cradle-to-grave influence over what a society learns about itself."

MATCH

In Gerbner's view, virtually all of TV's distortions of realty can be attributed to its obsession with demographics. The viewers that primetime sponsors most want to reach are white, middle-class, female and between 18 and 49—in short, the audience that purchases most of the consumer products advertised on the tube. Accordingly, notes Gerbner, the demographic portrait of TV's fictional characters largely matches that of its prime commercial targets and largely ignores everyone else. "Television" he concludes, "reproduces a world for its own best customers."

Among TV's more candid executives, that theory draws considerable support. Yet by pointing a finger at the power of demographics, Gerbner appears to contradict one of his major findings. If female viewers are so dear to the hearts of sponsors, why are female characters cast in such unflattering light? "In a basically male-oriented power structure." replies Gerbner, "you can't alienate the male viewer. But you can get away with offending women because most women are pretty well brainwashed to accept it." The Annenberg dean has an equally tidy explanation for another curious fact. Since the corporate world provides network television with all of its financial support, one would expect businessmen on TV to be portrayed primarily as good guys. Quite the contrary. As any fan of "Dallas①," "Dynasty" or "Falcon Crest" well knows, the image of the company man is usually that of a mendacious, dirty-dealing rapscallion. Why would TV snap at the hand that feeds it? "Credibility is the way to ratings," Proposes Gerbner. "This country has a populist② tradition of bias against anything big, including big business. So to retain credibility, TV entertainment shows businessman in relatively derogatory ways."

J. R. Ewing's hat, a foremost symbol of the show's inherent "Americanness" that contributed to its hold over audiences on a global scale, is currently held in the Smithsonian's National Museum of American History's collections.

电视剧 Dallas 的主人公 J. R. Ewing 的帽子,作为吸引全球观众的亮点,也被认为是该剧贯穿首尾的"美国性"的显著象征。目前这顶帽子也被纳入了史密斯索尼亚美国历史国家博物馆的馆藏。

In the medium's Hollywood-based creative community, the gospel of Gerbner finds some passionate adherents. Rarely have TV's best and brightest talents viewed their industry with

---

① Dallas:《豪门恩怨》,由美国哥伦比亚广播公司于 1978 年至 1991 年间推出的黄金时段电视剧,剧情围绕着从事石油与畜牧业的德克萨斯州富有的 Ewing 家族而展开。

② populist:平民主义的,民粹主义的思想,指倾向于社会平等的思想和情绪。

so much frustration and anger. The most sweeping indictment emanates from David Rintels, a two-time Emmy① -winning writer and former president of the Writers Guild of America, West②. "Gerbner is absolutely correct and it is the people who run the networks who are to blame," says Rintels. "The networks get bombarded with thoughtful, reality oriented scripts. They simply won't do them. They slam the door on them. They believe that the only way to get ratings is to feed viewers what conforms to their biases or what has limited resemblance to reality. From 8 to 11 o'clock each night, television is one long lie."

Innovative thinkers such as Norman Lear③, whose work has been practically driven off the tube, don't fault the networks so much as the climate in which they operate. Says Lear: "All of this country's institutions have become totally fixated on short-term bottom-line thinking. Everyone grabs for what might succeed today and the hell with tomorrow. Television just catches more of the heat because it's more visible." Perhaps the most perceptive assessment of Gerbner's conclusions is offered by one who has worked both sides of the industry street. Deanne Barkley, a former NBC vice president who now helps run an independent production house, reports that the negative depictions of women on TV have made it "nerve-racking" to function as a woman within TV. "No one takes responsibility for the social impact of their shows," says Barkley. "But then how do you decide where it all begins? Do the networks give viewers what they want? Or are the networks conditioning them to think that way?"

Gerbner himself has no simple answer to that conundrum. Neither a McLuhanesque④ shaman nor a Naderesque⑤ crusader, he hesitates to suggest solutions until pressed. Then out pops a pair of provocative notions. commercial television will never democratize its treatments of daily life, he believes, until it finds a way to broaden its financial base. Coincidentally, Federal Communications Commission⑥ chairman Mark Fowler seems to have arrived at much the same conclusion. In exchange for lifting such government restrictions on TV as the fairness doctrine and

---

① Emmy:艾米奖,颁奖对象侧重于娱乐电视剧的奖项,于1949年首次颁奖。其地位相当于电影奥斯卡奖,格莱美音乐奖或者是舞台剧托尼奖。

② Writers Guild of America, West: Writers Guild of America,美国影剧作家行会,包括Writers Guild of America, West (WGAW)以及Writers Guild of America, East (WGAE),代表所有电视剧和电影剧本作家以及电视与广播新闻节目雇员利益的工会组织。

③ Norman Lear(1922—):美国著名电视剧本作家、制片人,诸如*All in the Family*和*Sanford and Son*等多部美国经典电视剧的作者。

④ McLuhanesque:关于麦克卢恩的。赫伯特·马歇尔·麦克卢恩(Herbert Marshall McLuhan,1911—1980),加拿大教育家、哲学家和学者,同时也是文学评论家和传媒理论家,其媒体理论被视为该领域研究的奠基石。

⑤ Naderesque:关于纳德的。拉尔夫·纳德(Ralph Nader,1934—),美国律师、作家、演说家以及政治活动家。

⑥ Federal Communications Commission: 联邦通信委员会(FCC)是一个独立的美国联邦政府机构,由美国国会法令所授权创立,并由国会领导。联邦通信委员会是由1934年通信法案所创立,负责规定所有的非联邦政府机构的无线电频谱使用(包括无线电和电视广播),美国国内州际通信(包括固定电话网、卫星通信和有线通信)和所有从美国发起或在美国终结的国际通信。同时,委员会也是影响美国通信政策的一个重要因素。联邦通信委员会的权限涉及美国的50个州和华盛顿特区。

the equal-time rule, Fowler would impose a modest levy on station owners called a spectrum-use fee. Funds from the fees would be set aside to finance programs aimed at specialized tastes rather than the mass appetite. Gerbner enthusiastically endorses that proposal: "Let the ratings system dominate most of prime time but not every hour of every day. Let some programs carry advisories that warn: 'This is not for all of you. This is for nonwhites, or for religious people or for the aged and the handicapped. Turn it off unless you'd like to eavesdrop.' That would be a very refreshing thing."

ROLE

In addition, Gerbner would use to see viewers given an active role in steering the overall direction of television instead of being obliged to passively accept whatever the networks offer. In Britain, he points out, political candidates debate the problems of TV as routinely as the issue of crime. In this country, proposes Gerbner, "every political campaign should put television on the public agenda. Candidates talk about schools, they talk about jobs, they talk about social welfare. They're going to have to start discussing this all-pervasive force."

There are no outright villains in this docudrama①. Even Gerbner recognizes that network potentates don't set out to proselytize a point of view; they are simply businessmen selling a mass-market product. At the same time, their 90 million nightly customers deserve to know the side effects of the ingredients. By the time the typical American child reaches the age of reason, calculates Gerbner, he or she will have absorbed more than 30, 000 electronic "stories." These stories, he suggests have replaced the socializing role of the preindustrial church: they create a "cultural mythology" that establishes the norms of approved behavior and belief. And all Gerbner's research indicates that this new mythological world, with its warped picture of a sizable portion of society, may soon become the one most of us think we live in.

Who else is telling us that? Howard Beale and his eloquent alarms have faded into off network reruns. At the very least, it is comforting to know that a real life Beale is very much with us ...and really watching.

Questions to Consider

1. Waters reports extensive studies by George Gerbner and his associates that show that heavy television viewers have a generally "warped" view of reality, influenced by television's own "reality warp." Which viewers do you think would be affected most negatively by these "warped" viewpoints, and Why?
2. Gerbner's studies show that "55 percent of prime—time characters are involved in violent confrontations once a week; in reality, the figure is less than 1 percent." How do you explain these discrepancies? Why is "violent confrontation" so common on television?

---

① docudrama:实况戏剧。纪录片题材的影视作品,带有适当戏剧化的情节。

How does the violence you see on television affect you?

3. Lookclosely at those suggested causes and solutions that Waters have given. Which seem most reasonable to you? In general, is Waters's coverage of the issue balanced? Why or why not?
4. Do today's shows seem more accurate than those of ten years ago? Do you think most viewers want more "reality" on television? Why?
5. What do you think the relationship between television images and "real life" could be?

Lesson 12 Soaps Day and Night

日夜肥皂剧

RONALD BERMUN

Introduction

In this chapter from his book *How Television Sees Its Audience: A Look at the Looking Glass* (1987), Ronald Berman argues that modern-day soap operas are a form of the serial fiction of an earlier time, available and accessible to the masses. Still there are differences, and Berman points out many of the characteristics that make the soap opera a unique genre.

Berman contrasts nighttime and daytime soaps and finds marked class differences between the two. Nighttime characters tend to be more glamorous and have more money, so there is more fantasy involved, whereas daytime characters cut across a wider socioeconomic stratum and are therefore more "realistic." Both types of soap, however, enact a kind of "middle-class fantasy," where wealth is "the good," and it is this preoccupation with money and the self, Berman suggests, that places the genre within its contemporary cultural and social context.

Ronald Bermun is professor of Emeritus at the English department of University of California at San Diego. His books, among other things, include *Culture and Politics* (1984), *The Great Gatsby and Modern Times* (1994).

Text

STORIES AND SELVES

Serial fiction① isn't new; it began when publication caught up with demand. In the early part of the nineteenth century, books were expensive and writers like Dickens and Thackeray could not reach all their potential customers. Literacy had in effect become a commodity. For the Victorians the problem was solved by printing novels in monthly or even weekly installments. For a shilling the customer could get the latest chapter of *Pickwick Papers*②. He or she could join a sympathetic group of equals gathered around a London newsstand (or, for that matter, a newsstand in Bombay), anxious to know the fate of Little Nell③. Serial publication, like soap opera on television, brought together fiction and a mass public.

---

① serial fiction：即 periodical publication 或者 serial publication，分期刊登的文章或者是小说。

② *Pickwick Papers*：《匹克威克外传》，英国小说家狄更斯（Charles Dickens 1812—1870）的第一部小说，该小说最初分 19 期连载，在 20 个月之内出完。

③ Little Nell：Charles Dickens 小说 *The Old Curiosity Shop* 中的女主人公 Nell Trent 的昵称。

Emotions once reserved for high tragedy were drawn out of everyday life. Here is an excerpt from a letter to Dickens about the death of Paul Dombey in *Dombey and Son*: "Oh my dear dear Dickens! … I have so cried and sobbed over it last night, and again this morning: and felt my heart purified by those tears." Judging from other responses, this is, I think pretty much representative. One's deepest feelings were affected by stories about one's own time, place, and social condition. Horror and pity, once the subjects of Shakespeare or Sophocles, became feelings attached to life and death in the middle class.

Now the novel has been supplanted, and the work it used to do, telling us about daily life, has been taken on by other forms. They don't do it as well, but that matters little to their audience. who demand from our own kind of serial fiction a limited number of effects. The soap opera audience, although much less literate than the audience for the novel, wants also to know about self and social class, about money, about rising and falling in the world, and about love.

I suppose you could say that the soap opera has risen a notch or two in social class since the novel established cast and class as interests of fiction. The romance once associated with love is now attached to money. Although the broad range of daytime soaps concern themselves with jobs and careers, the nighttime programs are about big money. Like a historical novel, the soap of the eighties is about the various generations of a family. During the day this family tends to be organized around business or professions. At night, in a more fantastic world, it is gathered around oil wells or ranches—the struggle is not for survival but for control. Like so many little King Lears, the fathers of nighttime soaps are surrounded by the ungrateful young. This may be either a convenient literary strategy or a sign of the times. At any rate, the family of either day or nighttime soap opera is split around opposed interests. Parents and children disapprove of each other's business tactics or consultants or, now and then, lovers. But the essential fact in the structure of any soap is the family caught up in various ways with some kind of enterprise.

During the day we see more of communities than simply of Colbys① or Carringtons. There will be a greater variety of character, more minorities, more of a sense of necessity in choosing careers, mates, or opportunities. Daytime soaps are on a much smaller economic scale and will show us dramas about the fate of housemaids or police officers. Social class really means something on daytime soaps—it is not just a fantasy of wealth but something you can climb into or fall out of.

On either kind of soap love is probably less interesting than its after-effects. People are unquestionably drawn to each other, and acts of passion naturally result, but they are characterized by social self-consciousness. Men and women on soaps, before and after bed, ask themselves and each other if this has been "right' for them: if it suggests a break in their social lives; if it betrays their wives or husbands; what effect it has on their friends, acquaintances, former lovers, or spouses; and how it will affect business.

① Colbys:*The Colbys*,1985 年至 1987 年间,美国广播公司在黄金时段上映的肥皂剧。

This is all natural to domestic fiction. The real issues always have been the social effects of personal actions. And of course in an age such as our own, when both men and women work, one's real interest is reserved for the long haul, not for happy interludes. So that soaps, which may get steamy now and then, and which feature altogether wonderful characters like Susan Lucci① or Joan Collins②, nevertheless concentrate far more on lives, money, and careers than they do on love. A great American critic, Lionel Trilling③, once wrote that we learned from the novel "most of what we know about modern society, about class and its strange rituals, about power and influence and about money." With very little transposition the same could now be said about soaps. They don't teach as well, but they do show us what we know and they show us ourselves.

How does a soap proceed? Not like a movie, which has a beginning, a middle, and an end. Nor like a novel, which defines and develops characters. A soap is new every time we see it, even from Monday to Tuesday. This tends to be confusing to those of us educated under the old dispensation. If you cannot instantly disengage your expectations, to say nothing of your memory, you will not be able to watch a soap comfortably. It is a chronicle, not a history.

…

DRAMA OR MONOLOGUE?

The soap looks like a drama, and it involves adversarial figures and answering dialogue, but it does not really depend on interaction. The one great essential about soaps is that they are literally all talk. There really is very little action in proportion to production time.

In any drama the dialogue has some special meaning. It is shot through with particular themes and ideas, articulated through significant images. It corresponds to, is tailored for, individual characters. Ina drama, everyone has his or her own vocabulary. Very little of this is true for soaps. In fact, it can be said with little exaggeration that on a soap the dialogue doesn't have dramatic meaning. It may not have any meaning. That is because soap dialogue is not meant to further the action. It is a series of statements or expressions that show us not what people are thinking but what is on their minds, which is different. The soap script is designed to allow characters to empty themselves out, to cleanse themselves emotionally. Think not of the drama or the novel when looking at soap opera, but of the diary or journal.

Soap dialogue allows one to listen to oneself: It is almost purely expressive and subjective. Of course its subject will always be the self measuring its own claims to happiness, or stating its own consciousness, or simply letting off steam.

Soap dialogue has an odd resemblance to the talk of a patient to an analyst. The most common

---

① Susan Lucci：Susan Victoria Lucci，美国女演员，以其在日间肥皂剧 *All My Children* 中所塑造的 Erica Kane 这一角色而出名。该角色也因此被公认为美国偶像。

② Joan Collins：英国演员、作家和专栏作家，曾参演包括 *Dynasty* 在内的多部美国影视剧。

③ Lionel Trilling（1905—1975）：美国文学批评家、作家和教师。因其对文学的社会政治文化内涵的探索而被认为是美国 20 世纪伟大的批评家之一。

moment in soap conversation involves two people, one with personal emotional anguish that must be stated, and the other with no business but to witness that. Unhappiness does not really require a necessary cause—characters of soapland are unhappy from the beginning. They have been or are insufficiently loved; perhaps they have been wounded in their self-conception. Or they have been emotionally traumatized in the past. They seem to be constructs of some common psychological needs now popular. We all evidently need far more emotional gratification than we get. Even if we succeed in life we may be deeply deprived. Our own self-worth is rarely visible to others. Born with this attitude, soap opera people do not really need what have been called the "blocking characters"① of drama or the novel. Regardless of the opposition of villains, life on soaps would be psychologically unhappy. If Dickens had written a soap instead of a novel, David Copperfield would not have needed Uriah Heep to complicate his life②. He would have needed only to let us know that he was unhappy with himself, or uncertain about his career or sexual choices. Soaps have many villains, but most people make their own troubles for themselves.

What is the first rule of soap opera? No one should suffer in silence. Not to express all of one's anxiety would be an unthinkable deviation. There may be secrets suppressed in order to advance the plot, but no one ever hides the sources of his or her own discontent. They are all talked out. This is pretty much the opposite of real life, which may constitute one of the principal attractions of the soap opera. Few of us ever get to let the world know exactly how we feel. Clearly, the audience of soap opera is smitten not so much with melodrama③ as with psychodrama④.

...

The soap is full of nonverbal clues to character and feeling. To sigh is to have feelings. To wear a hat or especially a turban is (for women) the infallible sign of great wealth. To respond to animals or infants is to indicate moral value. To listen earnestly is to suggest moral purpose.

Even when tempered, as it is now by fantasy, the soap is about husbands and wives. Its central institution is the family. One of the basic soap plots is about the formation of a family, from the first attraction between two individuals to the social resonance caused by their eventual connection.

In the good old days of radio, where soaps originated, family problems tended to be simple and solutions tended to be moral. Domestic uncertainty and unhappiness were the great subjects, and they were looked at from a woman's point of view. Today we are much more likely to hear

---

① blocking characters：在影剧中阻碍主人公的次要人物。

② 在 Charles Dickens 的小说 *David Copperfield* 中，Uriah Heep 作为主人公的陪衬而出现，虽然他和 David Copperfield 有着相似的人生经历，却变得与 David 截然相反，为人尖酸刻薄。此句的意思是说，如果 *David Copperfield* 这部小说被改编成肥皂剧的话，David 将不需要 Uriah 这个角色来陪衬。

③ melodrama：情节剧，以夸张的情节和人物塑造来唤起观众情感的剧作。这里指夸张的情景。

④ psychodrama：心理剧，一种通过戏剧活动来探索人类梦境、渴望以及所面对问题的表演形式。这里指心理活动。

about issues, many of them involving social change. Soap characters are involved in running corporations and vineyards and oil wells. They brush up against politics (although most of the ideas are carefully washed out). They are threatened by technology; for example, on one of the nighttime soaps, the ongoing pollution of inherited property. We hear now in the soaps about abortion and computers, about working women and market trends.

Clearly the biggest issue of social change is the liberation of women. Since the soap is designed for a female audience, the issue is a natural. The news of the day tells us that more women are now in the work force and the soap responds by mixing career women in among housewives. Statistics indicate that many of these women are now executives and the soap shows us women in skyscraper offices running financial empires. The news reveals the new sexual morality and the soap is now about women attracted to (or suffering from) sexual freedom. The old standard problem of the soap opera, getting married, has been joined by the new one of extracting a "commitment" and maintaining a "relationship."

But for every social action there is bound to be a reaction. Not everyone in the audience is liberated. So the soaps keep men on in positions of authority—as physicians and lawyers and heads of households. Mothers continue to be best sources of love, sympathy, and advice. And, according to one survey, the soap is in some ways antifeminist:

> Conservative, nurturing women tended to be good characters, while evil women were career-oriented and nontraditional in their behavior. *All My Children's* Erica Kane Martin, who informed her mother that she was a feminist (November l, 1982, episode, and others), is the classic example of a selfish, ambitious, "bad" woman. This example suggests that soaps equate "good" with traditional, sex-typed behavior; that is, a "good" woman is not career-oriented and ambitious.

The information is interesting, but I'm not sure about the interpretation. The passage cited above seems to confuse character with occupation. Erica (or Alexis on *Dynasty*) would be what they are whether they had careers or were locked in a closet. And "badness" is relative—the audience is I think quite pleased to see Joan Collins sexually and financially triumphant. In fiction, good and bad are tricky terms—remember that Shylock and Iago① take all the curtain calls.

CHARACTER AND SOCIAL VALUES

The soap opera is never funny about anything. It would be as out of place to be witty on this kind of show as in a campaign for state assemblyman. It might even be said that the soap has less of a sense of humor than almost any other fictional genre. In a way this is understandable: Some of

① Shylock and Iago: Shylock,夏洛克,莎士比亚戏剧《威尼斯商人》中残酷无情的高利贷者;Iago,伊阿古,莎士比亚剧作《奥赛罗》中的阴险狡猾的人物。

the roles are already like cartoons and might lose their credibility if they were questioned. A sense of humor questions everything. But why are soaps so relentlessly serious? Serious especially about character and social values? There are comic characters even in *Hamlet* and *King Lear*. Is it the case that middle-class values or aspirations are too important for laughter? Or that the soap avoids any modality that might allow the viewer to look at the show in more than one designated way?

In soap opera, no social institution is ever satirized. The hospital and the ranch and the corporation all seem to be good by definition. The life they encourage, if lived rightly, seems to be just fine. This has several consequences for character. No one is ever allowed to be ambivalent about "basic" values. Characters may from time to time not know what they want, or make the wrong choice of bed, board, or career, but their philosophy is never in doubt. To see a soap requires more than one kind of suspension of disbelief. We have to accept that all its troubles occur in a social universe that really hasn't been responsible for causing them.

Erica Kane: She is the clothes queen in *All My Children*.

Erica Kane：*All My Children* 中的时装女王。

One of the big values on soap opera is money. The "bad" characters are corrupt in pursuit of it, but the money itself is okay. In fact, the "good" characters seem innocent enough in its pursuit. On certain soap operas what money does is fiercely admired by the cast and, one imagines, by the audience. Money and what it can buy are always on display and we are invited to pant over its power and uses. The set and costumes have come to matter increasingly, and soaps have become visual displays for haute couture①. Current nighttime soaps are very nearly pornographic about wealth. One doesn't know what matters most to the producers, Joan Collins's body or her wardrobe—probably the wardrobe. Her clothes are calculated to be the last word not in style or beauty but in the appearance of expense. As in the commercials she now does for Time and other magazines, they are "statements" about acquisition. Although Joan Collins is often viewed as a middle-aged sex goddess, she may be much more like Imelda Marcos than *Venus Geriatrix*②.

In the mid-1980s, the soaps seem to have moved away from middle-class actuality and toward middle-class fantasy. They are now about conspicuous consumption. In some ways the soaps are fictional versions of *Lifestyles of the Rich and Famous*③. But there is a real difference between interest in wealth and the depiction of wealth as a value in itself. Possibly the writers of *Dallas and*

---

① haute couture：高级女子时装业。

② Imelda Marcos（1929—）：菲律宾政客，第十任菲律宾总统费迪南德·马科斯的夫人，以其奢华的生活方式而出名；Venus Geriatrix 即 Venus Genetrix，意思是"mother Venus"，指的是罗马女神维纳斯——爱与美及丰产女神，这个称呼经常用于指代维纳斯（即希腊神话女神阿芙罗狄蒂）雕像。这句话的意思是，虽然 Joan Collins 经常被认为是中年性感女神，但她与 Imelda Marcos 更相像，而不是维纳斯。

③ *Lifestyles of the Rich and Famous*：美国在 1984 年至 1995 年间播出的电视剧，剧情以富有的娱乐明星、体育运动员以及商务人士穷奢极侈的生活方式为主题。

Dynasty are saying with a straight face what F. Scott Fitzgerald once wrote satirically: "The richer a fella is, the better I like him."

In more traditional fiction wealth is an object of suspicion, and its acquisition is part of a tension between ambition and surrender to its values. Especially in the last two centuries, the centuries both of the modern novel and the modern experience of "rising" into the "upper" middle class, getting money has been a major theme of both life and art. And serious literature has used the theme well. If one looks over Fitzgerald and Hemingway—or Balzac and Dickens—it's fairly plain that wealth has a Faustian① effect on character. It frees us from the ordinary human fate. We are no longer compelled by necessity. Which means that we are free to act out what we really are. Wealth allows character to reveal itself, finally, because there is no need any longer to subscribe to the hypocrisies of manners and morals. The rich, like Tom Buchanan in *The Great Gatsby*②, are free to be themselves. Or, like the inimitable Joan Collins, to show the world actual human desires unmediated by con-science or other social inhibitions. In great literature—and now and then on soaps—wealth really does free character and express nature. It certainly disposes of the merely social obstacles to self-expression.

…

DUALITIES

There are some characters on soaps, brilliantly acted, who escape the general fate. They are not reductive because money is for them a means to power—so is sex. Everything refers itself to a motive, and not merely the generalized desire for "happiness." J. R. Ewing③ of *Dallas*, Alexis④ of *Dynasty*, and Erica of *All My Children* are motivated by genuine self-interest and because of this are morally isolated from other characters on their shows. Those others, who serve as foils⑤ for Alexis and Erica and J. R., are radically innocent. They are convinced of two things in general: One is that the happiness of others is implied by their own, and the second is that the pursuit (and even capture) of happiness is a natural right. The burden of the many monologues and dialogues of soap opera is that there must be a solution to human problems. Since nothing is wrong with the world as it is, and since the pursuit of wealth, power, love and, "happiness" is normative, the failure to get what you want is only a failure of means.

---

① Faustian：浮士德，德国传说中的一个魔术师和炼金术士，他将灵魂卖给魔鬼，以换取力量和知识。德国作家歌德曾创作同名诗剧。

② Tom Buchanan in *The Great Gatsby*：Tom Buchanan 是美国小说家 F. Scott Fitzgerald（1896—1940）的代表作 *The Great Gatsby* 中的主要人物之一，出身豪门，身家百万。

③ J. R. Ewing：电视剧 *Dallas* 中主人公之一，其为人自私自利，贪婪成性，缺乏道德，时时找机会算计自己的对手。

④ Alexis：电视剧 *Dynasty* 中的女主人公，她为了击垮她的前夫 Blake，不惜赔上自己与 Krystle 的婚姻；她会不惜一切地疼爱自己的孩子，却时时忽略了他们自己真正的需要，总是以自己的意志来控制他们。

⑤ foils：与影剧中主要人物构成鲜明对比的角色。

The cast of *All My Children* has been forced to take a pay cut. Ratings have been down across the daytime board.

由于收视率的下降，*All My Children* 的演员被迫接受片酬削减的事实。

This philosophy underlies soap-opera motivation and discourse. The typical argument unfolded in a moment of truth on screen will be that if something had been done in the past, if some opportunity had been taken or some temptation resisted, then things in the present would have been uncritically good. If only the right advice had been listened to, or the rules observed more closely. This view, pretty much by definition, is the opposite of tragic and there will be some who call it the opposite of realistic. Nothing in the nature of things except for decisions accounts for happiness or unhappiness. No "Star-crossed" lovers for the soaps.

In his recent book *The Culture of Narcissism*, Christopher Lasch① has described a change in cultural definition: "The pursuit of self-interest, formerly identified with the rational pursuit of gain and the accumulation of wealth, has become a search for pleasure and psychic survival." The observation seems especially accurate for soap opera, which is in its own way a mirror of the times, except that on soaps, characters are liable to practice both kinds of self-interest at once. It is altogether fascinating to see how J. R., Erica, and Alexis link the two kinds of pleasure, money and sex. Most of their encounters in the bed-room lead to changes in stock options. And there is a kind of cross-fertilization, as attitudes conventional for business are transposed in love. It is no wonder that, at a time when the mass media's other forms ceaselessly exhort us to see ourselves as upwardly mobile consumers of every kind of property or pleasure, that these characters should have become cultural heroes. Joan Collins finds her natural métier, the advertisement; Larry Hagman② comes to symbolize American manners and mores on the television sets of Namibia, Chad, and Tongo; and Susan Lucci is a conglomerate of her own:

> Television's greatest villainess isn't really Alexis (Joan Collins) on "Dynasty." The real vixen in TV is Erica Kane (Susan Lucci) on the popular ABC soap opera "All My Children." The network has been literally holding its corporate breath waiting to see what Lucci might do once her contract ended. ...She was entertaining offers from all the networks and lots of other organizations too.

What do these great consumers of love and money bring to their shows? Unlike their foils, they are self-aware. They are capable of being jealous without cause, of bringing down destruction

---

① Christopher Lasch (1932—1994)：美国知名历史学家和社会学家，曾担任 Rochester 大学的教授，善于借助历史来促进美国社会对于无处不在的消费文化的体认。

② Larry Hagman(1931—)：美国影视演员、制片人以及导演，因在上世纪 80 年代的黄金时段电视剧 *Dallas* 中扮演 J. R. Ewing 而成名。

for a whim like the ancient gods. Like Alexis, they do what they want. Like Erica, they do what is easiest. But whatever they do is conceived as an extension of ordinary human possibility: They take the logic of the situation past the point that most of us dare to.

Their victims believe that happiness for one person means happiness for someone else as well. But Erica and company have given a certain amount of thought to the subject, and have concluded that their own happiness does not depend on that of anyone else. Nor need it make anyone else happy. They are perfectly subjective, images of psychological change in our national self-conception. The majority of innocent, striving characters of soap opera seem not to realize that there are those to whom the happiness of others is offensive.

This heightened sense of character and of its intensely subjective values, makes it difficult to agree that the soap opera is confined to domestic themes. One recent summary of studies on the subject concludes that the soap is "a world dominated by interpersonal relationships, where characters discuss romantic, marital, and family problems, and where health and work are major concerns within these contexts." Within limits this is true enough. But the soap does other kinds of work as well. In trying to keep up with the present it alters the old form. Right now, in the middle of the eighties, the major characters of the soaps are not very domestic. They display all the signs that we have come to associate with the personal liberation that marks this decade. They are alone, very much self-concerned, and interested in the various kinds of power, both material and emotional. They are not romantic—even though deep sexuality is hinted at, it turns out that sexual relationships are rarely ends in themselves. The major characters—those most enthusiastically accepted by the American (and even the world) audience—may live in family circumstances, but they go through sequential marriages and "relationships." If art imitates life, then these kinds of characters show the decade to itself.

My own guess, then, is that two kinds of social change are the underlying subjects of soap opera. One is fairly visible: These programs now translate news events into fiction. They show us the use and abuse of controlled substances. They have the latest attitudes toward alcoholism or sexual deviation. They are definitively about the new status of women—and, consequently, of men. They suggest the high incidence of crime in actual life and of terrorism. They contain characters far from the small town that was the origin of the genre, characters who step in from the vagueness of outer geography to the mise-en-scene① of Texas or Colorado. The "interpersonal relationships" of soap opera now are incredibly complicated because of the current history they are meant to represent. In this respect, then, the soap is almost literally a form of "news of the day."

But it is in a second respect that the soap displays social change more tellingly. It has two sets of characters, the simple and the complex, who tell us not about the news but about ourselves. The simple—who are often victims of the complex—represent in their innocent way all the hopes and desires of their audience. And their attitude is certainly representative: Without any sense of hubris

① mise-en-scene:法语,意指舞台演出、舞台调度、周围环境。

at all they demand from life every natural right that has been drafted since 1789①. They want happiness and in order to get it they construe the social, political, and psychological world as if it existed only to respond to human desires. These characters worry us even when they are blameless. Always talking of themselves, always invoking happy moments of their past, always demanding that the world listen to them, they seem to have sprung up from the shelves of self help and self-fulfillment. The complex characters are, paradoxically, more comfortable to understand. They hover on the edge of drama because they demand real "interaction." And in their powerful self-awareness and emotional selfishness they too help delineate the portrait of an age. Both kinds of characters unite to show some new social values, and we draw from their depiction an uneasy recognition of individualism concerned not with political freedom but with emotional indulgence. Are the soaps an art form? Not to me. Are they meaningful? Very much so. Better than most other forms of fiction in our time, they show us the passionate concern with the self that has been made possible by a new kind of cultural economy.

Questions to Consider

1. What does the author see as the similarities and differences between serial fiction of the nineteenth century and the soap operas of today?
2. According to Berman. "nothing in the nature of things except for decisions accounts for happiness or unhappiness" in soap operas. What does he mean by this statement, and what are its broader social and economic implications?
3. According to Berman's statement that "the soap opera is never funny about anything", why do you think soap operas are so serious in regard to character and social values?
4. From your experiences watching soap operas, do you find Berman's criticisms valid?

① 1789 年,法国大革命爆发,发布《人权宣言》。

Lesson 13 The Opera Winfrey Show and The Talk Show Furor

欧普拉·温弗瑞秀与脱口秀女王

STEVEN D. STARK

Introduction

Oprah Winfrey just might be the most powerful woman in America, and if not, certainly the most influential literary critic. In this selection from *Glued to the Set: The Sixty Television Shows and Events That Made Us What We Are Today* (1997), Steven D. Stark explains how she got that way. Tracing the evolution of daytime talk from Donahue to Jenny Jones, Stark analyzes the social forces behind this much vilified television genre in which Oprah is the reigning monarch. Finding in television a mirror image not of American realities but of American needs and desires, Stark thus provides a model for understanding the cultural significance of the tube. A frequent contributor to the *Atlantic Monthly* and the *New Yorker Magazine*, Stark is also a commentator for National Public Radio (NPR).

Oprah Winfrey gets a peck from her guest, US President George W Bush.

Oprah Winfrey 在节目中接受访谈嘉宾美国前总统小布什献吻。

Text

Start with these two basic premises:

1. Oprah Winfrey is probably the most celebrated and powerful black woman in U. S. history.

2. Oprah Winfrey is the undisputed leader of a television genre which has been more vehemently attacked by the establishment than any other in television history.

You don't have to be an Albert Einstein to recognize that these two propositions are related.

The modern daytime talk show—created by Phil Donahue① in the late 1960s, revolutionized by Oprah in the 1980s, and then transmogrified in the 1990s by everyone from Ricki Lake② to

① Phil Donahue: Phillip John "Phil" Donahue(1935—),美国公众媒体人物,作家以及电影制片人,以其主持的脱口秀节目 *The Phil Donahue Show* 而知名,曾获得艾米奖。

② Ricki Lake: Ricki Pamela Lake,美国女演员和电视节目主持人,以其主持的脱口秀节目而出名。

Jenny Jones①—is the newest genre to sweep television. On an average mid-nineties weekday, *The Oprah Winfrey Show* was watched by ten million Americans, mostly women, and the 20 or so other daytime talk shows in 1995 had a combined daily audience of around 50 million viewers—though many people undoubtedly watched a whole slew of these shows each day. Though these numbers were high, they pale when compared to those of the combined audiences that watch the violence of prime-time action shows or the local news.

Yet the talk-show genre was absolutely vilified by critics—blamed for everything from the culture's preoccupation with victimization to the general decline of civic discourse. Daytime talk generated a well-publicized crusade (led by two U. S. senators and former Secretary of Education William Bennett②) to purify the medium, not to mention a dozen or so critical books and hundreds of negative articles which joined these Washington officials in calling the new genre a "case study of rot" and "the pollution of the human environment."

Admittedly daytime talk shows are not for the squeamish or children—though one hopes that Bennett and his minions were as concerned about the millions who live full-time in economic and social surroundings far more squalid than anything on *The Maury Povich Show*③. The shows typically involve from two to six guests talking about their personal experiences, followed by boos, applause, tears, questions, and shouts from a studio audience modeled roughly on Howdy Doody's Peanut Gallery④. A typical week of mid-nineties programming on these shows was likely to include such topics as:

Leathermen Love Triangles
Bisexuals
Abusive Boyfriends
Men Engaged to Three Pregnant Women
Clueless Men
Women Who Marry Their Rapists
Runaway Teens
Secret Crushes

This was the genre where a man was surprisingly "confronted" with a secret admirer on *Jenny*

---

① Jenny Jones：加裔美籍喜剧演员以及脱口秀节目主持人，1991 至 2003 年间主持脱口秀节目 *The Jenny Jones Show*。

② William Bennett：William John Bennett（1943—），美国保守派学者、政客和政治理论家。曾担任老布什政府时期美国国家药品策略控制白宫办公室主任以及里根时代的教育部长。

③ *The Maury Povich Show*：由 Maurice Richard "Maury" Povich（1939—）主持的脱口秀节目。该节目经常受到电视评论员的指责，并被认为是垃圾电视节目。

④ Howdy Doody's Peanut Gallery：Howdy Doody 是儿童电视节目主持人；peanut gallery 最早是指一种特定的节目形式，期间观众可以通过向表演者投掷花生来表达对其表演的不满。Howdy Doody 采用同样的节目名称来指其由 40 个孩子组成的现场观众。

Jones, found the admirer was a man, and killed him after the show for humiliating him on national television. (The show was never broadcast due to the shooting.) "Rather than being mortified, ashamed, or trying to hide their stigma," two sociologists wrote of this genre, "guests willingly and eagerly discuss their child-molesting, sexual quirks, and criminal records in an effort to seek 'understanding' for their particular disease."

These shows obviously offer a distorted vision of America, thrive on feeling rather than thought, and worship the sound-bite rather than the art of conversation. Yet it's not like television hasn't been walking down these same paths in other forms every day for the past 50 years. If daytime talk has been preoccupied with sex, race, and family dysfunction, it may be because there is still so little discussion of those rather significant topics elsewhere on television, even in the nineties. All movements have their crazies. Yet when Oprah Winfrey can rank in a poll as the celebrity Americans believe to be most qualified to be president (far more than Bill Bennett, by the way), something significant is going on.

Just as vaudeville① was the root of much early American television, the circus and carnival with their freak shows influenced talk shows. Like any new television genre, these talk shows were a mixture of old programming types—many of which once dominated the daytime. Morning and afternoon talk, geared mostly to women, has a long TV history, beginning with Arthur Godfrey② and with Art Linkletter's *People Are Funny*③. From the soap opera, these new shows borrowed a feminine style of disclosure and a focus on issues considered to be of particular relevance to women, like family and relationships. Game shows were a rich source: From programs like *The Price is Right* the new talk shows learned how to involve an audience of ordinary people. From games like *Strike It Rich* and *Queen* for a Day they learned about the entertainment value of debasing "contestants" who will tell their sob story for money or fleeting fame. And from *Family Feud*④ they learned that conflict sells in the daytime. Throw in a smattering of TV religion (the televised confession and revelation so prominent on these shows), melodrama (Will the runaway teenager's father take her back?), and the news sensibility of Barbara Walters⑤, once an early-morning mainstay on Today, and the pieces were in place for a profitable genre—especially because daytime talk shows are so inexpensive to stage.

Like other popular forms of programming, these shows also mirrored their times. Phil Donahue created the genre because network television wasn't reflecting the serious concerns of many of its

---

① vaudeville:歌舞杂耍。提供多种短小节目的舞台娱乐演出,诸如滑稽节目、歌舞节目以及魔术表演。

② Arthur Godfrey:Arthur Morton Godfrey,美国电台以及电视主持人,娱乐节目演员。

③ *People Are Funny*:由 Arthur Gordon "Art" Linkletter(1912—2010)主持的美国电视游艺竞赛节目,该节目设计旨在激发人们的幽默感。

④ *Family Feud*:美国电视知识竞赛节目之一。

⑤ Barbara Walters:Barbara Jill Walters(1929—),美国广播记者以及作家,曾主持过晨间电视节目以及电视新闻杂志,美国广播公司晚间新闻记者。

women viewers. It began in 1967, at the dawn of the women's movement, when this Midwestern Catholic started a new type of daytime talk show in Dayton, Ohio, hosting for that first show atheist Madalyn Murray O'Hair①. Donahue's story was simple: "The average housewife is bright and inquisitive," he said, "but television treats her like a mental midget." His approach was to take TV talk out of its preoccupation with entertainment celebrities, and tackled instead (often with only one guest an hour) "difficult" women's issues that television wasn't addressing—sexism, artificial insemination, impotence, and homosexuality—combined with more traditional topics, like bathroom fixtures. "He flies in the face of TV tradition, which used to be that you didn't risk offending anyone," Steve Allen, former host of *The Tonight Show* said. Donahue also brilliantly added an active studio audience, usually composed almost entirely of women (though not by design—they're just the ones who showed up), which not only served as a kind of Greek chorus for the guests, but also asked many of the show's most penetrating questions.

For his part, Donahue the rebel frequently bounced about the crowd, microphone in hand, smashing the barrier between host and audience. It didn't hurt the show's populist appeal that it came to stations independently through syndication, rather than from a paternalistic network. In its heyday, *Donahue* also originated from Chicago—in the nation's heartland—rather than among the elites in New York. The more the women's movement progressed, however, the more well-educated women left home for the workplace, and found other outlets for their interests. That left Donahue and his imitators with a growing audience of less affluent, homebound women who often were full of anger and confusion, ignored as they were by more elite media. The women's movement first made Donahue, and then took away the cream of his audience who were interested in more serious topics.

Still, for over a decade he had the field to himself before along came a certain Oprah Winfrey in 1984. She was an empathetic black woman and former co-anchor of the local news in Baltimore. Oprah's advantage over Donahue was that, seeming to resemble her audience, she used that similarity to create a talk show which made the political more personal. Her program was infused with a therapeutic sensibility: Though Oprah did some politics, like her celebrated show in Forsyth County, Georgia, in 1987 (when white racists were on the march), she was more likely to do a show on abusive boyfriends, recovering alcoholics, or competitive sisters. The cause of many of the problems discussed on her show was not so much men, but the so-called rigid confines of traditional family. "What we are witnessing with the proliferating talk show is a social revolution which has at its core the demystification of the family" Michael Arlen, former TV critic for *The New Yorker*, would tell a reporter much later. Say good-bye *to Ozzie and Harriet*②!

Oprah's style was different, too. If Donahue was, at heart, a journalist exposing issues,

---

① Madalyn Murray O'Hair(1919—1995):美国无神主义活动家,美国无神主义组织的创立者,并于1963年至1986年间担任该组织主席。

② *Ozzie and Harriet*:*The Adventures of Ozzie and Harriet* 是美国广播公司在1952至1966年期间推出的情景剧。

Oprah ran what she called a "ministry"—the "church" being a branch of pop psychology which held that revealing problems, improving self esteem, and receiving empathy could cure just about anything, and empower women besides. Oprah hugged her guests, wept openly, and personally said good-bye to each member of the studio audience after a show. Even in 1996, Oprah spoke far more often on her shows than other hosts did. She confessed on the air that she had been sexually abused by relatives as a child, and in later years that she had smoked cocaine. On a show about dieting, she told the audience about the night she ate hot-dog buns drowned in syrup.

Oprah's race and street sass ("Hey Girl!") also made her more authentically hip, at least to her audience, than almost anyone else on television. Oprah would call her success an alternative to the "Twinkies and Barbie and Ken dolls①" that make up so much of television. "Racism remains the most difficult subject in America, and it is only really on the talk show that the raw hatred and suspicion that the races feel for each other is vented," Arlen had told that reporter. As a host who could walk the narrow line between the races, Oprah offered reassurance which others couldn't hope to match. That cultural bilingualism also allowed her to put together an audience coalition of the sort that Jesse Jackson② could only dream about.

With rock-and-roll in the 1950s, black artists had been swept aside so that more acceptable white singers could "cover" their songs. With daytime talk, the opposite occurred: Oprah's show soon wiped out *Donahue* in the ratings and everyone else, too. By 1994, *Working Woman* put Oprah's net worth at over $250 million: By then the show itself was grossing almost $200 million a year, had 55 percent more viewers than *Donahue* (its closest competitor), and enjoyed higher ratings on many days than *Today, Good Morning America*, and the *CBS Morning News*③ combined.

Understandably, Oprah's success bred imitators. Since other hosts couldn't hope to match her in identifying with the audience personally (Ricki Lake was a notable exception, as she went after younger viewers), they tried to win viewers by topping her with their list of sensationalistic topics and revelations. As TV news became ever more tabloid, these shows pushed the envelope even further. By 1992, even Donahue was tackling topics like "Safe Sex Orgies" and "What Happens When Strippers Get Old?" Other shows borrowed from the confrontational style of talk shows once run by Mort Downey Jr④. and turned Oprah's group hug into a daily talk riot with topics like "Wives Confront the Other Woman."

---

① Twinkies：美国最大的新鲜糕点产品分销商 Hostess Brands 经销的美国传统糕点，此处指的是 Twinkie the Kid，该传统糕点的吉祥物，同时也是州际糕点公司的注册商标；Barbie and Ken dolls：由美国 Mattel 玩具公司分别于 1959 年和 1961 年推出的情侣玩偶。

② Jesse Jackson：Jesse Louis Jackson, Sr. 美国黑人民权活动家，浸信会牧师。

③ *Today*：美国国家广播公司每天早晨播出的晨间新闻和脱口秀节目；*Good Morning America*：美国广播公司下属电视网络推出的晨间新闻和脱口秀节目；*CBS Morning News*：美国哥伦比亚广播公司推出的时长半小时的每日电视节目，以播报重大新闻故事为主。

④ Mort Downey Jr.：美国歌手、歌曲作家以及电视脱口秀节目主持人。

By the mid-1990s, an average day on these other shows revealed subjects like "Married Men Who Have Relationships with Their Next Door Neighbors," "Mothers Who Ran Off with Their Daughter's Fiancé," and "Drag Queens Who Got Makeovers." A 1995 study of these programs, done by a team of researchers at Michigan State University found that a typical one-hour show had:

> four sexual-activity disclosures, one sexual-orientation disclosure, three abuse disclosures, two embarrassing-situation disclosures, two criminal-activity disclosures and four personal-attribute disclosures, for a total of 16 personal disclosures. ...

These entertainment programs were selling more, however, than just their guests' disclosures or the "hot" topics which seemed to come straight out of the supermarket tabloids. They also purported to offer group therapy for the masses, at a price everyone could afford. As psychotherapist Murray Nossel once told a reporter, America is "the country that popularized psychoanalysis. Freud's theory of the psyche is that repression brings depression, whereas expression is liberating. Emotionally to cathart① in America, to reveal one's darkest secrets, is a desired social good in and of itself." Critics would have a field day pointing out the dangers of trying to provide such "therapy" on television, but that played right into the notion that elites were trying to keep the masses away from something that had once exclusively been available only to the well-to-do. After all, if daytime talk shows thrived on the violation of taboos, that was, in part, to stick a finger in the eye of those members of the Establishment who looked down on a television pursuit favored by the downscale.

Tom Cruise on May 23, 2005, jumped around the set, hopped onto a couch, fell to one knee and repeatedly professed his love for his new girlfriend Katie Holmes.

2005年5月23日,汤姆·克鲁斯在访谈现场,跳上沙发,单膝下跪,反复向他的新任女朋友 Katie Holmes 表白爱意。

The supporters of these shows also felt that they regularly received too little credit for tackling issues which mainstream television had traditionally ignored, like race and family dysfunction. "If people didn't get up there and talk about incest," Lee Fryd, director of media relations for the *Sally Jessy Raphael*② show once told a reporter, "it would never come to light." If these shows often presented what many considered a freak parade, others would argue that they had helped bring nonconformists further into the mainstream. Joshua Gamson, a cultural critic, once wrote:

---

① cathart:来自 catharsis,指情绪的净化或象征性清洗,尤指遗憾和恐惧,亚里士多德把他描述为悲剧对观众情绪的影响。

② *Sally Jessy Raphael*:Sally Angeline Lowenthal(1935—),美国脱口秀节目主持人,以其主持了二十年的脱口秀节目 *Sally* 而知名。

The story here is not about commercial exploitation but just about how effective the prohibition on asking and telling is in the United States, how stiff the penalties are, how unsafe this place is for people of atypical sexual and gender identities. You know you're in trouble when *Sally Jessy Raphael* (strained smile and forced tear behind red glasses) seems your best bet for being heard, understood, respected, and protected. That for some of us the loopy hollow light of talk shows seems a safe, shielding haven should give us all pause.

On the other hand, the values of these talk shows were oddly traditional—one reason why they posted such strong ratings with Bible Belt① females who considered themselves conservative. The parade of guests was almost always hooted down by the studio audience, which embodied a rather conventional view of morality (albeit one heavily tempered by empathy for victims). The parade of "trash," to use one critic's words, was also a way for those at home to feel better about themselves, since their lives were rarely as hopeless as what they could find here on the screen. Like so much else on TV, what these shows offered was a form of reassurance.

If these talk shows had a larger political consequence, it came with the administration of Bill Clinton, who accomplished little but empathized with everybody. He ran a kind of talk-show presidency—forged in the 1992 campaign with his appearance on *Donahue*, and continuing in that year into a second debate with George Bush and H. Ross Perot② which did away with journalist-questioners and substituted an inquiring studio audience like Oprah's. One of Clinton's principal contributions to our culture was to take the language and zeitgeist of the talk show and bring it into mainstream politics. After all, the "I feel your pain" trademark of his presidency first gained cultural prominence as a talk-show staple: The whole point of talk shows like Oprah's is to encourage "audience-victims" to "feel their pain" as a way of empowering themselves to strike back against those who seem more powerful.

Such a stance was undoubtedly a big reason why women, over time, supported Clinton so strongly. In fact, by 1996, the talk-show style and its celebration of victims was on display throughout both political conventions: There was Liddy Dole③'s Winfreyesque "among the delegates" talk to the Republican convention, Al Gore④'s speech recounting his dying sister's final moments, and the endless parade of the disease-afflicted. Our politics had been Opracized.

Yet if the nineties has been a decade tending to elevate feeling over thought and encourage a

---

① Bible Belt：美国南部以保守的福音派新教势力占主导地位的区域，包括德克萨斯州和俄克拉荷马州，俄亥俄河谷以南地区，西弗吉尼亚州中部地区，弗吉尼亚州以及马里兰州的一部分。该地区居民大多积极参与教会活动。

② H. Ross Perot：Henry Ross Perot，来自美国德克萨斯州的商人，曾于 1992 年和 1996 年两次参选美国总统。

③ Liddy Dole：Mary Elizabeth Hanford "Liddy" Dole(1939—)，美国政治家，曾在里根和老布什政府中任职，并曾担任北卡罗来纳州的参议员。

④ Al Gore：Albert Arnold "Al" Gore, Jr. (1948—)，美国第四十五任副总统，同时也是商人、作家以及环保活动家。

no-fault approach to behavior, the talk shows were hardly the only culprit, no matter what Bill Bennett thought. Few cultural movements of this magnitude proceed from the bottom up rather than the other way around. As Michiko Kakutani would point out in another context in the *New York Times*, the cult of subjectivity enveloping America came as much from Oliver Stone①, with his fantasies about JFK, and from "inventive" biographers like Joe McGinniss, as they came from Ricki Lake. Invective was as much a calling card of CNN's *Crossfire*② as it was of Montel and Jerry Springer③.

By late 1995, however, in response to criticisms by Bennett and others (and as ratings for the "confrontational" shows dropped by as much as a third), Oprah changed her mix of guests and topics too, moving away from tabloid psychology and toward less conventional, more "educational" subjects like anorexia and planning for old age. "She said to us that after 10 years and 2, 000 shows of mostly dysfunctional people, she felt it was time to start focusing on solutions," said Tim Bennett, Oprah's production-company president. At the same time, *The Rosie O'Donnell Show*④ rose to daytime prominence by essentially taking the old fifties' upbeat variety formula, popularized by Arthur Godfrey, and repackaging it with a likable female host, celebrity guests, and a nineties' zeitgeist.

But were even these small shifts something of a betrayal of a large portion of the talk show audience? What was always most striking about this form of "entertainment"—and what made it so different from anything else on television—was its never-ending portrait of despair and alienation. If the downtrodden who populated these shows popularized deviancy or celebrated the cheap confessional, they did it mostly as a plaintive cry for help. Yet Oprah had been there to bless them at the end of every weekday. "They are the people you'd ignore if you saw them in line at the supermarket instead of on TV," Wendy Kaminer, a cultural analyst, once wrote, but that was precisely the point. Talk television was yet another step in the 1990s' trend to democratization of the medium—this time to include the real have-nots. That may be why the elites responded with their usual rejoinder to let them eat cake.

Questions to Consider

1. What does Stark mean when he says that The *Oprah Winfrey Show* and its imitators "offer group therapy for the masses"?
2. What evidence does Stark provide to support his view that talk shows have had a special

---

① Oliver Stone:William Oliver Stone,美国电影导演和电影剧本作家。

② *Crossfire*:美国有线新闻网于1982年至2005年间推出的时事辩论电视节目。

③ Montel and Jerry Springer:Montel指的是*The Montel Williams Show*,由Montel Williams主持的脱口秀节目;Jerry Springer指的是Gerald Norman "Jerry" Springer,英裔美籍电视主持人,以其主持的脱口秀节目*The Jerry Springer Show*而出名。

④ *The Rosie O'Donnell Show*:美国国家广播公司于1996年至2002年间推出的,由影剧演员兼喜剧演员Rosie O'Donnell主持的日间电视脱口秀节目。

appeal to women?

3. Why does Stark say that talk shows are "oddly traditional", despite their often lurid content?
4. Explain what Stark means by saying that Bill Clinton "ran a kind of talk-show presidency."

Historical Perspective **历史视角**

Television

Robot S. Alley

Technically television① is in its fifties, culturally it is in its twenties. In the year 1926 there were practical demonstrations of living scenes viewed the instant they took place by audiences removed from the events. In London, Paris, and New York, the technology was similar and impressive. In 1927 the *New York Times* noted that television "outruns the imagination of all the wizards of prophecy." In that year the movies conquered the sound barrier with *The Jazz Singer*②. Radio emerged at the same time as a startling source of instant information and live entertainment. Depression, war, and technical difficulties combined to deter the development of television even as its two media partners flourished. The irony was that television, maturing in the 1950s, radically changed the face both of radio and cinema, thereby challenging the existence of each. Only as the two accommodated themselves to the young upstart did they find hope for survival.

By 1951 the commercial television networks had established their hegemony and were developing means of transmitting signals coast to coast. Beer sales rose as baseball invaded the medium, and at least one doctor dolefully predicted that children would have stunted feet from too little walking. By 1953, television had attracted the likes of Bob Hope, Groucho Marx, Lucille Ball, Fred Allen, Jack Benny, Edgar Bergen, and George Burns and Gracie Allen③. Thus radio, which had been a way of life for two generations of children, evaporated by the mid-1950s as quickly as it had burst upon us in the 1930s. Gone were the comedians and the dramas of a rainy

---

① 本文写于上世纪 80 年代初。

② *The Jazz Singer*:美国华纳兄弟公司于 1927 年推出的音乐剧,是第一部拥有同步对话配音的正片电影。该片的推出预示着无声电影时代的终结。

③ Bob Hope(1903—2003):美国演员、喜剧艺术家,曾参与广播电视节目以及影剧表演;Groucho Marx:Julius Henry "Groucho" Marx (1890—1977),美国喜剧演员以及电影明星,以其充满睿智的表演风格而出名;Lucille Ball:Lucille Désirée Ball(1911—1989),美国喜剧女演员、舞台表演艺术家,曾参与广播电视节目以及影剧表演,并曾担任影视公司主管;Fred Allen(1894—1956):喜剧演员,以其滑稽有趣的表演风格而出名,并在好莱坞星光大道上拥有属于其自己的一颗星;Jack Benny(1894—1974):喜剧演员、杂耍演员,曾参与广播电视与影剧表演,被认为是美国 20 世纪的主要娱乐演员之一;Edgar Bergen:Edgar John Bergen (1903—1978),美国演员,以其口技表演而出名;George Burns(1896—1996):喜剧演员、影视演员和作家;Gracie Allen:Gracie Ellen Rosalie Allen (1895—1964),女演员、喜剧演员 George Burns 的妻子,因以其在夫妻档喜剧 *Burns and Allen* 中的出色表现而出名,同时因为其对于电视表演所做出的杰出贡献而在好莱坞星光大道上拥有属于自己的一颗星。

afternoon. We were to discover that words, which had carried considerable weight, became conditioned by the visual.

The early 1950s was the era of television hearings—Kefauver and McCarthy①—and of the so-called "golden age" of television. That age lasted only a few brief years as it claimed the talents of writers, such as Paddy Chayefsky, Reginald Rose, and Rod Serling; directors, such as Delbert Mann, Arthur Penn, and Sidney Lumet; and a luxury of talent including Paul Newman, Sidney Poitier, Kim Stanley, Rod Steiger, and Joanne Woodward②. The remarkable success of the live anthological drama series that emerged with these personalities was all too short-lived. In the first place, the social comment of a play like *Marty* was in sharp contrast with the shiny world of the burgeoning number of eager sponsors. Second, the very success of television prompted a new breath of fresh air for cinema which began to drain talent from New York and consequently eliminate live television drama. Finally, the growing fear of both network executives and advertisers concerning controversial drama tended to stifle talent. Erik Barnouw③ dates the decline of these anthologies in the year 1955. Delbert Mann④ concurs. In a 1975 interview he noted that the early television dramas, starting in the late 1940s, appealed "to a small and rather specialized audience." As sets increased in number, the nature of the audience changed. The need to appeal to the mass audience was stimulated by the growing interest of manufacturers in advertising in the new medium. This coincided with the McCarthy era and the black listing of performers and writers. Mann noted that there was a pressure "not to offend." Thus was developed an inevitable pattern, of "restriction on the kind of material that could be used." Mann, like many other persons in the profession, left television for film by the end of the 1950s.

A great deal more was involved for television in the 1950s than fiction. The accident of

---

① Kefauver and McCarthy：Carey Estes Kefauver（1903—1963），美国政治家、民主党员，1939 至 1949 年期间任众议员，1949 年至 1963 年任美国参议员。上世纪 50 年代初期任参议院跨州商业犯罪特别调查委员会主席，该委员会在全国十四个城市举行过听证会，听取了六百多位证人的证词。其听证会受到了电视媒体的广泛关注；Joseph Raymond McCarthy（1908—1957），1947 年至 1957 年期间就任共和党参议员。上世纪 50 年代初期开始，他指责许多军队官员、新闻媒介内部工作人员和公众人物为共产党，并主持一个永久国会调查委员会以公开听证会的形式对他们进行调查。他的指控从未成立，1954 年他受到参议院的斥责。

② Paul Newman：Paul Leonard Newman（1925—2008），美国演员，曾荣获奥斯卡最佳男演员奖，三次金球奖，戛纳电影节奖和艾米奖；Sir Sidney Poitier（1927—），巴哈马裔美国演员以及外交官，以其在影剧中精湛的演技折服了观众，从而塑造了令人信服的黑人演员形象，1963 年荣获奥斯卡最佳男演员奖，并从 1997 年开始任巴哈马驻日本大使；Kim Stanley（1925—2001），女演员，主要从事舞台戏剧表演，曾因其在 *Cat on a Hot Tin Roof* 中的精彩表演而荣获艾米奖；Rod Steiger，Rodney Stephen "Rod" Steiger（1925—2002），美国演员；Joanne Woodward，Paul Newman 的遗孀，曾荣获奥斯卡最佳女演员奖。

③ Erik Barnouw（1908—2001）：美国历史学家，专注于美国电台电视广播历史研究。

④ Delbert Mann：Delbert Martin Mann，Jr.（1920—2007），美国电影电视导演，曾因为执导电影 *Marty* 而获得戛纳电影节金棕榈奖以及奥斯卡奖。

technological discovery gave control of the television networks to the radio people. Radio, while deeply involved in entertainment, was a news-oriented medium for much of the public. And it was centered in New York. Quite naturally, then, the use of television after 1950 included a considerable emphasis upon public events. Had the motion picture industry controlled the medium, it is not altogether certain that such emphasis would have been as strong. Located on the East Coast and in close proximity to political and social phenomena which were shaping the nation, network executives promoted the beginnings of a vast news network. (For CBS that meant Edward R. Murrow①.) David Halberstam② noted in an excellent two-part study of CBS in 1976 that

> television arrived simultaneously with the height of McCarthyism probably helped to narrow the parameters of journalistic freedom, but it was bound to happen anyway. Politically, television was simply too powerful a force, too fast, too immediate, with too large an audience, for the kind of easy journalistic freedom that radio and print reporters had enjoyed. [1]

Even in its restricted form television brought living drama into American homes regularly in its first decade. The Estes Kefauver Senate hearings on crime catapulted the senator into the Democratic nomination for vice-president by 1956. ABC moved quickly to televise the activities of the Army-McCarthy hearings③ in 1953. Concurrently millions of citizens had become more aware of the political process through the televising of the two party conventions of the previous year.

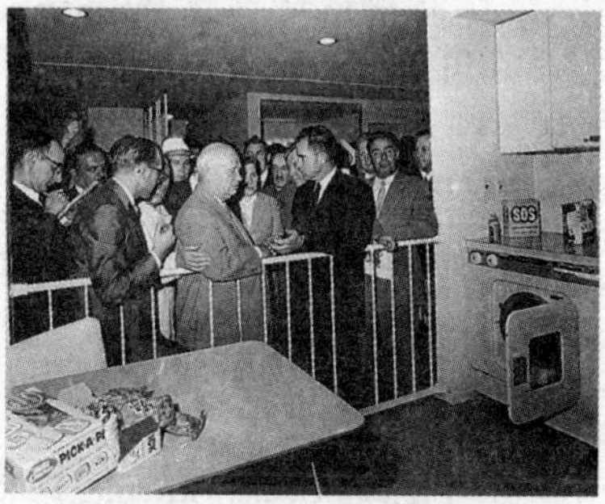

1959 年电视镜头中的尼克松与赫鲁晓夫的"厨房辩论"，让美国人感受到了资本主义的"优越性"。

The first pronouncements of Richard Nixon were televised, and his classic "Checkers" speech was delivered in 1952. Many Americans heard about "old soldiers" from General MacArthur in that' same year. In the aftermath of the Supreme Court's decision in *Brown vs. Board of*

① Edward R. Murrow：Edward Roscoe Murrow(1908—1965)，美国广播电台记者，电视新闻广播先驱，他主播的一系列电视新闻报道推动了美国参议院最终对麦卡锡进行斥责的决定。

② David Halberstam(1934—2007)：美国著名记者和作家，曾荣获普利策奖。

③ The Army-McCarthy hearings：美国陆军与参议员麦卡锡于 1954 年 3 月至 6 月期间举行的一系列听证会，其目的在于调查两者之间相互矛盾的指控，后者声称军队中存在着被共产主义者渗透的安全隐患。

"The Adventures of Ozzie & Harriet" debuted in 1944 on the CBS radio network. The show continued on radio until 1953 and on ABC-TV from 1952 to 1966

50 年代电视喜剧 Ozzie & Harriet 占据电视的大多数时间。

Education in 1955 came Little Rock and Governor Faubus①, and a changing domestic scene. From Sputnik② to the 1959 "kitchen debate③," television provided a window on the world beyond the United States.

The American public felt the influence of television entertainment through language, comic heroes and classic portrayals. The phenomenon of families gathered silently around a small box to watch Milton Berle④ or Sid Caesar⑤ exploded in the 1950s in a dozen different directions. The culture of postwar America was straining under the old melting pot philosophy, and much of the comedy of that decade sought to reestablish the mentality of a secure middle-class picket fence community of the 1930s.

The 1940s gave the American viewers its most enduring television figure, Ed Sullivan⑥ in 1948. A less remembered role was that played by E. G. Marshall⑦ in "Mary Poppins" in the year 1949. The next year the crucial decade began with Sid Caesar, Jack Benny, Burns and Allen and "Broadway Open House" (forerunner of "Tonight"). Live drama was highlighted by Helen Hayes⑧ in *Victoria Regina*. In the early years American cultural roots remained in the radio era, a phenomenon that would disappear by 1955. The classics, "I Love Lucy" and *Amahl and the Night Visitors*, were produced early in 1951. The next year there were

---

① Little Rock and Governor Faubus：1957 年黑人民权运动中，九位入学 Little Rock Central High School 的黑人学生受到了阿肯色州州长 Orval Faubus 的阻挠，时任美国总统的艾森豪威尔派遣美国 101 空降师以及阿肯色州国民警卫队介入，护送黑人学生入学。这被认为是黑人民权运动中的重要时刻之一。

② Sputnik：前苏联发射的一系列无人宇宙飞船的项目代号。其中第一颗卫星于 1957 年 10 月 4 日发射进入太空，这是历史上第一颗在轨运行的人造卫星。

③ "kitchen debate"：指的是 1959 年 6 月 24 日发生在时任美国副总统尼克松以及前苏联领导人赫鲁晓夫之间，在莫斯科开幕的美国国家展览上一系列关于两种制度优越性的争论。其直接起因是展会上美国公司所建的，用以代表资本主义美国市场经济成就的一整套厨房设施。

④ Milton Berle(1908—2002)：喜剧和影视演员，1948 年他成为了美国电视节目中的第一位主要电视明星，被称为 Uncle Miltie 和 Mr. Television。

⑤ Sid Caesar: Isaac Sidney "Sid" Caesar(1922—)，美国喜剧演员和作家，是上世纪 50 年代电视系列剧 *Your Show of Shows and Caesar's Hour* 中的领军人物。

⑥ Ed Sullivan：Edward Vincent "Ed" Sullivan(1901—1974)，美国娱乐剧作家、电视节目主持人，以其主持的电视综艺节目 *The Ed Sullivan Show*(1948—1971)而知名。

⑦ E. G. Marshall(1914—1998)：美国演员，以其在 60 年代电视剧 *The Defender* 和 70 年代电视剧 *The Bold Ones: The New Doctors* 中的角色而知名。

⑧ Helen Hayes(1900—1993)：女演员，其演艺生涯跨越了近七十年的时间，也为她赢得了"美国戏剧界的第一夫人"的美誉，她也是曾经获艾米奖、格莱美奖、奥斯卡奖和托尼奖四大奖项的十二人之一。

more comedians—"Ozzie and Harriet①", "Mr. Peepers," "Our Miss Brooks," and "My Little Margie." Sunday became the preserve of that special niche of television history called "Omnibus" and the sweaty hand of the forge became as well-known as Snap, Crackle, and Pop with the arrival of the Mark VII production "Dragnet②."

Along with the inauguration of President Eisenhower, Red Skelton③, Steve Allen④, and Danny Thomas⑤ took to television. *Marty*, deftly directed by Delbert Mann and consistently described as a high point in television drama, was also produced in 1953. That same year viewers might have caught James Dean⑥ in *A Long Time Till Dawn* and Richard Kiley⑦ in *P. O. W.*, a drama about brainwashing and the Korean War. The heart of the picket fence era was probably 1954. The new offerings included "Father Knows Best," "Lassie," "Walt Disney Presents," "Love That Bob" (Bob Cummings), and "Private Secretary" with Ann Sothern⑧. Live drama prospered in such offerings as *Twelve Angry Men*, written by Reginald Rose.

Little in the year 1955 warned Americans that their world was changing. Alfred Hitchcock entertained as did "The Honeymooners" and "Sergeant Bilko." "Captain Kangaroo" entered and became a traditional CBS figure for generations of children with Mr. Green Jeans⑨, Dancing Bear, and Bun Rabbit. Meanwhile, American viewers focused on the Past in drama and series. "Wyatt Earp" was the first, but "Gunsmoke" made it official; 1955 was the year the Westerns began. Drama was outstanding—Sidney Potier in *A Man Is Ten Feet Tall*, Raymond Massey and Lillian Gish in *The Day Lincoln Was Shot*, with Jack Lemmon as Wilkes Booth⑩, Barry Sullivan in *The Caine Mutiny*, Maurice Evans in The *Devil's Disciple*, Michael Redgrave in *She Stoops to Conquer*, Lee Grant in *Shadow of the Champ*, and Humphrey Bogart in Delbert Mann's production *of The Petrified Forest*. Rod Serling contributed Patterns. Perhaps "never again on this

---

① Ozzie and Harriet: *The Adventures of Ozzie and Harriet* 是美国广播公司在 1952 年至 1966 年期间推出的真人情景喜剧，由现实中 Nelson 家庭出演。该剧通过电台播出后大获好评，随后被搬上银幕，依旧大受欢迎，该剧也因此成为了上世纪 50 年代美国家庭生活的同义语。

② "Dragnet"：广播和电视罪案系列剧，讲述了忠于职守的洛杉矶警探 Sergeant Joe Friday 和其搭档们的故事。

③ Red Skelton(1913—1997)：喜剧演员，1937 年至 1971 年间成为家喻户晓的顶级广播和电视明星。

④ Steve Allen(1921—2000)：电视节目主持人和演员，以其主持的电视节目而出名，在好莱坞星光大道上拥有属于自己的两颗星。

⑤ Danny Thomas(1912—1991)：夜总会喜剧演员和电视情景喜剧演员，以其在电视情景喜剧 *Make Room for Daddy*, 以及综艺节目 *The Danny Thomas Show* 中的出色表现而知名。

⑥ James Dean(1931—1955)：电影演员，因其在影片 *Rebel Without a Cause* 中成功塑造的洛杉矶青年 Jim Stark 形象而被认为是美国文化的象征。

⑦ Richard Kiley(1922—1999)：演员，尤以其出色的配音表演而知名。

⑧ Ann Sothern(1909—2001)：影视演员，其演艺生涯跨越了六十年。因其在电影和电视上的成就，在好莱坞星光大道上拥有属于自己的两颗星。

⑨ Mr. Green Jeans：美国流行儿童电视节目 Captain Kangaroo 的搭档。

⑩ Wilkes Booth: John Wilkes Booth(1838—1865)，舞台演员，1865 年 4 月 14 日在华盛顿特区的福特剧场刺杀了时任美国总统的林肯。

stage" was the television epitaph for 1955.

The election year of 1956 saw themovement to Hollywood gather momentum. Film was replacing live drama, not always directly to its detriment but other effects were more subtle. Dramatically 1956 belonged to Rod Serling① and his *Requiem for a Heavyweight*.

In 1957 television offered "Maverick," "Perry Mason," "Wagon Train," "Leave It To Beaver," and "Have Gun, Will Travel." The Westerns were on their way as was Jack Paar②, who replaced Steve Allen that year on the "Tonight" show. Avid viewers may recall the maudlin conversations which Paar had with Hollywood personalities about bomb shelters and whether having one was cowardly.

Drama, now mostly on film, continued with high quality in 1958 with *The Bridge of San Luis Rey, The Days of Wine and Roses*, and *Little Moon of Alban*. Most lasting in impact was the "Untouchables," a product of Desilu③ which was also continuing to provide "I Love Lucy." The era of anthological dramatic shows was coming to an end with the television-film phase of 1955 and the discovery of video tape in 1957. "Studio One" moved to Hollywood in 1958, most other similar ventures faded and died. Even so, the last year of the decade offered some reason for hope that drama was not dead. There was Jason Robards in *For Whom the Bell Tolls*, George C. Scott in *Winterset*, Ingrid Bergman in *The Turn of the Screw*, and Laurence Olivier and Judith Anderson in *The Moon and Sixpence*. However, perhaps a greater harbinger of the 1960s was the debut of "Bonanza" that same year.

In the 1960s the stunning social dramas of the earlier decade became the live newscasts and made television fiction pale in comparison. The 1960 television debates between Richard Nixon and John Kennedy heralded the beginning of the decade of the newsman. A barrage of news-making events assailed the television viewer. If the event was not presented "live," it reached us within minutes thereafter—the Berlin Wall④, the missile crisis⑤, the assassination of John Kennedy and the subsequent killing of Lee Harvey Oswald⑥ "before our eyes," the reality of the war in Vietnam which every night on the news became more unreal, again assassination,

---

① Rod Serling: 1924—1975，美国剧本作家以及电视制片人，以其在上世纪50年代直播电视戏剧中的旁白而知名。

② Jack Paar(1918—2004)：美国广播和电视喜剧演员、脱口秀节目主持人，以其主持的脱口秀节目 *The Tonight Show* 而知名。

③ Desilu：全称为 Desilu Productions，由一对演员夫妻 Desi Arnaz 和 Lucille Ball 共同拥有、总部设在加利福尼亚州洛杉矶的影视制片公司。1967 年为 Gulf+Western 公司所收购，并被重命名为 Paramount Television。

④ the Berlin Wall：1961 年 8 月由前民主德国开建的将西柏林与东柏林分隔开的城墙。

⑤ the missile crisis：古巴导弹危机。1962 年 10 月发生在前苏联、古巴和美国之间，由前苏联在古巴部署洲际导弹而引起的严重对峙事件。

⑥ Lee Harvey Oswald(1939—1963)：前海军陆战队队员，根据政府调查，是刺杀美国总统约翰·肯尼迪的元凶，他于被逮捕之后在达拉斯被夜总会老板 Jack Ruby 枪杀。

Martin Luther King, Jr. and Robert Kennedy[1], riots at home from Watts in Los Angeles to Washington, D. C., men landing on the moon, and always the war in Southeast Asia. The Vietnam years were more devastating to our culture than perhaps any other event in our history. Distrust of government was rampant, with arrogance of power, depression and discontent among the dispossessed, fear and loathing to our youth, and deconstruction of decent models for children. Narcotics became a way of life for men called upon to commit mayhem abroad. Rising expectations and white stupidity created civil disorder from Watts to Washington. Television was there and it recorded a rare second chance in New Hampshire in February 1968 but America, after losing Robert Kennedy and Martin Luther King, Jr. to assassins, chose Richard Nixon. After that came Cambodia, Kent State[2], Attica[3], Agnew[4], Mitchell[5], Watergate[6], and pardons[7]. In June 1977 Johnny Carson[8] gave voice to many pent-up feelings when he noted upon the sentencing of John Mitchell and H. R. Haldeman[9] to minimum security prisons in Alabama that had it been you or I, we would have been put in a cell with Charles Manson[10]. Clearly dramatic and comedic television had considerable competition in those years.

Television exposed the Vietnam war to the public.

电视把越战暴露在了观众的面前,直接影响到了民众的反战情绪。

---

① Robert Kennedy: 1925—1968,美国政治家,被认为是现代美国自由主义的象征。美国总统约翰·肯尼迪的弟弟,并且在其任期内担任其内阁顾问。1961 年至 1964 年期间任美国司法部长。

② Kent State:肯特大学屠杀事件,也被称为五四屠杀事件。1970 年 5 月 4 日,肯特大学学生举行抗议活动反对美国入侵柬埔寨,遭到俄亥俄州国民警卫队开枪射杀,4 名学生身亡,9 名学生受伤。

③ Attica:阿提卡监狱暴动。1971 年,纽约州阿提卡监狱发生由一部分政治革命者领导、为争取更好的生活条件的暴动,州警察根据州长的命令采取武力行动,导致 39 人身亡。

④ Agnew: Spiro Theodore Agnew(1918—1996),第 39 任美国副总统,第 55 任马里兰州州长。1973 年夏,他被指控犯有勒索、骗税、受贿等多项罪名,并因此而受到司法部调查,最终被迫辞职。

⑤ Mitchell:John N. Mitchell(1913—1988),曾担任尼克松政府的美国司法部长,并于 1968 年至 1972 年担任尼克松的竞选经理,作为总统继任选举委员会主任,他是水门事件的幕后指使人之一,也是唯一一位被证实罪名成立的美国司法部长。

⑥ Watergate:水门事件,上世纪 70 年代发生在尼克松政府时期的政治丑闻,其直接起因是在位于华盛顿特区的水门办公楼内民主党全国委员会总部发生的非法闯入事件。水门事件最终导致了尼克松被迫辞去美国总统职务。

⑦ pardons:总统赦免令。此处是指在水门事件之后,尽管尼克松辞职之后,美国国会停止了对其的弹劾程序,但刑事调查的可能性依然存在。为此,继任总统杰罗德·福特于 1974 年9 月 8 日签署了对尼克松的总统赦免令。

⑧ Johnny Carson(1925—2005):美国电视主持人以及喜剧演员,以其主持的电视节目 *The Tonight Show Starring Johnny Carson* 而知名。

⑨ H. R. Haldeman: Harry Robbins "Bob" Haldeman(1926—1993),时任美国总统尼克松的白宫办公厅主任,水门事件的核心人物之一,最终因阴谋罪以及妨碍司法公正罪被捕判刑。

⑩ Charles Manson(1934—):美国罪犯,上世纪 60 年代晚期犯罪组织曼森家族的领导者。

In the history of commercial television there have been four distinct types of comedy. The earliest was the personality, Milton Berle or Jack Benny or George Burns. There followed quickly the situation comedies of the "Leave It to Beaver," "Father Knows Best," and "Ozzie and Harriet" variety. Mild doses of fun were sprinkled among basic Puritan moralisms. By the late 1950s a third type of comedy emerged in "The Real McCoys." The 1960s saw the flowering of this genre with "Car 54 Where Are You?," "Gilligan's Island," and "The Beverly Hillbillies." Each poked fun at an authority symbol—the law, the scientist and socialite, or the banking profession. Some, like "The Munsters" and "The Addams Family," seemed to take on all social conventions, but it would be foolish to make too much out of this because each show was also designed quite obviously to match the public mood which increasingly seemed to desire escape. Lucille Ball interestingly reversed the trend. Her early shows were slapstick. Her comedy of the 1960s was similar to the earlier Ann Sothern efforts. Only with the appearance, largely via CBS, of "The Mary Tyler Moore Show" and "All in the Family" did a fourth comedy type begin to dominate. In style these shows owed much to the earlier "Dick Van Dyke Show" (1961—66). Their substance was probably made possible by the pioneering on CBS of the Smothers Brothers① with social and political humor and on NBC by the freedom of "Laugh-In" with its sexual allusions, the former appearing first in 1965, the latter in 1968.

Of course even as the third comedy type dominated during the decade, the networks continued the traditional format with "My Three Sons," "Hazel," "That Girl," and "The Andy Griffith Show." The decline of the stand-up comic was a signal that the insatiable appetite of television, a new sketch every week, was beyond the capacity of comedians and writers. Indeed, this is a primary difficulty which television experiences unlike the theater, night club, or film. People like Johnny Carson have survived by creating a liturgy into which viewers enter as surely as the Sunday communicant. Thus the burden on the writers is largely relieved, but Carson is the exception and in that way has become a symbol of one important segment of the population. Carson makes trends and creates language styles. He is a primal popular cultural force, possibly more powerful than any other figure in the history of entertainment.

The decade of the 1960s was notable for three types of drama—police, Western, and medical. Apart from these types there were only a few dramatic series that survived long enough to remember—"The Defenders"(1962), "Combat" (1962), "Outer Limits" (1963), "East Side, West Side"(1963), "Mr. Novak" (1963), "Slattery's People" (1964), "Twelve O'clock High" (1964), "Star Trek" (1966), "The Bold Ones" (1969), "Room 222" (1969)—an average of one new series per year.

From their beginnings in 1955 the Westerns expanded to number fifteen by 1960. That number was reduced to five by 1965. By the end of the decade it had diminished to three including

① the Smothers Brothers:美国双簧戏,由两兄弟 Thomas 和 Richard 联袂演出,他们自己的电视综艺秀 *The Smothers Brothers Comedy Hour* 已成为美国在越战时期最具争议的电视节目。

"Bonanza" and "Gunsmoke." The history of police-detective drama is less consistent. When Americans entered their second ten years with television, they were watching "Naked City," "Peter Gunn," "Hawaiian Eye," "The Untouchables," and "The Detectives." "Dragnet" appeared and reappeared on the schedule during the same period. By 1964 there was not a single drama of this genre represented in network scheduling. In 1965 Quinn Martin①, most persistent purveyor of the police motif, introduced the long-running "FBI," and by 1969 the schedule included no less than seven police-private eye shows. The 1970s saw that proliferate into over twenty in the 1975-76 season. The police dramas have been dominated by three producing giants—Martin, Jack Webb②, and Spelling and Goldberg③.

Medical drama moved in and out of the television scene in this period with the two long-running series, "Ben Casey" and "Dr. Kildare" debuting in 1961 and departing in 1966. By 1969 a new set, "Marcus Welby," "Medical Center," and "The Bold Ones" gave viewers three opportunities to experience vicariously the treatment of obscure and not so obscure diseases.

Documentaries burgeoned in the 1960s. The networks, spurred on by an obvious interest in public events, focused on social events (national and international) for material from migrant workers to Vietnam. Simultaneously domestic unrest bubbled to the surface and cascaded across the land in 1967 and 1968.

When the history of the 1970s is written, the portion devoted to television will undoubtedly emphasize the enormous success of a new comedy art in the business. Norman Lear④, Grant Tinker⑤, and Larry Gelbart⑥ will carry the credits along with Carroll O'Connor⑦, Jean Stapleton⑧, Bea Arthur⑨, Mary Tyler Moore⑩, Cloris Leachman⑪, and Alan Alda⑫. The similarities between "M°A°S°H" and "Maude" are more felt than defined, but the commonality

---

① Quinn Martin(1922—1987):美国最成功的电视制片人之一,其制作的电视剧作品中至少有一部曾创造了连续在黄金时间档播出21年的业界传奇。

② Jack Webb(1920—1982):美国演员、电视制片人、导演和电视剧本作家,以其在广播和电视剧 *Dragnet* 中的饰演的 Sergeant Joe Friday 而知名。

③ Spelling and Goldberg:1972年成立的美国电视制片公司。

④ Norman Lear(1922—):美国电视剧本作家和制片人。

⑤ Grant Tinker(1925—):电视制片人,1981年至1986年期间曾任美国国家广播公司的首席执行官和董事会主席。

⑥ Larry Gelbart(1928—2009):美国剧作家。

⑦ Carroll O'Connor(1924—2001):美国演员、制片人以及导演,其电视生涯跨越了整整四十年。

⑧ Jean Stapleton(1923—):美国舞台和影视女演员。

⑨ Bea Arthur: Beatrice "Bea" Arthur(1922—2009),美国女演员和歌手,曾获得艾米奖和托尼奖。

⑩ Mary Tyler Moore(1936—):美国女演员,以其在电视情景喜剧中的角色而出名。

⑪ Cloris Leachman(1926—):美国舞台女演员和影视演员,曾八次获得艾米奖以及奥斯卡最佳女配角奖。

⑫ Alan Alda(1936—):美国演员、导演和剧本作家,曾五次获得艾米奖,六次获得金球奖,以其在电视剧 *M°A°S°H* 中的表演而知名。

was expressed both by audiences and actors. The flowering of the television comic short story may well be a most important cultural phenomenon. Beginning in 1971 the American public became conscious of Archie and Mary and Hawkeye. Every week these and other characters filled the screen with social bite in comic form. We laughed, often with a tear, and experienced what many knew finally to be reality joining hands with fantasy. Whatever new forms emerge for the 1980s, the television comedy of the 1970s had style and class and a social consciousness. Humanism dominated these shows and their companions—"The Bob Newhart Show," "Good Times," "The Jeffersons,"' "One Day at a Time," "Phyllis," and "The Odd Couple."

We were also deluged in this decade by an ever increasing assortment of gun-toting law enforcers. Television always upholds the law. It may be violent and sometimes in poor taste, but right does prevail. Not so in the movies or on the stage or in novels and magazines—these all offer alternatives to the triumph of the system. Television sustains it. To be sure not without criticism, but support there is, nonetheless. *Baretta*① may condone small-time crime, and *Kojak*② may bend the rules, but from *Starsky and Hutch*③ to *Barnaby Jones*④ to *Charlie's Angels*, the message is the same. Television has obviated certain cultural differences and leveled our language and dress. History may also affirm that it was the glue that held the clue to societal survival in the present decade. Certainly we all had television in common, and it has been affirming traditional social values. As early as 1968 the National Advisory Commission on Civil Disorders, commenting upon television coverage in 1967, noted:

Content analysis of television film footage shows that the tone of the coverage studied was more calm and "factual" than "emotional" and rumor-laden. ...Television newscasts during the periods of actual disorder in 1967 tended to emphasize law enforcement activities, thereby overshadowing underlying grievances and tensions. ...

In contrast to what some of itscritics have charged, television sometimes may have leaned over too far backward in seeking balance and restraint. [2]

Television is a massive power of promotion and persuasion and its immediacy to our every thought makes it a likely target when cultural leaders search for a culprit upon which to blame the general tone of our society. It is new, it is beyond our control, and it is electronic. Television is popular culture. Although many social critics condemn and deride what television offers, for the majority of American people television is a friend, warts and all. It has become, as well, a critic in comedy and, less often, drama, of the flaws in our society. James Brown has written:

---

① *Baretta*:美国广播公司于1975年至1978年期间推出的侦探电视系列剧,讲述了便衣侦探"Tony" Baretta办案的故事。

② *Kojak*:哥伦比亚广播公司于1973年至1978年推出的电视系列剧,讲述了纽约警探Theo Kojak办案的故事。

③ *Starsky and Hutch*:上世纪70年代由Spelling-Goldberg制片公司推出的电视剧。

④ *Barnaby Jones*:哥伦比亚广播公司于1973年至1980年推出的电视侦探系列剧,讲述了位于洛杉矶的一所私人侦探事务所内,公公和儿媳合作办案的故事。

The fact that the medium [television] produces several outstanding multi-hour presentations a month deserves more praise than the meager annual productivity of Broadway. Books have been with us since movable type for over 600 years. How many books of true significance and public acceptance are published annually? Daily newspapers have been around for more than a century. Movies have been on the scene three-quarters of a century. But radio was first heard clearly in the land in 1920. Television has elbowed its way through exuberant adolescence and is now just beyond its teens. As a mid-twenty-year old, it continues to try to find itself, to achieve its proper identity in society. [3]

In the early days the termeducational television was used to apply to those stations normally expected to be unaffiliated with a commercial network. It was not until February 1950 that the first non-commercial station, WOI-TV in Ames, Iowa, was licensed and began operation. It was the one-hundredth station to begin television broadcasting in America. Because of the slow beginning of educational television, most of the stations occupied UHF channels which the Federal Communications Commission (FCC) had begun to assign in 1952. As late as 1956 there were only twenty-four non-commercial, educational channels on the air, and most of those were struggling. Television set manufacturers completely ignored UHF on early sets, and it was not until a decree from Congress required it, that all sets began to be sold with UHF tuners incorporated. Even then, the technology that allowed snap-lock tuning of VHF channels was not installed with the UHF tuner, and this meant long years of invidious comparison with the ease of tuning Channels 2 through 13. This problem was coupled with the fact that the UHF signal was usually more difficult to receive and had a much more restricted range. As late as 1968 only 55 percent of American families could receive UHF. In 1977 most hotels and motels were still not equipped with sets capable of receiving UHF broadcasts.

The original National Educational Television (NET) network survived through grit and grants from a small number of major foundations. Finally, in 1967, Congress took direct action and established the Public Broadcast System with federal funding. It still required substantial fundraising by the local stations in order to guarantee survival. Since 1967, commercial networks have been quite guarded in their reactions to their new colleagues. Publications, such as TV Guide, have generally ignored the PBS activities except in the most obvious instances. Trade papers have tended to focus more attention on public policy regarding the new network than on the contributions it was making to television offerings.

Nevertheless, by 1975, with greater ease of reception becoming a reality for more and more of the viewing public, PBS began to attract more attention. There were two clear reasons—the huge success of "Sesame Street" and the prestigc garnered from British offerings, such as "Masterpiece Theatre" and "Upstairs, Downstairs." However, the financial difficulties of PBS affiliates did not abate. Inadequate staffing and generally poor pay characterized many of the less affluent PBS members in comparison with the more prosperous channels in New York, Los Angeles, Pittsburgh, San Francisco, and Boston. Most of the new programming sprang from these more fortunate affiliates. Auctions and scrambling for any size grants became a way of life for most stations. Threatened with economic collapse, the temptation has been real to emulate the commercial networks in their quest for ratings. Further, there is the constant danger of government interference in the affairs of PBS even though every effort is made to eliminate politics from the system. There has been considerable pressure from some lawmakers for PBS to serve broader publics since it uses tax dollars. PBS has continued to offer more and more excellent quality programming to a solid minority of citizens. Properly funded, it can provide a healthy stimulus to the three major commercial networks, as it serves a significant public of its own.

NOTES

1. David Halberstam, "CBS: The Network and the News and the Power and the Profits," The Atlantic Monthly, 237 (January 1976), 63.
2. Report of the National Advisory Commission on Civil Disorders (New York: New York Times, 1968), p. 373.
3. Ward Quaal and James Brown, Broadcast Management (New York: Hastings House, 1976), p. 440.

Chapter 5 Sports

The Cultural Implications in American Sports

美国体育运动中的文化内含

The United States seems to be a nation obsessed with sports, an obsession nowhere more evident than in some fans' virtual addiction to sports statistics. Somewhere there's probably a statistics maven① who knows the number of foot faults in the final 1956 Davis Cup② match or the most triples by a left-handed batter during Tuesday afternoon World Series③ games. Fans crave statistics, no matter how minute, as a way of measuring the achievements of their favorite athletes and teams—and perhaps also as a way of holding the memory of never-to-be-repeated athletic performances.

Yet during the early colonial period, early New England Puritans, aiming at a purer religious faith and stricter discipline of life, were quite hostile towards fun and games and repelled any idea of diversion and merry-making. Robert J. Higgs, in his comprehensive essay "Sports", traces the long history in which how the ruling class punished those who disobeyed and how sports became more and more popular despite of their sanction and prohibition, as he remarks that "the propensity of human nature [to play] will never be stilled."

It's not difficult to find further evidence of America's preoccupation with sports. Most daily newspapers allocate an entire section to sports reports and statistics; a number of national weekly and monthly publications concentrate exclusively on sports. Special sporting events such as the Super Bowl are consistently among the most highly rated TV broadcasts, and several cable networks are devoted solely to sports twenty-four hours a day. Americans play sports trivia games, call sports telephone hotlines, and participate in a multibillion dollar sports gaming industry; they display team logos on T-shirts, sweatshirts, baseball caps and countless other articles of clothing. Many colleges and universities capitalize on the prominence of their sports programs to increase enrollments and donations.

Sports can affect fans in surprisingly intense ways. We all probably know people whose moods fluctuate with the fortunes of their favorite team. They yell and holler hysterically when their supported team wins, and they sullen, or even cry when their team loses. Indeed, entire cities rejoice when their team brings home a championship, and our national mood lifts when an American underdog takes a medal at the Olympics or when the "Dream Team" squashes an

① maven:〈口语〉行家,内行。

② Davis Cup:戴维斯杯网球锦标赛。

③ World Series:世界职业棒球联盟系列赛,始于 1903 年,每年秋季十月份举行。

opponent. Given this obsession, it's no wonder that professional athletes are among our most revered—and highly paid—citizens, and their success in sporting field seems to have opened many doors in their later career.

How can we explain the popularity of professional sports and its appeal among all walks of life? The essays in the first part of this chapter offer views about the role of sports in American life in general, and in the essay "Sport and American Dream" by Jeffrey Schrank, the author delves deeper into the fancy of sports, arguing that sports are not only games, but rather "ritualistic enactments of the American Dream." It is a dream to participate, to compete, to expand, to explore, and most important of all, to win. No wonder many sports critics including television commentator Dick Schaap's lament for the days when sportsmanship was more important to professional athletes than their next contract.

The essays in the second part of this chapter examine sports in a larger context from different perspectives of politics, race, and gender. There is no gainsaying that America is still being the pace-setter in many international sports events and disciplines, at least in terms of medal counts, being outnumbered only recently by China on the 2008 Summer Olympics Games. And sports and games, perceived in this way, also become quitesymbolic of nationalist sentiments and patriotism. And James Combs, in his book *Polpop*, from which the essay "Jockpop: Popular Sports and Politics" is selected, thus disentangles the complicated relationship between sports and politics in many ways with substantive examples and clairvoyant insights.

In "The Black and White Truth about Basketball," the media commentator and newspaper columnist Jeff Greenfield pays attention to the phenomenal dominance of black players in basketball field and summarizes on the different features of white and black basketball players, thus revealing the black and white truth about this sport which now has taken over football as the national pastime of America.

The Philadelphia Phillies have won the World *Series*, and another season of baseball is done.

费城 Phillies 赢得 2008 年美国职业棒球联赛。

Obviously, sports can influence the way we speak and the way we feel, our notions of teamwork and individuality, success and failure, and male and female roles. From sports we learn how to deal with pressure, adversity, and physical pain and we discover models of grace, skill, and style. As you read the selected essays in this chapter, think of the sports you play and watch, of the athletes you admire, of the role sports play (or have played) in your life.

Lesson 14 Sports and the American Dream

体育运动与美国梦

JEFFREY SCHRANK

Introduction

Professional sports play a large role in the lives of many Americans, and in this essay, Jeffrey Schrank, a social commentator who often examines the interaction between the media and society, offers a detailed analysis on sports to see how it reflects the American character and our wishes, values, and beliefs.

In detailing how sports mirrors American culture, Schrank suggests that different sports appeal to Americans for different reasons and reveal different aspects of the American character. His underlying premise is that a country can trace its national preoccupations, attitudes, and aspirations in its popular sports. For example, football, in which the goal is to gain territory against an opponent, may more accurately reflect contemporary American values than does baseball, a game in which "aggression is subservient to finesse." He then goes further, arguing that sports serve as "ritualistic enactments of the American Dream."

Text

Sports is a ritual, an acting out of a myth or series of myths. A sport that can be considered a national pastime can be expected to reflect national values and wishes. Sports that capture the national fancy are ritualistic enactments of the American Dream①. Baseball is still called our national pastime but is rapidly being replaced by American football. That football should become our "national pastime" is understandable to those who can see sports as reflections of national character.

American football is passionately concerned with the gain and loss of land, of territory. The football field is measured and marked with all the care of a surveyor and the ball's progress noted to the nearest inch. Football is a precise game and its players are often trained like a military unit on a mission to gain territory for the mother country. The players are the popular heroes but the coaches and owners run the game, using the players to carry out their plans—there is comparatively little room for individual initiative. A score comes as the result of a strategic series of well-executed

① 此句意为:那些全民追捧的体育项目堪称美国梦的仪式化再现。

Baseball Field 棒球场一隅

maneuvers and is bought on the installment plan, yard by yard①.

The regulation and almost military precision of American football is a reflection of national psychology. Even the words we use to describe the game include throwing the bomb, marching down field, game plan (which has become nearly a national phrase for any field, from selling toothpaste to covering up political scandals), guards, executions, blitz, zone, platoon, squad, drills, attack, drives, marching bands for entertainment, stars on helmets, lines that can be blasted through, and even war paint. Much of the verbal similarity comes from the fact that war was originally the ultimate game, played within the confines of certain rules agreed upon by both "teams."

Seattle Seahawks Vs. Detroit Lions NFL Nov 8th 2009.
2009 年度美国橄榄球联盟赛上西雅图海鹰对阵底特律雄狮。

Football, more than any other sport, is a game for spectators to watch superhuman, mythical heroes. Football is a sport that more people watch than play. The game requires too many people, too much space and is simply too dangerous for the weekend athlete. The size and speed of professional players and their uniforms make them into heroic figures capable of feats that invite admiration but not imitation. The football spectator is in awe of the armored monsters. The viewer of a golf match or even baseball or tennis dreams of going out the next day and doing likewise, but football is played only by the gods who can run the 100-yard dash in ten seconds, stand six feet three and weight 260 pounds.

The demise of baseball as our national pastime reflects a change in national character. The change does not mean the disappearance of baseball, merely its relocation to a position as just another game rather than the game. Professor John Finlay of the University of Manitoba, writing in *Queen's Quarterly*, compares baseball to an acting out of the robber baron stage of capitalism whereas football more clearly reflects a more mature capitalism② into which we are now moving. Hence, the rise in popularity of football and apparent decline in baseball. He notes that Japan, still in the early stages of capitalism, has taken avidly to baseball but not to football. It is not a question of Japanese physique serving as a determinant since rugby has a large Asian following. He predicts that when their capitalism moves into a higher stage. The Japanese will move on to football, as

① 此句意为：要得分就要做好一系列的组织决策并分步执行，一点一点实现。installment，原意是"分期付款"。

② John Finlay 教授将棒球喻为资本主义的强盗资本家阶段，而将美式橄榄球比作其成熟阶段。robber baron，强盗资本家，指 19 世纪后期那些通过不正当手段大肆掠夺资源而一时暴发的资本家。

have Americans.

Baseball is a game of a quieter age when less action was needed to hold interest, when going to the park was enjoyable (baseball is still played in ball parks while football is played in stadiums), when aggression was subservient to finesse. Baseball players did not need exposure as college players to succeed as football players do; they play a relatively calm game almost daily instead of a bruising gladiatorial contest weekly. Baseball has room for unique and colorful characters, while football stresses the more anonymous but effective team member. Baseball is a game in which any team can win at any given contest and there are no favorites; only football has real "upsets." Football's careful concern with time adds a tension to the game that is lacking in the more leisurely world of baseball.

Football has replaced baseball as the favorite American spectator sport largely because of television. A comparison between a telecast of a football game on one channel and a baseball game on another could reveal baseball as a game with people standing around seemingly with little to do but watch two men play catch. Football would appear as twenty-two men engaged in almost constant, frenzied action. To watch baseball requires identification with the home team; to watch football requires only a need for action or a week of few thrills and the need for a touch of vicarious excitement.

Baseball is a pastoral game, timeless and highly ritualized; its appeal is to nostalgia and so might enjoy periods of revitalization in comparison to football. But for now, the myth of football suits the nation better.

According to a 1974 Harris survey①, baseball has already been statistically dethroned. In a sports survey a cross section of nearly fourteen hundred fans was asked, "Which of these sports do you follow?"

The decision to play or "follow" a certain sport is also the decision to live a certain myth. The team violence of football, the craftiness of basketball, the mechanistic precision of bowling, the auto racer's devotion to machinery are all subworlds within the universe of sport.

Tiger Woods Wins 2005 Mater Pick.

2005年度高尔夫赛场上夺冠的老虎·伍兹。

Golf, for example, is a unique subworld, one of the few left as a sport (unlike hunting, which does not involve scoring or teams) in which the game is played between man and nature. The winner of a match is one who has beaten the opponent, but the game itself is a person versus the environment. To understand the appeal of golf it is again necessary to consider the game as a ritual

① Harris survey:美国民意测验组织,成立于1956年。

reenactment of an appealing myth.

Golf, perhaps more than any other sport, has to be played to be appreciated. Millions who never played football can enjoy the game on TV, but only a dedicated participant can sit through two hours of televised golf. Golf is growing in participation but still has the stigma of an upper class game. Eighty percent of the nation's golfers must play on 20 percent of the nation's courses that are open to the public. The ratio of public to private facilities hurts public participation in the game but mirrors the inequities of society and provides a convenient status symbol for those who can afford club membership. Its TV audience is not the largest of any sport but it is the most well heeled①.

Golf is a reenactment of the pioneer spirit. It is man versus a hostile environment in search of an oasis. The goal is a series of lush "greens," each protected by natural hazards such as water, sand and unmanageably long grass. The hazards are no threat to physical life but they are to the achievement of success. Golf is a journey game with a constantly changing field. Golfers start the eighteen-hole journey, can rest at a halfway point and then resume until they return to near the point of origination.

The winner of the match is one who has fallen victim to the fewest hazards and overcome the terrain. Many golf courses have Indian names as if to remind the golfer of the frontier ethos. A local course called Indian Lakes invites golfers to use either one of two courses—the Iroquois trail or the Sioux trail②.

Golf, like baseball, is a pastoral sport—with a high degree of tensions and drama but relatively little action. It is a game in which players are constantly in awe of the magic flight of the golf ball. To hit any kind of ball 100 or 200 or more yards with accuracy or to hit a small target from 150 yards is an amazing feat to be appreciated only by those who have at least tried the game. Golf is very likely the most difficult game to master, yet one in which the average player occasionally hits a shot as good as the best of any professional. It is this dream of magic results that keeps the golfer on course.

Questions to Consider

1. What role, in this essay, does Schrank give sports in defining the American Dream? Do you find his observations persuasive, or do you think he makes too much of the role of sports?
2. According to your own experiences, do you believe your own favorite sports reveal anything about your values and wishes?
3. Schrank wrote this essay in 1977. Nowadays, some people would argue that basketball has overtaken football as America's national pastime. What do you think the current popularity of basketball says about the American national character, and how might this shift fit

① heeled：有钱的；此句意为：尽管高尔夫在所有运动中电视观众最少，但这些观众却是最富有的。

② Iroquois 和 Sioux 都是美国殖民地时期的印第安部落。

Schrank's analysis of changing American preferences for certain sports?

4. What do you think is the national sport of China, table tennis, badminton, or any other sports? Then try to analyze what kind of national values and aspirations does this national sport reflect?

Lesson 15 Jockpop: Popular Sports and Politics

大众体育运动与政治

JAMES COMBS

Introduction

The following essay is excerpted from James Combs's book, *Polpop*①, a study of the way in which popular culture affects our political ideas and images. In "Jockpop", Combs looks at how playing and watching sports shapes our thoughts and actions in the realm of politics. Combs's basic premise is that "the 'lessons of sports' help orient us to the world." He argues that we are drawn to sports in large part because they teach us about "competition, teamwork, risk-taking, aggression and defense, winning and losing"; and voters and politicians alike apply these lessons to the world of politics.

Combs identifies a number of ways in which sports and politics are interrelated. Sporting events provide a setting for political rituals and symbols, such as raising the American flag, singing the national anthem and other expressions of patriotism. Sports provide metaphors and images politicians use in appealing to voters, explaining their policies, and promoting themselves and their programs. Sporting events, particularly international ones, may in addition take on political and national significance; and here Combs cites the victory of the American ice hockey team over the Soviet Union in the 1984 Olympics as an example of how a simple game can take on dramatic political overtones.

Text

SPORTS AND LEARNING

In the famous opening sequence of the movie *Patton*②, General Patton (George C. Scott) delivered a speech to an audience of soldiers. He said in part:

> Men, all this stuff you've heard about America not wanting to fight, wanting to stay out of the war, is a lot of horse dung. Americans traditionally love to fight. All real Americans love the sting of battle. When you were kids you all admired the champion marble shooter,

---

① *Polpop*:本书于 1984 年首次出版,书名系作者揉合 Politics 和 Pop Culture 两个词而成。

② *Patton*:美国 1970 年由 Fox 公司拍摄的传记影片《巴顿将军》,主要以 George S. Patton (1885—1945)将军在二战中的事迹为题材。

the fastest runner, the big league ballplayers, the toughest boxers. Americans play to win all the time. I wouldn't give a hoot in hell for a man who lost and laughed. That's why Americans have never lost, and will never lose a war, because the very thought of losing is hateful to Americans.

Let us reflect a moment, as General Patton urges, on growing up. When we were kids, we all quickly learned the importance of sports. Playing was fun, and indeed gave us a chance to prove ourselves. We discovered that organized sports at school and the Little League gave us an opportunity to play. We discovered that some could play better than others, that winning was valued, that there was a huge adult interest in sports. We found that there was a big world of sports in which adult athletes played before gigantic audiences for large amounts of money and glory. We adopted heroes among athletes in high school, or more remotely in the pro leagues①. We attempted to bat, or dribble or pass like them, even to act like them. If we hung around locker rooms or played, we heard the slogans: "Quitters never win, and winners never quit." some of us experienced the "thrill of victory and the agony of defeat." We heard the speeches at sports banquets. We won letters, were cheerleaders and pom-pom girls②, went to the school games. We talked about sports, followed college and pro sports, maybe even dreamed dreams of athletic glory.

And what effect did it all have on us? Specifically here, what impact does the play-world of sports have on politics? Like the other areas of the American play-world, popular sports is not "just a game." Rather, we learn much about the world from sports. Whether consciously or not, the "lessons of sports" help to orient us to the world③. It is not an idle metaphor when we speak of the "game of life." For games, and what we are told about games, give us much learning about life, and even politics. Sports is a form of play which we early on learn is important, come to value, and link to "real life."

SPORTS AND POLTICS

The dramatization of the American Dream in sports suggests that sports has important meanings for us. It is likely that we "read into" sports a variety of messages, including political ones. So we should expect that sports would have political meanings and realize that these meanings have not been lost on politicians and observers of politics. Sometimes the sports-politics connection is obvious, some-times subtle, but it is nevertheless there. For if sports is a key part of our cultural mythology and is a play-setting for the dramatization of American myths, then its relevance for the world of politics and government exists. Therefore, we can explore some of the

① pro leagues：职业联赛。pro 是 professional 的简写。

② pom-pom girl：啦啦队手持绒球（pom-pon）的表演队员。

③ 本句意为：无论有意识与否，"体育之所学"都有助于我们适应现实世界。

political meanings and uses of sports: sports as a setting for political *ritual*; as a metaphor for political rhetoric; as a dramatic microcosm of political *conflicts*; and as a political *resource*. We will consider these in turn.

SPORTS AS A SETTING FOR POLITICAL RITUAL

Remember that we have stressed the ways that popular culture is a political teacher. We learn things about ourselves as political beings from the social messages that a popular play-form communicates. An important part of our political socialization was through patriotic ritual at school—saluting the flag, saying the Pledge of Allegiance, school spirit assemblies. But this is not the only setting for such symbolic dramas. We all remember the patriotic rituals attached to sporting events—the national anthem, raising the flag, color guards, and so forth. We would feel uneasy if a high school or college football game did not include such patriotic rituals.

These generalized rituals are more or less universal. Indeed, we commonly expect sporting events to be clothed in not only political symbolism, but also religious symbolism as well. We all recall the invocations given before games, the players all praying in the huddle, and singing "God Bless America." Patriotic and religious symbols are, of course, closely linked in sports ritual. The presence of such ritual underscores that the event is not merely a game, but a play-event conducted with proper deference by participants and audience to transcendent values①. The appeal is very largely to the moral community, as when the invocation prays that the players conduct the game with respect to moral values. Thus, the folk drama of sports comes to be imbued with patriotic rituals which remind us not only in what country the game is being played, but that the game occurs in the context of national values.

Now when a political crisis ensues, such patriotic ritual takes on a more intensely felt meaning. During the Iranian crisis②, it was common for football game rituals to recognize the hostages through moments of silence immediately before the national anthem was played, a dramatic reminder with political significance. Immediately after the release of the hostages, the 1981 Super Bowl③ became a festive setting for the ritual recognition of that celebrated event—everyone there wore yellow ribbons, and even the Superdome had a massive yellow ribbon on the outside.

But when the country is divided over some political issue, political rituals at sports events can become controversial and excessive. During the height of the Vietnam War, there was a clear increase in the number of college football halftime shows that involved patriotic themes and

① 此句意为:这些仪式的存在突出性地说明体育项目不仅仅是游戏,而是表明比赛者和观众对一些普世价值观念的尊重。

② Iranian crisis:伊朗人质危机(1979—1981),1979 年在美伊两国关系紧张之时,伊朗部分人围攻美国驻伊朗大使馆,66 名美国人被作为人质扣押。

③ Super Bowl:超级杯,美国橄榄球联盟(National Football League)举行的年度锦标赛。

pageantry. Indeed, in 1970 ABC① refused to televise a halftime show planned by the University of Buffalo band which dramatized antiwar, antiracist, and antipollution themes through music and skits on the grounds that it would be a "political demonstration." But later that season ABC did televise a halftime show at the Army-Navy game which honored Green Berets② who had just conducted an unsuccessful raid on a prisoner of war camp in North Vietnam, including statements by military officers critical of antiwar activity at home. So it depends upon whose moralistic myth is to be ritualized! Such incidents do remind us that sports involve the affirmation of cultural myths, since sports "participates" in the social order. Thus, "negative" rituals which celebrate a counter-myth conflict with the traditional patriotic function that sporting rituals have served.

In the past, political rituals which celebrated the symbols of government seemed especially appropriate for sporting events, since major sports seemed to embody so nicely aspects of the American Dream. If myths of the State come to be disbelieved or doubted, then such rituals may ring hollow for many people. One may wonder what sorts of feelings playing the national anthem before a game conjures up in our breasts. But whether we still believe or not the fact remains that sports is a major stage for the dramatization of political symbols.

SPORTS AS A METAPHOR FOR POLITICAL RHETORIC

Politicians like to draw upon familiar symbols to illustrate some political point, and sports offer familiar and widely used metaphors. The language of the locker room permeates politics, sports is a major repository of American mythology so politicians can utilize the analogy, safely assuming wide familiarity with the "lessons" of sports. Since politics has many game-like aspects, reference to the dynamics of sporting games as similar to "the game of politics" is natural. Both coaches and political figures seem to believe in the necessity of inspiration, which is the most common political use of sports analogies, allegories, parables, and so on.

US Athelete Jesse Owens Won the 100-Meter Sprint in the 1936 Berlin Olympics.

1936 年柏林奥运会上美国运动员杰西·欧文斯夺得男子 100 米金牌。

The "values" of sports can also be for a variety of political uses. In particular, sports can illustrate the "truth" of either moralistic or materialistic myths. The American sports creed includes many tenets, most of which can be used to support or illustrate different political messages. Even though there is wide popular consensus that sports makes us "better citizens," what that means is subject to interpretation. For instance, Americans repeatedly agree on the positive lessons of sports: e.g., sports are

① ABC:系美国广播公司(American Broadcasting Company)的首字母缩写,现隶属迪斯尼公司。

② Green Berets:绿色贝雷帽,美国特种部队(US Army Special Forces)的别称,60 年代冷战期间,由肯尼迪推动组成,因士兵头戴绿色贝雷帽而得此称号。

worthwhile because they teach us "self-discipline"; sports are good because they promote "fair play" and sports are positive because they teach "respect for authority and good citizenship." However, such virtues can be variously interpreted.

Let us illustrate this by reference to two often competing aspects of the sports creed: sportsmanship and winning. The ideal of sportsmanship has persisted in political rhetoric as a norm by which the game is supposed to be played, i. e., that one plays fair, enjoys the contest, and accepts victory with magnanimity and defeat with grace. Being a "good sport" was a trait admirable in all areas of life. The "truth" of sports was not whether one won or lost, but how you played the game. A "sportsman" was a gentleman committed to excellence, but within ethical bounds and without cheap tactics. Such an image smacks of the "Ivy League" pop books of an earlier age about sports heroes such as Frank Merriwell①.

This venerable notion has been applied to democratic politics again and again. In a classic book about democracy, we learn that sportsmanship, on the field or in politics, consists of such attitudes as tolerating and honoring the opposition being a gracious winner and loser: and playing "the game of politics" within the bounds of rules and fair play.

This motif is complicated by a conflicting norm: winning. Winning isn't everything, goes Lombardi's Law②, it's the only thing. Nice guys, Durocher's Dictum has it, finish last③. The winning motif is related to the idea of sports as war, in which winning takes precedence over gentlemanly traits, and indeed where sportsmanship is a hindrance to victory. The implicit locker room message is often that since winning is paramount, any means, including bending or breaking the rules, unfair play, and intimidation, are justified. At the extreme, this can justify the virtue of sheer winning in politics. Indeed, the Nixon Administration's fondness for sports metaphors was thought to have contributed to the "Watergate mentality," i. e., that the political world is a game of winners and losers locked in relentless strife, and since the "other side" are rogues and will do anything to win, we are justified in being just as nasty as them in order to win. The famous "Plumbers" office④ in the basement of the Nixon White House, consisting of those assigned to conduct break-ins, dirty tricks, and the like, had a sign that paraphrased Lombardi: "Winning in politics isn't everything, it is the only thing."

---

① Frank Merriwell:美国作家 Gilbert Patten(1866—1945)在其连环故事中塑造的主人公,他是体育健将,更是匡扶正义的英雄;本句意为:这种形象让人想到早期"常春藤联盟"流行读物中的体育英雄弗兰克·梅瑞维尔。

② Lombardi's Law:Vince Lombardi(1913—1970),美国橄榄球传奇人物,曾在60年代出任 Green Bay Packers 教练,获得无数奖杯。他始终把目标定位在取得胜利。"胜利不是最重要的,是唯一重要的"即出自他的语录。

③ Dictum:格言;此句源于1946年7月5日布鲁克林道奇队(1958年更名为洛杉矶道奇队)经理 Leo Durocher 对纽约巨人队的评论,后被媒体扭曲为"Nice guys finish last";屡次否认无果之后,Leo Durocher 后来曾借用此句作为其自传的书名。

④ The "Plumbers" Office:白宫特殊调查组(White House Special Investigations Unit)的别名,于1971年尼克松在位时成立,负责防止机密外泄,在"水门事件"发生后曾阻碍调查的展开。

The sportsmanship theme is explicitly stated in political rhetoric, but the winning theme, by emphasis, implicitly suggests to us the necessity of aggressiveness, cunning, and even violence. In areas such as business and politics, the sports metaphor reflects the tension we feel about these two values. In business, for example, we believe that pursuit of material goals all should be bound by the competitive rules of capitalism and moral rules derived from, say, religion; but we also recognize and even admire the business sharpie who makes lots of money by circumventing the rules, participating in underhanded and even illegal deals, and perhaps even using intimidation and violence. Our fascination with the superrich, instant millionaires and gangsters stems in part from the popular belief that one cannot make it without being a scoundrel. Similarly it has been widely believed since Machiavelli① that one cannot acquire and use power unless you are not bound by moral rules. Since politics, like sports, is a mean and competitive world, the winners have to be equal to the task. Getting the "material" of power and prestige in politics requires violating morality. Like the Godfather, you have to make people offers they can't refuse.

In American culture, our attitudes toward the conflicting values have roots in the worldview termed Social Darwinism. As a metaphor drawn from the theory of evolution the Social Darwinists argued that business and politics were hard struggles in which the fittest survived and dominated. For this viewpoint sports offers evidence that life is like that, and thus politics is by necessity that way. Therefore, we warn people in charge who use power less bound by moral restraints. But if we take the more "civilized" view of this sportsmanship motif, business and politics, like sports, should be tamed and made fair. For the political rhetorician sports offer analogies of both motifs, although the "winning" ethic is usually not blatantly said. In any case, it is an indication of a tension in our attitudes toward American politics as to which sports metaphor we think most applicable to politics.

SPORTS AS A DRAMATIC MICROCOSM OF POLITICAL CONFLICTS

The old saw② has it that sports reflect society. If sports is a mirror of our conflicts, certainly when our divisions are politicized, sports become a dramatic microcosm of political conflicts. If groups experience material or moral lapses, they may be dramatized on the playing field. We have already mentioned how the post-World War Ⅱ civil rights revolution was reflected in sports. Many other domestic conflicts work their way into sports. For example, it is nowadays popularly thought that America is a society of litigants eternally suing each other. Certainly this is reflected in sports, which involves a great deal of litigation over the status of players, franchises, fans, the media, and so on. If Americans think that as a people we spend a great deal of time in court, they certainly are reinforced in that view by reading the sports page.

① Niccolo Machiavelli (1469—1527):尼科洛·马基雅维里,文艺复兴时期意大利杰出的政治家、哲学家和作家,强调势力政治,为取得目的而不择手段,著有《君主论》和《战争的艺术》等著作。

② saw:这里指"proverb",意即"谚语"。

Adolph Hitler watches the 1936 Berlin Olympic Games at his showcase stadium with Italian Crown Prince.

1936 年希特勒和意大利皇储在柏林观看奥运会。

Perhaps the most spectacular way in which sports come to be infested with politics involves international political conflicts. It is no secret that international sports—the Olympics, international track and field meets, even professional sports—often become embroiled in political controversies between nations.

The quadrennial Olympic Games are the most important dramatic forum with political overtones. Nations are interested in "proving" the superiority of their political values by success at the Olympic Games. The Nazis tried to prove the superiority of the "Aryan race" at the 1936 Olympics, but the dramatic scenario backfired somewhat by the success of American black runners. Communist countries such as the Soviet Union and East Germany invest great resources into Olympic success, since this dramatizes the alleged superiority of "socialist man." Terrorists are attracted to such games to dramatize their cause, as was the case with the Palestinian group that kidnapped the Israeli athletes at the Munich Olympics of 1972①.

But the most memorable recent incident involving the United States occurred at the 1980 Winter Olympics. In late 1979, in an already volatile Middle East following the Iranian Revolution and the hostage crisis, the Soviet Union invaded Afghanistan. This was the culmination of a complex series of political events that signified the crisis of "detente②" between the United States and the Soviet Union, and brought the world into one of those periods of international tension. Further, it was an election year in the United States, which made the role of American public opinion all the more crucial in the crisis. It became politically for important for President Carter to respond to these developments, given the chauvinistic and retributive mood of the country. So he dispatched the fleet, agitated for Persian Gulf resistance to Soviet expansion, and cut off the shipment of some trade materials to the Russians.

But he did something else too: he called for a boycott of the 1980 Summer Olympic Games in Moscow. He sent boxer Muhammad Ali to Africa to enlist support for the boycott. He advocated and arranged "alterative" games to be held somewhere other than Russia. He pressured NBC to not televise the Soviet Olympics and stopped American companies from Olympic-related shipments to the Soviets. He sought the support of the athletes themselves, and of the international sports community. The political purpose, of course, was to symbolically (and in some measure, tangibly) "punish" the Soviets for the Afghanistan intervention.

In themidst of the new tension, a dramatic sports even occurred which demonstrated how play can have political significance. At the Winter Olympics in Lake Placid, New York, the American

① 1972 年慕尼黑奥运会上,巴勒斯坦恐怖分子挟持并杀害了 11 名以色列运动员和 1 名德国警察。

② détente:[法语]绥靖政策,指尼克松 70 年代初上台后为缓和冷战气氛而实施的外交政策。

hockey team unexpectedly upset the Soviets, 4-3. This triumph and then later when the Americans won the gold medal by defeating the Finns, brought an outpouring of rejoicing and national pride. This outburst, which included many people who knew absolutely nothing about hockey, was clearly related to the new international tensions with the Soviets. The defeat of the Soviet hockey team was not "just a game." Boycotting the Olympic Games for political reasons dramatized the importance accorded international sporting matches. Inviting the triumphant U. S. Winter Olympic team to the White House, including the cowboy-hatted hockey team, became the focus for national congratulations, and gave a dramatic role to a President up for re-election.

An international sporting event conducted in the midst of a political crisis, then, can take on an intensely patriotic flavor, and, if victorious, people can feel as if through play they have "won" some sort of political victory. It focuses political emotion onto the drama of the game, and thus gives us deep patriotic pride. Politicians and the news media recognized the political significance of the event, and gave it great play. The triumph gave occasion for political ritual at the White House, associating the even formally with patriotic symbols and offering ritual thanks to the athletes. The drama did nothing to undo Soviet political intentions, but it did help people to deal with their athletes about international tensions and their own country's worth. The Olympic triumph signaled a new patriotic fervor in the United States, and helped to revive the moralistic myth about our "mission" in the world and national superiority. The hockey match and the national outburst it caused was a dramatic microcosm of a political crisis.

SPORTS AS A POLITICAL RESOURCE

Since sports are valued popular play-activities, it is common for politicians to use sports and sports figures for a wide variety of political purposes. Like religion and show business, sports offer the politician association with something nonpolitical that large numbers of people are attracted to. Not only do politicians use the rhetoric of sports for political purposes, they also express their interest in sports to dramatize their commonality. Candidates campaigning for office attend sporting events, mention the local team and seek the endorsement of famous athletes. Endorsement-seeking illustrates how politics seeks out popular culture. The endorsement of a famous athlete somehow gives the aspiring politician a kind of popular status and humanity he might not earn otherwise. The athlete is an embodiment of both material and moral success on the playing-field, and the politician seems to think that with the association some of the heroic magic might rub off. All this is nothing new: both Al Smith and Herbert Hoover sought the endorsement of Babe Ruth① in 1928! But it doesn't always work. Gerald Ford had an endless list of athletes who endorsed him in 1976, but he lost the election anyway. Ford and other politicians have been

① Al Smith (1837—1944):美国政客,曾任第42届纽约州州长。Herbert Hoover(1874—1964):第31届美国总统。Babe Ruth(1895—1948):George Herman Ruth, Jr. 的昵称,美国著名棒球运动员。

accused of being "jock-sniffers[①]," zealously exploiting their relationship to athletes and athletics, but the transfer of magic is not guaranteed.

President Carter did not appear to be a jock-sniffer, but he was aware of the political uses of participation in sports. He cultivated his Southern regional tie, including hunting, fishing, and wading in hip-boots for bait. He reigned over slow-pitch softball games between the White House staff and the press. He became the First Jogger, and was photographed jogging in long distance races with troops in Korea. President Reagan liked to ride, and professed himself a sports fan. It is always difficult to tell the extent to which sports participation by politicians stems from their desire to stay healthy and enjoy strenuous activity, or from their awareness that such activities are popular, and by participating they communicate to the public their common human interest. In any case, most recent Presidents have cultivated some form of popular leisure activity—golf, touch-football, sailing, etc. However, if some of the recent revelations about President John Kennedy's "favorite leisure activity" are true, then it must be said that although golf and jogging have their virtues as sports, so does his, although the former type is most politically acceptable and performable in public.

Since sports figures do become popular embodiments of heroic success, the celebrity status they enjoy can become a resource for successful political recruitment. Having played college football or even some professional sport seems to have helped a wide variety of political figures, ranging from Ford to Supreme Court Justice Byron "Whizzer" White[②] (a former All-American) and former baseball pitcher and House member Wilmer "Vinegar Bend" Mizell[③]. Former NBA

Former NBA Player Bill Bradley turned into New Jersey senator(1979—1997).
美国前NBA球员比尔·布拉德利摇身化为新泽西州议员(1979—1997)。

① jock-sniffer:意指那些和运动员套近乎的人,jock在俚语中即指运动员。Gerald Ford (1913—2006):第38届美国总统。

② Byron White (1917—2002):美国橄榄球前运动员,1962被肯尼迪总统任命为最高法院的副法官。

③ Wilmer Mizell (1930—1999):美国棒球联赛投手,曾任三届(1969—1975)国会众议院议员。

star Bill Bradley① became Senator from New Jersey at least partially on his sports celebrity. Congressman Jack Kemp② of New York ran for Congress in the city he was an NFL quarterback, stressed how quarter-backing gave him leadership qualities, and used the rhetoric of football for political purposes. It may be the case in the future that more politicians will be drawn from the ranks of well-known sports figures.

CONCLUSION

We have not exhausted the complex relationships between popular sports and political culture, but the above should give the reader the idea of some of the major linkages. As long as Americans are sports crazy, we should expect that sports will have political relevance, and that "the game of politics" will be conducted in a culture that includes sports as a value.

Questions to Consider

1. In your opinion, do you think sports and games carry strong political overtones? Should this political influence on sports be lessened? Is winning the only thing of sports? How should the players accept victory and defeat in order to be "a gracious winner and loser?"
2. What are some of the "eternal human truths" and "specific cultural truths" that Combs says we learn from sports? Can you think of others? Would everyone agree that these are "truths"?
3. Combs divides the main part of his essay into four sections, each dealing with a different way in which sports is connected to politics. In your opinion, which of these four seems the most influential? Think of examples, other than those mentioned by Combs, to support your opinion.
4. Apply Combs's idea that we learn values and truths through sports to an area in our culture other than politics. For example, how does sports affect our notions of religion, education, or work?

---

① Bill Bradley (1943—):美国 NBA 前白人球员,曾于 1967—1977 年效力纽约尼克斯队,退役后当选新泽西州议员。

② Jack Kemp (1935—2009):美国前橄榄球职业球员,曾任九届(1971—1989)国会议员。

Lesson 16 The Black and White Truth about Basketball

篮球运动中的黑—白真理

JEFF GREENFIELD

Introduction

Jeff Greenfield (1943—), a political and media analyst for ABC News and a syndicated newspaper columnist, has written extensively about contemporary American culture, focusing on politics, sports, and the media. Originally published in 1975, the essay which follows has been widely anthologized since then and was updated by the author in 1988.

Greenfield's thesis is that there are two different styles—"black style" and a "white style"—of playing basketball and that these result from differences in the environments the players grow up in. So, although his analysis of basketball focuses on the game and how it's played, Greenfield also looks closely at broader cultural influences. This essay is notable both for its controversial thesis and for its rhetorical technique: this is an excellent example of an essay of comparison and contrast, in which "black" and "white" basketball are carefully contrasted in terms of their style, how they evolved, and how different players embody each style.

Text

The dominance of black athletes over professional basketball is beyond dispute. Two-thirds of the players are black, and the number would be greater were it not for the continuing practice of picking white bench warmers for the sake of balance. Over the last two decades, no more than three white players have been among the ten starting players on the National Basketball Association's All-Star team, and in the last quarter century, only two white players—Dave Cowens and Larry Bird of the Boston Celtics①—have ever been chosen as the NBA's Most Valuable Player.

And at a time when a baseball executive could lose his job for asserting that blacks lacked "the necessities" to become pro sports executives and when the National Football League still has not hired a single black head coach, the NBA stands as a pro sports league that hired its first black head coach in 1968 (Bill Russell) and its first black general manager in the early 1970s (Wayne Embry

---

① Dave Cowens (1948—):1970 年起效力波士顿凯尔特人队,1973 年获得 NBA 最有价值球员称号; Larry Bird (1956—):1978 年起效力凯尔特人队,曾于 1984、1985、1986 连续三年获得过 NBA 最有价值球员称号。

of the Milwaukee Bucks)①. What discrimination remains—lack of equal opportunity for speaking engagements and product endorsements—has more to do with society than with basketball②. .

This dominance reflects a natural inheritance: Basketball is the pastime of the urban poor. The current generation of black athletes are heirs to a tradition more than half a century old. In a neighborhood without the money for bats, gloves, hockey sticks and ice skates, or shoulder pads, basketball is an eminently accessible sport. "Once it was the game of the Irish and Italian Catholics in Rockaway and the Jews on Fordham Road in the Bronx," writes David Wolf in his brilliant book, *Foul*! "It was recreation, status, and a way out." But now the ethnic names have been changed: Instead of the Red Holzimans, Red Auerbachs, and the McGuire brothers, there are Julius Ervings and Michael Jordans, Ralph Sampsons and Kareem Abdul-Jabbars③. And professional basketball is a sport with national television exposure and million-dollar salaries.

But the mark on basketball of today's players can be measured by more than money or visibility. It is a question of style. For there is a clear difference between "black" and "white" styles of play that is as clear as the difference between 155th Street at Eighth Avenue④ and Crystal City, Missouri. Most simply (remembering we are talking about culture, not chromosomes), "black" basketball is the use of superb athletic skill to adapt to the limits of space imposed by the game. "White" ball is the pulverization of that space by sheer intensity⑤.

It takes a conscious effort to realize how constricted the space is on a basketball court. Place a regulation court (ninety-four by fifty feet) on a football field, and it will reach from the back of the end zone to the twenty-one-yard line; its width will cover less than a third of the field. On a baseball diamond, a basketball court will reach from home plate to first base. Compared to its principal indoor rival, ice hockey, basketball covers about one-fourth the playing area. Moreover, during the normal flow of the game, most of the action takes place on the third of the court nearest the basket. It is in this dollhouse space that ten men, each of them half a foot taller than the average man, come together to battle each other.

There is, thus, no room; basketball is a struggle for the edge: the half step with which to cut

---

① Bill Russell(1934—):美国退役篮球运动员,曾效力于波士顿凯尔特人队;Wayne Embry(1937—):退役美国篮球运动员,曾效力于密尔沃基雄鹿队。

② speaking engagements and product endorsements, 指为运动员产品代言和推广的活动,以此谋取利益。整句话大意为:如果有什么歧视存在的话——如发言和产品代言机会不均等——这更多与社会而不是与篮球有关。

③ Red Holziman (1920—98)、Red Auerbach (1917—2006) 以及 Dick McGuire (1926—2010) 和 Al McGuire (1928—2001) 都曾是美国 NBA 白人球员和教练,而 Julius Erving (1950—)、Michael Jordan (1963—)、Ralph Sampson (1960—) 和 Kareem Abdul-Jabbar (1947—) 都是前美国 NBA 黑人球员。

④ 指纽约第八大道 155 街,靠近黑人社区哈莱姆。在美国,黑人常常居住在城市内城,而白人则往往会住在郊外。

⑤ 此句意为:"黑人篮球"利用技巧的娴熟来适应有限的场地,而"白人篮球"则纯粹是场地上激烈打拼。作者试图要说明这种区分没有指涉黑人和白人在篮球上孰优孰劣,或者黑人有打篮球的天赋等歧视之意。

around the defender for a lay-up①, the half second of freedom with which to release a jump shot, the instant a head turns allowing a pass to a teammate breaking for the basket. It is an arena for the subtlest of skills: the head fake, the shoulder fake, the shift of body weight to the right and the sudden cut to the left. Deception is crucial to success; and to young men who have learned early and painfully that life is a battle for survival, basketball is one of the few pursuits in which the weapon of deception is a legitimate tactic rather than the source of trouble.

If there is, then, the need to compete in a crowd, to battle for the edge, then the surest strategy is to develop the *unexpected*: to develop a shot that is simply and fundamentally different from the usual methods of putting the ball in the basket. Drive to the hoop, but go under it and come up the other side; hold the ball at waist leve1 and shoot from there instead of bringing the ball up to eye level; leap into the air, but fall away from the basket instead of toward it. All these tactics, which a fan can see embodied in the astonishing play of the Chicago Bulls' Michael Jordan, take maximum advantage of the crowding on the court. They also stamp uniqueness on young men who may feel it nowhere else.

"For many young men in the slums," David Wolf writes, "the school yard is the only place they can feel true pride in what they do, where they can move free of inhibitions and where they can, by being spectacular, rise for the moment against the drabness and anonymity of their lives. Thus, when a player develops extraordinary 'schoo1 yard' moves and shots… [they] become his measure as a man."

So the moves that begin as tactics for scoring soon become calling cards②. You don't just lay the ball in for an uncontested basket; you take the ball in both hands, leap as high as you can, and slam the ball through the hoop. When you jump in the air, fake a shot, bring the ball back to your body, and throw up a shot, all without coming back down, you have proven your worth in uncontestable fashion.

This liquid grace is an integral part of "black" ball, almost exclusively the province of the playground player. Some white stars like Bob Cousy, Billy Cunningham, and Doug Collins had it, and the Celtics' Kevin McHale has it now③: the body control, the moves to the basket, the free-ranging mobility. Most of them also possessed the surface ease that is integral to the "black" style; an incorporation of the ethic of mean streets—to "make it" is not just to have wealth but to have it without strain④. Whatever the muscles and organs are doing, the face of the "black" star

---

① lay-up:(篮球术语)单手打板投篮。

② calling cards:手中可用的牌,意指黑人可以发挥特长的地方。

③ Bob Cousy (1928—)、Billy Cunningham (1943—)、Doug Collins (1951—)、Kevin McHale (1957—)都是 NBA 退役白人球员。

④ an…strain:此句大意为:这体现了居住在穷街陋巷中的黑人的生活态度——"成功"并不仅仅指获得(财富),而是要表明毫不费力地获得。要让社会知道黑人的特长,但不用炫耀。言外之意还是要表明黑人社会地位的低下。

almost never shows it. Magic Johnson[①] of the Lakers can bring the ball down court with two men on him, whip a pass through an invisible opening, cut to the basket, take a return pass, and hit the shot all with no more emotion than a quick smile. So stoic was San Antonio Spurs' great George Gervin[②] that he earned the nickname "Ice Man." (Interestingly, a black coach like Boston's K. C. Jones exhibits far less emotion on the bench than a white counterpart like Dick Motta or Jack Ramsey.)

If there is a single trait that characterizes "black" ball it is leaping ability. Bob Cousy, ex-Celtic great and former pro coach, says that "when coaches get together, one is sure to say, 'I've got the one black kid in the country who can't jump.' When coaches see a white boy who can jump or who moves with extraordinary quickness, they say, 'He should have been born black, he's that good.'"

Don Nelson[③], now a top executive with the Golden State Warriors, recalls that back in 1970, Dave Cowens, then a relatively unknown graduate of Florida State, prepared for his rookie pro season[④] by playing the Rucker League, an outdoor competition in Harlem playgrounds that pits pros against college kids and playground stars. So ferocious was Cowens' leaping ability, Nelson says, that "when the summer was over, everyone wanted to know who the white son of a bitch was who could jump so high." That's another way to overcome a crowd around the basket—just go over it.

Speed, mobility, quickness, acceleration, "the moves"—all of these are catch-phrases that surround the "black" playground athlete, the style of play. So does the most racially tinged of attributes, "rhythm." Yet rhythm is what the black stars themselves talk about: feeling the flow of the game, finding the tempo of the dribble, the step, the shot. It is an instinctive quality (although it stems from hundreds of hours of practice), and it is one that has led to difficulty between system-oriented coaches and free-form players.

NBA Spanish Player Pau Gasol of Los Angeles Lakers.

美国NBA洛杉矶湖人队西班牙籍球员加索尔。

"Cats from the street have their own rhythm when they play," said college dropout Bill Spivey[⑤], onetime New York high school star. "It's not a matter of somebody setting you up and you shooting. You feel the shot. When a coach holds you back, you lose the feel and it isn't fun anymore."

---

① Magic Johnson (1959—): 原名 Earvin Johnson,美国 NBA 退役球员,于 1979 入选湖人队,被称为"魔术师约翰逊"。

② George Gervin (1952—): 美国 NBA 退役球员,曾效力圣安东尼奥马刺队和芝加哥公牛队。

③ Don Nelson (1940—): 曾为美国 NBA 球员,现为 NBA 金州勇士队总教练。

④ 新球员职业赛季;rookie:新球员。

⑤ Bill Spivey (1929—1995): 曾为美国大学体育联盟赛(NCAA)中锋球员。

When legendary Brooklyn playground star Connie Hawkins was winding up his NBA career under Laker coach Bill Sharman, he chafed under the methodical style of play. "He's systematic to the point where it begins to be a little too much. It's such an action-reaction type of game that when you have to do everything the same way, I think you lose something."

There is another kind of basketball that has grown up in America. It is not played on asphalt playgrounds with a crowd of kids competing for the court; it is played on macadam driveways by one boy with a ball and a backboard nailed over the garage; it is played in gyms in the frigid winter of the rural Midwest and on Southern dirt courts. It is a mechanical, precise development of skills. It is a game without frills, without flow, but with effectiveness. It is "white" basketball: jagged, sweaty, stumbling, intense. Where a "black" player overcomes an obstacle with finesse and body control, a "white" player reacts by outrunning or overpowering the obstacle.

By this definition, the Boston Celtics are a classically "White" team. They rarely suit up a player with dazzling moves; indeed such a player would probably make Red Auerbach swallow his cigar. Instead, the Celtics wear you down with execution, with constant running, with the same play run again and again and again. The rebound by Robert Parrish① triggers the fast break, as everyone races downcourt; the ball goes to Larry Bird, who pulls up and takes the shot or who drives and then finds Danny Ainge or Kevin McHale free for an easy basket.

Perhaps the most definitively "white" position is that of the quick forward, one without great moves to the basket, without highly developed hosts, without the height and mobility for rebounding effectiveness. So what does he do?

Michael Jordan on the slamdunk contest.

扣篮大赛上的迈克尔·乔丹。

He runs. He runs from the opening jump to the final buzzer②. He runs up and down the court, from base line to base line, back and forth under the basket, looking for the opening, the pass, the chance to take a quick step, the high percentage shot. To watch San Antonio's Mark Olberding or Detroit's Bill Lambeer③, players without speed or obvious moves, is to wonder what they are doing in the NBA—until you see them swing free and throw up a shot that, without demanding any apparent skill, somehow goes in the basket more frequently than the shots of many of their more skilled teammates. And to have watched the New York Knicks' (now U. S.

---

① Robert Parrish (1953—):美国 NBA 黑人球员,曾于 1980—1994 年效力于波士顿凯尔特人队。

② final buzzer: 比赛结束嗡鸣信号。

③ Mark Olberding (1956—):美国 NBA 退役球员,曾于 1975—1982 年效力于圣安东尼奥马刺队;Bill Lambeer (1957—):NBA 白人球员,于 1982 年转会底特律活塞队。

Senator) Bill Bradley①, or the Celtics' John Havlicek②, is to have watched "white" ball at its best.

Havlicek or Lambeer, or the Laker's Kurt Rambis, stand in dramatic contrast to Michael Jordan or to the Philadelphia 76ers' legend, Julius Erving. Erving had the capacity to make legends come true, leaping from the foul line and slam-dunking the ball on his way down; going up for a lay-up, pulling the ball to his body, and driving under and up the other side of the rim, defying gravity and probability with impossible moves and jumps. Michael Jordan of the Chicago Bulls has been seen by thousands spinning a full 360 degrees in midair before slamming the ball through the hoop.

When John Havlicek played, by contrast, he was the living embodiment of his small-town Ohio background. He would bring the ball down court, weaving left, then right, looking for a path. He would swing the ball to a teammate, cut behind the pick, take the pass, and release the shot in a flicker of time. It looked plain, unvarnished. But it was a blend of skills that not more than half a dozen other players in the league possessed.

To former pro Jim McMillian③, a black who played quick forward with "white" attributes, "it's a matter of environment. Julius Erving grew up in a different environment from Havlicek. John came from a very small town in Ohio. There everything was done the easy way, the shortest distance between two points. It's nothing fancy; very few times will he go one-on-one. He hits the lay-up, hits the jump shot, makes the free throw, and after the game you look up and say, 'How did he hurt us that much?'"

Coach Steve Alford of New Mexico Lobos.
新墨西哥灰狼队教练史蒂夫·阿福德。

"White" ball, then, is the basketball of patience, method and sometimes brute strength. "Black" ball is the basketball of electric self expression. One player has all the time in the world to perfect his skills, the other a need to prove himself. These are slippery categories, because a poor boy who is black can play "white" and a white boy of middle-class parents can play "black." Bill Cartwright④ of the New York Knicks and Steve Alford⑤ of the Dallas Mavericks are athletes who seem to defy these categories.

And what makes basketball the most intriguing of sports is how these styles do not necessarily

① Bill Bradley (1943—)：美国前 NBA 白人球员，曾于 1967—1977 年效力纽约尼克斯队，退役后当选新泽西州议员。

② John Havlicek (1940—)：美国前 NBA 白人球员，于 1962 年入选波士顿凯尔特人队，效力 16 个赛季。

③ Jim McMillian (1948—)：美国黑人球员，曾于 1976—1978 效力纽约尼克斯队。

④ Bill Cartwright (1957—)：美国前 NBA 黑人球员，曾分别效力于纽约尼克斯（1979—1988）、芝加哥公牛队（1988—1994）和西雅图超音速队（1994—1995）。

⑤ Steve Alford (1964—)：美国前 NBA 白人球员，现为新墨西哥州大学队总教练。

clash; how the punishing intensity of "white" players and the dazzling moves of the "blacks" can fit together, a fusion of cultures that seems more and more difficult in the world beyond the out-of-bounds line①.

Questions to Consider

1. As you read, notice the form of Greenfield's essay as well as its content. What organizational and descriptive techniques does he use to convey his ideas clearly and persuasively? Do you find yourself agreeing with his points? Why or why not?
2. What reasons does Greenfield give for the predominance of African Americans in professional basketball? Are his reasons related primarily to race, class, environment, or to a combination of all three?
3. How does the "white style" of basketball differ from the "black style," as Greenfield describes them? How does he account for these differences? Why do you think Greenfield uses quotation marks around "black" and "white" throughout his essay?
4. When this essay was first published in *Esquire* in 1975, it sparked some controversy. Do you find anything controversial or potentially offensive in Greenfield's analysis? Do you think he wanted to cause controversy? If so, why? In determining your answer, consider the author's final paragraph as well as the comparisons he makes with other professional sports in paragraph 2.

---

① a fusion of cultures: 两种文化的融合；本句意为：两种文化的融合在篮球场内似乎还可以实现，但出了这个场地却困难重重。

Historical Perspective 历史视角

Sports

体育运动

ROBERT J. HIGGS

What is sport? The truth is that no one knows, and the challenge to define it, or at least to describe its characteristics, has engaged the attention of some of the best scholars of our time, always with beneficial results but never with answers that satisfy completely. Says Johan Huizinga[①] in *Homo Ludens*, a book that is *sine qua non*[②] on any aspect of the subject of sport, "In our heart of hearts we know that none of our pronouncements is absolutely conclusive." Like Tennyson's flower in the crannied wall[③], we know that sport is, but we do not know with certainty what it is. Nevertheless, we are compelled to seek understanding of anything that so engages the interest of mankind as sport or play. In fact, play has become so important that it can no longer be left exclusively to the players. The influence of games on societies, from "the bloody Roman spectacles" to the staged demonstrations of the modern Olympiad and the Super Bowl[④], is simply staggering. Sport, as one observer has claimed, is the new opiate of the masses, as it has probably always been, though never so freely administered as in the modern world.

Drawing upon earlier works, Paul Weiss[⑤] in *Sport: A Philosophic Inquiry* has grappled admirably with the problem of definitions and provided worthwhile distinctions among sport, play, and game, but does not, and indeed cannot, remove the overlap that exists in the common understanding of the terms. Since time and space do not allow me to delve into the nuances that Weiss establishes, I must, out of necessity, proceed, not on differences of opinion between him and others, but upon some common ground of agreement, with an invitation to the interested scholar to go directly to the sources himself.

"'Sport', 'athletics', 'games', and 'play'," says Weiss, "have in common the idea of

---

① Johan Huizinga (1872—1945)：荷兰历史学家，文化历史学奠基人之一，本文提到的著作 *Homo Ludens* 于 1938 年出版。

② sine qua non: [拉丁] 不可或缺的。

③ 此处借指英国诗人 Alfred Tennyson (1809—92) 的名诗 "Flower in the Crannied Wall": I pluck you out of the crannies, /I hold you here, root and all, in my hand, / Little flower—but if I could understand / What you are, root and all, and all in all, / I should know what God and man is.

④ Super Bowl：超级杯，美国橄榄球联盟(National Football League)举行的年度锦标赛。

⑤ Paul Weiss (1901—2002)：美国哲学家，1946 年执教耶鲁大学，本文所指的著作 *Sport*：*A Philosophic Inquiry* 于 1969 年出版。

being cut off from the workaday world." Here he is in agreement with Huizinga as he is with Roger Caillois[①] who claims that play is *free, separate, uncertain, unproductive*, and governed by both rules and make-believe. "Sport," as Weiss reminds us, "means" to disport, "that is, to divert and amuse." Hence in this study I regard sport as that aspect of culture by which men divert themselves from labor as opposed to work. This important distinction between labor and work is well made by Hannah Arendt[②] in *The Human Condition* in her discussion of the difference between *animal laborans*, laboring animal, and *homo faber*, man the maker or artist, which is so succinctly implied in the phrase "the work of our hands and the labor of our body." Today it is essential to realize that in professional sports, especially in professional sports, the athlete is quite often player, laborer, and artist all, one who laboriously sculpts a life of meaning out of his physical nature. Though lines between different activities frequently become blurred, in this chapter I regard sport as a diversion from labor. I am considering sport as "unnecessary" action in the sense that it is not required for survival as are forms of labor, such as farming. I must also add that I regard sport as an activity that requires the expenditure of a substantial amount of physical energy, more than that needed to play a game of bridge or checkers, though these too are certainly forms of play and diversions from labor.

"What is play? What is serious?" Huizinga asks. The Puritans would have had far less difficulty in answering these questions than we would today. For them, any effort not devoted to the good of the colony was to be eschewed, and games did not seem to lend themselves to the general welfare. In 1621 Governor Bradford[③] rebuked the young men he found "in ye streete at play, openly; some pitching ye barr and some at stooleball, and shuck like sports." There should not be, in the governor's view, any "gameing or revelling in ye streets" nor if we are to judge from the incident of the maypole of Merry Mount any reveling in the country either. "Had the leaders at Plymouth, Salem, and Boston been in Parliament in 1643 they would have voted with the majority that all copies of the *Book of Sports* be seized and burned" (Krout: 10).

The Puritan hostility to games took the form of official prohibition and even punishment. In 1647 in Massachusetts Bay a court order was issued against shuffleboard, and in 1650 the same injunction was extended against "bowling or any other play or games in or about houses of common entertainment" (Manchester: 16). In 1693 in eastern Connecticut a man "was fined twelve shillings and sentenced to six hours in the stocks for playing ball on the Sabbath.... Apparently, either he was playing alone or his teammates were let go with a warning, since he was the only man convicted" (Twombly: 18). The Puritan attitude toward fun and games in the view of many is perhaps best illustrated in Macaulay's[④] remark that bearbaiting was stopped not because it gave

① Roger Caillois (1913—1978):法国学者,对文学批评、哲学和社会学都产生过影响。

② Hannah Arendt (1906—1971):德国犹太裔政治理论家,1941 年为躲避纳粹迫害而移民美国,她的著作主要涉及政治、权力和集权主义等主题。

③ Bradford (1590—1657):全名 William Bradford,早期英国殖民者,曾多次当选普利茅斯长官。

④ Thomas B. Macaulay (1800—1859):英国诗人,历史学家和政治家,在维多利亚时期曾担任财政部主计长等职。

pain to the bear but because it provided pleasure to the spectators.

The "Detestation of Idleness" was not confined toNew England. In Virginia in 1619 "the assembly decreed that any person found idle should be bound over to compulsory work; it prohibited gaming at dice or cards, strictly regulated drinking, provided penalties for excess in apparel and rigidly enforced Sabbath observance"(Dulles: 5). Interdictions against racing within the city limits of New Amsterdam were issued in 1657, and two years later Governor Peter Stuyvesant① proclaimed a day of fast on which would be forbidden "all exercise and games of tennis, ball-playing, hunting, fishing, plowing, and sowing, and moreover all unlawful practices such as dice, drunkenness—" (Manchester: 17). Restriction of activities in some form on Sunday could be found wherever the new American civilization was extended on the frontier.

As John A. Krout, Foster Rhea Dulles, and others have pointed out thetheocracy did not represent all of New England, and the narrow sanctions of the ruling class had in the long run little chance of being obeyed. The human propensity to play could not be stilled. Sport grew not only in New England but all along the frontier. Hunting and fishing flourished frequently as a means gaining food but also as a form of diversion. Forests and rivers seemed to contain an endless supply of game and fish, and many availed themselves of the abundance. "Even Cotton Mather fished. Samuel Sewall tells of the time when the stern old Puritan went out with line and tackle and fell into the water at Spy Pond, 'the boat being ticklish'"(Dulles: 25). For those who have read Mather's prose, this is a pleasing image indeed.

The growth ofrecreation, even during the latter part of the seventeenth century, can be inferred from the journal of Sarah Kembell Knight②, who wrote of her travels through Connecticut in 1704: "Their diversions in this part of the country are on lecture days and training days mostly" on the former there is riding from town to town... and on training days the youth divert themselves by shooting at the targets, as they call it (but is very much resembles a pillory). When he that hits nearest the white has some yards of red ribbon presented to him, which being tied to his hatband, he is led away in triumph, with great applause, as the winners of the Olympiak Games" (Dulles: 29).

At the beginning of the nineteenth century there was a widediversity of amusements in the North, at least as reported by President Timothy Dwight③ of Yale: "The principal amusements of the inhabitants are visiting, dancing, music, conversation, walking, riding, sailing, shooting at a mark, draughts, chess, and unhappily, in some of the larger towns, cards and dramatic exhibitions... Our Countrymen also fish and hunt. Journeys and young men play at foot-ball, cricket, quoits, and at many other sports of an athletic cast, and in the winter are peculiarly fond of skating. Riding in a sleigh, or sledges, is also a favorite diversion in New England" (Saveth: 72—3). Ninepins, skittles, and bowls were common at inns in the North for the convenience of

---

① Peter Stuyvesant (c. 1612—1672):荷兰早期殖民者,曾任新阿姆斯特丹长官。

② Sarah Kembell Knight (1666—1727):早期殖民时期波士顿女教师,其日记详细记述了当时的世态人情。

③ Timothy Dwight (1752—1817):美国教育家、学者,曾任耶鲁大学第八任校长(1795—1817)。

the guests, while in the South shooting matches were preferred, with "beef shooting" being one of the favorite forms.

The sports that seemed to attract the most attention in the South, however, were cockfighting and horse-racing. According to Hugh Jones in 1724, "the common planters don't much admire labour or any other manly exercise except Horse racing, nor diversion, except Cock-Fighting, in which some greatly delight." In tones suggestive of William Byrd, he adds, "This Way of Living and the Heat of the Summer make some very lazy, who are then said to be Climate-struck" (Dulles: 35).

While the foreign traveler, especially the English, as Henry Adams① notes, "charged the Virginians with fondness for horse-racing and cock-fighting, betting and drinking, … the popular habit which most shocked them, and with which books of travel filled pages of description was the so-called rough and tumble fight. The practice was not one on which authors seemed likely to dwell; yet foreigners like Weld, and Americans like Judge Longstreet in 'Georgia Scenes' united to give it a sort of grotesque dignity like that of the bull-fight, and under their treatment it became interesting as a popular habit" (Saveth: 74).

The rough and tumble, Adams argues, did not originate in Virginia, but came to America from England, as did, according to Jennie Holliman, most American sports, excepting those practices learned from the Indians, such as methods of hunting and trapping deer and bear, the use of bows and arrows, fishing at night with lights on canoes, lacrosse, and even rolling the hoop. Still the predominant influence was from abroad. The gun itself is a good example. "Up to 1830," says Holliman, "a few fine guns had been made in America, but they did not sell to an advantage simply because they were not imported." The same was true for fishing equipment, twine, tackles, hooks, flies, and rods, which came from Holland as well as England. Sleighs also came from Holland while bridles, harness, and saddles came from England" (Holliman: 6-7).

Cockfighting eventually disappeared in the South except in a few isolated areas but horse-racing, as everyone knows, has grown into both a major sport and industry with interest in the Triple Crown② equaling that of the World Series and the Super Bowl. Wagering for the 1977 Kentucky Derby exceeded $3,500,000, breaking all previous records.

The history of horse-racing has to a large extent been the history of selective breeding of which Diomed and Messenger③ provide excellent examples. Diomed was brought to Virginia in 1798 and came to be held in such esteem that his death in 1808 caused almost as much mourning as that for Washington in 1799. Messenger, bred by the Earl of Grosvenor on his Yorkshire farm,

---

① Henry Adams (1838—1918):美国学者、小说家和历史学家,其最主要著作包括《亨利·亚当斯的教育》。

② Triple Crown: 美国"三冠王",包括肯塔基德比赛(Kentucky Derby)、普瑞克尼斯奖金赛(Preakness Stakes)和贝尔蒙特奖金赛(Belmont Stakes)三项经典赛马比赛。

③ Diomed (1777—1808):英国著名纯血马,英国艾普逊德比赛冠军,后来作为种公马被引入美国;Messenger (1780—1808),英国纯血马,美国独立战争后不久作为种马引入参加繁育。

was brought to America a few years after the Revolution by Thomas Berger of Pennsylvania. Prized as a stud, Messenger was the sire of a long line of racing immortals, including American Eclipse, who defeated Sir Henry of Virginia at the Union course on Long Island in 1823, the first intersectional race that illustrated once and for all the popular appeal of the sport. Another offspring of Messenger was Hambletonian, the horse that turned harness racing into a national mania. "In the 1850's, the nation worshipped Hambletonian. It bought commemorative plates on which his likeness was inscribed. Children talked about him as if he were human" (Twombly: 30). Spurred on by the creation of Jockey clubs, the establishment of race courses, and support of the aristocracy, horse-racing became America's first organized sport and has remained unquestionably one of its most popular.

The wide interest in the turf helped to bring about the rise of sporting literature in the three decades before the Civil War. The first sporting magazine in America was the *American Turf Register*, published in Baltimore in 1829 by John Stuart Skinner①. Ten years later Skinner sold the *Register to* William Trotter Porter② who had already begun his own weekly sporting publication called *Spirit of the Times*, one of the most famous of all American publications and a reservoir of history of American popular culture from 1831 to 1861. Prominent among contributors to this magazine was Thomas B. Thorpe, who inaugurated "the Big Bear school of humor," and the Englishman Henry William Herbert③ who wrote under the pen name of "Frank Forester" and who introduced "something of the English point of view of sport for sport's sake" (Manchester: 77).

Baseball, like horse-racing, has its roots in the nineteenth century and also like horse-racing owes more perhaps to the English than we are inclined to admit. The myth that Abner Doubleday④ invented baseball is totally without foundation. "The rules of baseball attributed to Doubleday in 1839 were identical to those in a rule book for the English game of rounders published in London in 1827" (Twombly: 43). In America rounders became known as town ball and was played at Harvard as early as 1829. In *The Book of Sport* (1827) Robert Carver related that many Britons, like the Americans, were calling the game by a new name, "base ball," and that it was "becoming a distinct threat to cricket." Both the game and the new name caught on quickly in America, and by the 1850s the *Spirit of the Times* was calling it "The National Game." By the 1880s daily attendance at the games was some sixty thousand. It has become "far and away the leading spectator sport."

As Foster Rhea Dulles has observed, the role of colleges in the rise of sports in the decades after the Civil War was not one of leadership. The only sport that undergraduates developed was football, and again the English influence is incontrovertible. Basketball, in fact, is the only

① John Stuart Skinner (1788—1851):美国著名律师、出版商和编辑。

② William Trotter Porter (1809—1858):美国体育记者和报纸编辑,早期体育杂志创办人。

③ Henry William Herbert (1807—1858):英国小说家和体育专栏作家。

④ Abner Doubleday (1819—1893):美国军官,美国内战中任盟军将领,许多人将棒球的创立归功于他。

James A. Naismith, the inventor of basketball.
篮球发明者奈史密斯博士也是一位伟大的教练。

popular American ball game whose origins are not English, being invented by James A. Naismith① in Springfield, Massachusetts, in 1891. American football evolved from soccer to Rugby to "American" Rugby and finally to the game we know today. While the basic forms derived from England, the Americans had long demonstrated a fondness for games of mayhem. Harvard, for example, "had a festival in the early 1800's which qualified vaguely as football. It was called Bloody Monday, but the upperclassmen mostly kicked the freshmen and only occasionally the ball" (Dulles: 223-24). Though it was essentially soccer instead of Rugby, what is called the first intercollegiate football game took place in 1869 between Princeton and Rutgers at New Brunswick. Rutgers won, no thanks to the player who, becoming confused and endearing himself to all future generations, kicked the ball through Princeton's goal. The first contest was played before a small crowd but approximately twenty years later Princeton played Yale before a crowd of almost forty thousand. Thus long before the turn of the century football was well established as a mass spectator sport.

The one overriding fact concerning sport in America is its phenomenal growth. From William Bradford's injunction against games on Christmas Day in 1621 to Super Sunday 1977 there has been a complete reversal of attitudes. A few facts on salaries of the super stars tell much of the story. Fran Tarkenton estimates his net worth at \$7,000,000, Kareem Abdul-Jabbar is earning \$2,500,000 for five years with the Lakers, Jim "Catfish" Hunter \$1,000,000 more than that for the same period of time with the Yankees, and Muhammad Ali grossed over \$16,000,000 in 1976②.

Muhammad Ali vs. Sonny Liston.
前世界拳王阿里宣传照片。

How did such changes occur? No one seems to be able to offer any conclusive answers except the human love of sport and the need for heroes. One thing is undeniable, however, and that is the contention that the widespread acceptance of sport was brought about in part by the revolution in technology in the decades after the Civil War. Says John R. Betts, "Ante-bellum sport had capitalized on the development of the steamboat, the railroad, the telegraph, and the penny press, and in succeeding decades the role of technology in the

---

① James A. Naismith (1861—1939): 加拿大裔美国人，创立了篮球运动并最早制定了其规则。

② Fran Tarkenton (1940—): 美国职业橄榄球运动员，退役后曾创立软件开发公司；Kareem Abdul-Jabbar (1947—)，美国 NBA 退役球员，1969 年入选 NBA，曾分别效力于密尔沃基雄鹿队(1969-75)和洛杉矶湖人队(1975—89)；Jim "Catfish" Hunter (1946—1999)，美国棒球运动员，曾于 1975 至 1979 年效力于纽约 Yankees 棒球队；Muhammad Ali (1942—)，美国前拳击手，曾三次夺得世界超重量级冠军，被认为是美国有史以来最伟大的拳击手之一。

rise of sport proved even more significant. ”

Of major importance in the promotion of sports has been the press, a major product of technology. Following the lead of the *Spirit of the Times*, new periodicals drawing attention to sport began to appear after the war. Among these were *Baseball Magazine, Golfer's Magazine, Yachting, and Saturday Evening Post*. Newspapers from coast to coast began to devote more and more space to sports until finally they had a section of their own. ” Frank Luther Mott① designated the years 1892—1914 as a period in news-paper history when sporting news underwent remarkable development, being segregated on special pages, with special makeup pictures, and news writing style. ” Books, too, continued to arouse interest, especially among the younger generation. Among the many writers bringing dreams of fair play and heroism to millions of American youth were Gilbert Patten (Burt L. Standish), Henry Barbour, Zane Grey, and Edward Stratemeyer②. The champion producer of all in this group of juvenile writers was Gilbert Patten who wrote a Frank Merriwell③ story once a week for nearly twenty years and had only one nervous breakdown. Estimates of the sales of Merriwell novels run as high as five hundred million copies.

The press helped bring together heroes and hero worshippers, but other developments also played crucial roles in the expansion of sports. It would be hard, for example, to overestimate the importance of the railroad and the telegraph in the spread of games. Because of the growing rail network, the Cincinnati Red Stockings④ could travel from Maine to California, and John L. Sullivan⑤ could go on a grand tour of athletic clubs, opera houses, and theaters. Revolution in mass transit meant mass audiences, and for those who could not come to the games the telegraph provided instant news of results. The Atlantic cable, electrification, radio, and television all influenced sport in profound ways that are still only vaguely understood. Because of technology the city of New Orleans could build in 1974 a bronzed-topped stadium with a gigantic screen for instant replays at a total cost of over $285,000,000. As Wells Twombly asks, “Was this only the beginning…or was it the end?”

---

① Frank Luther Mott (1888—1964)：美国历史学家和新闻教育家，曾任爱荷华大学大学新闻系主任多年，1942年被任命为密苏里大学新闻学院院长。

② Gilbert Patten (1866—1945)：美国作家，笔名 Burt L. Standish，创作了众多关于 Frank Merriwell 的脍炙人口的故事；Henry Barbour (1870—1944)，美国作家，创作了大量体育故事通俗读物；Zane Grey (1872—1939)，美国作家，以创作冒险小说和英雄人物故事见长；Edward Stratemeyer (1862—1930)，美国出版商和儿童题材作家。

③ Frank Merriwell：Gilbert Patten 在其连环故事中塑造的主人公，他是体育健将，更是匡扶正义的英雄。

④ 俄亥俄州的辛辛那提红衣球队成立于1869，是美国首个职业棒球队。

⑤ John L. Sullivan (1858—1918)：美国超重量级拳击手，也是拳击改戴手套前的最后一位赤拳搏击冠军。

Works Cited

Arendt, Hannah. *The Human Condition*. Chicago: University of Chicago Press, 1958, p. 85.

Betts, John R. *America's Sporting Heritage,* 1850-1950. Reading, Mass.: Addison-Wesley, 1974.

Caillois, Roger. *Man, Play, and Games*. Translated by Meyer Barash. New York: Free Press, 1961.

Dulles, Foster Rhea. *America Learns to Play: A History of Popular Recreation, 1607-1940*. New York: Appleton-Century, 1940.

Edwards, Harry. *The Revolt of the Black Athlete*. New York: Free Press, 1969.

Finley, M. I., and H. W. Pleket. *The Olympic Games: The First Thousand Years*. New York: Viking, 1976.

Gardiner, E. Norman. *Athletics of the Ancient World*. London: Oxford University Press, 1930.

Haley, Bruce. *Sports and the Victorian World*. Western Humanities Review, 22 (1968), p. 115-25.

Henderson, Robert W. *Early American Sport*. New York: The Grolier Club, 1937. Reprint. Cranbury, N. J.: Associated University Presses, 1977.

Holliman, Jennie. *American Sports (1785-1835)*. 1931. Reprint. Philadelphia: Porcupine Press, 1975.

Huizinga, Johan. *Homo Ludens: A Study of the Play Element in Culture*. Boston: Beacon, 1960.

Kaye, Ivan. *Good Clean Violence: A History of College Football*. Philadelphia: Lippincott, 1973.

Krout, John A. *Annals of American Sport,* Vol. 15, Pageant of America Series. New Haven, Conn.: Yale University Press, 1929.

Lardner, John. *White Hopes and Other Tigers*. Philadelphia: Lippincott, 1956.

Manchester, Herbert. *Four Centuries of American Sport, 1490-1890*. 1931. Reprint. New York: Benjamin Bloom, 1968.

Menke, Frank G. *The Encyclopedia of Sport*. 5th ed. Cranbury, N. J.: A. S. Barnes, 1975.

Olsen, Jack. *The Black Athlete: A Shameful Story*. New York: Time-Life Books, 1968.

Patten, Cilbert (Burt L. Standish). *Frank Merriwell's "Father": An Autobiography* (Norman: University of Oklahoma Press, 1964), p. 181.

Robinson, Rachel S. *Sources for the History of Greek Athletics*. Cincinnati, Ohio: University of Cincinnati Press, 1955.

Rosenstein, Jay. "Sweating Cold", *Playboy*, April 1977, pp. 106, 112, 238-240.

Saveth, Edward N. (ed.), "The United States in 1800", Henry Adams: The Education Of Henry Adams and Other Selected Writings (New York: Washington Square Press), p. 72-73.

Scott, Jack. *The Athletic Revolution*. New York: Free Press, 1971.

Strutt, Joseph. *The Sports and Pastimes of the People of England*. 1833. Reprint. New York: A. M. Kelley, 1970.

Twombly, Wells. *200 Years of Sport in America* (New York: McGraw-Hill, 1976), p. 18.

Weiss, Paul. *Sport: A Philosophic Inquiry* (Carbondale: Southern Illinois University Press, 1969), p. 134.

Chapter 6 Film

Making Hollywood Dreams
电影:制造"好莱坞"梦

It's Friday night. You park in an exhausted-filled subterranean garage① or a vast asphalt lot② surrounding a mall. You make your way into the neon-lit mega-eight-plex③, where you and a companion or two pay half a day's salary for tickets, a tub of artery-clogging popcorn, and a couple of ten-gallon sodas. You wind your way through a maze of corridors to the theater of your choice, where a psychedelic montage④ filling the screen is soon replaced by the first of an interminable series of quick-cutting, MTV-style previews, as you bathe in rolling quadraphonic surround-sound⑤. You sink into your space-age plastic seat and kick back, surrending to the waves of sound and images…

Such is moviegoing of the 1990s and still so in the first decade of the new century. Gone are the nickel matinee⑥ and the discount double-feature⑦, newsreel⑧, cartoons, and comic short subjects, and the driven-in⑨, where many a pair of teenagers learned human anatomy in the back seat of a Chevy⑩.

The external trappings of the moviegoing experience may have changed, but the reasons people go are still pretty much the same: to get out of the house and escape the routine of their daily lives; to be part of a communal group sharing an experience; to find a romantic setting where conversation is at a minimum; to indulge, for one night, in an orgy of junk food; and, above all, to be entertained and, perhaps, touched emotionally. So strong is the draw of motion pictures that

---

① an exhausted-filled subterranean garage: 停满车的地下车库。

② a vast asphalt lot: 沥青铺的大型停车场,此处指露天停车场。

③ mega-eight-plex: 有八个大型剧场的电影院。

④ montage:蒙太奇在法语是"剪接"的意思,指一种电影中镜头组合的理论。蒙太奇一般包括画面剪辑和画面合成两方面,电影将一系列在不同地点,从不同距离和角度,以不同方法拍摄的镜头排列组合起来,叙述情节,刻画人物。当不同的镜头组接在一起时,往往会产生各个镜头单独存在时所不具有的含义。

⑤ quadraphonic surround-sound: 四声道环绕声。

⑥ nickel matinee: 票价为 5 美分的日场电影。

⑦ double feature: (电影)两场连映。

⑧ newsreel:(旧时在电影院播放的)新闻短片。

⑨ driven-in: 影院、餐厅、银行等的免下车服务,此处指可坐在车内观看的露天影院。

⑩ Chevy:雪佛兰,汽车品牌。

Americans fork over billions of dollars a year on domestic movies alone.

As there are many reasons for going to the movie, so there are many ways of explaining their popularity and studying their influence within the fabric of contemporary culture. From a sociological perspective, movies can reflect, define, or even redefine social norms, and—in the work of politically focused filmmakers like Spike Lee①—depict urgent social problems within the relative safety of the big screen. From a psychological perspective, viewers identify with the character and project their own feelings into the action, giving them a deep emotional connection to a protagonist along with feelings of tension and, ultimately release. From a literary perspective, movies can be interpreted in terms of genres—horror movies, or crime drama or menaced-female stories—or in terms of plot, characterization, imagery, and so forth. From an economic perspective, movies may be seen primarily as a consumable product, defined solely by the marketplace. To the cultural critic, this economic influence might seem to be negative, reducing a potentially powerful artistic form to the lowest common denominator. The capitalist observer might see such forces as positive, however, because they encourage the worldwide spread of American cultural values. Finally, from a semiological perspective, movies are ripe with symbolic imagery, from the multiple associations possible in a character's name to the way images are juxtaposed in the editing. On the other hand, interpreting a movie or a group of movies is not unlike interpreting a television program or group of programs. Here too you must suspend any personal feelings of aesthetic judgments that you may have about your subject. As with any semiotic analysis, your object is to interpret the cultural significance of your topic, not to give it a thumbs up or a thumbs down. Thus, you may find it more rewarding to interpret those films that promise to be culturally meaningful rather than simply choosing your favorite flick. Determining whether a movie is culturally meaningful in the prewriting stage, of course, may be something of a hit-or-miss affair; you may find that your first choice does not present you with any particularly interesting grounds for interpretation. That's why it can be helpful to consider factors—such as enormous popularity or widespread critical attention—that seem to set off a particular movie as being special. Of course, cult favorites, while often lacking in critical or popular attention, can also be signs pointing toward their more self-selected audiences and so are perfectly good candidates for analysis. Academy Award candidates are also pretty reliable as cultural signs.

The readings in this chapter focus on different aspects of film criticism and the art and business of moviemaking in the United States. Linda Seger follows with a screenwriter's how-to-do-it guide for the creation of the kind of archetypal characters that made *Star Wars* one of the most popular movies of all time. The secret of film making as a sort of "myth" is uncovered in her article. Gary Johnson offers a historical survey of the Western, one of the most archetypal and iconographic of Hollywood genres. The next selection tackles racial issues, with Jessica Hagedorn

---

① Spike Lee：斯派克·李（1957—），美国著名黑人导演。他所涉及的题材大都与黑人的出路、觉醒、种族歧视有关。

surveying a tradition of American filmmaking in which Asian women are presented as either tragic or trivial. The chapter ends up with Sidney Pollack's profound analysis of both commercial and artistic features of filmmaking in Hollywood.

As you read and think about film and the film industry, you may find that you want to pick and choose among these various approaches, incorporating parts of any number of them into your own theoretical analyses.

Moviegoing is America's NO. 1 leisure activity—97% of moviegoers go with at least one other person. 69% of all Americans go to the movies at least once every year. Characters on screen can serve a social function for moviegoers. When people watch a film, they show physiological evidence of empathizing with characters.

看电影是美国人首选的娱乐休闲方式。据统计,97% 的美国人会和家人或朋友一起去看电影,69% 的美国人每年至少去一次电影院。看电影时,他们会随着电影情节的发展或欢喜,或悲伤。

Lesson 17 Creating the Myth
制造神话

LINDA SEGER

Introduction

To be a successful screenwriter, Linda Seger, a script consultant and author who has given professional seminars on filmmaking around the world, suggests in this selection from *Making a Good Script Great* (1987), you've got to know your archetypes. Seger reveals the secret behind the success of such Hollywood creations as *Star Wars*'s Luke Skywalker① and tells you how you can create such heroes yourself. In this "how to" approach to the cinema, Seger echoes the more academic judgments of such semioticians of film as Umberto Eco②—the road to popular success in mass culture is paved with cultural myths and clichés.

Text

All of us have similar experiences. We share in the life journey of growth, development, and transformation. We live the same stories, whether they involve the search for a perfect mate, coming home, the search for fulfillment, going after an ideal, achieving the dream, or hunting for a precious treasure. Whatever our culture, there are universal stories that form the basis for all our particular stories. The trappings might be different, the twists and turns that create suspense might change from culture to culture, the particular characters may take different forms, but underneath it all, it's the same story, drawn from the same experiences.

Many of the most successful films are based on these universal stories. They deal with the basic journey we take in life. We identify with the heroes because we were once heroic (descriptive) or because we wish we could do what the hero does (prescriptive). When Joan Wilder③ finds the jewel and saves her sister, or James Bond④ saves the world, or Shane⑤ saves the family from the evil ranchers, we identify with the character, and subconsciously recognize the

---

① Luke Skywalker: 美国科幻系列片《星球大战》(*Star Wars*)主要人物,下文提到的 Princess Leia, Obi-Wan Kenobi, R2D2, Darth Vader 等均为片中角色。

② Umberto Eco (1932—):意大利符号学家和作家,其学术代表作为《开放的作品》。

③ Joan Wilder: 美国惊险片《绿宝石》(*Romancing the Stone*, 1984)及其续集《尼罗河宝石》(*The Jewel of the Nile*,1985)女主角。

④ James Bond:系列小说和电影 007 的男主角。其身份是英国情报机构军情六处(MI6)的特务,代号 007。

⑤ *Shane*:美国西部片《原野奇侠》(*Shane*, 1953)男主角。

story as having some connection with our own lives. It's the same story as the fairy tales about getting the three golden hairs from the devil, or finding the treasure and winning the princess. And it's not all that different a story from the caveman killing the woolly beast or the Roman slave gaining his freedom through skill and courage. These are our stories—personally and collectively—and the most successful films contain these universal experiences.

Some of these stories are "search" stories. They address our desire to find some kind of rare and wonderful treasure. This might include the search for outer values such as job, relationship, or success, or for inner values such as respect, security, self expression, love, or home. But it's all a similar search.

Some of these stories are "hero" stories. They come from our own experiences of overcoming adversity as well as our desire to do great and special acts. We root for the hero and celebrate when he or she achieves the goal because we know that the hero's journey is in many ways similar to our own.

We call these stories *myths*. Myths are the common stories at the root of our universal existence. They're found in all cultures and in all literature, ranging from the Greek myths to fairy tales, legends, and stories drawn from all of the world's religions.

A myth is a story that is "more than true." Many stories are true because one person, somewhere, at some time, lived it. It is based on fact. But a myth is more than true because it is lived by all of us, at some level. It's a story that connects and speaks to us all.

Some myths are true stories that attain mythic significance because the people involved seem larger than life, and seem to live their lives more intensely than common folk. Martin Luther King, Jr. [①], Gandhi[②], Sir Edmund Hillary[③], and Lord Mountbatten[④] personify the types of journeys we identify with, because we've taken similar journeys—even if only in a very small way.

Other myths revolve around make-believe characters who might capsulize for us the sum total of many of our journeys. Some of these make-believe characters might seem similar to the characters we meet in our dreams. Or they might be a composite of types of characters we've met.

In both cases, the myth is the "story beneath the story." It's the universal pattern that shows us that Gandhi's journey toward independence and Sir Edmund Hillary's journey to the top of Mount Everest contain many of the same dramatic beats. And these beats are the same beats that

---

① Martin Luther King, Jr. (1929—1968): 小马丁·路德·金,美国著名民权运动领袖。

② Gandhi (1869—1948): 莫罕达斯·卡拉姆昌德·甘地(Mohandas Karamchand Gandhi),尊称圣雄甘地,印度民族主义运动和国大党领袖。

③ Sir Edmund Hillary (1919—2008): 著名登山家,生于新西兰的奥克兰,1953 年 5 月 29 日和尼泊尔夏尔巴人丹增(Tenzing)创造了人类首次登顶珠峰的历史。

④ Lord Mountbatten (1900—1979):L. Louis Mountbatten,英国海军元帅,1942 年任盟军联合作战司令,1943 年起任东南亚战区盟军总司令,率部收复缅甸。1947 年任印度总督,提出"蒙巴顿方案",使印度和巴基斯坦分治。1979 年在爱尔兰被炸身亡。

Rambo takes to set free the MIAs①, that Indiana Jones takes to find the Lost Ark②, and that Luke Skywalker takes to defeat the Evil Empire.

Indiana Jones is the central protagonist of the Indiana Jones franchise. Since his first appearance in *Raiders of the Lost Ark,* he has become a worldwide star. In 2003, he was ranked as the second greatest movie hero of all time by the American Film Institute.

印第安纳·琼斯是系列惊险片《印第安纳·琼斯》(又译《夺宝奇兵》系列)主人公。自其在《夺宝奇兵1》之《法柜奇兵》出现以来,已成为世界知名的电影人物。2003年,印第安纳·琼斯位列美国电影学会评选的银幕英雄第二名。

In *Hero with a Thousand Faces*, Joseph Campbell③ traces the elements that form the hero myth. "In their own work with myth, writer Chris Vogler④ and seminar leader Thomas Schlesinger⑤ have applied this criteria to *Star Wars*. The myth within the story helps explain why millions went to see this film again and again."

The hero myth has specific story beats that occur in all hero stories. They show who the hero is, what the hero needs, and how the story and character interact in order to create a transformation. The journey toward heroism is a process. This universal process forms the spine of all the particular stories, such as the *Star Wars* trilogy.

The Hero Myth

1. In most hero stories, the hero is introduced in ordinary surroundings, in a mundane world, doing mundane things. Generally, the hero begins as a non-hero, innocent, young, simple, or humble. In *Star Wars*, the first time we see Luke Skywalker, he's unhappy about having to do his chores, which consists of picking out some new droids for work. He wants to go out and have fun. He wants to leave his planet and go to the Academy, but he's stuck. This is the setup of most myths. This is how we meet the hero before the call to adventure.

① Rambo takes to set free the MIAs:在美国著名动作片明星史泰隆(Sylvester Stallone)主演的影片《第一滴血2》(1985)中,主人公兰博前往越南解救战俘。MIA: Missing in Action,战斗中的失踪人员。

② Indiana Jones takes to find the Lost Ark:《夺宝奇兵》(*Raiders of the Lost Ark*)是好莱坞著名的寻宝题材影片,1981年度票房冠军。片中主人公印第安纳·琼斯(Indiana Jones)是考古学教授,受美国军方所托寻找"法柜"。

③ Joseph Campbell (1904—1987): 美国著名学者、神话学大师。《千面英雄》(*The Hero with a Thousand Faces*, 1948)是奠定其在神话学权威地位的巨著,是神话学的经典作品。

④ Chris Vogler: 好莱坞知名剧本顾问,长期从事剧本预读、挑选和创作,著有剧作家创作指南 *The Writer's Journey: Mythic Structure For Writers*。

⑤ Thomas Schlesinger:好莱坞知名剧本顾问、剧作家,并长期从事剧本创作教学与研讨工作。

2. Then something new enters the hero's life. It's a catalyst that sets the story into motion. It might be a telephone call, as in *Romancing the Stone*, or the German attack in *The African Queen*, or the holograph of Princess Leia in *Star Wars*. Whatever form it takes, it's a new ingredient that pushes the hero into an extraordinary adventure. With this call, the stakes are established, and a problem is introduced that demands a solution.

3. Many times, however, the hero doesn't want to leave. He or she is a reluctant hero, afraid of the unknown, uncertain, perhaps, if he or she is up to the challenge. In *Star Wars* Luke receives a double call to adventure. First, from Princess Leia in the holograph, and then through Obi-Wan Kenobi, who says he needs Luke's help. But Luke is not ready to go. He returns home, only to find that the Imperial Stormtroopers have burned his farmhouse and slaughtered his family. Now he is personally motivated, ready to enter into the adventure.

4. In any journey, the hero usually receives help, and the help often comes from unusual sources. In many fairy tales, an old woman, a dwarf, a witch, or a wizard helps the hero. The hero achieves the goal because of this help, and because the hero is receptive to what this person has to give.

There are a number of fairy tales where the first and second son are sent to complete a task, but they ignore the helpers, often scorning them. Many times they are severely punished for their lack of humility and unwillingness to accept help. Then the third son, the hero, comes along. He receives the help, accomplishes the task, and often wins the princess.

In *Star Wars*, Obi-Wan Kenobi is a perfect example of the "helper" character. He is a kind of mentor to Luke, one who teaches him the Way of the Force and whose teachings continue even after his death. This mentor character appears in most hero stories. He is the person who has special knowledge, special information, and special skills. This might be the prospector in *The Treasure of the Sierra Madre*① or the psychiatrist in *Ordinary People*②, or Quint *in Jaws*③, who knows all about sharks, or the Good Witch of the North who gives Dorothy the ruby slippers in *The Wizard of OZ*④. In *Star Wars*, Obi-Wan gives Luke the light saber that was the special weapon of the Jedi Knight. With this, Luke is ready to move forward and do his training and meet adventure.

5. The hero is now ready to move into the special world where he or she will change from the ordinary into the extraordinary. This starts the hero's transformation, and sets up the obstacles that must be surmounted to reach the goal. Usually, this happens at the first Turning Point of the story and leads into Act Two development. In *Star Wars*, Obi-Wan and Luke search for a pilot to take them to the planet of Alderaan, so that Obi-Wan can deliver the plans to Princess Leia's father. These plans are essential to the survival of the Rebel Forces. With this action, the adventure is

① *The Treasure of the Sierra Madre*:《碧血金沙》(1948),亨弗莱·鲍嘉(Humphrey Bogart)主演。

② *Ordinary People*:罗伯特·雷德福(Robert Redford)1980 年拍摄的导演处女作《普通人》,该片获当年奥斯卡最佳导演及最佳影片奖。

③ *Jaws*:著名导演斯皮尔伯格(Steven Spielberg)1975 年拍摄的首部惊险巨制《大白鲨》。

④ *The Wizard of OZ:* 电影《绿野仙踪》(1939)。

ready to begin.

6. Now begin all the tests and obstacles necessary to overcome the enemy and accomplish the hero's goals. In fairy tales, this often means getting past witches, outwitting the devil, avoiding robbers, or confronting evil. In Homer's *Odyssey* it means blinding the Cyclops①, escaping from the island of the Lotus-Eaters②, resisting the temptation of the singing Sirens③, and surviving a shipwreck. In *Star Wars* innumerable adventures confront Luke. He and his cohorts must run to the *Millennium Falcon*, narrowly escaping the Stormtroopers before jumping into hyperspace. They must make it through the meteor shower after Alderaan has been destroyed. They must evade capture on the Death Star, rescue the Princess, and even survive a garbage crusher.

7. At some point in the story the hero often hits rock bottom. He often has a "death experience," leading to a type of rebirth. In *Star Wars* Luke seems to have died when the serpent in the garbage-masher pulls him under, but he's saved just in time to ask R2D2 to stop the masher before they're crushed. This is often the "black moment" at the second turning point, the point when the worst is confronted, and the action now moves toward the exciting conclusion.

Star Wars is an American epic space opera franchise conceived by George Lucas. The first film in the franchise was originally released on May 25, 1977, by 20th Century Fox, and became a worldwide pop culture phenomenon, followed by two sequels, released at three-year intervals.

Sixteen years after the release of the trilogy's final film, the first in a new prequel trilogy of films was released, again released at three-year intervals, with the final film released on May 19, 2005.

《星球大战》是美国著名导演—制作人乔治·卢卡斯所制作拍摄的一系列科幻电影。从1970年代到1980年代,卢卡斯出品了《星球大战》三部曲,1990年代末开始他拍摄了最初的三部曲之前的故事,又叫"星战前传"。自1977年首部星战片上映以来,星战系列影片及漫画、游戏等相关产品已成为全球性的流行文化现象。图为《星球大战前传3:西斯的复仇》(Episode III-REVENGE OF THE SITH,2005)。

8. Now, the hero seizes the sword and takes possession of the treasure. He is now in charge, but he still has not completed the journey. Here Luke has the Princess and the plans, but the final confrontation is yet to begin. This starts the third-act escape scene, leading to the final climax.

9. The road back is often the chase scene. In many fairy tales, this is the point where the devil chases the hero and the hero has the last obstacles to overcome before really being free and safe.

① Cyclops:荷马史诗《奥德赛》中的独眼巨人。

② the island of Lotus-Eaters:《奥德赛》中讲到,离开特洛伊城的第10天,奥德修斯和他的随从来到了一个岛上。岛上的居民只以莲花(忘忧树)的果实和花为食物。这种神奇的植物魔力极大,谁只要吃了它,就会忘记往事,陷入恍恍惚惚的昏睡状态。

③ Sirens:《奥德赛》中的塞壬女妖,常用歌声诱惑过路的航海者而使航船触礁沉没,船员则成为塞壬的腹中餐。

His challenge is to take what he has learned and integrate it into his daily life. He must return to renew the mundane world. In *Star Wars*, Darth Vader is in hot pursuit, planning to blow up the Rebel Planet.

10. Since every hero story is essentially a transformation story, we need to see the hero changed at the end, resurrected into a new type of life. He must face the final ordeal before being "reborn" as the hero, proving his courage and becoming transformed. This is the point, in many fairy tales, where the Miller's Son becomes the Prince or the King and marries the Princess. In *Star Wars*, Luke has survived, becoming quite a different person from the innocent young man he was in Act One.

At this point, the hero returns and is reintegrated into his society. In *Star Wars*, Luke has destroyed the Death Star, and he receives his great reward.

This is the classic "Hero Story". We might call this example a *mission* or *task myth*, where the person has to complete a task, but the task itself is not the real treasure. The real reward for Luke is the love of the Princess and the safe, new world he had helped create.

A myth can have many variations. We see variations on this myth in James Bond films (although they lack much of the depth because the hero is not transformed), and in *The African Queen*①, where Rose and Allnutt must blow up the *Louisa*, or in *Places in the Heart*②, where Edna overcomes obstacles to achieve family stability.

The *treasure myth* is another variation on this theme, as seen in *Romancing the Stone*. In this story Joan receives a map and a phone call which forces her into the adventure. She is helped by an American birdcatcher and a Mexican pickup truck driver. She overcomes the obstacles of snakes, the jungle, waterfalls, shootouts, and finally receives the treasure, along with the "prince."

Whether the hero's journey is for a treasure or to complete a task, the elements remain the same. The humble, reluctant hero is called to an adventure. The hero is helped by a variety of unique characters. S/he must overcome a series of obstacles that transform him or her in the process, and then faces the final challenge that draws on inner and outer resources.

The Healing Myth

Although the hero myth is the most popular story, many myths involve healing. In these stories, some character is "broken" and must leave home to become whole again.

The universal experience behind these healing stories is our psychological need for rejuvenation, for balance. The journey of the hero into exile is not all that different from the weekend in Palm Springs③, or the trip to Hawaii to get away from it all, or lying still in a hospital

① *The African Queen:* 美国影片《非洲女王号》(1951)。Rose 和 Allnutt 为片中女主角和男主角名。

② *Places in the Heart:* 美国影片《我心深处》(1984),Edna 为片中女主角名。

③ Palm Springs: 棕榈泉,美国科罗拉多沙漠的 Coachella 山谷内的绿洲城市,著名度假胜地。

bed for some weeks to heal. In all cases, something is out of balance and the mythic journey moves toward wholeness.

Being broken can take several forms. It can be physical, emotional, or psychological. Usually it's all three in the process of being exiled or hiding out in the forest, the desert, or even the Amish farm in *Witness*①, the person becomes whole, balanced, and receptive to love. Love in these stories is both a healing force and a reward …

Combination Myths

Many stories are combinations of several different myths. Think of *Ghostbusters*②, a simple and rather outrageous comedy about three men saving the city of New York from ghosts. Now think of the story of "Pandora's Box." It's about the woman who let loose all manner of evil upon the earth by opening a box she was told not to touch. In *Ghostbusters*, the EPA③ man is a Pandora figure. By shutting off the power to the containment center, he inadvertently unleashes all the ghosts upon New York City. Combine the story of "Pandora's Box" with a hero story and notice that we have our three heroes battling the Marshmallow Man. One of them also "gets the Princess" when Dr. Peter Venkman finally receives the affections of Dana Barrett. By looking at these combinations, it is apparent that even *Ghostbusters* is more than "just a comedy".

*Tootsie*④ is a type of reworking of many Shakespearean stories where a woman has to dress as a man in order to accomplish a certain task. These Shakespearean stories are reminiscent of many fairy tales where the hero becomes invisible or takes on another persona, or wears a specific disguise to hide his or her real qualities. In the stories of "The Twelve Dancing Princesses" or "The Man in the Bearskin," disguise is necessary to achieve a goal. Combine these elements with the transformation themes of the hero myth where a hero (such as Michael) must overcome many obstacles to his success as an actor and a human being. It's not difficult to understand why the *Tootsie* story hooks us.

Archetypes

A myth includes certain characters that we see in many stories. These characters are called *archetypes*. They can be thought of as the original "pattern" or "character type" that will be found on the hero's journey. Archetypes take many forms, but they tend to fall within specific categories.

Earlier, we discussed some of the helpers who give advice to help the hero—such as the wise old man who possesses special knowledge and often serves as a mentor to the hero.

The female counterpart of the wise old man is the good mother. Whereas the wise old man has

---

① *Witness*:美国惊险片《目击证人》(1985)。

② *Ghostbusters*:美国奇幻喜剧片《捉鬼敢死队》(1984)。

③ EPA: US Environmental Protection Agency 美国国家环境保护局。

④ *Tootsie:* 美国影片《窈窕淑男》(1982),Dustin Hoffman(达斯汀·霍夫曼)主演。

superior knowledge, the good mother is known for her nurturing qualities, and for her intuition. This figure often gives the hero particular objects to help on the journey. It might be a protective amulet, or the ruby slippers that Dorothy receives in *The Wizard of OZ* from the Good Witch of the North. Sometimes in fairy tales it's a cloak to make the person invisible, or ordinary objects that become extraordinary as in "The Girl of Courage," an Afghan fairy tale about a maiden who receives a comb, a whetstone, and a mirror to help defeat the devil.

Many myths contain a *shadow figure*. This is a character who is the opposite of the hero. Sometimes this figure helps the hero on the journey, other times this figure opposes the hero. The shadow figure can be the negative side of the hero which could be the dark and hostile brother in "Cain and Abel," the stepsisters in "Cinderella," or the Robber Girl in "The Snow Queen." The shadow figure can also help the hero, as the whore with the heart of gold who saves the hero's life, or provides balance to his idealization of woman.

Many myths contain *animal archetypes* that can be positive or negative figures. In "St. George and the Dragon," the dragon is the negative force which is a violent and ravaging animal, not unlike the shark in *Jaws*. But in many stories, animals help the hero. Sometimes there are talking donkeys, or a dolphin which saves the hero, or magical horses or dogs.

The *trickster* is a mischievous archetypical figure who is always causing chaos, disturbing the peace, and generally being an anarchist. The trickster uses wit and cunning to achieve his or her ends. Sometimes the trickster is a harmless prankster or a "bad boy" who is funny and enjoyable. More often, the trickster is a con man, as in *The Sting*①, or the devil, as in *The Exorcist*② who demanded all the skills of the priest to outwit him. The "Till Eulenspiegel③" stories revolve around the trickster, as do the Spanish picaresque novels. Even the tales of Tom Sawyer have a trickster motif. In all countries, there are stories that revolve around this figure, whose job it is to outwit.

"Mythic" Problems and Solutions

We all grew up with myths. Most of us heard or read fairy tales when we were young. Some of us may have read Bible stories, or stories from other religions or other cultures. These stories are part of us. And the best way to work with them is to let them come out naturally as you write the script.

Of course, some filmmakers are better at this than others. George Lucas④ and Steven Spielberg⑤ have a strong sense of myth and incorporate it into their films. They both have spoken

① *The Sting:* 黑色幽默片《骗中骗》(1973),罗伯特·雷德福与保罗·纽曼主演。

② *The Exorcist:* 美国恐怖片《驱魔人》(1973)。

③ Till Eulenspiegel: 德国民间传说中的爱捉弄人的捣蛋鬼。

④ George Lucas (1944—): 乔治·卢卡斯,美国著名导演、制片人和编剧,代表作为史诗式作品《星球大战》和《夺宝奇兵》系列(与斯皮尔伯格合作)。

⑤ Steven Spielberg (1946—): 史蒂文·斯皮尔伯格,美国著名电影导演和制片人,曾三次荣获奥斯卡奖,有史以来电影总票房最高的导演。代表作《辛德勒名单》、《大白鲨》、《E. T.》、《侏罗纪公园》等等。

about their love of the stories from childhood, and of their desire to bring these types of stories to audiences. Their stories create some of the same sense of wonder and excitement as myths. Many of the necessary psychological beats are part of their stories, deepening the story beyond the ordinary action-adventure.

Myths bring depth to a hero story. If a filmmaker is thinking only about the action and excitement of a story, audiences might fail to connect with the hero's journey. But if the basic beats of the hero's journey are evident, a film will often inexplicably draw audiences, in spite of critics' responses to the film.

Take *Rambo* for instance. Why was this violent, simple story so popular with audiences? I don't think it was because everyone agreed with its politics. I do think Sylvester Stallone is a master at incorporating the American myth into his filmmaking. That doesn't mean it's done consciously. Somehow he is naturally in sync with the myth, and the myth becomes integrated into his stories.

Clint Eastwood① also does hero stories, and gives us the adventure of the myth and the transformation of the myth. Recently Eastwood's films have given more attention to the transformation of the hero, and have been receiving more serious critical attention as a result.

All of these filmmakers—Lucas, Spielberg, Stallone, and Eastwood—dramatize the hero myth in their own particular ways. And all of them prove that myths are marketable.

Questions to Consider

1. How does Seger define the "hero myth" ?
2. Seger is writing to aspiring screenwriters. How does her status as an industry insider affect her description of heroic archetypes?
3. In your own words, explain what Seger means by "the healing myth".
4. What is an "archetype" in film?
5. Explain the myths and archetypal characters *The Lord of the Rings* series include.

---

① Clint Eastwood (1930—)：克林特·伊斯特伍德，美国演员、电影导演。曾是颇具代表性的硬汉明星，并两度获得奥斯卡最佳导演奖。

Lesson 18 The Western

西部片

GARY JOHNSON

Introduction

If England has King Arthur and the Knights of the Round Table, America has John Wayne① and the gunslinging cowboys of the Old West. Constituting one of the most popular and enduring of Americans mythologies, the Western—whether inscribed in dime novels②, in the cinema, or on TV—reflects the bedrock American belief that, in Richard Schickel's words③, "complex moral conflicts can be plausibly resolved in clear clean violent action." In this excerpt from the online magazine *ImagesJournal. com*, Gary Johnson offers an overview of the cinematic history and impact of this most American of art forms, explaining why despite periods of temporary decline, the Western has never vanished into the sunset of popular culture. Johnson is the publisher of *ImagesJournal. com*, a quarterly that focuses on movies, television, videos and other popular visual arts.

Text

The Western has left an indelible mark on the world. Thanks to Hollywood, virtually everyone knows the ingredients of the Western—the lassos and the Colt. 45s④; the long-horned steer and the hanging trees; the stagecoaches and the Stetson hats; the outlaws and the lawmen; the gamblers and the gunfighters. And virtually everyone knows the settings of the Western—the red rock monoliths of Monument Valley⑤; the jagged, snowcapped peaks of the Teton Range⑥; the treeless expanses of the prairie. The iconography of the Western is the largest and richest of all the film genres, and Hollywood has burned it into the minds of moviegoers from Dodge City⑦ to

---

① John Wayne (1907—1979):约翰·韦恩,著名西部片明星。代表作包括《关山飞渡》(*Stagecoach*, 1939)、《红河》(*Red River*, 1948)、《搜索者》(*The Searchers*, 1956)、《大地惊雷》(*True Grit*, 1969)等。

② dime novel:廉价畅销小说。

③ Richard Schickel (1933—):美国作家、纪录片制作人及影评人。

④ Colt 45:美国著名枪械制造商柯尔特公司的点45手枪。

⑤ Monument Valley:纪念谷,位于美国犹他州和亚利桑那州接壤处,著名旅游景地,许多西部片在此取景。

⑥ Teton Range:堤顿山脉,落基山北段的一部分。

⑦ Dodge City:道奇城,位于美国堪萨斯州西南部。

Timbuktu①.

Part of the allure of the Western was its very simplicity. As critic Richard Schickel said, because "everyone wore a six-shooter, complex moral conflicts could be plausibly resolved in clear, clean violent action" (Buscombe, pg. 11). This decisiveness allowed the West to take on mythical dimensions, to become a place where great legends could be born. These myths and legends were embodied by Western heroes such as Wyatt Earp, Doc Holliday, Wild Bill Hickok, Buffalo Bill Cody, Calamity Jane, Jesse James, and Billy the Kid②.

Equally important, especially in the first half of the twentieth century, was the immediacy of the American West. When Hollywood first set up shop, the last great frontier was so close at hand that gunslingers/lawmen like Wyatt Earp drifted to Hollywood to serve as consultants on movie sets. This closeness to the West made the Western myths tangible and all the more powerful.

At the heart of the Western, and not to be underestimated, was physical action—runaway stagecoaches, Indian raids, bank holdups, posse pursuits, and cattle stampedes. The Western resolved its conflicts through violent brawls and gunplay, reestablishing the moral order with an exhilarating BANG! during the final reel.

Hollywood sold its stories about the West to an eager American public, providing us with a wide range of Westerns, from the series Westerns of Gene Autry③ and Roy Rogers④ with their clean-cut stars, fun-loving sidekicks, and guitar strumming singalongs to the obsessed, revenge-bent heroes of Anthony Mann⑤'s majestic 1950s Westerns.

The Western provided infinite variety on a relatively small stable of situations and plots, with conflicts often growing out of several archetypal situations: ranchers vs. farmers (*Shane and Man without a Star*), Indians vs. settlers (*The Searchers* and *Hondo*), and outlaws vs. civilization (*My Darling Clementine*⑥ and *High Noon*⑦). Robert Warshow⑧ in his influential essay "Movie Chronicle: The Westerner" described the Western as "an art form for connoisseurs, where the spectator derives his pleasure from the appreciation of minor variations within the working out of a pre-established order" (Warshow, pg. 66).

---

① Timbuktu:廷巴克图,又译为"丁布各都",现名通布图(Tombouctou),坐落在尼日尔河河道和萨赫勒地区陆地通道的交汇处。

② 这七人皆为历史上真实的西部名人,都在多部西部片中出现。

③ Gene Autry(1907—1998):美国牛仔乡村音乐的代表人物。进入好莱坞以后,他创作了大量带有西部风格的歌曲。

④ Roy Rogers(1911—1998):罗伊·罗杰斯,40年代好莱坞最为杰出的歌手之一,1935年从影,从50年代初期开始主演西部片。

⑤ Anthony Mann(1902—1967):安东尼·曼,美国导演、编剧,曾执导一系列著名西部片。

⑥ *My Darling Clementine*:西部片《侠骨柔情》(1946),约翰·福特导演,亨利·方达主演。

⑦ *High Noon*:西部片《正午》(1952),弗雷德·金尼曼导演,贾利·古柏、格蕾丝·凯利主演。

⑧ Robert Warshow(1917—1955):罗伯特·沃肖,美国作家、评论家,他对西部牛仔片与黑帮片的研究尤为突出。

Stagecoach is a 1939 American Western film directed by John Ford, starring John Wayne in his breakthrough role. It follows a group of strangers riding on a stagecoach through dangerous Apache territory. Lauded as one of the most influential films ever made, the film won two Oscars. Orson Welles argued that it was a perfect textbook of film making and claimed to have watched it more than 40 times during the making of *Citizen Kane*.

《关山飞渡》是美国20世纪福克斯影片公司于1939年摄制的一部黑白影片，也是好莱坞著名导演约翰·福特和著名影星约翰·韦恩的西部片代表作之一。从这部影片开始两个"约翰"携手共创了西部片30年的辉煌。在美国电影学院(AFI)评选的20世纪最佳100部电影中，《关山飞渡》位列第63位。

Many filmmakers felt at ease with the Western and made their best movies within the genre. In a short speech before the Director's Guild①, director John Ford② (who had directed movies from many different genres) went on record as saying, "My name's John Ford. I make Westerns." Directors such as Ford, Budd Boetticher③, Anthony Mann, and Sam Peckinpah④ excelled at prying unsuspected complexities and ironies out of well-worn stories of the American West. As a result, in John Ford's *The Searchers* we have much more than a simple quest to find a young girl kidnapped by Indians; we have the story of a quest that will never end, for the story's hero, Ethan Edwards (John Wayne), can never become part of the civilization he strives to restore. And in Anthony Mann's *The Naked Spur*, we have much more than the simple story of a bounty hunter (Jimmy Stewart) bringing home a body, we have a story where vengeance and self-destruction are intertwined. "He's not a man. He's a sack of money."

Some actors became closely identified with the Western, including Tom Mix⑤, W. S. Hart⑥, Roy Rogers, Gene Autry, and Audie Murphy⑦—but for many people, no one epitomized the Western like John Wayne. With a towering stature and a steely gaze, Wayne dominated his

---

① Director's Guild: 美国导演工会(Director's Guild of America,简称DGA)，是涵盖美国电影、电视、舞台剧、广播等艺术领域的导演行业工会。

② John Ford(1894—1973)：约翰·福特，美国最伟大和最多产的导演之一，四次获得奥斯卡最佳导演奖。代表作有《愤怒的葡萄》(*Grapes of Wrath*,1940)，《青山翠谷》(*How Green Was My Valley*,1941)以及许多著名的西部片，被称为西部片的第一位大师。

③ Budd Boetticher(1916—2001)：巴德·伯蒂彻，美国电影导演、编剧、演员。1956年至1960年导演了一批西部片如《单骑血战》(*Buchanan Rides Alone*,1958)，《蛮山野侠》(*Comanche Station*,1960)等。

④ Sam Peckinpah(1925—1984)：山姆·佩金法，美国编剧、导演。他导演的西部片有《午后枪声》(*Ride the High Country*,1962)、《日落黄沙》(*The Wild Bunch*,1969)等。

⑤ Tom Mix(1880—1940)：汤姆·麦克斯，早期西部片明星。他是好莱坞最早因扮演西部片中的牛仔形象而成名的演员。

⑥ W. S. Hart(1864—1946)：威廉姆·哈特，美国默片时代的演员、编剧、导演和制片人。

⑦ Audie Murphy(1924—1971)：奥迪·墨菲，美国电影编剧、演员，一生出演过近50部影片，大部分为西部片。

movies like a national monument dominates the land. His image has worked its way into the American consciousness as a metaphor for America itself, its strength, its determination, and its reliability. A quick survey of his movies—from *Stagecoach* to *The Man Who Shot Liberty Valance*①—is very nearly a list of the greatest Westerns ever made. While Wayne owns the top echelon by himself, a host of other actors have made powerful contributions to the genre, including Henry Fonda②, James Stewart③, Gary Cooper④, Joel McCrea⑤, Randolph Scott⑥, and Clint Eastwood⑦.

Hollywood fed us a steady diet of Western myths, legends, and heroes for over five decades. And in the process, the Western myth engulfed American popular culture—from clothes (denim jackets, jeans, and cowboy boots) to children's toys (cap guns, rubber-tipped arrows, and tom toms). Its lexicon entered our language ("round-up," "hog-tied," and "bury the hatchet"). The Western held our interest (with only minor lapses) until postwar cynicism ate away at the American psyche and we started doubting the heroes of the West. Gradually then the West began to fade away, struggling in spasms of violence in *The Wild Bunch* and the Spaghetti Westerns of Italy⑧, until the Western hardly seemed relevant anymore. And not until the 1990s arrived (with films such as *Dances with Wolves* and *Unforgiven*) did it seem possible that the Western could survive in any form other than dewy-eyed nostalgia.

The Western Survives

The Western limped through the 1980s with few hopes for a recovery. *Silverado* (1985) attempted to pump up the old clichés and stock situations with rapid-fire editing, larger-than-life images, and a tongue-in-cheek attitude, but for all its verve, the movie wasn't genuine. Its well-rehearsed crescendos carried the aura of movie brats gussying up an old form. Audiences largely stayed away. Even Clint Eastwood's *Pale Rider* disappointed with its cloning of *Shane*. *Young Guns* strived to create a teenage audience for the Western by giving us Brat Pack alumni in Western garb.

---

① *The Man Who Shot Liberty Valance*: 西部片《双虎屠龙》(1962—),约翰·福特导演,约翰·韦恩、詹姆斯·斯图尔特主演。

② Henry Fonda(1905—1982):亨利·方达,美国著名演员。代表作《愤怒的葡萄》、《侠骨柔情》、《十二怒汉》(*12 Angry Men*,*1957*)等。

③ James Stewart(1908—1997):詹姆斯·斯图尔特,美国著名演员。代表作《费城故事》(*The Philadelphia Story*,1940),《双虎屠龙》等。

④ Gary Cooper(1901—1961):贾利·古柏,美国著名演员,曾在上百部影片中扮演英雄,是有史以来获奥斯卡奖最多的一位男演员。《约克军曹》(*Sergeant York*,1941)和《正午》是其最受欢迎的两部影片。

⑤ Joel McCrea(1905—1990):乔尔·麦克雷,美国演员,从1946年起出演了一系列西部片。

⑥ Randolph Scott(1898—1987):兰道夫·斯科特,美国演员,二次大战后以出演西部片为主。

⑦ Clint Eastwood(1930—):克林特·伊斯特伍德,美国著名演员、导演、制片人。他曾是颇具代表性的硬汉明星,并两度获得奥斯卡最佳导演奖。代表作《荒野大镖客》(*A Fistful Of Dollars*,1964)、《杀无赦》(*Unforgiven*,1992)等。

⑧ Spaghetti Westerns of Italy: 意大利西部片(又称"意大利面西部片"),60年代兴起的新西部片,因为大多数由意大利公司投资拍摄而得名。如今它被用来标示任何由欧洲电影工作者投资拍摄的西部片。

While modestly successful at the box office, *Young Guns* pointed down a dead-end path.

Dances with Wolves is an American epic western film developed by director/star Kevin Costner over five years. With a budget of only $22 million, the film had high production values and won 7 Academy Awards including Best Picture. It is considered one of the best films of the 1990s and is credited as a leading influence for the revitalization of the Western genre of filmmaking in Hollywood. In 2007, *Dances with Wolves* was selected for preservation in the United States National Film Registry by the Library of Congress as being "culturally, historically, or aesthetically significant."

《与狼共舞》是凯文·科斯特纳在1990年执导并主演的一部史诗影片。它在西部片逐步走向衰落的时候取得了辉煌的成功,横扫当年奥斯卡,震惊世界影坛。它不但重新唤起了人们对西部英雄的缅怀和关注,更以一个全新的角度和视点,把旧西部电影中被忽略和丑化的印第安部族作为主要角色,重现了他们不为人知的真实面貌和真挚情感,堪称世界电影史上一部永垂不朽的西部传奇。

As it struggled into the 1990s, the Western finally discovered salvation in the form of Kevin Costner①'s *Dances with Wolves.* It packed in audiences and carted away the Academy Award for Best Picture. And soon afterwards, the TV miniseries *Lonesome Dove*② (based on Larry McMurtry③'s Pulitzer Prize-winning novel) attracted a huge following. Eastwood's *Unforgiven* followed in 1992. It's a magnificent meditation on the Old West, filled with bitter ironies and brutal violence meted out by lawmen and outlaws alike. *Unforgiven* took home the Best Picture Academy Award in 1992.

A variety of Westerns then soon appeared, from The *Quick and the Dead*, an inspired but hyperactive fusion of horror movie sensibilities and Spaghetti Western situations, to *Posse*, a black Western with a rap soundtrack. The legendary Gunfight at the OK Corral provided the material for two movies, Lawrence Kasdan④'s ambitious but stodgy *Wyatt Earp* and George Cosmatos⑤'s intermittently dazzling *Tombstone.*

Even with the minor resurgence of the Western in the 1990s, the Western exists in limbo. It still has the power to fan the sparks of imagination, but our distance from the West has weakened its

---

① Kevin Costner(1955—):凯文·科斯特纳,美国著名演员、导演。1990年,他首次担任导演和制片,拍摄了史诗作品《与狼共舞》,获得了十二项奥斯卡奖提名并最终获得了七项大奖。

② *Lonesome Dove*:《寂寞之鸽》,1989年美国哥伦比亚广播公司(CBS)根据Larry McMurty原著改编的西部电视片。

③ Larry McMurty(1936—):拉里·麦克默蒂,美国小说家、剧作家。其作品主要以美国老西部或现代的德克萨斯为背景。

④ Lawrence Kasdan(1949—):劳伦斯·卡斯丹,美国导演、制片、编剧。导演代表作《义海倾情》(*Wyatt Earp*,1994),编剧代表作《法柜奇兵》(*Raiders of the Lost Ark*,1981)等。

⑤ George Cosmatos(1941—2005):乔治·科斯马图斯,意大利导演。代表作《卡桑德拉大桥》(*The Cassandra Crossing*, 1976)、《第一滴血2》(*Rambo: First Blood* Part II,1985)等。

authority. While the West once represented a simpler time in America's history, we now see that the power of the gun (as shown in *Unforgiven* and *Tombstone*) could make lawmen just as dangerous as the outlaws. And although justice may have been swift; it was not necessarily fair and at times it was absolutely deadly. As the myths and heroes of the American West fade away, the Western becomes just another genre, a genre that becomes more remote with each passing year.

Works Cited

Buscombe, Edward (ed.). *The BFI Companion to the Western*. New York: Da Capo Press, 1991.

Warshow, Robert. *The Immediate Experience*. New York: Anchor Books, 1964.

Questions to Consider

1. What, according to Johnson, accounts for the popularity of the Western?
2. What does Johnson say are some of the archetypal situations dramatized by the typical Western?
3. At what point did the Western begin to decline in popularity in Johnson's view?
4. If the classic Westerns offer their viewers "dewy-eyed nostalgia", what new perspectives do the Westerns in 1990s add to the genre?

Lesson 19 Asian Women in Film: No Joy, No Luck

电影中的亚洲女性:无喜无福

JESSICA HAGEDORN

Introduction

Why do movies always seem to portray Asian women as tragic victims of history and fate? Jessica Hagedorn (born in 1949) asks in this essay, which originally appeared in *Ms. Even* such movies as *The Joy Luck Club*, based on Amy Tan's① breakthrough novel that elevated Asian American fiction to bestseller status, reinforce old stereotypes of the powerlessness of Asian and Asian American women. A screenwriter and novelist, Hagedorn calls for a different kind of storytelling that would show Asian women as powerful controllers of their own destinies.

Text

Pearl Of the Orient. Whore. Geisha. Concubine. Whore. Hostess. Bar Girl. Mamasan. Whore. China Doll. Tokyo Rose. Whore. Butterfly. Whore. Miss Saigon. Whore. Dragon Lady. Lotus Blossom. Gook. Whore. Yellow Peril. Whore. Bangkok Bombshell. Whore. Hospitality Girl. Whore. Comfort Woman. Whore. Savage. Whore. Sultry. Whore. Faceless. Whore. Porcelain. Whore. Demure. Whore. Virgin. Whore. Mute. Whore. Model Minority. Whore. Victim. Whore. Woman Warrior. Whore. Mail-Order Bride. Whore. Mother. Wife. Lover. Daughter. Sister.

As I was growing up in the Philippines in the 1950s, my fertile imagination was colonized by thoroughly American fantasies. Yellow face variations on the exotic erotic loomed larger than life on the silver screen. I was mystified and enthralled by Hollywood's skewed representations of Asian women: sleek, evil goddesses with slanted eyes and cunning ways, or smiling, sarong-clad South Seas "maidens" with undulating hips, kinky black hair and white skin darkened by makeup. Hardly any of the "Asian" characters were played by Asians. White actors like Sidney Toler and Warner Oland played "inscrutable Oriental detective" Charlie Chan② with taped eyelids and a singsong, chop suey accent. Jennifer Jones was a Eurasian doctor swept up in a doomed

---

① Amy Tan:谭恩美,美籍华裔女作家,代表作有《喜福会》(*The Joy Luck Club*)、《灶神之妻》(*The Kitchen God's Wife*)、《接骨师之女》(*The Bonesetter's Daughter*)等。

② Charlie Chan:陈查理,是美国作家厄尔·德尔·比格斯(Earl Derr Biggers)笔下的一名华人探长。之后陈查理被拍成电影。关于陈查理的前 15 部电影都是由 Warner Oland 主演,在 Warner Oland 去世后,改由 Sidney Toler 主演。

"interracial romance" in *Love Is a Many Splendored Thing*. In my mother's youth, white actor Luise Rainer① played the central role of the Patient Chinese Wife in the 1937 film adaptation of Pearl Buck's novel *The Good Earth*. Back then, not many thought to ask why; they were all too busy being grateful to see anyone in the movies remotely like themselves.

Cut to 1960: *The World Of Suzie Wong,* another tragic East-West affair. I am now old enough to be impressed. Sexy, sassy Suzie (played by Nancy Kwan②) works out of a bar patronized by white sailors, but doesn't seem bothered by any of it. For a hardworking girl turning nightly tricks to support her baby she manages to parade an astonishing wardrobe in damn near every scene, down to matching handbags and shoes. The sailors are also strictly Hollywood, sanitized and not too menacing. Suzie and all the other prostitutes in this movie are cute, giggling, dancing sex machines with hearts of gold. William Holden plays an earnest, rather prim, Nice Guy painter seeking inspiration in The Other. Of course, Suzie falls madly in love with him. Typically, she tells him, "I not important," and "I'll be with you until you say—Suzie, go away." She also thinks being beaten by a man is a sign of true passion and is terribly disappointed when Mr. Nice Guy refuses to show his true feelings.

Next in Kwan's short-lived but memorable career was the kitschy 1961 musical *Flower Drum Song*, which, like *Suzie Wong*, is a thoroughly American commercial product. The female roles are typical of Hollywood musicals of the times; women are basically airheads, subservient to men. Kwan's counterpart is the Good Chinese Girl, played by Miyoshi Umeki③, who was better playing the Loyal Japanese Girl in that other classic Hollywood tale of forbidden love, *Sayonara*. Remember? Umeki was so loyal, she committed double suicide with actor Red Buttons. I instinctively hated *Sayonara* when I first saw it as a child, now I understand why. Contrived tragic resolutions were the only way Hollywood got past the censors in those days. With one or two exceptions, somebody in these movies always had to die to pay for breaking racial and sexual taboos.

Until the recent onslaught of films by both Asian and Asian American filmmakers, Asian Pacific women have generally been perceived by Hollywood with a mixture of fascination, fear, and contempt. Most Hollywood movies either trivialize or exoticize us as people of color and as women. Our intelligence is underestimated, our humanity overlooked, and our diverse cultures treated as interchangeable. If we are "good," we are childlike, submissive, silent, and eager for

---

① Luise Rainer:德国著名女演员,在根据赛珍珠小说《大地》(*The Good Earth*)改编的电影中饰女主角。

② Nancy Kwan: 关南施,1939 年生于吉隆坡,原籍广东番禺,母亲为美国人。1960 年凭借派拉蒙影片《苏丝黄的世界》(*The World Of Suzie Wong*)一举成名,成为首位在西方电影界成名的亚洲女演员。她的成功为以后打入西方电影界的亚洲裔演员提供了很大的帮助。

③ Miyoshi Umeki: 美籍日裔演员,在电影《花鼓戏》(*Flower Drum Song*)中扮演主角。她出演了电影《樱花恋》(*Sayonara*)并获得 1957 年奥斯卡最佳女配角奖。

sex (see France Nuyen'[1] s glowing performance as Liat in the film version of *South Pacific*) or else we are tragic victim types (see *Casualties of War*, Brian De Palma's graphic 1989 drama set in Vietnam). And if we are not silent, suffering doormats, we are demonized dragon ladies—cunning, deceitful, sexual provocateurs. Give me the demonic any day—Anna May Wong[2] as a villain slithering around in a slinky gown is at least gratifying to watch, neither servile nor passive. And she steals the show from Marlene Dietrich in Josef von Sternberg's *Shanghai Express*. From the 1920s through the 1930s, Wong was our only female "star." But even she was trapped in limited roles, in what filmmaker Renee Tajima has called the dragon lady/lotus blossom dichotomy.

Cut to 1985: There is a scene toward the end of the terribly dishonest but weirdly compelling Michael Cimino[3] movie *Year of the Dragon* (cowritten by Oliver Stone) that is one of my favorite twisted movie moments of all time. If you ask a lot of my friends who've seen that movie (especially if they're Asian), it's one of their favorites too. The setting is a crowded Chinatown nightclub. There are two very young and very tough Jade Cobra gang girls in a shoot-out with Mickey Rourke, in the role of a demented Polish American cop who, in spite of being Mr. Ugly in the flesh—an arrogant, misogynistic bully devoid of any charm —wins the "good" Asian American anchorwoman in the film's absurd and implausible ending. This is a movie with an actual disclaimer as its lead-in, covering its ass in advance in response to anticipated complaints about "stereotypes."

My pleasure in the hard-edged power of the Chinatown gang girls in *Year of the Dragon* is my small revenge, the answer to all those Suzie Wong "I want to be your slave" female characters. The Jade Cobra girls are mere background to the white male foreground/focus of Cimino's movie. But long after the movie has faded into video-rental heaven, the Jade Cobra girls remain defiant, fabulous images in my memory, flaunting tight metallic dresses and spiky cock's-comb hairdos streaked electric red and blue.

Mickey Rourke looks down with world-weary pity at the unnamed Jade Cobra girl (Doreen Chan) he's just shot who lies sprawled and bleeding on the street: "You look like you're gonna die, beautiful."

JADE COBRA GIRL: "Oh yeah? [blood gushing from her mouth] I'm proud of it."

ROURKE: "You are? You got anything you wanna tell me before you go, sweetheart?"

---

① France Nuyen: 在电影《南太平洋》(*South Pacific*,1958)和《喜福会》(*The Joy Luck Club*, 1993)中都扮演重要角色。

② Ann May Wong: 黄柳霜,第一位美籍华人好莱坞影星,在约瑟夫·冯·斯登堡(Josef von Sternberg)导演的电影《上海快车》(*Shanghai Express*,1932)中扮演女主角。

③ Michael Cimino: 美国著名导演,其编导的《猎鹿人》(*The Deer Hunter*, 1978)获得奥斯卡最佳影片及最佳导演两项大奖。1985 年与奥利佛·斯通(Oliver Stone)合作了电影《龙年》(*Year of the Dragon*)。米基·洛克(Mickey Rourke)为该电影主演,扮演对抗纽约华人黑帮的美国警察。

JADE COBRA GIRL: "Yeah. [pause] Fuck you."

Cut to 1993: I've been told that like many New Yorkers, I watch movies with the right side of my brain on perpetual overdrive. I admit to being grouchy and overcritical, suspicious of sentiment, and cynical. When a critic like Richard Corliss① of *Time* magazine gushes about *The Joy Luck Club* being "a fourfold *Terms of Endearment*," my gut instinct is to run the other way. I resent being told how to feel. I went to see the 1993 eight-handkerchief movie version of Amy Tan's best-seller with a group that included my ten-year-old daughter. I was caught between the sincere desire to be swept up by the turbulent mother-daughter sagas and my own stubborn resistance to being so obviously manipulated by the filmmakers. With every flashback came tragedy. The music soared, the voice-overs were solemn or wistful, tears, tears, and more tears flowed onscreen. Daughters were reverent, mothers carried dark secrets.

I was elated by the grandness and strength of the four mothers and the luminous actors who portrayed them, but I was uneasy with the passivity of the Asian American daughters. They seemed to exist solely as receptors for their mothers' amazing life stories. It's almost as if by assimilating so easily into American society, they had lost all sense of self.

In spite of my resistance, my eyes watered as the desperate mother played by Kieu Chinh② was forced to abandon her twin baby girls on a country road in war-torn China. (Kieu Chinh resembles my own mother and her twin sister who suffered through the brutal Japanese occupation of the Philippines.) So far in this movie, an infant son had been deliberately drowned, a mother played by the gravely beautiful France Nuyen had gone catatonic with grief, a concubine had cut her flesh open to save her dying mother, an insecure daughter had been oppressed by her boorish Asian American husband, another insecure daughter had been left by her white husband, and so on. ... The overall effect was numbing as far as I'm concerned, but a man sitting two rows in front of us broke down sobbing. A Chinese Filipino writer even more grouchy than me later complained, "Must ethnicity only be equated with suffering?"

Because change has been slow, *The Joy Luck Club* carries a lot of cultural baggage. It is a big-budget story about Chinese American women, directed by a Chinese American man, cowritten and coproduced by Chinese American women. That's a lot to be thankful for. And its box office success proves that an immigrant narrative told from female perspectives can have mass appeal. But my cynical side tells me that its success might mean only one thing in Hollywood: more weepy epics about Asian American mother-daughter relationships will be planned.

---

① Richard Corliss: 美国《时代》周刊的专职作家，主要写电影评论。

② Kieu Chinh: 越南裔美国女演员，在《喜福会》(*The Joy Luck Club*, 1993)中扮演一个绝望的母亲，在战争年代为了逃生抛弃了自己的双胞胎女儿。

The Joy Luck Club is a 1993 American film about the relationships between Chinese-American women and their Chinese mothers. It is based on the 1989 novel of the same name by Amy Tan, who co-wrote the screenplay with Ronald Bass. The film was produced by Oliver Stone and directed by Wayne Wang. The cast is notable for consisting primarily of Asian American women. The film reveals the hidden pasts of the older women and explores cultural conflict and the relationships between mothers and daughters.

《喜福会》是一部讲述美籍华裔妇女和她们的中国母亲之间关系的美国电影,拍摄于1993年。它以谭恩美1989年出版的同名小说为蓝本,由奥利弗·斯通出品,王颖导演,电影的演员阵容因主要由亚裔美籍妇女组成而引人注目。该影片揭示了母亲们隐藏的往事,探索了母女之间的关系和文化冲突。

That the film finally got made was significant. By Hollywood standards (think white male; think money, money, money), a movie about Asian Americans even when adapted from a best-seller was a risky proposition. When I asked a producer I know about the film's rumored delays, he simply said, "It's still an Asian movie," surprised I had even asked. Equally interesting was director Wayne Wang's initial reluctance to be involved in the project; he told the *New York Times,* "I didn't want to do another Chinese movie."

Maybe he shouldn't have worried so much. After all, according to the media, the nineties are the decade of "Pacific Overtures" and East Asian chic. Madonna①, the pop queen of shameless appropriation, cultivated Japanese high-tech style with her music video "Rain," while Janet Jackson faked kitschy orientalia in hers, titled "If." Critical attention was paid to movies from China, Japan, and Vietnam. But that didn't mean an honest appraisal of women's lives. Even on the art house circuit, filmmakers who should know better took the easy way out. ...

Nineteen ninety-three also brought Tran Anh Hung's② *The Scent of Green Papaya*, a different kind of Vietnamese memento—this is a look back at the peaceful, lush country of the director's childhood memories. The film opens in Saigon, in 1951. A willowy ten-year-old girl named Mui comes to work for a troubled family headed by a melancholy musician and his kind, stoic wife. The men of this bourgeois household are idle, pampered types who take naps while the women do all the work. Mui is male fantasy: she is a devoted servant, enduring acts of cruel mischief with patience and dignity; as an adult, she barely speaks. She scrubs floors, shines shoes, and cooks with loving care and never a complaint. When she is sent off to work for another wealthy musician, she ends up being impregnated by him. The movie ends as the camera closes in

① Madonna: 麦当娜,美国摇滚女歌星。文中提到的"Rain"是麦当娜1995《情难忘——性感情歌精选辑》(*Something to remember*)中的一首。

② Tran Anh Hung: 陈英雄,越南裔法国导演,其导演的《番木瓜飘香》(*The Scent of Green Papaya*)获1993年奥斯卡"最佳外语片"提名奖。该影片讲述了小女孩梅在两个家庭环境中的生活境遇和成长经历。

on Mui's contented face. Languid and precious, *The Scent of Green Papaya* is visually haunting, but it suffers from the director's colonial fantasy of women as docile, domestic creatures. Steeped in highbrow nostalgia, it's the arty Vietnamese version of *My Fair Lady* with the wealthy musician as Professor Higgins, teaching Mui to read and write.

And then there is Ang Lee's tepid 1993 hit, *The Wedding Banquet*①—a clever culture-clash farce in which traditional Chinese values collide with contemporary American sexual mores. The somewhat formulaic plot goes like this: Wai-Tung, a yuppie landlord, lives with his white lover Simon, in a chic Manhattan brownstone. Wai-Tung is an only child and his aging parents in Taiwan long for a grandchild to continue the family legacy. Enter Wei-Wei, an artist who lives in a grungy loft owned by Wai-Tung. She slugs tequila straight from the bottle as she paints and flirts boldly with her young, uptight landlord, who brushes her off. "It's my fate. I am always attracted to handsome gay men," she mutters. After this setup, the movie goes downhill, all edges blurred in a cozy nest of happy endings. A pregnant, suddenly complacent Wei-Wei gives in to family pressures—and never gets her life back.

> "It takes a man to know what it is to be a real woman."
>
> ——SONG LILING in *M. Butterfly*②

Ironically, two gender-bending films in which men play men playing women reveal more about the mythology of the prized Asian woman and the superficial trappings of gender than most movies that star real women. The slow-moving *M. Butterfly* presents the ultimate object of Western male desire as the spy/opera diva Song Liling, a Suzie Wong/Lotus Blossom played by actor John Lone with a five o'clock shadow and bobbing Adam's apple. The best and most profound of these forays into cross-dressing is the spectacular melodrama *Farewell My Concubine*③ directed by Chen Kaige. Banned in China, *Farewell My Concubine* shared the prize for Best Film at the 1993 Cannes Film Festival with Jane Campion's *The Piano*. Sweeping through 50 years of tumultuous history in China, the story revolves around the lives of two male Bejing Opera stars and the woman who marries one of them. The three characters make an unforgettable triangle, struggling over love, art, friendship, and politics against the bloody backdrop of cultural upheaval. They are as capable of casually betraying each other as they are of selfless, heroic acts. The androgynous Dieyi, doomed to play the same female role of concubine over and over again, is portrayed with great vulnerability, wit, and grace by male Hong Kong pop star Leslie Cheung. Dieyi competes

① *The Wedding Banquet*: 电影《喜宴》，由著名导演李安导演，获柏林电影节金熊奖及金马奖最佳影片。主要表述了中国人特有的家庭伦理观点与同性恋的碰撞。

② *M. Butterfly*: 电影《蝴蝶君》，由 David Cronenber 根据 David Henry Hwang 的同名舞台剧改编。Jeremy Irons 和 John Lone 主演。

③ *Farewell My Concubine*:《霸王别姬》，由陈凯歌导演，张国荣、张丰毅、巩俐主演，获 1993 年戛纳国际电影节最高奖项——金棕榈奖。

with the prostitute Juxian (Gong Li) for the love of his childhood protector and fellow opera star, Duan Xiaolou (Zhang Fengyi).

Farewell My Concubine, a 1993 Chinese film directed by Chen Kaige, is one of the central works of the Fifth Generation movement that brought Chinese film directors to world attention. Similar to other Fifth Generation films like *To Live* and *The Blue Kite, Farewell My Concubine* explores the effect of China's political turmoil during the mid-20th century on the lives of individuals, families, and groups, in this case, two stars in a Peking opera troupe and the woman who comes between them. The film is an adaptation of the novel by Lilian Lee. *Farewell My Concubine* remains to date the only Chinese-language film to win the Cannes Palme d'Or.

《霸王别姬》,1993年由陈凯歌导演的电影,是为中国电影带来世界性关注的第五代导演的主要作品之一。与其他的第五代导演作品如《活着》和《蓝风筝》类似,《霸王别姬》探索了20世纪中叶中国的政治风暴对个人、家庭和群体生活的影响,在这部电影里,是两位京剧团的明星和他们之间的一个女人。这部电影改编自李碧华的小说,她也是电影剧本作者之一。直到今天,《霸王别姬》仍然是唯一一部获得金棕榈奖的中文电影。

Cheung's highly stylized performance as the classic concubine-ready-to-die-for-love in the opera within the movie is all about female artifice. His sidelong glances, restrained passion, languid stance, small steps, and delicate, refined gestures say everything about what is considered desirable in Asian women—and are the antithesis of the feisty outspoken woman played by Gong Li. The characters of Dieyi and Juxian both see suffering as part and parcel of love and life. Juxian matter-of-factly says to Duan Xiaolou before he agrees to marry her: "I'm used to hardship. If you take me in, I'll wait on you hand and foot. If you tire of me, I'll... kill myself. No big deal." It's an echo of Suzie Wong's servility, but the context is new. Even with her back to the wall, Juxian is not helpless or whiny. She attempts to manipulate a man while admitting to the harsh reality that is her life.

Dieyi and Juxian are the two sides of the truth of women's lives in most Asian countries. Juxian in particular—wife and ex-prostitute—could be seen as a thankless and stereotypical role. But like the characters Gong Li has played in Chinese director Zhang Yimou's films, *Red Sorghum, Raise the Red Lantern*, and especially *The Story Of Qiuju*, Juxian is tough, obstinate, sensual, clever, oafish, beautiful, infuriating, cowardly heroic, and banal. Above all, she is resilient. Gong Li is one of the few Asian Pacific actors whose roles have been drawn with intelligence, honesty and depth. Nevertheless, the characters she plays are limited by the possibilities that exist for real women in China.

"Let's face it. Women still don't mean shit in China," my friend Meeling reminds me. What she says so bluntly about her culture rings painfully true, but in less obvious fashion for me. In the Philippines, infant girls aren't drowned, nor were their feet bound to make them more desirable. But sons were and are cherished. To this day men of the bourgeois class are coddled and prized, much like the spoiled men of the elite household in *The Scent of Green Papaya*. We do not have a geisha tradition like Japan, but physical beauty is overtreasured. Our daughters are protected virgins or primed as potential beauty queens. And many of us have bought into the image of the white man as our handsome savior: G. I. Joe①.

Buzz magazine recently featured an article entitled "Asian Women/L. A. Men," a report on a popular hangout that caters to white men's fantasies of nubile Thai women. The lines between movies and real life are blurred. Male screenwriters and cinematographers flock to this bar-restaurant, where the waitresses are eager to "audition" for roles. Many of these men have been to Bangkok while working on film crews for Vietnam War movies. They've come back to L. A., but for them, the movie never ends. In this particular fantasy the boys play G. I. Joe on a rescue mission in the urban jungle, saving the whore from herself. "A scene has developed here, a kind of R-rated *Cheers*," author Alan Rifkin② writes. "The waitresses audition for sitcoms. The customers date the waitresses or just keep score."

Colonization of the imagination is a two-way street. And being enshrined on a pedestal as someone's Pearl of the Orient fantasy doesn't seem so demeaning, at first; who wouldn't want to be worshipped? Perhaps that's why Asian women are the ultimate wet dream in most Hollywood movies; it's no secret how well we've been taught to play the role, to take care of our men. In Hollywood vehicles, we are objects of desire or derision; we exist to provide sex, color and texture in what is essentially a white man's world. It is akin to what Toni Morrison③ calls "the Africanist presence" in literature. She writes: "Just as entertainers, through or by association with blackface, could render permissible topics that otherwise would have been taboo, so American writers were able to employ an imagined Africanist persona to articulate and imaginatively act out the forbidden in American culture." The same analogy could be made for the often titillating presence of Asian women in movies made by white men.

Movies are still the most seductive and powerful of artistic-mediums, manipulating us with ease by a powerful combination of sound and image. In many ways, as females and Asians, as audiences or performers, we have learned to settle for less—to accept the fact that we are either decorative, invisible, or one-dimensional. When there are characters who look like us represented in a movie, we have also learned to view between the lines, or to add what is missing. For many of us, this way of watching has always been a necessity. We fill in the gaps. If a female character is presented as a mute, willowy beauty, we convince ourselves she is an ancestral ghost—so smart she doesn't have to speak at all. If she is a whore with a heart of gold, we claim her as a tough feminist icon. If she is a sexless, sanitized, boring nerd, we embrace her as role model for our daughters, rather than the tragic whore. And if she is presented as an utterly devoted saint suffering nobly in silence, we lie and say she is just like our mothers. Larger than life. Magical and insidious. A movie is never just a movie, after all.

---

① G. I. Joe:原为美国玩具厂商Hasbro生产的军事可动人偶,后用来指"特种部队"(G. I. Joe),不惜赴汤蹈火来伸张正义的人物。

② Alan Rifkin: 美国 *Details* 杂志的特约编辑,他的主要作品 *Signal Hill* 获得2004年南加州书商奖。

③ Toni Morrison: 托尼·莫里森,美国黑人女作家,1993年获诺贝尔文学奖。

Questions to Consider

1. According to Hagedorn, what are the stereotypes of Asian women as presented in Hollywood movies?
2. What is the chronology of Asian women in film that Hagedorn presents, and why do you think she gives us a historical overview?
3. Discuss the box office success of *The Joy Luck Club* and a Chinese Filipino writer's complaint "Must ethnicity only be equated with suffering?" in view of the traditional images of Asian women.
4. Why does Hagedorn say that the film *The Joy Luck Club* "carries a lot of cultural baggage"?
5. What sort of images of Asian women does Hagedorn imply that she would prefer to see?

Lesson 20 The Way We Are

我们何以如是

SYDNEY POLLACK

Introduction

If anyone knows American moviemaking, it's Sidney Pollack[1]. A director of more than sixteen films—including *The Way We Were, Tootsie*, *Out of Africa*, and *The Firm*—and an occasional actor (Dustin Hoffman's agent in *Tootsie*), Pollack has had an unparalleled opportunity to observe the changing tastes of the American viewing public and the movie industry's response to those changes. In the following article, a transcript of an address Pollack delivered at a conference about the influence of the popular media on American values, Pollack suggests that changes in the moral fabric of our society are responsible for the kinds of movies we see today, not vice versa.

When he looks at contemporary America, Pollack finds a conspicuous lack of the "kind of scrupulous ethical concern for the sanctity of life" that prevailed in past decades and was reflected in motion pictures of the time, when there were less frequent and less graphic scenes of violence, when characters were esteemed for their humility and personal integrity, and when explicit sexuality was found only in "stag" films, not in mainstream theaters. Many people today, Pollack notes, are nostalgic for the "old values" and believe that movies should encourage the return of these values rather than reflecting current values. Pollack disagrees, however, pointing out that, although screenwriters and directors may want their movies to reflect some moral content, the economics of the industry require first and foremost that movies be entertaining, and therefore, they must appeal to a buying audience whose values may be very different from those of the reformers.

Out of Africa is a film released in 1985. The story based loosely on the autobiographical book *Out of Africa* written by Isak Dinesen (the pseudonym of the author Karen Blixen), which was published in 1937, with additional material from Dinesen's book *Shadows on the Grass* and other sources. This film received 28 film awards, including seven Academy Awards.

影片《走出非洲》在1985年公映。影片故事大体以伊萨克·蒂内森(作家凯伦·白烈森的笔名)1937出版的自传《走出非洲》为基础,添加了蒂内森的《草地上的影子》中的素材和其他素材。这部影片获得过28个电影奖项,包括7项奥斯卡金像奖。

① Sidney Pollack (1934—2008):西德尼·波拉克,美国著名导演,共获得46项奥斯卡提名。他的《走出非洲》赢得7项奥斯卡奖,其中包括波拉克本人的最佳导演和最佳影片奖。

Text

I know your concerns have to do with American values and whether those values are being upheld or assaulted by American entertainment—by what I and others like me do. But which values exactly?

In the thirties, forties, and fifties, six men in the Valley, immigrants really, ran the movie industry. Our society was vastly different. The language of the movies was a language of shared values. If you put forward a virtuousness on the part of your hero, everybody responded to it.

When Sergeant York①, played by Gary Cooper, refused to endorse a breakfast cereal, knowing he'd been asked because he'd won the Medal of Honor, he said: "I ain't proud of what I've done. You don't make money off of killing people. That there is wrong." We expected him to behave that way.

But society's values have changed. That kind of scrupulous, ethical concern for the sanctity of human life doesn't exist in the same way, and that fact is reflected in the movies. There's a nostalgia now for some of the old values, but so many people embrace other expressions of values that it's hard to say these other expressions aren't reality.

Their idea of love, for example, is a different idea of love. It's a much less chaste, much less idealized love than was depicted in the earlier films. We are seeing some sort of return to the ideal of marriage. There was a decade or two when marriage really lost its popularity, and while young people are swinging toward it again, I don't believe one could say that values have not changed significantly since the thirties, forties, and fifties.

Morality, the definitions of virtue, justice, and injustice, the sanctity of the individual, have been fairly fluid for American audiences in terms of what they choose to embrace or not embrace.

Take a picture like *Dances With Wolves*. You could not have made it in the thirties or forties. It calls into question every value that existed in traditional Westerns. It may not reflect what everybody thinks now, but it expresses a lot of guilty re-evaluation of what happened in the West, the very things shown in the old Westerns that celebrated the frontier.

OUT OF HOLLYWOOD

Before they can be anything else, American movies are a product. This is not good or bad, this is what we've got. A very few may become art, but all of them, whatever their ambitions, are first financed as commodities. They're the work of craftsmen and artists, but they're soon offered for sale.

Whether we say that we're "creating a film" or merely "making a movie," the enterprise itself is sufficiently expensive and risky that it cannot be, and it will not be, undertaken without the hope

① Sergeant York:《约克军曹》,1941 年美国电影,由贾利・古柏(Gary Cooper)主演。

of reward. We have no Medicis① here. It takes two distinct entities, the financiers and the makers, to produce movies, and there is a tension between them. Their goals are sometimes similar, but they do different things. Financiers are not in the business of philanthropy. They've got to answer to stockholders.

Of course, the controlling influence in filmmaking hasn't changed in 50 years: it still belongs to the consumer. That's the dilemma and, in my view, what we're finally talking about. What do you do about culture in a society that celebrates the common man but doesn't always like his taste?

If you operate in a democracy and you're market-supported and -driven, the spectrum of what you will get is going to be very wide indeed. It will range from trash to gems. There are 53,000 books published in this country every year. How many of them are really good? Tired as I may be of fast-food-recipe, conscienceless, simple-minded books, films, TV, and music, the question remains, who is to be society's moral policeman?

Over the course of their first 30 or 40 years, the movies were a cottage industry, and the morality that was reflected in them was the morality of the early film pioneers. Now, film studios are tiny divisions of multinational corporations, and they feel the pressure for profits that happens in any other repeatable-product business. They look for a formula. Say you get the recipe for a soft drink and perfect it; once customers like it, you just repeat it and it will sell. More fortunes have been lost than made in the movie business pursuing such a formula, but unfortunately today, more junk than anything else is being made pursuing it. And film companies are folding like crazy.

Since we are in the democracy business, we can't tell people what they should or shouldn't hear, or support, or see, so they make their choices. The market tries to cater to those choices, and we have what we have.

MAKING FILMS

Are American films bad? A lot of them surely are, and so are a lot of everybody else's, the way a lot of anything produced is bad—breakfast cereals, music, most chairs, architecture, mail-order shirts. There probably hasn't been a really beautiful rake since the Shakers② stopped making farm implements. But that is no excuse.

I realize that I am a prime suspect here, but I'm not sure that you really understand how odd and unpredictable a business the making of films actually is. It just doesn't conform to the logic or rules of any other business. It's always been an uneasy merger of two antithetical things: some form of art and sheer commerce.

If the people who make films get the money that is invested in them back to the people who finance them, then they'll get to make more. We know that the business of films is to reach as

① Medicis：梅第奇家族是13世纪至17世纪时期在欧洲拥有强大势力的意大利佛罗伦萨名门望族。梅第奇家族是科学、建筑及艺术的赞助者，在文艺复兴时期起了很大的促进作用，被称为文艺复兴教父。

② Shakers：震教徒（Shakers），又称为震教教友会（Shaking Quakers），属于基督再现信徒联合会，1774年由安·李（Ann Lee，1736—1784）在美国建立的贵格会支派，现已基本消亡。

many people as possible. That works two ways; it's not just a market discipline. You have to remember that most of us who are doing this got into it for the romance, the glory, the applause, the chance to tell stories, even to learn, but rarely for the money. The more people you reach, the greater your sense of success. Given the choice, I'd rather make the whole world cry than 17 intellectuals in a classroom.

But, paradoxically, if you are the actual maker of the film—not the financier—you can't make films and worry about whether they'll reach a large audience or make money, first, because nobody really knows a formula for what will make money. If they did, I promise you we would have heard about it, and studios would not be going broke. Second, and much more practically, if you spent your time while you were making the film consciously thinking about what was commercial, then the real mechanism of choice—the mechanism that is your own unconscious, your own taste and imagination, your fantasy—would be replaced by constant reference to this formula that we know doesn't work.

So the only practical approach a filmmaker can take is to make a film that he or she would want to see. This sounds arrogant, but you try to make a movie for yourself, and you hope that as many people as possible will like it too. If that happens, it's because you've done something in the telling of the story that makes people care. One of the things that makes a film distinct from other American business products is this emotional involvement of the maker. A producer of autoparts can become pretty emotional about a sales slump, but it isn't the same thing. His product hasn't come from his history; it isn't somehow in the image of his life; and it lacks mystery. It is entirely measurable and concrete, which is certainly appropriate in the manufacture of auto parts. I wouldn't want to buy a carburetor from a neurotic, mixed-up auto manufacturer.

Fortunately for those of us in film, no such standards apply. Quite the contrary, in fact. No matter what his conscious intentions are, the best part of what the filmmaker does—the part, when it works, that makes you want to see the film—doesn't come from a rational, consciously controllable process. It comes from somewhere inside the filmmaker's unconscious. It comes from making unlikely connections seem inevitable, from a kind of free association that jumps to odd or surprising places, conclusions that cause delights, something that creates goose pimples or awe.

This conference has suggested a question: While you're actually making the movie, do you think about whether or not it will be doing the world any good? I can't answer it for filmmakers in general. For myself, candidly, no, I don't.

I try to discover and tell the truth and not be dull about it. In that sense, the question has no significance for me. I assume that trying to discover the truth is in itself a good and virtuous aim. By truth I don't mean some grand, pretentious axiom to live by; I just mean the truth of a character from moment to moment. I try to discover and describe things like the motives that are hidden in day-to-day life. And the truth is rarely dull. If I can find it, I will have fulfilled my primary obligation as a filmmaker, which is not to bore the pants off you.

Most of us in this business have enormous sympathy for Scheherazade①—we're terrified we're going to be murdered if we're boring. So our first obligation is to not bore people; it isn't to teach.

Most of the time, high-mindedness just leads to pretentious or well-meaning, often very bad, films. Most of the Russian films made under communism were of high quality in terms of craft, but they were soporific because their intent to do good as it was perceived by the state or an all-knowing party committee was too transparent.

I'm sure that you think the person in whose hands the process actually rests, the filmmaker, could exert an enormous amount of control over the film's final worthiness. The question usually goes like this: Should filmmakers pander to the public, or should they try to elevate public taste to something that many at this conference would find more acceptable? Is the job of an American filmmaker to give the public what it wants or what the filmmaker thinks the public should have? This doesn't leave much doubt as to what you think is the right answer.

But framing your question this way not only betrays a misunderstanding of how the filmmaking process works but also is just plain wishful thinking about how to improve society. I share your nostalgia for some of those lost traditional values, but attempting to reinstall them by arbitrarily putting them into movies when they don't exist in everyday life will not get people to go to the movies or put those values back into life. I wish it were that simple.

ENGAGING AN AUDIENCE

This conference is concerned with something called popular culture and its effect on society, but I am concerned with one film at a time and its effect. You are debating whether movies corrupt our souls or elevate them, and I'm debating whether a film will touch a soul. As a filmmaker, I never set out to create popular culture, and I don't know a single other filmmaker who does.

Maybe it's tempting to think of Hollywood as some collective behemoth grinding out the same stories and pushing the same values, but it's not that simple. Hollywood, whatever that means, is Oliver Stone castigating war in *Born on the Fourth of July*② and John Milius celebrating it in *The Wind and the Lion*③. It's Walt Disney and Martin Scorcese④. It's Steven Spielberg and Milos Foreman⑤. It's *Amadeus*⑥ and *Terminator*⑦ and hundreds of choices in between.

---

① Scheherazade: 谢赫拉莎德,《一千零一夜》中苏丹的新娘。

② *Born on the Fourth of July*:《生于 7 月 4 日》,美国越战题材影片,导演奥利弗·斯通(Oliver Stone)。

③ *The Wind and the Lion*:《黑狮震雄风》,惊险影片,导演约翰·米利厄斯(John Milius)。

④ Martin Scorcese(1942—):马丁·斯科塞斯,公认的美国战后最具影响力的电影导演之一。

⑤ Milos Foreman(1932—):米洛斯·福尔曼,是自捷克新浪潮中诞生的最具国际知名度的导演,代表作《飞越疯人院》(*One Flew Over the Cuckoo's Nest*)。

⑥ *Amadeus*:电影《莫扎特传》,导演米洛斯·福尔曼(Milos Forman)。

⑦ *Terminator*:影片《终结者》,美国系列科幻动作片,著名男演员阿诺德·施瓦辛格(Arnold Schwarzenegger)主演。

I don't want to defend Hollywood, because I don't represent Hollywood—I can't, any more than one particular writer can represent literature or one painter art. For the most part, the impulse toward all art, entertainment, culture, pop culture, comes from the same place within the makers of it. The level of talent and the soul, if you'll forgive the word again, is what finally limits it.

At the risk of telling you more than you need to know about my own work, I make the movies I make because there is in each film some argument that fascinates me, an issue I want to work through. I call this a spine or an armature because it functions for me like an armature in sculpture—something I can cover up and it will support the whole structure. I can test the scenes against it. For me, the film, when properly dramatized, adds up to this idea, this argument.

But there are lots of other ways to go about making a film, and lots of other filmmakers who do it differently. Some filmmakers begin knowing exactly what they want to say and then craft a vehicle that contains that statement. Some are interested in pure escape. Here's the catch. The effectiveness and the success of all our films is determined by exactly the same standards—unfortunately, not by the particular validity of their message but by their ability to engage the concentration and emotions of the audience.

Citizen Kane is a 1941 American drama film, directed by and starring Orson Welles. The film is often considered the greatest of all time and is particularly praised for its innovative cinematography, music and narrative structure. *Citizen Kane* was Welles' first feature film. The film was nominated for Academy Awards in nine categories; it won an Academy Award for Best Writing (Original Screenplay) by Herman Mankiewicz and Welles.

《公民凯恩》是1941年的美国电影，导演是奥森·威尔斯。这部影片被认为是史上最伟大的电影，尤其是它在电影摄影、配乐和叙事结构方面的创新广受赞誉。《公民凯恩》是导演奥森·威尔斯的处女作。该片获得奥斯卡奖9项提名，由海尔曼·曼凯维契和威尔斯完成的剧本获得最佳编剧（原创剧本）奖。

*Citizen Kane*① is an attack on acquisition, but that's not why people go to see it. I don't have any idea if the audience that saw *Tootsie* thought at any conscious level that it could be about a guy who became a better man for having been a woman; or that *The Way We Were*, a film I made 20 years ago, may have been about the tension between passion, often of the moment, and wisdom, often part of a longer view; or that *Out Of Africa* might be about the inability to possess another individual and even the inability of one country to possess another. That's intellectual and stuffy. I just hope the audiences were entertained. …

---

① *Citizen Kane*: 美国影片《公民凯恩》，影片以一位报业大亨凯恩之死揭开了序幕，并通过他的人生经历和事业的兴衰史，见证了一桩资本主义神话下的复杂真相。该片在世界电影史上具有重要地位。

AN AMERICAN AESTHETIC?

In some circles, American films suffer by comparison with European films precisely because a lot of our movies seem to be the product of little deliberation and much instinct. It's been said of European movies that essence precedes existence, which is just a fancy way of saying that European movies exist in order to say something. Certainly one never doubts with a European film that it's saying something, and often it just comes right out and says it.

American films work by indirection; they work by action and movement, either internal or external, but almost always movement. Our films are more narratively driven than others, which has a lot to do with the American character and the way we look at our lives. We see ourselves and our lives as being part of a story.

Most of our movies have been pro the underdog, concerned with injustice, relatively anti-authority. There's usually a system—or a bureaucracy—to triumph over.

More often than not, American movies have been affirmative and hopeful about destiny. They're usually about individuals who control their own lives and their fate. In Europe, the system was so class-bound and steeped in tradition that there was no democratization of that process.

There's no prior education required to assimilate American movies or American culture. American culture is general, as opposed to the specificity of Japanese or Indian culture. America has the most easily digestible culture.

Our movies seem artless. The best of them keep us interested without seeming to engage our minds. The very thing that makes movies so popular here and abroad is one of the primary things that drives their critics to apoplexy, but seeming artlessness isn't necessarily mindlessness. There's a deliberate kind of artlessness in American movies that has come from a discipline or aesthetic long ago imposed by the marketplace. Our movies began as immigrants' dreams that would appeal to the dreams of other immigrants, and this aesthetic has led American films to transcend languages and cultures and communicate to every country in the world.

THE FILMMAKER'S RESPONSIBILITY

It has been suggested to some extent in this conference that I ought to study my own and American filmmakers' responsibilities to the public and to the world. I realize I have responsibilities as a filmmaker, but I don't believe that they are as a moralist, a preacher, or a purveyor of values. I know it's tempting to use filmmaking as such, but utility is a poor standard to use in art. It's a standard that has been and is still used by every totalitarian state in the world.

My responsibility is to try to make good films, but "good" is a subjective word. To me at any rate, "good" doesn't necessarily mean "good for us" in the narrow sense that they must elevate our spirits and send us out of the theater singing, or even that they must promote only those values that some think are worth promoting.

Good movies challenge us, they provoke us, they make us angry sometimes. They present points of view we don't agree with. They force us to clarify our positions in opposition to them, and they do this best when they provide us with an experience and not a polemic.

Somebody gave the okay to pay for *One Flew Over the Cuckoo's Nest*①, *Driving Miss Daisy*②, *Stand By Me*③, *Moonstruck*④, *Terms of Endearment*⑤, and *Amadeus*, and despite conventional wisdom that said those films could not be successful, those decisions paid off handsomely because there are no rules. Studio executives and other financiers do exceed themselves. They take chances. They have to, and we have to hope that they'll do it more often.

What we see in movie theaters today is not a simple reflection of today's economics or politics in this country but is a sense of the people who make the movies, and they vary as individuals vary. So what we really want is for this very privileged process to be in the best hands possible, but I know of no force that can regulate this except the moral climate and appetites of our society.

What we're exporting now is largely a youth culture. It's full of adolescent values; it's full of adolescent rage, love, rebelliousness, and a desire to shock. If you're unhappy with their taste—and this is a free market—then an appetite has to be created for something better. How do we do that? Well, we're back to square one: the supplier or the consumer, the chicken or the egg? Let's not even ask the question; the answer is both.

Of course filmmakers ought to be encouraged toward excellence, and audiences ought to be encouraged to demand it. How? That's for thinkers and social scientists to figure out. I have no idea. But if I had to play this scene out as an imaginary dialogue, I might say that you must educate the consumer first, and the best places to start are at school and at home. And then you would say that that is my job, that popular entertainment must participate in this education. And I would say, ideally, perhaps, but I do not think that will happen within a system that operates so fundamentally from an economic point of view. On an individual basis, yes, one filmmaker at a time; as an industry, no. An appetite or market will have to exist first.

That's not as bad as it sounds, because in the best of all possible worlds, we do try to satisfy both needs: entertain people and be reasonably intelligent about it. It can be done, and it is done more often than you might think. It's just very difficult.

It's like the two Oxford dons who were sitting at the Boarshead. They were playwrights, grousing because neither one of them could get produced, neither one could get performed. One turned to the other and said, "Oh, the hell with it. Let's just do what Shakespeare did—give them entertainment."

---

① *One Flew Over the Cuckoo's Nest*:《飞越疯人院》,美国70年代社会政治电影的代表作,获得1975年奥斯卡最佳影片、最佳导演、最佳改编剧本、最佳男主角和最佳女主角等五项主奖。

② *Driving Miss Daisy*:美国影片《为戴西小姐开车》,讲述一名黑人司机与一位白人老妇雇主之间的故事,获得1990年奥斯卡最佳影片、最佳女主角等4个奖项。

③ *Stand By Me*:影片《伴我同行》,讲述青春期边缘几个孩子苦乐参半的故事。

④ *Moonstruck*:电影《月色撩人》,这是一部关于爱情和家庭的轻喜剧。

⑤ *Terms of Endearment*:电影《母女情深》,该片被认为是80年代最感人肺腑的影片之一,以人生酸甜苦辣来诠释母女复杂亲情关系,获得1983年奥斯卡最佳导演、最佳影片等5项大奖。

Questions to Consider

1. Do you agree with Pollack's notions of artistic integrity, especially his assertions that a filmmaker's prime goal should be to entertain an audience and that movies simply reflect the surrounding society?
2. When Pollack asserts that he'd "rather make the whole world cry than 17 intellectuals in a classroom," what is he implying about his—and other filmmakers'—motivations?
3. According to Pollack, "Most of the time, high-mindedness just leads to pretentious or well-meaning, often very bad, films." Do you agree? If not, can you give some examples to refute his opinion?
4. Pollack describes his interest in making "films about arguments" and giving "each side a strong argument." What does he mean? Do you think movies that balance two sides of an "argument" are "more interesting" than those with clear-cut "good guys" and "bad guys?"
5. What is Pollack's definition of good movies in the last section? Do you think what good movies can do according to his view ("Good movies challenge us, they provoke us, they make us angry sometimes. They present points of view we don't agree with. They force us to clarify our positions in opposition to them.") actually imply that movies contribute to the creation of the values of the society?

Historical Perspective 历史视角

Film

电影

Robert A. Armor

The date was December 28, 1895. The place was the basement of a cafe in Paris. The audience was the first public one to pay its way to watch movies, paying to be fascinated by moving images of a baby eating his meal, workers leaving a factory, and a train rushing into a station. The scenes were taken from ordinary life, but the experience was far from ordinary. This event was produced by the Lumière brothers①, but the technology that led to this moment had been the result of the imagination and persistence of many inventors, both in Europe and America.

Eadweard Muybridge② in 1877 had discovered that sequential still photographs of a horse running could be placed in a series and "projected" in such a manner as to make the photographic image of the horse appear to be running. In New Jersey in the late 1880s Thomas Edison③ and his crew led by William Dickson④ developed the idea of putting photographs on a single piece of continuous film, and George Eastman⑤ supplied the film. For projection Edison decided on the Kinetoscope, a peephole machine through which the film could be shown to one person at a time. Several creative inventors worked on the idea of a projector, but it was finally the Lumière brothers who were able to adapt Edison's ideas and develop the first practical means of allowing many people to view a movie simultaneously. The history of this new art form was then to be written in light.

Once the photographic technology had been developed, the next stage was to decide what to do with it. Obviously audiences could not long be enthralled by shots of a baby eating and would demand more. Both the Lumières and Edison attempted to expand the cinematic subject matter;

---

① Lumière brothers: 卢米埃兄弟(Auguste Marie Louis Nicholas,1862—1954; Louis Jean,1864—1948),法国人,电影和电影放映机的发明者。

② Eadweard Muybridge(1830—1904):埃德沃德·迈布里奇,英国摄影师,他因使用多个相机拍摄运动的物体而著名。

③ Thomas Edison(1847—1931):托马斯·爱迪生,举世闻名的美国发明家。爱迪生一生共有约两千项创造发明,为人类的文明和进步做出了巨大的贡献。

④ William Dickson(1860—1935):威廉·迪克森,法国-苏格兰人,发明家,在托马斯·爱迪生的公司研制出电影摄像机和活动电影放映机。

⑤ George Eastman(1854—1932):乔治·伊士曼,美国发明家,柯达公司创办人以及胶卷发明人。

but it was another Frenchman, George Méliès[①], who first achieved major success at telling a story with film. He was a magician who used the medium as part of his act, but in the process he began to depict plot as well as action. His most famous film was *A Trip to the Moon*[②] (1902) which described a fanciful space voyage.

In order to develop a narrative process for film, the filmmaker had to learn to manipulate both space and time, to change them, and to move characters and action within them much as a novelist does. What Méliès had begun, others, especially Edison and his new director of production, continued. Edwin S. Porter[③] learned how to use dissolves and cuts between shots to indicate changes in time or space, or both; the result was *The Great Train Robbery* (1903). This Western, shot in the wilds of New Jersey, told the complete story of a train robbery, the chase of the bandits, and their eventual defeat in a gunfight with the posse. Cross-cutting allowed Porter to show in sequence activities of both the posse and the bandits that were supposed to take place at the same time.

Businessmen began to realize the financial potential for movies. While movies were first shown as part of other forms of entertainment, they soon became the featured attraction themselves. By 1905 the first nickelodeon had opened in Pittsburgh, where customers each paid a nickel to see a full program of a half dozen short films. The opening of theaters completed the elements necessary for an industry: product, technology, producer, purchaser, and distributor.

In 1907, a would-be playwright came to Edison with a filmscript for sale. Edison did not like the script, but he hired its author, David Wark Griffith[④], as an actor. Griffith refused to use his real name, but he needed money and accepted the job. Thus began the career of the man who would turn this entertainment into an art. He began making films himself shortly. His tastes in plots were melodramatic, but his interests in technique were both innovative and scientific. Guided by his cameraman, Billy Bitzer, he began to experiment with editing and shots, finding many ideas for cinematic technique in the sentimental novels and poems of nineteenth-century literature. Gradually he persuaded both audiences and company bosses to accept the idea of a more complicated plot told in a lengthy movie. The result was the first major, long film. In 1915, after unheard-of amounts of time in production, Griffith released *The Birth of a Nation*, a story of the South during the Civil War and Reconstruction. The racial overtones of the film caused considerable controversy, but the power

① George Méliès(1861—1938):乔治·梅里爱,法国电影导演,世界第一位电影艺术家。他创造了快动作、慢动作、停机再拍、叠印、淡出、淡入等特技摄影,把电影技艺变成了电影艺术,并且引进了戏剧因素,创造了故事片。

② *A Trip to the Moon*:法国影片《月球旅行家》(1902),乔治·梅里爱导演,表现了一群天文学家乘坐炮弹到月球探险的情景。本片不仅开创了科幻片的先河,而且使电影上升为施展幻想的平台和提供娱乐的工具,被认为是电影史上的里程碑。

③ Edwin S. Porter(1870—1941):埃德温·S·波特,美国早期导演,曾在托马斯·爱迪生的公司工作。

④ David Wark Griffith(1875—1948):大卫·格里菲斯,美国导演,被认为是对早期电影发展做出极大贡献的开创性人物。

of the images and the timing of the editing created a work of art whose aesthetic excellence is not questioned. In response to the criticism of his racial views, the next year Griffith directed *Intolerance*, which interwove four stories of intolerance into a single film. Griffith was to continue as one of America's leading directors until audiences began to lose their taste for melodrama, and other directors had learned his methods. He had been responsible for launching the careers of several directors, such as Raoul Walsh①, and Frank Powell②, and numerous actors, such as Lillian and Dorothy Gish③, Mary Pickford④, and H. B. Walthall.

While Griffith was learning how to get the most from screen actors, Thomas Ince⑤ was polishing the art of telling a story efficiently. In the early 1900s, he directed a few films (*Civilization*, 1916, is the best known), but he quickly turned his attention to production, leaving the details of directing to others under his close supervision. His talent was for organization, and today he is credited with perfecting the studio system. Film is actually a collaborative art, and Ince learned how to bring the talents of many different people into a system that produced polished films, without the individualizing touches found in those films of Griffith or others who work outside the strict studio system.

One man who learned his trade from Griffith was Mack Sennett⑥. Sennett worked for Griffith for a few years as a director and writer, but his interests were more in comedy than in melodrama. In 1912 he broke away and began to work for an independent company, Keystone⑦. Here he learned to merge the methods of stage slapstick comedy with the techniques of film; the results were the Keystone Cops, Ben Turpin⑧, and Charlie Chaplin⑨. Sennett's films used only the barest plot outline as a frame for comic gags that were improvised and shot quickly. From the Sennett method, Charlie Chaplin developed his own technique and character. He began making shorts under the direction of Sennett, but in 1915 he left and joined with Essenay which agreed to let him write and direct his own films at an unprecedented salary. Here he fleshed out his tramp

---

① Raoul Walsh(1887—1980):美国导演、演员,美国电影艺术与科学学院(Academy of Motion Picture Arts and Sciences)的创始人之一。

② Frank Powell:弗兰克·鲍威尔,美国默片时代的导演、编剧。

③ Lillian and Dorothy Gish(1893—1993):莉莲·吉许,美国著名女演员、电影活动家,出演过格里菲斯许多重要影片中的女主角。

④ Mary Pickford(1892—1979):玛丽·璧克馥,著名女演员,美国电影艺术与科学学院的创始人之一。

⑤ Thomas Ince(1882—1924):托马斯·因斯,美国默片时代的演员、导演、编剧和制片人,被称为“西部片之父”。

⑥ Mack Sennett(1880—1960):麦克·塞纳特,1909年后参加格里菲斯的摄制组,1912年建立启斯东影片公司。他对美国电影的最大贡献在于首创了传送带生产式的制片方式。

⑦ Keystone Cops:启斯东电影公司,设立于1912年,1915年为“铁三角公司”所吸收。

⑧ Ben Turpin(1869—1940):美国默片时代的喜剧演员。

⑨ Charlie Chaplin(1889—1977):查理·卓别林,英国著名电影演员、导演、制片人。他一生共拍摄过80余部喜剧片,在电影史上著名的影片有《淘金记》(*The Gold Rush*,1925)、《城市之光》(*City Lights*,1931)、《摩登时代》(*Modern Times*,1936)、《大独裁者》(*The Great Dictator*,1940)等。

character; one of his first films for Essenay was *The Tramp*① (1915). He continued making films that combined his own comic sense and acrobatic movements with social commentary and along with Mary Pickford became one of the first "stars." Later he made features, such as *The Gold Rush* (1925) and *Modern Times* (1936). Sennett and Chaplin began a period of great film comedy. Buster Keaton② combined a deadpan look with remarkable physical ability and timing. He too began making shorts, but soon was directing and starring in features, such as *The General* (1926). Harold Lloyd③ (*The Freshman*, 1925) and Harry Langdon④ (*The Strong Man*, 1926) also created comic characters that demonstrated their individuality and imagination.

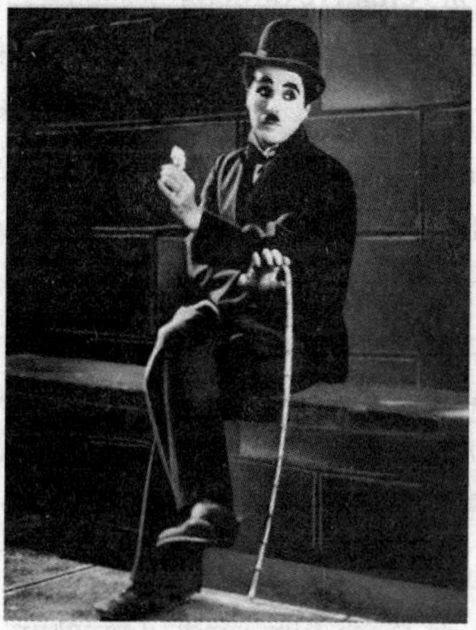

As one of the most creative and influential personalities of the silent-film era, Charlie Chaplin endowed comedy movie with the greatest power to give pleasure and relief to so many human beings when they needed it. His working life in entertainment spanned over 75 years, from the Victorian stage and the Music Hall in the United Kingdom as a child performer, until close to his death at the age of 88. In 1999, the American Film Institute ranked Chaplin the 10th greatest male screen legend of all time.

在无声电影时期查理·卓别林是最有才能和影响最大的人物之一。作为演员,他那戴着圆顶硬礼帽、手持竹拐杖、留着一撇小胡子的流浪汉形象被称为银幕上的不朽经典;作为导演,他用《淘金记》、《城市之光》、《摩登时代》、《大独裁者》等作品为现代喜剧电影奠定了基础;而作为一位从无声片时代成功过渡到有声片时代的喜剧大师,他留给后世的精神财富更是难以估量。

From these ingredients came the studio system and the star system. The demands of the moviegoing audiences created a need for a great number of films, and small companies were unable to meet the demands. Adolph Zukor⑤ at Paramount⑥ and Marcus Loew⑦, Louis B. Mayer⑧, and Irvin Thalberg at Metro-Goldwyn-Mayer quickly learned the means of applying American business methods to this new industry. They bought out their competition and eventually controlled film production, distribution, and exhibition. Even the actors and directors got into the

① *The Tramp*: 美国影片《流浪汉》(1915)。查理·卓别林在其中扮演的流浪汉是他最成功的银幕形象之一。

② Buster Keaton(1895—1966):巴斯特·基顿,美国导演、演员、编剧。

③ Harold Lloyd(1893—1971):哈罗德·劳埃德,美国喜剧片演员。1952年美国电影艺术与科学学院授予他奥斯卡特别奖。

④ Harry Langdon(1884—1944):哈里·兰登,美国默片时代的著名喜剧演员、编剧。

⑤ Adolph Zukor: 阿道夫·祖科,出生于匈牙利,1903年转行进入电影放映业,1912年成立了Famous Players公司。

⑥ Paramount:派拉蒙影业公司,是美国著名的电影制片和发行公司。

⑦ Marcus Loew(1870—1927):马尔科斯·洛夫,美国商业大亨和电影产业的先驱,Loews Theatres和米高梅电影公司(Metro-Goldwyn-Mayer,简称MGM)的创建人。

⑧ Louis B. Mayer(1882—1957):路易·B·梅耶,好莱坞工业大鳄,著名制片人,米高梅公司创建人。

act as Chaplin, Griffith, Pickford, and Douglas Fairbanks joined together to create United Artists[①], intended at first to distribute the various productions of its founders. Later it too became a studio force, along with Columbia, Fox, Warners, and others.

With the studios came the stars. The public hungered for new heroes and new sex objects, and the studios were quick to give the public what it wanted. Along with the stars who had been established in the early 1900s came the new generation of the 1920s: Rudolph Valentino[②], Gloria Swanson[③], Clara Bow[④]. The stars soon became the nucleus of American myth, and the public followed the stars' affairs, marriages, and extravagant lives with keen interest. This was the stuff Hollywood was made of. Fortunately there were behind these stars creative directors, such as Cecil B. DeMille[⑤], Eric Von Stroheim, and Henry King, who were able to mold the talents of the stars into movies.

During the 1920s American films dominated the worldwide industry, but they were greatly influenced and enhanced by developments and personalities from Europe. The Russians Sergei Eisenstein[⑥] (*Potemkin*, 1925) and V. I. Pudovkin[⑦] (*Mother*, 1926) were especially influential in their understanding of montage (the relationship of the images to each other and the meaning that results). American interest in fantasy was influenced both directly and indirectly by *The Cabinet of Dr. Caligari*[⑧] (1919) directed by the German Robert Wiene[⑨] and *Destiny* (1921) directed by an Austrian working in Germany, Fritz Lang[⑩].

Some Europeans came to America to make films: Ernst Lubitsch[⑪], Victor Seastrom[⑫], and F. W. Murnau[⑬], for examples. The influence on American film of these films and filmmakers was

---

① United Artists: 联美公司,1919 年由卓别林等创办的一家电影发行公司。

② Rudolph Valentino(1895—1926):鲁道夫·瓦伦蒂诺,美国默片时代的著名演员。

③ Gloria Swanson(1897—1983):葛洛丽亚·斯旺森,美国女演员,20 年代跻身于无声片影后之列,演艺生涯一直延续到 60 年代。

④ Clara Bow(1905—1965):克拉拉·鲍,美国女星,有"性感女郎"之称。

⑤ Cecil B. DeMille(1881—1959):美国著名电影导演、编剧、制片人,派拉蒙公司创始人之一,电影生涯从 1910 年代持续到 50 年代末。

⑥ Sergei Eisenstein(1898—1948):谢尔盖·爱森斯坦,前苏联著名电影导演、电影艺术理论家、教育家。1922 年,他在《左翼艺术战线》杂志上发表了第一篇纲领性的美学宣言《杂耍蒙太奇》,引起了长期的争论,并对整个电影艺术的发展产生了深远的影响。《战舰波将金号》(*Potemkin*, 1925)为其代表作。

⑦ V. I. Pudovkin(1893—1953):前苏联电影导演、编剧、演员,其蒙太奇理论颇有影响。

⑧ *The Cabinet of Dr. Caligari*:德国惊悚片《卡里加里博士》(1919),罗伯特·威恩导演。

⑨ Robert Wiene(1873—1938):罗伯特·威恩,德国导演,电影史上德国表现主义的代表人物。

⑩ Fritz Lang(1890—1976):弗里茨·朗,德国著名编剧、导演,与希区柯克、卓别林等人并列于电影百人之列,被认为是电影史上影响最大的导演之一。代表作《M 就是凶手》(*M*,1931)等。

⑪ Ernst Lubitsch(1892—1947):恩斯特·刘别谦,德国著名导演,擅长执导喜剧片与歌舞片。他 1922 年到好莱坞发展,取得巨大成功。

⑫ Victor Seastrom(1879—1960):瑞典著名电影导演、编剧和演员。

⑬ F. W. Murnau(1888—1931):F·W·茂瑙,德国导演,1926 年转往好莱坞,在美国拍摄的《日出》被认为是德国默片的颠峰之作。

profound; they left their strong impression on what came to be known as the Hollywood movie.

The story surrounding the coming of sound to movies is a complex and complicated one. The idea of connecting sound to the visuals was an old one; Edison had in fact entered the movie business because he was searching for visuals to go with the phonograph he was already marketing. To convert the movie technology to sound was expensive. Despite development of the necessary technology (most notably in this country by Lee de Forest①), the industry was reluctant to invest in the change. In the mid-1920s Western Electric developed a method for putting the sound on a disk that could be roughly synchronized with the film. None of the big studios could be convinced to try it, but Warners Brothers was about to be forced out of business by the other, larger companies. It had little to lose and decided to take the risk. For a year Warners distributed a program with short sound films of slight interest, but on October 6, 1927, it premiered *The Jazz Singer*② with Al Jolson③. Sound was used to help tell the story, and the public loved it. Quickly, Warners established its financial base, and other studios rushed to emulate them; but problems developed. Studios had to reequip themselves. The camera, which had been struggling to free itself and discover new methods of expression, found itself confined to a large box and immobile. Actors had to learn to speak to their audiences, and exhibitors had to invest in sound projectors and speakers. Once the problems were overcome, however, the marriage of sound to the visuals became a natural extension of the art.

The period between the coming of sound and World War II was dominated by the studios. They controlled the production—including story, the role of the directors, and the selection of actors—distribution, and exhibition (they owned their own theaters). In the 1930s America went to the movies; by the end of the decade some eighty million people saw a movie every week. The studios provided them with the means to live out their fantasies, find heroes, and escape from the Depression.

One factor directly affecting the films of the 1930s was censorship. Hollywood movies in the late 1920s and early 1930s had become rather open in their use of sex, and the scandals in the private lives of the stars shocked the public even as it hungered for vicarious living. Fear of government intervention and of the Depression forced the studios to censor themselves. They established the Hays Office④ under the directorship of Will Hays⑤, former postmaster-general, and this office published a strict moral code for on-screen activities and language. The results

---

① Lee de Forest(1873—1961):德·福雷斯特,美国发明家,真空三极管的发明人,“无线电之父”。

② *The Jazz Singer*:美国爱情歌舞片《爵士歌王》(1927),Alan Crosland 导演,Al Jolson 主演。有人把它看作电影史上第一部有声长片。

③ Al Jolson(1886—1950):艾尔·乔森,20 世纪初期百老汇舞台和后来银幕上最有名的歌星和演员之一。

④ Hays Office: 海斯办公室,威尔·海斯主持的“美国电影协会”(Motion Picture Association of America)的俗称。

⑤ Will Hays(1879—1954):威尔·海斯,1912 至 1922 年任邮政部长。1922 年,他转向电影业,成为美国电影制片人和发行人协会(MPPDA)的第一任主席,主持制定“电影生产法典”(后人简称“海斯法典”)。

stifled creativity, but the new moral tastes of the public were satisfied.

The stars captured the public's imagination as in no other time in American popular culture: Fred Astaire and Ginger Rogers, Jean Harlow, Clark Gable and Vivien Leigh, Edward C. Robinson, and Marlene Dietrich. The comics maintained the traditions of the silent comedians: Charlie Chaplin continued to make movies and was joined by the Marx brothers①, Mae West, and W. C. Fields.

Gone with the Wind is a 1939 American epic romance-drama film adapted from Margaret Mitchell's 1936 novel of the same name. Produced by David O. Selznick and starring Clark Gable and Vivien Leigh, it tells a story of the American Civil War and Reconstruction Era from a white, southern point of view. It received ten Academy Awards (8 competitive, 2 honorary), a record that stood for twenty years; in the American Film Institute's inaugural Top 100 Best American Films of All Time list of 1998, it was ranked number four. Today, it is still considered one of the greatest and most popular films of all time.

根据玛格丽特·米切尔的小说《飘》改编,由克拉克·盖博和费雯·丽饰演男、女主角的《乱世佳人》在文化与商业上都获得了极大的成功。在1940年的奥斯卡奖中,本片独得包括最佳影片在内的十项大奖,此记录在20年后才被打破;在1998年美国电影协会评选的20世纪最伟大100部电影中它排名第四;而在商业上,《乱世佳人》是美国史上售出票数最多者,并有许多研究指出在考虑通胀后,它是美国史上票房最高的电影。

At the same time, the directors had to find a path through the maze created by the studios, the Hays Office, and the stars. They had to bring all these divergent elements together and make movies. Men such as John Ford and Howard Hawks② created their own visions of America and discovered methods of capturing the American myth on film. Many of the directors of the period were immigrants: Josef von Sternberg③, Alfred Hitchcock④, Fritz Lang, Otto Preminger⑤, and Frank Capra⑥. Each discovered for himself the essence of this country and its people. Perhaps that

---

① Marx brothers:影史上最成功的美国喜剧团体之一,堪称无厘头的鼻祖,热衷于塑造或癫狂或装傻充愣的人物,表现荒诞不经的内容,并凭此独步20世纪30年代的喜剧电影界。

② Howard Hawks(1896—1977):霍华德·霍克斯,美国电影导演,一生拍过47部电影,类型多样,被称为"类型片大师"。

③ Josef von Sternberg(1894—1969):约瑟夫·冯·史登堡,奥地利美籍导演、编剧。代表作《上海风光》(*The Shanghai Gesture*,1941)等。

④ Alfred Hitchcock(1899—1980):阿尔弗雷德·希区柯克,原籍英国,是一位闻名世界的电影导演,惊悚悬疑片大师。在长达六十年的艺术生涯中,他拍摄了超过五十部电影。代表作《蝴蝶梦》(*Rebecca*,1941),《惊魂记》(*Psycho*,1961)等。

⑤ Otto Preminger(1905—1986):奥托·普雷明格,美国演员、导演、制片人,出生于维也纳。

⑥ Frank Capra(1897—1991):弗兰克·卡普拉,美国著名导演,出生于意大利,被称为"好莱坞最伟大的意大利人"。他六次获得奥斯卡最佳导演奖提名,获奖三次。代表作《一夜风流》(*It Happened One Night*,1934)等。

essence was most fittingly expressed in a film that came at the end of the prewar period, *Citizen Kane*(1941), the first film Orson Welles① directed.

The war changed the industry. Many residents of Hollywood took time off to participate in the war effort. Some like John Ford and Frank Capra made films for the government. Others like Fritz Lang continued to make commercial films, but they were propaganda-oriented and helped build morale. The stars went to the battle areas to entertain the troops. Even studio space was commandeered to produce war documentaries, and war films became a dominant fictional genre.

After the war the rate of change accelerated. Anti-trust suits broke up the large companies and forced them to sell their theaters. And television began to keep the public at home. The movie industry responded with attempts at expanding the medium to attract new interests: 3-D, CinemaScope, Technicolor; and it continues to experiment: quadraphonic sound, sensurround, holographic images, and giant leaps in special effects have been tried.

However, in responding to competition from television, the use and type of subject matter has taken precedence over the development of technology. The movie makers have thought it necessary to give the public something that cannot be beamed into private living rooms. The results have been increased depiction of explicitness in sex and violence. Both sex and violence have been staples of the movies since the beginning, but the contemporary cinema has found new methods of enticing the public with them.

As the major Hollywood studios began to lose their domination of the American movie industry and turn their attention to television production, the leadership was taken up by independent producers and directors, making their own films and then distributing them through the networks originally established by the Hollywood companies. Stanley Kubrick②, Robert Altman③, Arthur Penn④, Peter Bogdanovich⑤, and Francis Ford Coppola⑥ have provided America with a new group of filmmakers, men who have demonstrated a certain independence of subject and method. Part of the void left by the diminishing importance of Hollywood has been

① Orson Welles(1915—1985):奥逊·威尔斯,是美国电影史上集演员、导演、编剧、制片人等多种角色于一身的电影天才。《公民凯恩》是其影响最大的作品。

② Stanley Kubrick(1928—1999):斯坦利·库布里克,美国著名导演。其作品《奇爱博士》(*Dr. Strangelove*,1964)、《2001 太空漫游》(*2001: A Space Odssey*,1968)、《发条橙》(*A Clockwork Orange*,1971)等都是电影史上的经典之作。

③ Robert Altman(1925—2006):罗伯特·奥特曼,美国著名导演,是迄今囊括金棕榈奖、金狮奖和金熊奖的两位导演之一。代表作《陆军野战医院》(*M. A. S. H.*,1970)、《纳什维尔》(*Nashville*,1975)等。

④ Arthur Penn(1922—):阿瑟·佩恩,美国著名导演,其作品《邦妮和克莱德》(*Bonnie and Clyde*,1967)被认为"新好莱坞电影"的开篇之作。

⑤ Peter Bogdanovich(1939—):彼得·博格达诺维奇,编剧、导演、演员,是美国在 60 年代末到 70 年代大量涌现的新一代导演的代表。

⑥ Francis Ford Coppola(1949—):弗朗西斯·福特·科波拉,美国著名导演,多次获得奥斯卡奖。代表作《教父》三部曲(1972,1974,1990)、《对话》(*The Conversation*,1974)、《现代启示录》(*Apocalypse Now*,1979)等。

filled by foreign filmmakers whose films have been greeted with enthusiasm by American audiences. Ingmar Bergman①, François Truffaut②, and Federico Fellini③ have dominated, but for the first time countries outside of Europe have begun to leave their mark. Japan has been especially productive.

Perhaps, however, the most important change in movies in recent years has been in the audience. By no means the number of people who went to the movies in the late 1930s still do, but those who do go are younger and more knowledgeable about film. They read the books, subscribe to film journals, watch filmed interviews with movie people on television, and read daily reviews. Many in today's audience are college-educated and have taken film courses while in school; they can talk intelligently about montage, jump cuts, and fade outs. It is for this audience that *Scenes from a Marriage*④ is imported from Europe and *Star Wars* is made.

---

① Ingmar Bergman(1918—2007):英格玛·伯格曼,瑞典著名导演,杰出的电影剧作家,"作者电影"的代表。代表作《野草莓》(*Wild Strawberries*,1957)、《第七封印》(*The Seventh Seal*,1967)等。

② François Truffaut(1932—1984):弗朗索瓦·特吕弗,法国电影新浪潮运动中最具影响力的导演,电影"作者论"的主要倡导者。代表作《四百击》(*The Four Hundred Blows*, 1959),《最后一班地铁》(*The Last Metro*,1980)等。

③ Federico Fellini(1920—):费德里柯·费里尼,意大利著名的电影艺术家,编剧、导演和演员。代表作《八部半》(*Eight and a Half*,1963)等。

④ *Scenes from a Marriage*: 瑞典电影《婚姻生活》(1973),英格玛·伯格曼导演。

Chapter 7 American Icons

The Worshipped Characters for the Public
美国偶像

In the fall of 2001, Michael Jordan came out of retirement for the second time to return to active play in the NBA. After months of speculation, the build-up to Jordan's reappearance was enormous, promising to make it one of the media events of the year. But then, literally overnight, the national mood changed, and by the time Jordan soared towards his first postretirement slam dunk, America had rediscovered a different kind of national hero, one who prompted us to reappraise just what heroism means. And so, at least for the time, Michael Jordan's preeminent stature as an American icon was redefined as a new set of icons suddenly emerged.

In this chapter, you will read about America's cultural icons, about those figures—some entirely fictional and others quite real—who have been mythologized into larger-than-life symbols that capture our imagination by embodying our deepest values and desires. An icon is not simply a popular figure or celebrity (though he or she often is in our entertainment culture); an icon is someone, or something, that has a meaning , a cultural significance that goes beyond any particular qualities he, she , or it might have.

It is not difficult to find that most icons today are from the entertaining world. But it was not true in the past. For America's traditional heroes and cultural icons weren't entertainers at all; they were men like George Washington and Abraham Lincoln, who dedicated their lives to building and preserving their country, or like Frederick Douglass① and Martin Luther King Jr., who struggled to win for their people the rights that their country promised. And they were women like Susan B. Anthony and Eleanor Roosevelt②, who helped redefine the place of women in American political life. It has only been in the era of mass culture that entertainers have come to replace such traditional icons, beginning with the Golden Age of Hollywood and baseball, when names like Clark Gable, Greta Garbo, and Babe Ruth③ came to represent the emerging center of American desire.

Somehow, the trend of American life had been strongly towards celebrity worship. American culture had been dedicated to the celebrity of wealth, fame, and entertainment. Few Americans even

---

① Frederic Douglas (1818—1895): 19 世纪著名黑人废奴主义者,作家、演说家、社会活动家。

② Susan B. Anthony (1820—1906): 早期美国女权运动领导者。Eleanor Roosevelt (1884—1962): 富兰克林·罗斯福总统妻子,著名社会活动家。

③ Babe Ruth (1895—1948): 美国早期著名棒球运动员.

seemed to notice or care that these weren't the values that their country had been founded upon.

That so many of America's cultural icons have been subsumed, or even created, to serve commercial interests is a sign of just how profoundly America has embraced the values of a consumer culture. And few icons have been left out of the consumer stampede. Political icons like Martin Luther King Jr. have been appropriated for telecommunications pitch, and the great scientist Albert Einstein's image has been splashed across more ad campaigns than we can count. For their part, George Washington and Abraham Lincoln are the names of sales events. Very little, it seems, is too sacred not to be used for commercial purposes. Or is it that consumerism itself has become sacred?

The readings in this chapter analyze a range of American characters, some of whom have been used for marketing purposes and others who function as American heroes, real and fictional, serving as vehicles for clandestinely conveying the American values. Michael Eric Dyson starts with an interpretation of the cultural significance of Michael Jordan, a reading of a real-world superman. Gary Engle follows with an analysis of the original Superman, a cartoon hero who, Engle argues, is very much a symbol of the American way. Emily Prager comes next with an analysis of one of America's favorite characters, Barbie-iconic toy that continues to shape American childhoods, especially the girlhoods.

Frederic Douglas

Susan Anthony

Clark Gable

Greta Garbo

Lesson 21 Be Like Mike? Michael Jordan and the Pedagogy of Desire

想像迈克一样吗?——迈克尔·乔丹和欲望的启示

MICHAEL ERIC DYSON

Introduction

It's hard to keep up with Michael Jordan. Not only is it impossible to beat him on the court, but you can't even figure out what to call him these days. A former NBA megastar? Well, he's retired twice and has come back once, which has become an appropriate addition to the legend that Michael Eric Dyson analyzes in this selection. Situating Jordan within the context of American social and cultural history, Dyson shows what basketball, and everything that goes with it, means in America, especially for African American youth. And it isn't just air time. A professor of African and Afro-American studies at the University of North Carolina at Chapel Hill, Michael Eric Dyson is author of *Reflecting Black: African-American Cultural Criticism* (1993), from which this essay is taken, *Making Malcolm: The Myth and Meaning of Malcolm X* (1995), and *Between God and Gangsta Rap: Bearing Witness to Black Culture* (1996), and *Holler if You Hear Me: Searching for Tupac Shakur* (2001).

Text

Michael Jordan is perhaps the best, and best-known, athlete in the world today. He has attained unparalleled cultural status because of his extraordinary physical gifts, his marketing as an icon of race-transcending American athletic and moral excellence, and his mastery of a sport that has become the metaphoric center of black cultural imagination. But the Olympian sum of Jordan's cultural meaning is greater than the fluent parts of his persona as athlete, family man, and marketing creation. There is hardly cultural precedence for the character of his unique fame, which has blurred the line between private and public, between personality and celebrity, and between substance and symbol. Michael Jordan stands at the breach between perception and intuition, his cultural meaning perennially deferred from closure because his career symbolizes possibility itself, gathering into its unfolding narrative the shattered remnants of previous incarnations of fame and yet transcending their reach.

Jordan has been called "the new DiMaggio①" and "Elvis in high-tops," indications of the herculean cultural heroism he has come to embody. There is even a religious element to the near

① Joe DiMaggio (1914—1999): 50 年代美国著名棒球运动员,1954 年与玛丽莲·梦露结婚。

worship of Jordan as a cultural icon of invincibility, as he has been called a "savior of sorts," "basketball's high priest", and "more popular than Jesus," except with "better endorsement deals". But the quickly developing cultural canonization① of Michael Jordan provokes reflection about the contradictory uses to which Jordan's body is put as a seminal cultural text and ambiguous symbol of fantasy, and the avenues of agency and resistance available especially to black youth who make symbolic investment in Jordan's body as a means of cultural and personal possibility, creativity, and desire.

I understand Jordan in the broadest sense of the term to be a public pedagogue②, a figure of estimable public moral authority whose career educates us about productive and disenabling forms of knowledge, desire, interest, consumption, and culture in three spheres: the culture of athletics that thrives on skill and performance, the specific expression of elements of African American culture, and the market forces and processes of commodification expressed by, and produced in, advanced capitalism. By probing these dimensions of Jordan's cultural importance, we may gain a clearer understanding of his function in American society.

Athletic activity has shaped and reflected important sectors of American society. First, it produced communities of common athletic interest organized around the development of highly skilled performance. The development of norms of athletic excellence evidenced in sports activities cemented communities of participants who valorized rigorous sorts of physical discipline in preparation for athletic competition and in expressing the highest degree of athletic skill. Second, it produced potent subcultures that inculcated in their participants norms of individual and team accomplishment. Such norms tapped into the bipolar structures of competition and cooperation that pervade American culture. Third, it provided a means of reinscribing Western frontier myths of exploration and discovery-as-conquest onto a vital sphere of American culture. Sports activities can be viewed in part as the attempt to symbolically ritualize and metaphorically extend the ongoing quest for mastery of environment and vanquishing of opponents within the limits of physical contest.

Air Jordan 飞人乔丹挑战引力

Fourth, athletic activity has served to reinforce habits and virtues centered in collective pursuit of communal goals that are intimately connected to the common good, usually characterized within athletic circles as "team spirit." The culture of sport has physically captured and athletically articulated the mores, folkways, and dominant visions of American society, and at its best it has been conceived as a means of symbolically embracing and equitably pursuing the just, the good, the true, and the beautiful. And finally, the

① canonize: 把……当作圣者。
② pedagogue: 教师,教员。

culture of athletics has provided an acceptable and widely accessible means of white male bonding. For much of its history, American sports activity has reflected white patriarchal privilege, and it has been rigidly defined and socially shaped by rules that restricted the equitable participation of women and people of color.

Black participation in sports in mainstream society, therefore, is a relatively recent phenomenon. Of course, there have existed venerable traditions of black sports, such as the Negro (baseball) Leagues[①], which countered the exclusion of black bodies from white sports. The prohibition of athletic activity by black men in mainstream society severely limited publicly acceptable forms of displaying black physical prowess, an issue that had been politicized during slavery and whose legacy extended into the middle of the twentieth century. Hence, the potentially superior physical prowess of black men, validated for many by the long tradition of slave labor that built American society, helped reinforce racist arguments about the racial regimentation of social space and the denigration of the black body as an inappropriate presence in traditions of American sport[②].

Coupled with this fear of superior black physical prowess was the notion that inferior black intelligence limited the ability of blacks to perform excellently in those sports activities that required mental concentration and agility. These two forces—the presumed lack of sophisticated black cognitive skills and the fear of superior black physical prowess—restricted black sports participation to thriving but financially handicapped subcultures of black athletic activity. Later, of course, the physical prowess of the black body would be acknowledged and exploited as a supremely fertile zone of profit as mainstream athletic society literally cashed in on[③] the symbolic danger of black sports excellence.

Because of its marginalized status within the regime of American sports, black athletic activity often acquired a social significance that transcended the internal dimensions of game, sport, and skill. Black sport became an arena not only for testing the limits of physical endurance and forms of athletic excellence—while reproducing or repudiating ideals of American justice, goodness, truth, and beauty—but it also became a way of ritualizing racial achievement against socially imposed barriers to cultural performance.

In short, black sport activity often acquired a heroic dimension, as viewed in the careers of figures such as Joe Louis, Jackie Robinson, Althea Gibson, Wilma Rudolph, Muhammad Ali,

---

① Negro (baseball) League: 黑人(棒球)联赛,由非裔球队组成,起始于1920年,1950年代后基本停赛。

② 此句大意为:为美国社会的建立付出了一份艰辛劳动的黑人有着强壮的体魄,但他们参与体育活动却会招致种族纷争乃至诋毁,这说明了传统社会对黑人的歧视。

③ cash in on: 从……中获利;利用。

and Arthur Ashe[①]. Black sports heroes transcended the narrow boundaries of specific sports activities and garnered importance as icons of cultural excellence, symbolic figures who embodied social possibilities of success denied to other people of color. But they also captured and catalyzed the black cultural fetishization of sport as a means of expressing black cultural style, as a means of valorizing craft as a marker of racial and self-expression, and as a means of pursuing social and economic mobility.

It is this culture of black athletics, created against the background of social and historical forces that shaped American athletic activity, that helped produce Jordan and help explain the craft that he practices. Craft is the honing of skill by the application of discipline, time, talent, and energy toward the realization of a particular cultural or personal goal. American folk cultures are pervaded by craft, from the production of cultural artifacts that express particular ethnic histories and traditions to the development of styles of life and work that reflect and symbolize a community's values, virtues, and goals. Michael Jordan's skills within basketball are clearly phenomenal, but his game can only be sufficiently explained by understanding its link to the fusion of African American cultural norms and practices, and the idealization of skill and performance that characterize important aspects of American sport. I will identify three defining characteristics of Jordan's game that reflect the influence of African American culture on his style of play.

First, Jordan's style of basketball reflects the *will to spontaneity*. I mean here the way in which historical accidence is transformed into cultural advantage, and the way acts of apparently random occurrence are spontaneously and imaginatively employed by Africans and African Americans in a variety of forms of cultural expression. When examining Jordan's game, this feature of African American culture clearly functions in his unpredictable eruptions of basketball creativity. It was apparent, for instance, during game two of the National Basketball Association 1991 championship series between Jordan's Chicago Bulls and the Los Angeles Lakers, in a shot that even Jordan ranked in his all-time top ten. Jordan made a drive toward the lane, gesturing with his hands and body that he was about to complete a patent Jordan dunk shot[②] with his right hand. But when he spied defender Sam Perkins slipping over to oppose his shot, he switched the ball in midair to his left hand to make an underhanded scoop shot instead, which immediately became known as the "levitation" shot. Such improvisation, a staple of the will to spontaneity, allows Jordan to expand his vocabulary of athletic spectacle, which is the stimulation of a desire to bear witness to the revelation of truth and beauty compressed into acts of athletic creativity .

---

① Joe Louis(1914—1981)：美国非裔职业重量级拳击手，被认为是历史上最伟大的重量级拳击手之一。Jackie Robinson(1919—1972)：美国职业棒球大联盟现代史上第一位非裔美国人(美国黑人)球员。Althea Gibson(1927—2003)：女子网球运动员，第一位赢得温布顿赛的美国黑人。Wilma Rudolph(1940—1994)：美国非裔短跑选手，是奥运会历史上最伟大的女子短跑运动员之一。Muhammad Ali(1942—)：拳王阿里，世界重量级拳击冠军。Arthur Ashe(1943—1993)：网坛明星，美国第一位赢得男单大满贯的非裔运动员。

② dunk shot:（篮球的）扣篮，塞篮。

Second, Jordan's game reflects the *stylization of the performed self*. This is the creation and projection of a sport persona that is an identifying mark of diverse African American creative enterprises, from the complexly layered jazz experimentation of John Coltrane①, the trickstering and signifying comedic routines of Richard Pryor②, and the rhetorical ripostes and oral significations of rapper Kool Moe Dee③. Jordan's whole game persona is a graphic depiction of the performed self as flying acrobat, resulting in his famous moniker "Air Jordan." Jordan's performed self is rife with④ the language of physical expressiveness: head moving, arms extending, hands waving, tongue wagging, and legs spreading.

He has also developed a resourceful repertoire of dazzling dunk shots that further express his performed self and that have garnered him a special niche within the folklore of the game: the cradle jam, rock-a-baby, kiss the rim, lean in, and the tomahawk. In Jordan's game, the stylization of a performed self has allowed him to create a distinct sports persona that has athletic as well as economic consequences, while mastering sophisticated levels of physical expression and redefining the possibilities of athletic achievement within basketball.

Finally, there is the subversion of perceived limits through the use of *edifying deception*, which in Jordan's case centers around the space/time continuum. This moment in African American cultural practice is the ability to flout widely understood boundaries through mesmerization and alchemy, a subversion of common perceptions of the culturally or physically possible through the creative and deceptive manipulation of appearance. Jordan is perhaps most famous for his alleged "hang time," the uncanny ability to remain suspended in midair longer than other basketball players while executing his stunning array of improvised moves. But Jordan's "hang time" is technically a misnomer and can be more accurately attributed to Jordan's skillful athletic deception, his acrobatic leaping ability, and his intellectual toughness in projecting an aura of uniqueness around his craft than to his defiance of gravity and the laws of physics.

…

The African American aspects of Jordan's game are indissolubly linked to the culture of consumption and the commodification of black culture. Because of Jordan's supreme mastery of basketball, his squeaky-clean image, and his youthful vigor in pursuit of the American Dream, he has become, along with Bill Cosby⑤, the quintessential pitchman⑥ in American society. Even his highly publicized troubles with gambling, his refusal to visit the White House after the Bulls' championship season, and a book that purports to expose the underside of his heroic myth have barely tarnished his

① John Coltrane(1926—1967):美国黑人爵士乐手,著名萨克斯演奏家、作曲家和乐队领导者。

② Richard Pryor(1940—2005):被称为美国喜剧开路人的著名黑人演员。

③ Kool Moe Dee(1962—):美国著名黑人说唱乐歌手。

④ rife with: 充满的;充斥的。

⑤ Bill Cosby(1937—):美国黑人喜剧演员。

⑥ pitchman:摊贩;推销员。

All-American image. Jordan eats Wheaties①, drives Chevrolets, wears Hanes②, drinks Coca-Cola, consumes McDonald's, guzzles Gatorade③, and, of course, wears Nikes. He and his shrewd handlers have successfully produced, packaged, marketed, and distributed his image and commodified his symbolic worth, transforming cultural capital into cash, influence, prestige, status, and wealth. To that degree, at least, Jordan repudiates the sorry tradition of the black athlete as the naif who loses his money to piranha-like financial wizards, investors, and hangers-on. He represents the new-age athletic entrepreneur who understands that American sport is ensconced in the cultural practices associated with business, and that it demands particular forms of intelligence, perception, and representation to prevent abuse and maximize profit.

From the very beginning of his professional career, Jordan was consciously marketed by his agency Pro-Serv as a peripatetic vehicle of American fantasies of capital accumulation and material consumption tied to Jordan's personal modesty and moral probity. In so doing, they skillfully avoided attaching to Jordan the image of questionable ethics and lethal excess that plagued inside traders and corporate raiders on Wall Street during the mid-eighties, as Jordan began to emerge as a cultural icon. But Jordan is also the symbol of the spectacle-laden black athletic body as the site of commodified black cultural imagination. Ironically, the black male body, which has been historically viewed as threatening and inappropriate in American society (and remains so outside of sports and entertainment), is made an object of white desires to domesticate and dilute its more ominous and subversive uses, even symbolically reducing Jordan's body to dead meat (McDonald's McJordan hamburger), which can be consumed and expelled as waste.

Jordan's body is also the screen upon which is projected black desires to emulate his athletic excellence and replicate his entry into reaches of unimaginable wealth and fame. But there is more than vicarious substitution and the projection of fantasy onto Jordan's body that is occurring in the circulation and reproduction of black cultural desire. There is also the creative use of desire and fantasy by young blacks to counter, and capitulate to, the forces of cultural dominance that attempt to reduce the black body to a commodity and text that is employed for entertainment, titillation, or financial gain. Simply said, there is no easy correlation between the commodification of black youth culture and the evidences of a completely dominated consciousness.

…

Basketball is the metaphoric center of black juvenile culture, a major means by which even temporary forms of cultural and personal transcendence of personal limits are experienced. Michael Jordan is at the center of this black athletic culture, the supreme symbol of black cultural creativity in a society of diminishing tolerance for the black youth whose fascination with Jordan has helped sustain him. But Jordan is also the iconic fixture of broader segments of American society, who see in him the ideal figure: a black man of extraordinary genius on the court and before the cameras, who by virtue of his magical skills and godlike talents symbolizes the meaning

① Wheaties:一种因为篮球冠军著名的谷类食品。

② Hanes:美国著名服装品牌。

③ Gatorade:"佳得乐",美国运动型饮料一大品牌。

of human possibility, while refusing to root it in the specific forms of culture and race in which it must inevitably make sense or fade to ultimate irrelevance ①.

Jordan also represents the contradictory impulses of the contemporary culture of consumption, where the black athletic body is deified, reified, and rearticulated within the narrow meanings of capital and commodity. But there is both resistance and consent to the exploitation of black bodies in Jordan's explicit cultural symbolism, as he provides brilliant glimpses of black culture's ingenuity of improvisation as a means of cultural expression and survival. It is also partially this element of black culture that has created in American society a desire to dream Jordan, to "be like Mike."

This pedagogy of desire that Jordan embodies, although at points immobilized by its depoliticized cultural contexts, is nevertheless a remarkable achievement in contemporary American culture: a six-foot-six American man of obvious African descent is the dominant presence and central cause of athletic fantasy in a sport that twenty years ago was denigrated as a black man's game and hence deemed unworthy of wide attention or support. Jordan is therefore the bearer of meanings about black culture larger than his individual life, the symbol of a pedagogy of style, presence, and desire that is immediately communicated by the sight of his black body before it can be contravened by reflection.

In the final analysis, his big black body—graceful and powerful, elegant and dark—symbolizes the possibilities of other black bodies to remain safe long enough to survive within the limited but significant sphere of sport, since Jordan's achievements have furthered the cultural acceptance of at least the athletic black body. In that sense, Jordan's powerful cultural capital has not been exhausted by narrow understandings of his symbolic absorption by the demands of capital and consumption. His body is still the symbolic carrier of racial and cultural desires to fly beyond limits and obstacles, a fluid metaphor of mobility and ascent to heights of excellence secured by genius and industry. It is this power to embody the often conflicting desires of so many that makes Michael Jordan a supremely instructive figure for our times.

Questions to Consider

1. What does Dyson mean by the term "public pedagogue"?
2. What social forces have caused black athletes to assume "a heroic dimension" in American life, according to Dyson?
3. What evidence does Dyson provide to show that Jordan's skills express African American "cultural norms and practices"?
4. What connection does Dyson make between Jordan's athletic skills and America's "culture of consumption"?
5. How do you understand the author's analysis of the meaning of the black body reflected in Jordan?

① 此句表明乔丹现象的矛盾之处：一方面需要跳出种族领域来看出其文化价值，也就是大部分美国人所理解的乔丹身上体现的人之无限能力；另一方面，离开种族来谈乔丹，实际上本身就失去了意义产生的依据。

Lesson 22 What Makes Superman So Darned American?

超人何以成为十足的美国人?

GARY ENGLE

Introduction

Since his initial appearance in a June 1938 comic book, and through countless more radio serials, books, toys, Web sites, video games, movies, and television shows—including his latest incarnation in the hit WB show Smallville—Superman has fought for "truth, justice, and the American way." In this semiotic analysis of the enduring appeal of Superman, Gary Engle argues why the Man of Steel —whom Engle views as the ultimate immigrant—has dominated the pantheon of American characters for so many years. Of all our heroes, Engle claims, Superman alone " achieves truly mythic stature, interweaving a pattern of beliefs, literary conventions, and cultural traditions of the American people more powerfully and more accessibly than any other cultural symbol of the twentieth century, perhaps of any period in our history." A specialist in popular culture, Engle is a professor of English at Cleveland State University. In addition to over two hundred magazine and journal articles, he has also written *The Grotesque Essence: Plays from American Minstrel Style* (1978).

Text

When I was young I spent a lot of time arguing with myself about who would win in a fight between John Wayne and Superman. On days when I wore my cowboy hat and cap guns, I knew the Duke would win because of his pronounced superiority in the all-important matter of swagger. There were days, though, when a frayed army blanket tied cape-fashion around my neck signaled a young man's need to believe there could be no end to the potency of his being. Then the Man of Steel was the odds-on[①] favorite to knock the Duke for a cosmic loop. My greatest childhood problem was that the question could never be resolved because no such battle could ever take place. I mean, how would a fight start between the only two Americans who never started anything, who always fought only to defend their rights and the American way?

Now that I'm older and able to look with reason on the mysteries of childhood, I've finally resolved the dilemma. John Wayne was the best older brother any kid could ever hope to have, but he was no Superman.

Superman is *the* great American hero. We are a nation rich with legendary figures. But

---

① odds-on: 大半有希望赢的。

among the Davy Crocketts① and Paul Bunyans② and Mike Finks③ and Pecos Bills④ and all the rest who speak for various regional identities in the pantheon of American folklore, only Superman achieves truly mythic stature, interweaving a pattern of beliefs, literary conventions, and cultural traditions of the American people more powerfully and more accessibly than any other cultural symbol of the twentieth century, perhaps of any period in our history.

The core of the American myth in *Superman* consists of a few basic facts that remain unchanged throughout the infinitely varied ways in which the myth is told—facts with which everyone is familiar, however marginal their knowledge of the story. Superman is an orphan rocketed to Earth when his native planet Krypton explodes; he lands near Smallville and is adopted by Jonathan and Martha Kent, who inculcate in him their American middle-class ethic; as an adult he migrates to Metropolis where he defends America—no, the world! no, the Universe!—from all evil and harm while playing a romantic game in which, as Clark Kent, he hopelessly pursues Lois Lane, who hopelessly pursues Superman, who remains aloof until such time as Lois proves worthy of him by falling in love with his feigned identity as a weakling. That's it⑤. Every narrative thread in the mythology, each one of the thousands of plots in the fifty-year stream of comics and films and TV shows, all the tales involving the demigods of the Superman pantheon—Superboy, Supergirl, even Krypto the superdog—every single one reinforces by never contradicting this basic set of facts. That's the myth, and that's where one looks to understand America.

Superman: the man of steel
眼望前方,目光深邃的超人

It is impossible to imagine Superman being as popular as he is and speaking as deeply to the American character were he not an immigrant and an orphan. Immigration, of course, is the overwhelming fact in American history. Except for the Indians, all Americans have an immediate sense of their origins elsewhere. No nation on Earth has so deeply embedded in its social

---

① Davy Crockett(1786—1836):美国19世纪拓荒传奇英雄。

② Paul Bunyan:美国传说中的伐木巨人,力大无穷。

③ Mike Fink:密西西比河上的海盗,美国垦荒时期有许多夸大其实的超人传说,Mike Fink就是其中一个。

④ Pecos Bill:美国民间传说中的英雄。

⑤ 《超人》故事概要:超人出生在克利普顿星(Krypton),外星名"卡艾尔"(Kar-El)。当他还是婴儿的时候,被他的父亲"乔艾尔"(Jor-El)和母亲"拉娜"(Lara)单独放进太空船中,当他乘坐的太空船离开时,他出生的星球发生大爆炸。他的太空船降落在地球,他被美国堪萨斯州斯莫尔镇(Smallville)肯特农场的一对夫妇收养,改名为"克拉克·肯特"(Clark Kent)。长大后,他在大都会做记者。Lois Lane是超人的女友/妻子,报社女记者。

consciousness the imagery of passage from one social identity to another: the *Mayflower*[①] of the New England separatists, the slave ships from Africa and the subsequent underground railroads toward freedom in the North, the sailing ships and steamers running shuttles across two oceans in the nineteenth century, the freedom airlifts in the twentieth. Somehow the picture just isn't complete without Superman's rocket ship.

Like the peoples of the nation whose values he defends, Superman is an alien, but not just any alien. He's the consummate and totally uncompromised alien, an immigrant whose visible difference from the norm is underscored by his decision to wear a costume of bold primary colors so tight as to be his very skin. Moreover, Superman the alien is real. He stands out among the hosts of comic book characters (Batman is a good example) for whom the superhero role is like a mask assumed when needed, a costume worn over their real identities as normal Americans. Superman's powers—strength, mobility, x-ray vision and the like —are the comic-book equivalents of ethnic characteristics, and they protect and preserve the vitality of the foster community in which he lives in the same way that immigrant ethnicity has sustained American culture linguistically, artistically, economically, politically, and spiritually. The myth of Superman asserts with total confidence and a childlike innocence the value of the immigrant in American culture.

From this nation's beginnings Americans have looked for ways of coming to terms with the immigrant experience. This is why, for example, so much of American literature and popular culture deals with the theme of dislocation, generally focused in characters devoted or doomed to constant physical movement. Daniel Boone[②] became an American legend in part as a result of apocryphal stories that he moved every time his neighbors got close enough for him to see the smoke of their cabin fires. James Fenimore Cooper's[③] Natty Bumppo spent the five long novels of the Leatherstocking saga drifting ever westward, like the pioneers who were his spiritual offspring, from the Mohawk valley of upstate New York to the Great Plains where he died. Huck Finn[④] sailed through the moral heart of America on a raft. Melville's Ishmael[⑤], Wister's Virginian[⑥], Shane, Gatsby, the entire Lost Generation, Steinbeck's Okies, Little Orphan Annie[⑦], a thousand

---

① *The Mayflower*: 五月花号(1620 年英国清教徒去美洲时所乘的船)。

② Daniel Boone(1734—1820):美国边疆开拓者,是美国历史上最著名的拓荒者之一。

③ James Fenimore Cooper (1789—1851):美国小说家,他最有成就的作品,如《皮袜子故事集》五部曲,对美国的西部小说产生很大影响。Natty Bumpo 是小说中的主要人物。

④ Huck Finn:马克・吐温名著《哈克历险记》中的人物。

⑤ Ishmael:麦尔维尔(Melville)小说《白鲸》中的叙述者。

⑥ Owen Wister(1860—1938):西部小说作家,其作品 *The Virginian: a Horseman of the Plains* 1920 年出版。

⑦ Jack Schaefer (1907—1991)1949 年出版西部小说 *Shane*,后被改编成电影。著名作家斯坦贝克(Steinbeck)1939 年小说 *The Grapes of the Wrath* (《愤怒的葡萄》)描述大萧条期间,从奥克拉荷马到加州寻找工作的农业工人(Okies)的生活。Gatsby 是菲兹杰拉德著名小说《了不起的盖茨比》中的主要人物。The Little Orphan Annie 是漫画家 Harod Gray (1894—1968)笔下的喜剧人物。

fiddle-footed cowboy heroes of dime novels① and films and television—all in motion, searching for the American dream or stubbornly refusing to give up their innocence by growing old, all symptomatic of a national sense of rootlessness stemming from an identity founded on the experience of immigration.

Individual mobility is an integral part of America's dreamwork. Is it any wonder, then, that our greatest hero can take to the air at will? Superman's ability to fly does more than place him in a tradition of mythic figures going back to the Greek messenger god Hermes② or Zetes the flying Argonaut③. It makes him an exemplar in the American dream. Take away a young man's wheels and you take away his manhood. Jack Kerouac and Charles Kuralt④ go on the road; William Least Heat Moon⑤ looks for himself in a van exploring the veins of America in its system of blue highways; legions of gray-haired retirees turn Air Stream trailers and Winnebagos⑥ into proof positive that you can, in the end, take it with you. On a human scale, the American need to keep moving suggests a neurotic aimlessness under the surface of adventure. But take the human restraints off, let Superman fly unencumbered when and wherever he will, and the meaning of mobility in the American consciousness begins to reveal itself. Superman's incredible speed allows him to be as close to everywhere at once as it is physically possible to be. Displacement is, therefore, impossible. His sense of self is not dispersed by his life's migration but rather enhanced by all the universe that he is able to occupy. What American, whether an immigrant in spirit or in fact, could resist the appeal of one with such an ironclad immunity to the anxiety of dislocation?

In America, physical dislocation serves as a symbol of social and psychological movement. When our immigrant ancestors arrived on America's shores they hit the ground running, some to homestead on the Great Plains, others to claw their way up the socioeconomic ladder in coastal ghettos. Upward mobility, westward migration, Sunbelt relocation—the wisdom in America is that people don't, can't, mustn't end up where they begin. This belief has the moral force of religious doctrine. Thus the American identity is ordered around the psychological experience of forsaking or losing the past for the opportunity of reinventing oneself in the future. This makes the orphan a potent symbol of the American character. Orphans aren't merely free to reinvent themselves. They are obliged to do so.

When Superman reinvents himself, he becomes the bumbling Clark Kent, a figure as immobile as Superman is mobile, as weak as his alter ego is strong. Over the years commentators have been fond of stressing how Clark Kent provides an illusory image of wimpiness onto which

---

① dime novel：廉价畅销小说。

② Hermes：[希神]赫耳墨斯(众神的使者,并掌管商业、道路等)。

③ Argonaut：[希神]英雄阿尔戈。乘阿尔戈号船随大英雄伊阿宋(Jason)到海外觅取金羊毛的英雄。

④ Jack Kerouac(1922—1969)：美国垮掉派代表小说家。《在路上》是杰克·凯鲁亚克的第二部小说。Charles Kuralt(1934—1997)：美国 CBS 电视新闻记者,著名的旅行作家。

⑤ William Least Heat Moon(1939—)：美国著名旅行作家,写过游记 *Blue Highways: A Journey Into America*,讲述了穿行在美国小城镇中的旅程。

⑥ Air Stream trailers："气流",美国旅用拖带式居住车品牌。Winnebagos：美国著名房车品牌。

children can project their insecurities about their own potential (and, hopefully, equally illusory) weaknesses. But I think the role of Clark Kent is far more complex than that.

During my childhood, Kent contributed nothing to my love for the Man of Steel. If left to contemplate him for too long, I found myself changing from cape back into cowboy hat and guns. John Wayne, at least, was no sissy that I could ever see. Of course, in all the Westerns that the Duke came to stand for in my mind, there were elements that left me as confused as the paradox between Kent and Superman. For example, I could never seem to figure out why cowboys so often fell in love when there were obviously better options: horses to ride, guns to shoot, outlaws to chase, and savages to kill. Even on the days when I became John Wayne, I could fall victim to a never-articulated anxiety about the potential for poor judgment in my cowboy heroes. Then, I generally drifted back into a worship of Superman. With him, at least, the mysterious communion of opposites was honest and on the surface of things.

What disturbed me as a child is what I now think makes the myth of Superman so appealing to an immigrant sensibility. The shape-shifting between Clark Kent and Superman is the means by which this mid-twentieth-century, urban story—like the pastoral, nineteenth-century Western before it—addresses in dramatic terms the theme of cultural assimilation.

At its most basic level, the Western was an imaginative record of the American experience of westward migration and settlement. By bringing the forces of civilization and savagery together on a mythical frontier, the Western addressed the problem of conflict between apparently mutually exclusive identities and explored options for negotiating between them. In terms that a boy could comprehend, the myth explored the dilemma of assimilation—marry the school marm and start wearing Eastern clothes or saddle up and drift further westward with the boys.

The Western was never a myth of stark moral simplicity. Pioneers fled civilization by migrating west, but their purpose in the wilderness was to rebuild civilization. So civilization was both good and bad, what Americans fled from and journeyed toward. A similar moral ambiguity rested at the heart of the wilderness. It was an Eden in which innocence could be achieved through spiritual rebirth, but it was also the anarchic force that most directly threatened the civilized values America wanted to impose on the frontier. So the dilemma arose: In negotiating between civilization and the wilderness, between the old order and the new, between the identity the pioneers carried with them from wherever they came and the identity they sought to invent, Americans faced an impossible choice. Either they pushed into the New World wilderness and forsook the ideals that motivated them or they clung to their origins and polluted Eden.

The myth of the Western responded to this dilemma by inventing the idea of the frontier in which civilized ideals embodied in the institutions of family, church, law, and education are revitalized by the virtues of savagery: independence, self-reliance, personal honor, sympathy with nature, and ethical uses of violence. In effect, the mythical frontier represented an attempt to embody the perfect degree of assimilation in which both the old and new identities came together, if not in a single self-image, then at least in idealized relationships, like the symbolic marriage of reformed cowboy and displaced school marm that ended Owen Wister's① prototypical Virginian, or the mystical masculine bonding between representatives of an ascendant and a vanishing America—Natty Bumppo and Chingachgook②, the Lone Ranger③ and Tonto. On the Western frontier, both the old and new identities equally mattered.

As powerful a myth as the Western was, however, there were certain limits to its ability to speak directly to an increasingly common twentieth century immigrant sensibility. First, it was pastoral. Its imagery of dusty frontier towns and breathtaking mountainous desolation spoke most affectingly to those who conceived of the American dream in terms of the nineteenth-century immigrant experience of rural settlement. As the twentieth century wore on, more immigrants were, like Superman, moving from rural or small-town backgrounds to metropolitan environments. Moreover, the Western was historical, often elegiacally so. Underlying the air of celebration in even the most epic and romantic of Westerns—the films of John Ford④, say, in which John Wayne stood tall for all that any good American boy could ever want to be—was an awareness that the frontier was less a place than a state of mind represented in historic terms by a fleeting moment glimpsed imperfectly in the rapid wave of westward migration and settlement. Implicitly, then, whatever balance of past and future identities the frontier could offer was itself tenuous or illusory.

…

Under such circumstances, finding a believable and inspiring balance between the old identity and the new, like that implicit in the myth of the frontier, was next to impossible. The images and characters that did emerge from the immigrant communities were often comic. Seen over and over in the fiction and popular theater of the day was the figure of the *yiddische Yankee*⑤, a jingoistic optimist who spoke heavily accented American slang, talked baseball like an addict without understanding the game, and dressed like a Broadway dandy on a budget—in short, one who didn't understand America well enough to distinguish between image and substance and who paid for the mistake by becoming the butt of a style of comedy bordering on pathos. So ingrained was this stereotype in popular culture that it echoes today in TV situation comedy.

---

① Owen Wister (1860—1938): 欧文·威斯特被誉为美国"西部牛仔小说之父",在美国文学中占有重要地位。他创作的小说《弗吉尼亚人》被视为西部牛仔小说形成的标志。

② Chingachgook: Cooper 小说中的人物, Chingachgook 是美国原住民生活与文化的表征;故事主人翁 Bumppo 与 Chingachgook 的友谊,代表的是两个有巨大差异的种族和文化之间的友谊。

③ Lone Ranger: 独行侠,游侠。*The Lone Ranger* (《游侠传奇》)在美国最早是一出电台节目,诞生于上世纪 30 年代,之后被改编成电影、电视、漫画、小说等多种形式。《游侠传奇》的主人公 the Lone Ranger 是一名戴着面具的游侠,他原本是德州骑警,在追捕一伙不法之徒时险些送命,在印第安人 Tonto 的治疗和照顾下逐渐康复,并从此戴上面具、骑着白马和 Tonto 一起在西部旷野惩恶扬善。

④ John Ford(1894—1973):约翰·福特是美国最伟大和最多产的导演之一,曾四次获得奥斯卡最佳导演奖。在他的影片里,主人公多是硬汉,彪悍刚毅的男性成为福特镜头下、在文明与野蛮的夹缝中挣扎的西部英雄。

⑤ *yiddische Yankee:* yiddish,〈俚〉犹太人的。Yankee:〈俚〉美国人,美国佬。

Throughout American popular culture between 1880 and the Second World War the story was the same. Oxlike Swedish farmers, German brewers, Jewish merchants, corrupt Irish ward healers, Italian gangsters —there was a parade of images that reflected in terms often comic, sometimes tragic, the humiliation, pain, and cultural insecurity of people in a state of transition. Even in the comics, a medium intimately connected with immigrant culture, there simply was no image that presented a blending of identities in the assimilation process in a way that stressed pride, self-confidence, integrity, and psychological well-being. None, that is, until Superman.

The brilliant stroke in the conception of Superman—the sine qua non① that makes the whole myth work—is the fact that he has two identities. The myth simply wouldn't work without Clark Kent, mild mannered newspaper reporter and later, as the myth evolved, bland TV newsman. Adopting the white-bread image of a wimp is first and foremost a moral act for the Man of Steel. He does it to protect his parents from nefarious sorts who might use them to gain an edge over the powerful alien. Moreover, Kent adds to Superman's powers the moral guidance of a Smallville upbringing. It is Jonathan Kent, fans remember, who instructs the alien that his powers must always be used for good. Thus does the myth add a mainstream white Anglo-Saxon Protestant② ingredient to the American stew. Clark Kent is the clearest stereotype of a self-effacing, hesitant, doubting, middle-class weakling ever invented. He is the epitome of visible invisibility, someone whose extraordinary ordinariness makes him disappear in a crowd. In a phrase, he is the consummate figure of total cultural assimilation, and significantly, he is not real. Implicit in this is the notion that mainstream cultural norms, however useful, are illusions.

Though a disguise, Kent is necessary for the myth to work. This uniquely American hero has two identities, one based on where he comes from in life's journey, one on where he is going. One is real, one an illusion, and both are necessary for the myth of balance in the assimilation process to be complete. Superman's powers make the hero capable of saving humanity; Kent's total immersion in the American heartland makes him want to do it. The result is an improvement on the Western: an optimistic myth of assimilation but with an urban, technocratic setting.

…

In light of the graphic detail, it seems hardly coincidental that Superman's real, Kryptonic name is Kal-El, an apparent neologism by George Lowther, the author who novelized the comic strip in 1942. In Hebrew, *el* can be both root and affix. As a root, it is the masculine singular word for God. Angels in Hebrew mythology are called *benei Elohim* (literally, sons of the Gods), or *Elyonim* (higher beings). As an affix, *el* is most often translated as "of God," as in the plenitude of Old Testament given names: Ishma-el, Dani-el, Ezeki-el, Samu-el, etc. It is also a common form for named angels in most Semitic mythologies: Israf-el, Aza-el, Uri-el, Yo-el, Rapha-el, Gabri-el and—the one perhaps most like Superman—Micha-el, the warrior angel and Satan's principal adversary.

The morpheme *Kal* bears a linguistic relation to two Hebrew roots. The first, *kal*, means

① sine qua non: 必要的条件,必具的资格,必需的东西。

② White Anglo-Saxon Protestant: 也称 WASP,即有着英国人血统的新教徒,通常指美国主流的白人。

"with lightness" or "swiftness" (faster than a speeding bullet in Hebrew?). It also bears a connection to the root *hal*, where *h* is the guttural *ch* of *chutzpah*. *Hal* translates roughly as "everything" or "all." *Kal-el*, then, can be read as "all that is God," or perhaps more in the spirit of the myth of Superman, "all that God is." And while we're at it, *Kent* is a form of the Hebrew *kala*. In its *k-n-t* form, the word appears in the Bible, meaning "I have found a son."

I'm suggesting that Superman raises the American immigrant experience to the level of religious myth. And why not? He's not just some immigrant from across the waters like all our ancestors, but a real alien, an extraterrestrial, a visitor from heaven if you will, which fact lends an element of the supernatural to the myth. America has no national religious icons nor any pilgrimage shrines. The idea of a patron saint is ludicrous in a nation whose Founding Fathers① wrote into the founding documents the fundamental if not eternal separation of church and state②. America, though, is pretty much as religious as other industrialized countries. It's just that our tradition of religious diversity precludes the nation's religious character from being embodied in objects or persons recognizably religious, for such are immediately identified by their attachment to specific sectarian traditions and thus contradict the eclecticism of the American religious spirit.

In America, cultural icons that manage to tap the national religious spirit are of necessity secular on the surface and sufficiently generalized to incorporate the diversity of American religious traditions. Superman doesn't have to be seen as an angel to be appreciated, but in the absence of a tradition of national religious iconography, he can serve as a safe, nonsectarian focus for essentially religious sentiments, particularly among the young.

In the last analysis, Superman is like nothing so much as an American boy's fantasy of a messiah③. He is the male, heroic match for the Statue of Liberty, come like an immigrant from heaven to deliver humankind by sacrificing himself in the service of others. He protects the weak and defends truth and justice and all the other moral virtues inherent in the Judeo-Christian tradition, remaining ever vigilant and ever chaste. What purer or stronger vision could there possibly be for a child? Now that I put my mind to it, I see that John Wayne never had a chance.

Questions to Consider

1. Why does Superman's status as "an immigrant and an orphan" make him deeply American, according to Engle?
2. What is the significance of Superman's ability to fly?
3. Why does Engle see physical dislocation as being so typically American?
4. What is the significance of Superman's two identities, according to Engle?
5. How does the author's analysis of Superman's outstanding characters help you understand American culture in general?

---

① Founding Fathers: 建国之父们、开国元勋,指美国建国时的一些伟人如华盛顿、杰弗逊、富兰克林等。

② 美国宪法第一修正案确定不立国教。

③ messiah:(民族的)救星。

Lesson 23 Our Barbies, Ourselves

我们的芭比，我们自己

EMILY PRAGER

Introduction

Barbie is now seen everywhere in the world. But little girls should know that Barbie is not drawn to scale. In this tongue-in-cheek essay on the role Barbie has played in her life, Emily Prager reveals the damaging effect of a doll that establishes such an impossible standard of physical perfection for little girls—and for little boys who grow up expecting their girlfriends to look like Barbie. Not only contemplating what Barbie has done to her but also thinking aloud about the relation between the bodily contour of Barbie and the conventional male peeping, Prager is really at her best in uncovering the patriarchally self-conflicting demand on women. Emily prager is a columnist with the *New York Times* and an essayist and fiction writer of a dozen of books.

Text

I read an astounding obituary in the *New York Times* not too long ago. It concerned the death of one Jack Ryan. A former husband of Zsa Zsa Gabor①, it said, Mr. Ryan had been an inventor and designer during his lifetime. A man of eclectic creativity, he designed Sparrow and Hawk missiles when he worked for the Raytheon Company, and, the notice said, when he consulted for Mattel he designed Barbie.

Ken, Barbie's boyfriend
时现时隐的芭比男友

If Barbie was designed by a man, suddenly a lot of things made sense to me, things I'd wondered about for years. I used to look at Barbie and wonder, what's wrong with this picture? What kind of woman designed this doll? Let's be honest: Barbie looks like someone who got her start at the Playboy Mansion. She could be a regular guest on *The Howard Stern Show*②. It is a fact of Barbie's design that her breasts are so out of proportion to the rest of her body that if she were a human woman, she'd fall flat on her face.

If it's true that a woman didn't design Barbie, you don't know how

① Zsa Zsa Gabor: 匈牙利裔美国演员，生于布达佩斯，原名莎丽·嘉宝，1936 年当选匈牙利小姐，1941 年移居美国，以离婚七次和有大量珠宝收藏闻名。

② *The Howard Stern Show*: 美国脱口秀节目。

much saner that makes me feel. Of course, that doesn't ameliorate the damage. There are millions of women who are subliminally sure that a thirty-nine-inch bust and a twenty-three-inch waist are the epitome of lovability. Could this account for the popularity of breast implant surgery?

I don't mean to step on anyone's toes here. I loved my Barbie. Secretly, I still believe that neon pink and turquoise blue are the only colors in which to decorate a duplex condo①. And like many others of my generation, I've never married, simply because I cannot find a man who looks as good in clam diggers as Ken②.

The question that comes to mind is, of course, Did Mr. Ryan design Barbie as a weapon? Because it is odd that Barbie appeared about the same time in my consciousness as the feminist movement③—a time when women sought equality and small breasts were king. Or is Barbie the dream date of weapons designers? Or perhaps it's simpler than that: Perhaps Barbie is Zsa Zsa if she were eleven inches tall. No matter what, my discovery of Jack Ryan confirms what I have always felt: There is something indescribably masculine about Barbie—dare I say it, phallic. For all her giant breasts and high-heeled feet, she lacks a certain softness. If you asked a little girl what kind of doll she wanted for Christmas. I just don't think she'd reply, "Please, Santa, I want a hard-body."

Barbie, a model for girls.
永远的芭比,永远的偶像。

On the other hand, you could say that Barbie, in feminist terms, is definitely her own person. With her condos and fashion plazas and pools and beauty salons, she is definitely a liberated woman, a gal on the move. And she has always been sexual, even totemic. Before Barbie, American dolls were flat-footed and breastless, and ineffably dignified. They were created in the image of little girls or babies. Madame Alexander④ was the queen of doll makers in the fifties, and her dollies looked like Elizabeth Taylor in *National Velvet*. They represented the kind of girls who looked perfect in jodhpurs, whose hair was never out of place, who grew up to be Jackie Kennedy⑤—before she married Onassis. Her dolls' boyfriends were figments of the imagination, figment with large portfolios and three-piece suits and presidential aspirations, figments who could keep dolly in the style to which little girls of the fifties were programmed to become accustomed, a style that spasm-ed with the sixties and the appearance

① duplex condo: 二联式公寓。

② Ken 是芭比的男朋友,穿着中长裤(clam diggers)的 Ken 在市面上曾经非常流行。

③ the feminist movement: 女权运动是指美国历史上妇女争取政治、经济和社会权利的活动,包括选举权、财产权以及婚姻、工资待遇和社会福利等。

④ Madame Alexander:亚历山大女士娃娃的创建者。

⑤ Jackie Kennedy (1929—1994):美国前总统肯尼迪夫人,肯尼迪总统遇刺后,杰奎琳于 1968 年嫁给希腊船王 Onassis。

of Barbie. And perhaps what accounts for Barbie's vast popularity is that she was also a sixties woman: into free love and fun colors, anti-class, and possessed of real, molded boyfriend, Ken, with whom she could chant a mantra.

But there were problems with Ken. I always felt weird about him. He had no genitals, and, even at age ten, I found that ominous. I mean, here was Barbie with these humongous breasts, and that was OK with the toy company. And then, there was Ken with that truncated, unidentifiable lump at his groin. I sensed injustice at work. Why, I wondered, was Barbie designed with such obvious sexual equipment and Ken not? Why was his treated as if it were more mysterious than hers? Did the fact that it was treated as such indicate that somehow his equipment, his essential maleness, was considered more powerful than hers, more worthy of the dignity of concealment? And if the issue in the mind of the toy company was obscenity and its possible damage to children, I still object. How do they think I felt, knowing that no matter how many water beds they slept in, or hot tubs they romped in, or swimming pools they lounged by under the stars, Barbie and Ken could never make love? No matter how much sexuality Barbie possessed, she would never turn Ken on. He would be forever withholding, forever detached. There was a loneliness about Barbie's situation that was always disturbing. And twenty-five years later, movies and videos are still filled with topless women and covered men. As if we're all trapped in Barbie's world and can never escape.

God, it certainly has cheered me up to think that Barbie was designed by Jack Ryan. …

Questions to Consider

1. Why does Prager say "a lot of things made sense" to her after she learned Barbie was designed by a man?
2. What is Prager's attitude toward Ken? And how is it related to her feminist fighting gesture?
3. How do Madame Alexander dolls differ from Barbies?